C000292896

STRE

Gloucestershire

ublished in 2001 by

, a division of
s Publishing Group Ltd
ron Quays, London E14 4JP

lour edition 2001
impression with revisions 2003

-540-08100-0

p's 2003

Ordnance Survey®

oduct includes mapping data licensed
rdnance Survey® with the permission
Controller of Her Majesty's Stationery
© Crown copyright 2003. All rights
ed. Licence number 100011710.

t of this publication may be
uced, stored in a retrieval system or
itted in any form or by any means,
nic, mechanical, photocopying,
ng or otherwise, without the
sion of the Publishers and the
ght owner.

ce Survey and the OS Symbol are
ered trademarks of Ordnance Survey,
ional mapping agency of Great Britain.

d and bound in Spain
fosa-Quebecor

Contents

III **Key to map symbols**

IV **Key to map pages**

VI **Route planning**

X **Administrative and Postcode boundaries**

1 **Street maps** at 2½ inches to 1 mile

140 **Street maps** at 1¼ inches to 1 mile

190 **Street maps** at 2½ inches to 1 mile

193 **Street maps of centres of Cheltenham, Bristol and Gloucester** at 5 inches to 1 mile

197 **Town maps** of Chipping Norton, Evesham, Faringdon and Ross-on-Wye

199 **Index** of towns and villages

201 **Index** of streets, hospitals, industrial estates, railway stations, schools, shopping centres, universities and places of interest

Digital Data

The exceptionally high-quality mapping found in this atlas is available as digital data in TIFF format, which is easily convertible to other bitmapped (raster) image formats.

The index is also available in digital form as a standard database table. It contains all the details found in the printed index together with the National Grid reference for the map square in which each entry is named .

For further information and to discuss your requirements, please contact Philip's on 020 7644 6932 or james.mann@philips-maps.co.uk

CROFT FARM SCHOOL CAMP Pg 182 A6

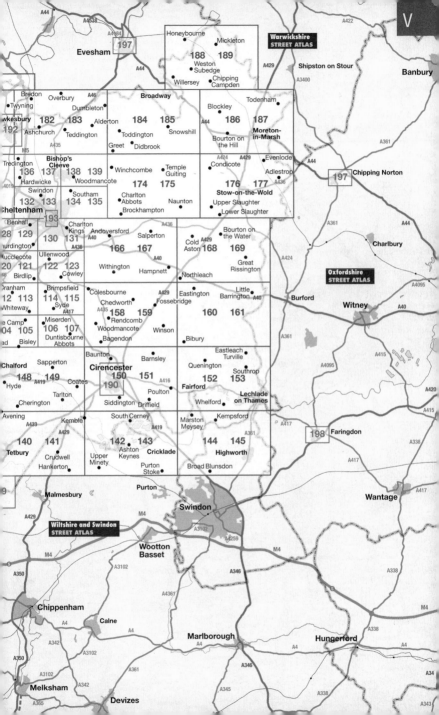

V

Honeybourne
Mickleton

Warwickshire
STREET ATLAS

Shipston on Stour

Banbury

A422

A4538

A44

Evesham

197

188   189

Weston
Subedge
Willersey

Chipping
Campden

A429

A3400

A44

A44

A361

Bredon
Overbury
Dumbleton

Broadway

Blockley

Todenham

Twyning

wkesbury   182   183   Alderton

184   185

Snowshill

186   187

A44

Moreton-
in-Marsh

192

Ashchurch   Teddington

Toddington

Bourton
on the
Hill

M5

Greet   Didbrook

Evenlode

197   Chipping Norton

Tredington   136   Bishop's
Cleeve

138   139

Winchcombe

Temple
Guiting

A424
Condicote

Adlestrop

A44   A436

Hardwicke   137

Woodmancote

174   175

176   177

Swindon   Southam

132   133   134   135

Charlton
Abbots
Brockhampton

Naunton

Stow-on-the-Wold

Upper Slaughter

A361

A44

heltenham

Lower Slaughter

A436

Charlbury

Benhall

Charlton
Kings

Andoversford   Salperton

Bourton
on the
Water

28   129   130   131

166   167

Cold
Aston   A429   168   169

A424

urdington   A436

A40

A361

Oxfordshire
STREET ATLAS

A4095

ucclecote   Ullenwood

122   123

Cowley

Withington

Hampnett

Northleach

Great
Rissington

Burford

Witney   A40

20   121   Birdlip

A40

Branham   Brimpsfield

12   113   114   115   Syde

A417

Colesbourne   A429   Eastington

Little
Barrington   A40

160   161

A361

Whiteway

Chedworth

Fossebridge

A4095

e Camp   Miserden

104   105   106   107

A435
Rendcomb

158   159

Winson

Bibury

Eastleach
Turville

Duntisbourne
Abbots

Woodmancote

Bagendon

04   105   Bisley

Chalford   Sapperton

Baunton

Barnsley

Quenington   Southrop

A420

148   149   Coates

Cirencester

150   151

152   153

Hyde   A419   Tarlton

190

A416   Poulton

Fairford

A415

Cherington

Siddington   Driffield

Whelford

Lechlade
on Thames

Avening   Kemble

South Cerney

A433

A429

A419

Marston
Meysey

Kempsford

198   Faringdon

A338

140   141   142   143

Cricklade

144   145

A417

Tetbury   Crudwell

Upper
Minety   Ashton
Keynes

Highworth

Hankerton

Purton
Stoke   Broad Blunsdon

A338

9

Malmesbury   Purton

Wantage

Swindon

A429   M4   M4

A3102

Wiltshire and Swindon
STREET ATLAS

A4259

M4   Wootton
Basset

A346

A338

M4

A350   A3102

A4361

Chippenham

Calne   A4

A338

M4

A4

A350   A342

Marlborough   A4

Hungerford   A4

A346

A34

A3102

A361

A346

A338

Melksham   A342

A3102

A345

A343

Devizes   A365

Route planning

Scale

0 1 2 3 4 5 6 7 8
0 1 2 3 4 5 miles

IX

Route planning

Scale

0 1 2 3 4 5 6 7 8

0 1 2 3 4 5 miles

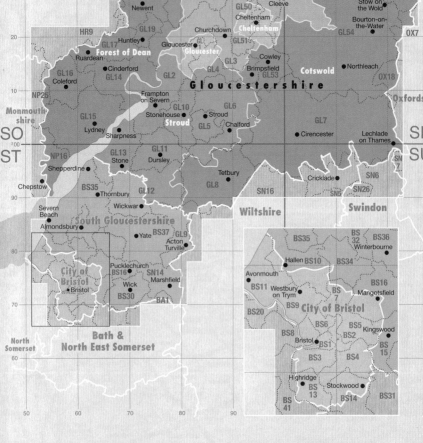

X

Major administrative and Postcode boundaries

County and unitary authority boundaries
District boundaries
Postcode boundaries
Area covered by this atlas

Scale
0 — 5 — 10 — 15 km
0 — 5 — 10 miles

SO | SP

Worcestershire

Warwickshire

WR11 | CV36

County of Herefordshire

WR13

WR11

Chipping Camden

GL55

Broadway

Moreton-in-Marsh

Ledbury ● HR8

GL20

Tewkesbury

GL52

Winchcombe ●

GL56

Staunton

GL19

Tewkesbury

Bishop's Cleeve

Stow on the Wold

Newent ●

GL18

GL50

Cheltenham

Churchdown

Cheltenham

Bourton-on-the-Water

HR9

GL19

GL51

GL54

OX7

Huntley ●

GL17

Gloucester

GL1

Forest of Dean

Ruardean ●

Gloucester

Cowley ●

Cotswold

Northleach ●

Cinderford ●

GL14

GL2

GL4

Brimpsfield ●

GL53

OX18

GL16

Coleford

GL3

Gloucestershire

NP25

Frampton on Severn

GL10

GL6

GL7

Oxfords

Stonehouse ●

Stroud ●

Chalford ●

GL15

GL5

Cirencester ●

Lechlade on Thames

Lydney ●

Sharpness ●

Monmouth shire

SO

ST

200

GL11

Dursley ●

Tetbury ●

GL8

SN7

SU

SF

NP16

GL13

Stone ●

GL12

SN16

SN6

SN26

SN5

Shepperdine ●

Cricklade ●

Chepstow ●

BS35

Thornbury ●

Wickwar ●

Wiltshire

Swindon

Severn Beach

South Gloucestershire

Yate ●

BS37

GL9

Acton Turville ●

Almondsbury ●

City of Bristol

Pucklechurch ●

BS16

SN14

Marshfield ●

Wick ●

BS30

BA1

North Somerset

Bath & North East Somerset

BS35

BS32

BS36

Winterbourne

BS34

Hallen ●

BS10

Avonmouth ●

BS11

Westbury on Trym ●

BS7

BS16

Mangotsfield ●

BS20

BS9

City of Bristol

BS6

BS5

Kingswood

BS8

Bristol ●

BS1

BS2

BS15

BS3

BS4

Highridge ●

BS13

Stockwood ●

BS14

BS31

BS41

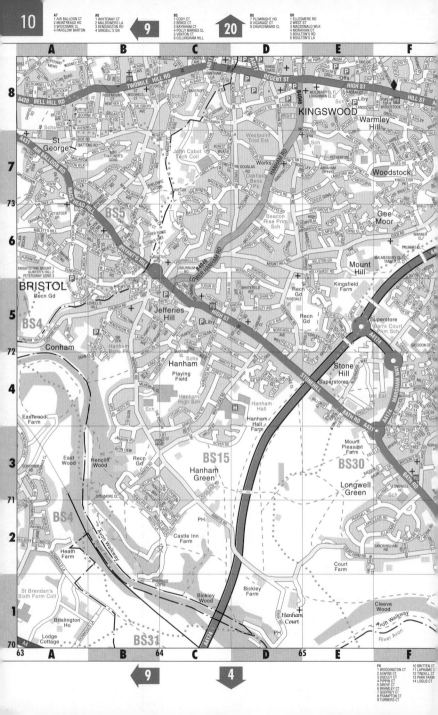

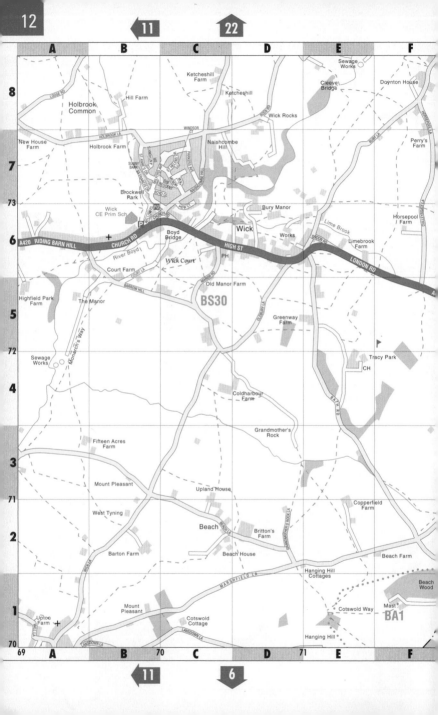

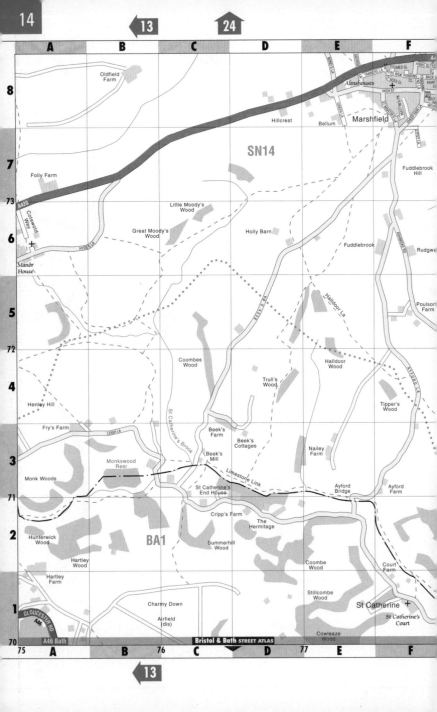

Wiltshire STREET ATLAS

SN14

BA1

Map labels:

Greenview Farm
Garston Farm
Star Farm
Bond's Wood
Woodlands
Newleaze Wood
Doncombe Scrubs
Doncombe Hill
East End
Marshfield Prim Sch
Ringswell
Ringswell Common
Sewage Wks
Doncombe Brook
Cloud Wood
Colerne
Henleyhill Barn
Woodleaze Barn
Henley Hill
Marshfield Wood
Henleyhill Plantation
Barracks
Raizes Plantation
Raizes Wood
The Raizes
West Lodge
The Warren
Ashwicke Grange
International Sch of Choueifat
Centre Plantation
Ashwicke Home Farm
Pixtonsgreen
East Lodge
Colerne Airfield
Motcombe Farm
Clift Wood
Cherry Wood
Diamond Wood
Longley Wood
Bandywell Wood
PH
Motcombe Wood
Orchard Wood
Hunters Hall
Dicknick Wood
The Rocks
Abbotscombe Wood
Breach Wood
Ryder's Wood
Oakleigh
Draught Wood
Westwood Farm
West Wood
Limestone Link
Oakford Farm
Three Shires Stone
Bath Rd

A B C D E F

79 80

8 7 73 6 5 72 4 3 71 2 1 70

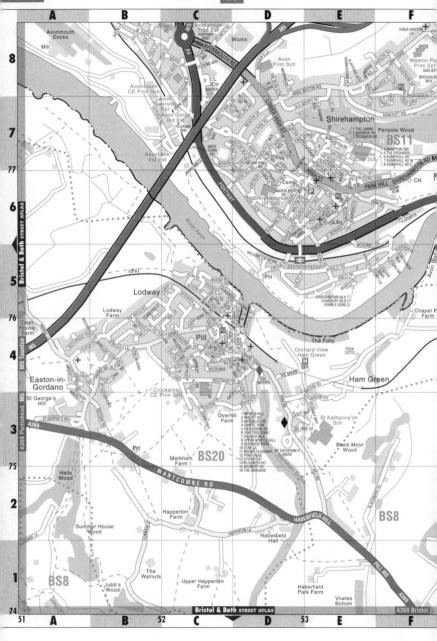

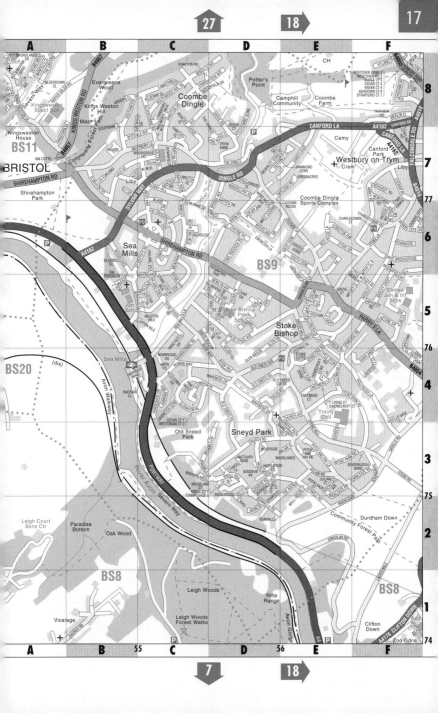

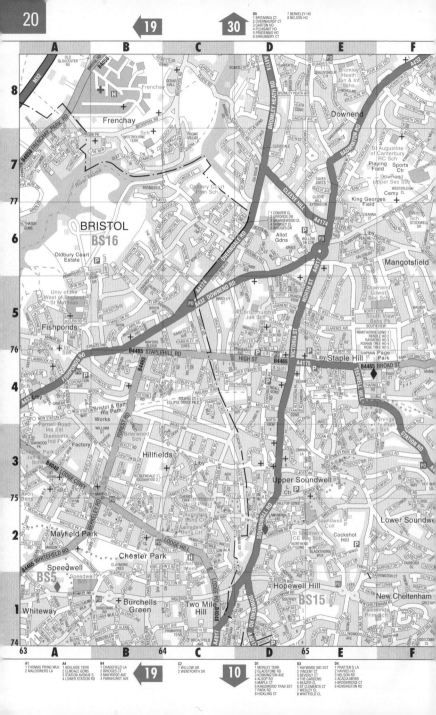

M4

Chy   8

Whitehouse
Farm

Lyde
Green

Lydegreen
Farm

Newlands

Hallen
Farm

Green Tree
Farm

Grove
Farm

New
England

Blackhorse

Vinney
Green

Emerson's
Green Prim
Sch

PO

Superstore

7

77

Emerson's
Green

THE
ROSARY

Bristol & Bath Railway Path

Works
(dis)

THE VALE

6

arley Close
Prim
Sch

Shortwood
Farm

CHITTERING RD

Shortwood
Lodge

Vinney Green
Secure Unit

BS16

5

Teaching Unit

P

COSSHAM ST

The
Vale

Pomphrey

Rock House
Farm

POMPHREY HILL

MAIN RD   Shortwood   SHORTWOOD HILL

76

B4465

Orchard
Farm

PH

Community Forest Path

Gingell's
Farm

B4465   4

Mangotsfield
Sch

Rodway
Hill

Lodge
Farm

Long
Plantation

Siston
Court

Siston   3

75

Deers Wood
Prim Sch

Syston
Farm

CH

Hanging
Wood

St Anne's
Bridge

A4175

Withy
Bed

2

BS15

NEW CHELTENHAM

FISHER RD

Siston
Hill

Cherryorchard
Farm

Myrtle
Farm

Mill
Farm

Siston Brook

BS30

Tut's
Wood

Goose
Green

Brook
Farm

Meadow
Farm

Webb's Heath
Farm

1

WEBBS HEATH

Mounds Court
Farm

74

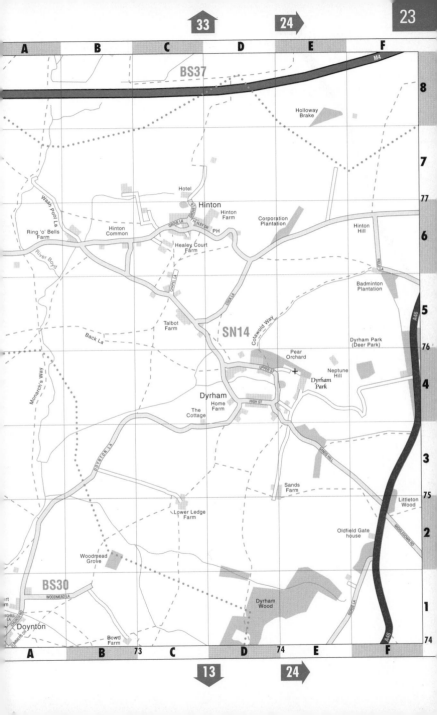

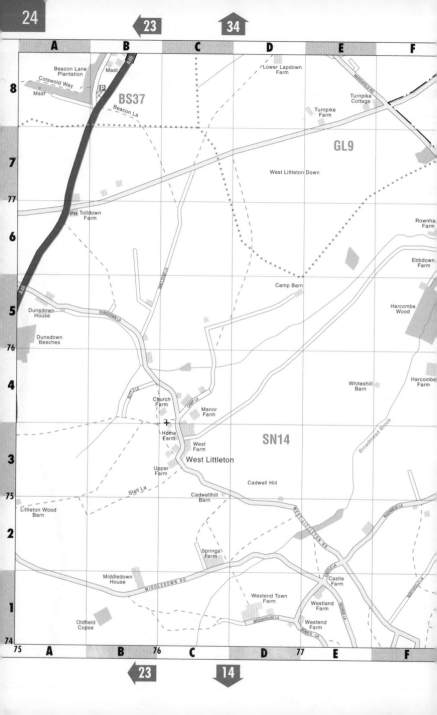

35

| A | B | C | D | E | F |

8

Kington Down Farm

Fox Covert

West Kington

Brook Farm

7

Down Farm

HOLLYBUSH LN

DRIFTON HILL

Mill House

Latimer Farm

✚

77

Broadmead Brook

6

Hazel Grove

Shirehill Farm

Lower Shirehill Farm

Gunning's Wood

SN14

5

Wiltshire STREET ATLAS

76

Hillcrest Farm

4

Maggs Farm

Plough Farm

New Homestead Farm

THE CREST

Rushmead Farm

Mountain Bower

Highfield Cottage

3

Downthorns Farm

75

BUSHMEAD LA

Martor Ind Est

Culverslade

2

Home Farm

Upper Wraxall

A420 Chippenham

DEVANT RD

Hillcrest Farm

PH

A420

Upper Farm

The Shoe

✚ Cemy

1

Northfield House

A420

74

| A | B | C | D | E | F |

79

80

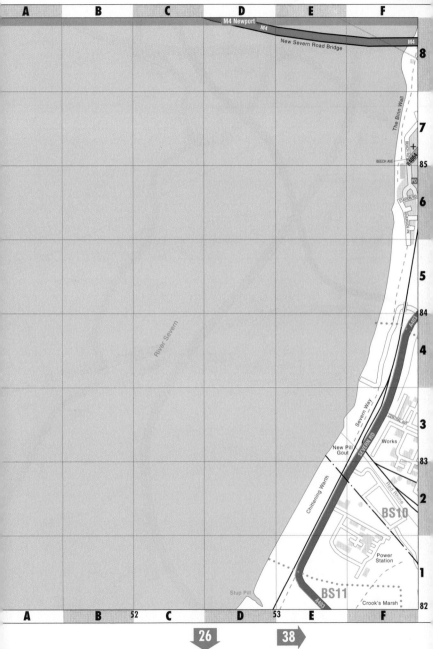

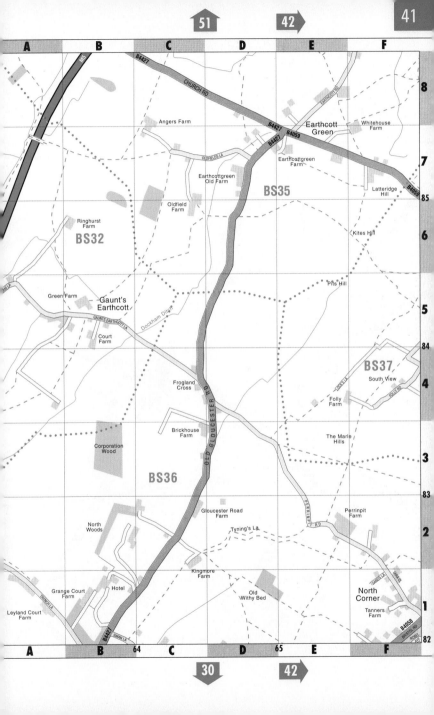

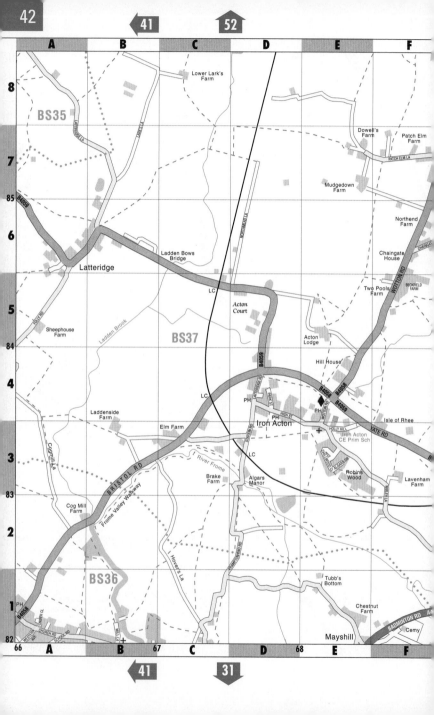

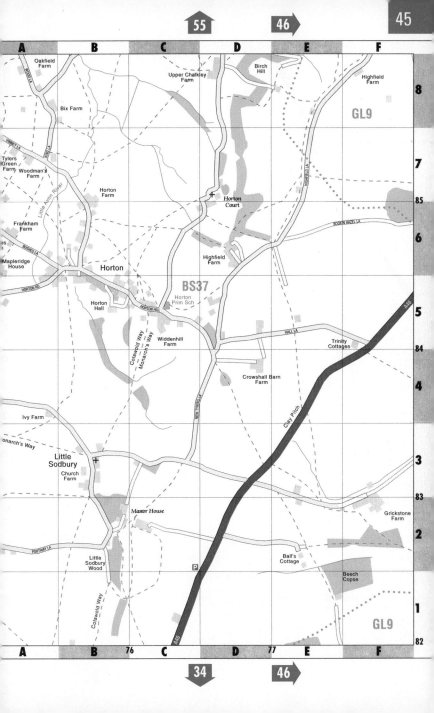

45
56

8

Swangrove
House

Petty France
Farm

Hotel

Petty France

7

Bodkin
Wood

85

Bodkin Hazel
Wood

Worcester Clump

Worcester Avenue

6

Shepherd's
Lodge

Withy
Bed

Little
Badminton
Farm

Little
Badminton

5

American
Barn

Seven Mile Plantation

GL9

CHURCH LA

WELL LA

84

BS37

Peaked Down
Clump

4

Badminton

Deer Park

Mount
Pond

3

Landing Strip

Park
Pond

M

83

Slait
Lodge

Badminton
House

2

Castle
Barn

The Tyning

Bath
Lodge

Bath Verge

ROACH'S LA

SHOP LA

PO

HIGH ST

THE LINES

SCHOOL LA

MILL LA

Badminton

Vicarage
Plantation

1

Badminton
Farm

OLD DOWN RD

SWAN RD

Ca
Fa

82

45
35

A46

Marshfield Path

BODKIN DRAIN LA

A46

A433

A433

A B C D E F

8

Duchess's
Clump

Hundred Acres
Farm

GL9

Sandy Farm

Badminton
Down

Luckley
Brake

7

Ivy Leaze
Cottage

85

Luckley Farm

Lord's
Copse

Wick Farm

6

SN14

Cherry
Orchard

CHERRY ORCHARD LA

North End
Farm

North End
House

Brook
End

5

Luckington
Cty Prim Sch

PH

SHERSTON RD

Luckington
Court

Lyppiatt
Barn

The Farm

Luckington
Court
Gardens

84

THE MERCHANTS

CHAPEL
ROW

CHURCH RD

4

Hermit's Cell

Allengrove
Farm

ALLENGROVE LA

Luckington

POLAD SQUARE

Allen Grove

Hebden Leaze
Farm

Macmillan Way

3

Oak
Plantation

83

Alderton

GL9

Giant's
Cave

PO

2

Townfield
Farm

Splash
Pond

Hebden
Leaze

Fatting
Barn

1

Hebden
Farm

B4040

82

A B 82 C D 83 E F

BRISTOL RD

SHOPWORTH RD

Wiltshire STREET ATLAS

A   B   C   D   E   F

8

Severn Road
Bridge

M48

Mast

Severn

7

Aust
Cliff

89

New House
Farm

Old
Passage

6

Old Passage
House

Aust Warth

5

Cake Pill

Cake Pill
Gout

88

Northwick Oaze

Severn Way

Asnum
Copse

4

Lords Rhine

Bilsham Rhine

3

Northwick Pig
Farm

BS35

Bils
Fa

87

WARTH LA

AUST RD

Laural
Farm

Church
Farm

Northwick
Redwick & Northwick
CE Sch

2

Mill
Farm

B4055

Manor
Farm

SEVERN RD

NORTHWICK RD

WARTH LA

DANGER
AREA

Holm Rhine

Red
Lodge

Rifle Range

North Worthy
Farm

1

REDWICK RD

Severn
Lodge
Farm

REDWICK RD   B4064

BLANDS ROW

New
Passage

B403

B4055

M4

86

54   A   55   B   C   D   56   E   F

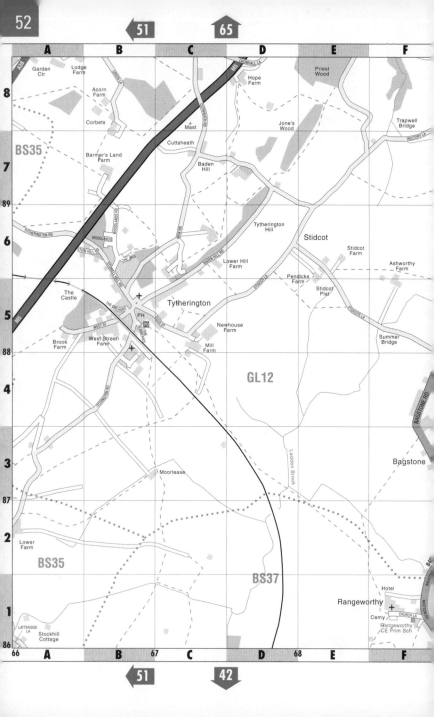

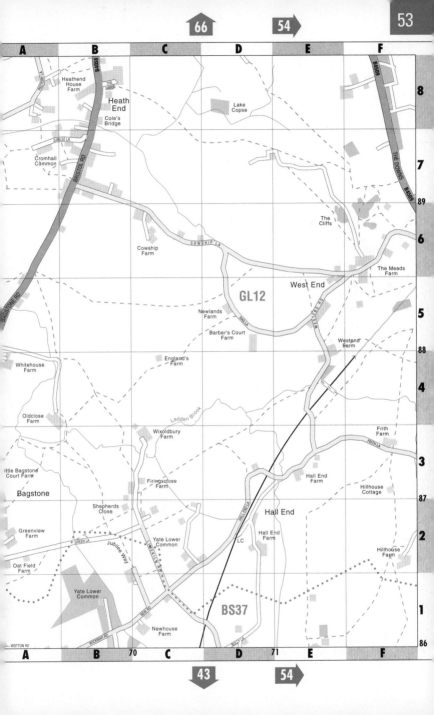

55
69

8

Kilcott Mill

Hammouth Hill

Hammouth Hill Wood

Monarch's Way

Cotswold Way

Midger Nature Reserve

Midger Wood

Midger Wood

Whitewell Wood

GL8

Nan Tow's Tump

7

Lower Kilcott

Lizens Wood

GL12

Back Common

Field Barn

Apsimore Barn

89

6

Monarch's Way
Cotswold Way

Curtis Mill

Stickstey Wood

Upper Kilcott

Ridge Wood

Cfaypit Wood

Miry Wood

Hobbyhorse Wood

5

Small Coombe

Bangel Wood

88

Hennel Bottom

Church Wood

Starveall Farm

4

Barley Ridge

Upton Coombe

Starveall

Tump Barn

Beech Lane Farm

3

ST JOHN'S LA
BACK ST

Warren Farm

Blackwell's

GL9

Hawkesbury Upton

87

PARK ST

NEWTOWN
SANDPITS LA

2

Folly Farm

Hinnegar

Britain Bottom

Back Warren

1

FRANCE LA

SANDPITS LA

Dunkirk Farm

A433

Swangrove

The Gorses

Ragged Castle (Folly)

86

Dunkirk

A46

55
46

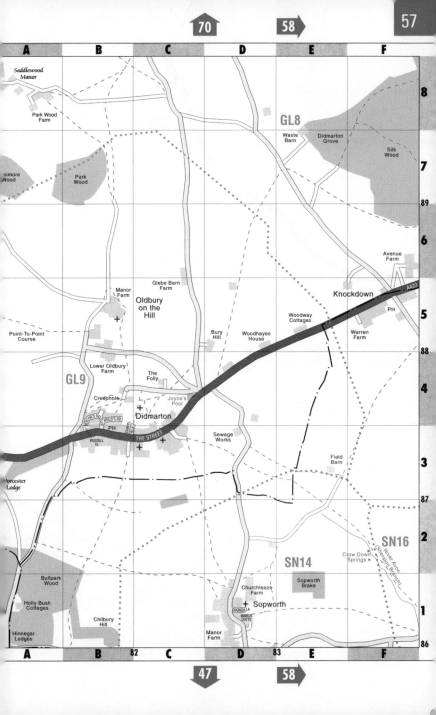

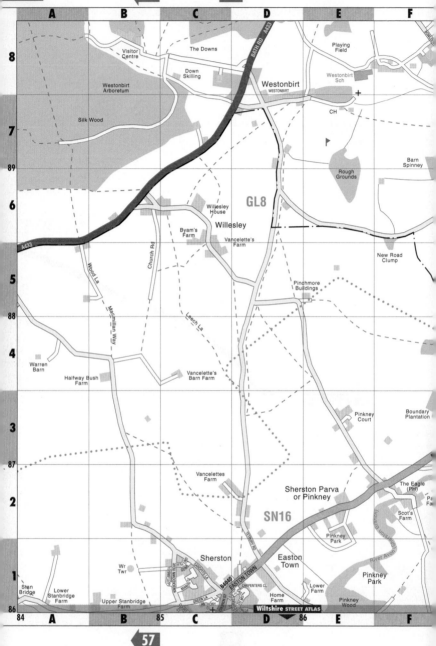

8

7

89

6

5

88

4

3

87

2

1

86

A B 85 C D 86 E F

BATH RD A433

The Downs

Down Skilling

Playing Field

Visitor Centre

Westonbirt
WESTONBIRT

Westonbirt Sch

Westonbirt Arboretum

Silk Wood

CH

Barn Spinney

Rough Grounds

GL8

Willesley House

Byam's Farm

Willesley

Vancelette's Farm

New Road Clump

A433

Wood La

Church Rd

Pinchmore Buildings

Macmillan Way

Leech La

Warren Barn

Halfway Bush Farm

Vancelette's Barn Farm

Pinkney Court

Boundary Plantation

Vancelettes Farm

Sherston Parva or Pinkney

The Eagle (PH)

SN16

Scot's Farm

Pinkney Park

Stan Bridge

Lower Stanbridge Farm

Wr Twr

Sherston

Upper Stanbridge Farm

B4040

GREEN LA

ANTHONY CL

EASTON TOWN

CARPENTERS CL

Easton Town

Home Farm

Lower Farm

Pinkney Park

Pinkney Wood

Wiltshire STREET ATLAS

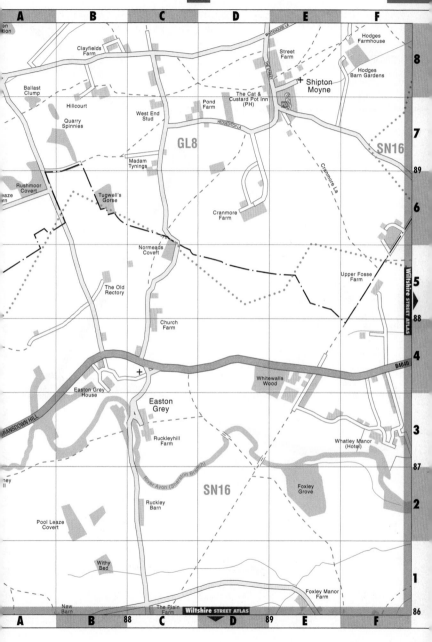

Clayfields Farm

Ballast Clump

Hillcourt

Quarry Spinnies

West End Stud

Madam Tynings

Rushmoor Covert

Tugwell's Gorse

Normeads Covert

The Old Rectory

Church Farm

Easton Grey House

Easton Grey

Ruckleyhill Farm

Ruckley Barn

Pool Leaze Covert

Withy Bed

New Barn

The Plain Farm

Pond Farm

The Cat & Custard Pot Inn (PH)

Street Farm

Shipton Moyne

Hodges Farmhouse

Hodges Barn Gardens

HEDGEDITCH LA

THE STREET

WHITEHOUSE LA

Cranmore Farm

Cranmore La

Upper Fosse Farm

Whitewalls Wood

Whatley Manor (Hotel)

Foxley Grove

Foxley Manor Farm

River Avon (Sherston Branch)

RANSDOWN HILL

B4040

GL8

SN16

SN16

A B C D E F

8

89

7

6

5

88

4

87

3

2

86

1

88 89

Wiltshire STREET ATLAS

CHEPSTOW
(CAS-GWENT)

NP16

NP26

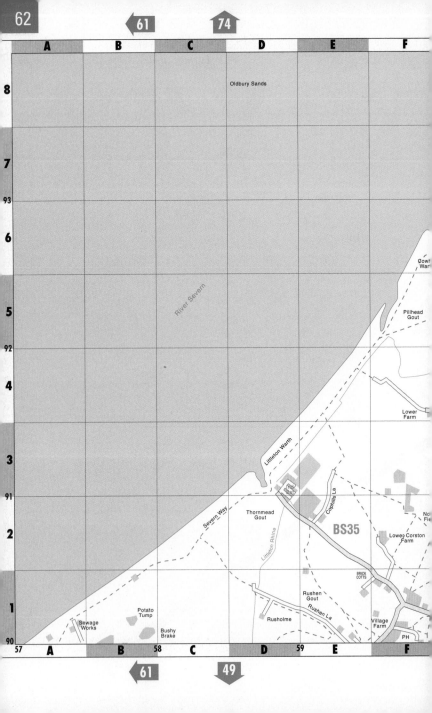

A B C D E F

8

Oldbury Sands

7

93

6

Cowl
War

5

River Severn

Pillhead
Gout

92

4

Lower
Farm

3

Littleton Warth

91

Frog
Land

Cophills La

Thornmead
Gout

BS35

No
Fie

2

Littleton Rhine

Severn Way

Lower Corston
Farm

BRICK
COTTS

1

Rushen Gout

Potato
Tump

Rushen La

Village
Farm

Sewage
Works

Rusholme

PH

90

Bushy
Brake

57 A B 58 C D 59 E F

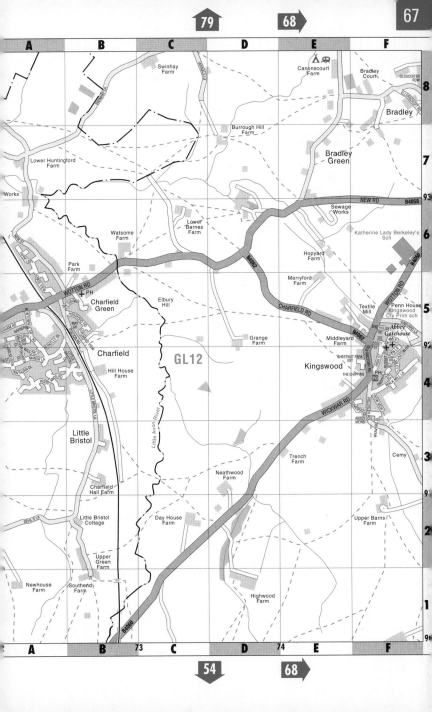

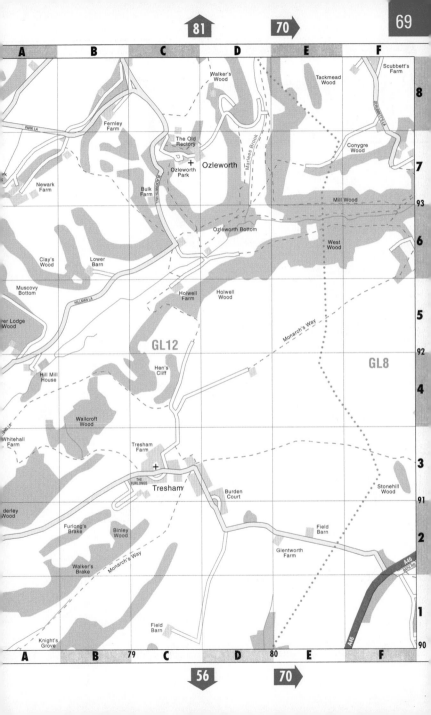

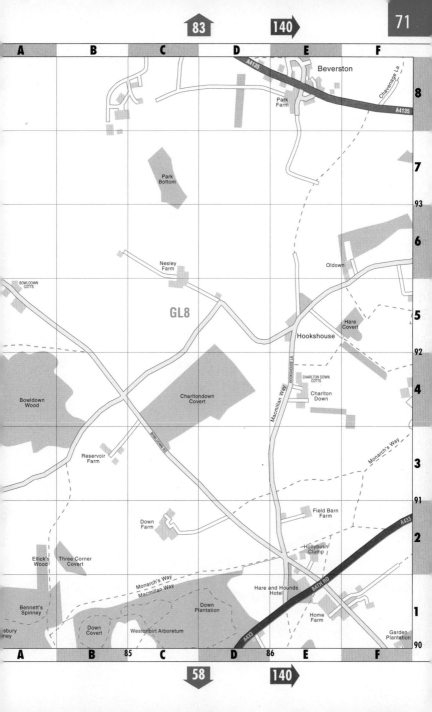

A B C D E F

8
7
93
6
5
92
4
3
91
2
1
90

A4135 Beverston

Chavenage La

Park Farm

A4135

Park Bottom

Nesley Farm

Oldown

BOWLDOWN COTTS

GL8

Hare Covert

Hookshouse

Bowldown Wood

Charltondown Covert

CHARLTON DOWN COTTS

Charlton Down

Macmillan Way

Monarch's Way

Reservoir Farm

BOWLDOWN RD

Field Barn Farm

A433

Down Farm

Hollybush Clump

BATH RD

Ellick's Wood

Three Corner Covert

Monarch's Way

Macmillan Way

Hare and Hounds Hotel

Home Farm

Bennett's Spinney

Down Plantation

Westonbirt Arboretum

Down Covert

A433

Garden Plantation

sbury ney

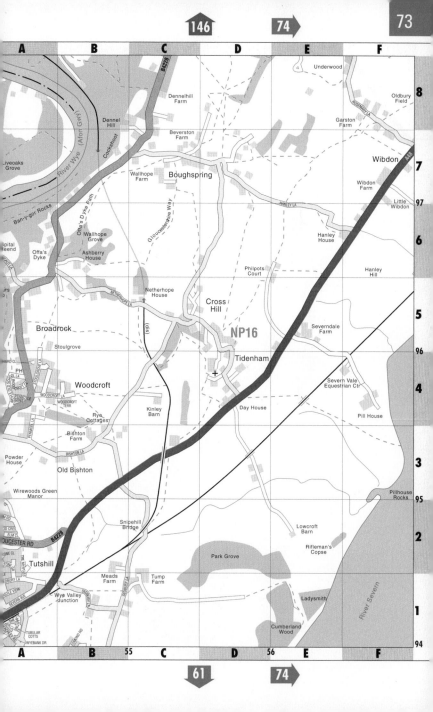

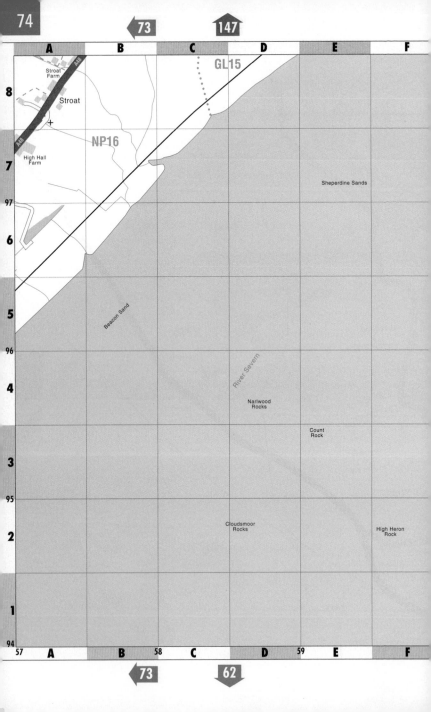

A B C D E F

8

Hills Flats

7

97

GL13

6

River Severn

The Ledges
White House

Chapel House

Severn Way

Manor Farm

BURDON RD

The Laurels

5

96

PH

Shepperdine Farm

4

North Ham Corner

Shepperdine Farm

Shepperdine

Brickhouse Farm

3

Shepperdine Withybed

BS35

95

Harecrest La

Jobscreen Farm

SHEPPERDINE RD

2

Lowgoods Farm

Power Station

Knight's Farm

Mast

Visitor Ctr

HILLS

1

94

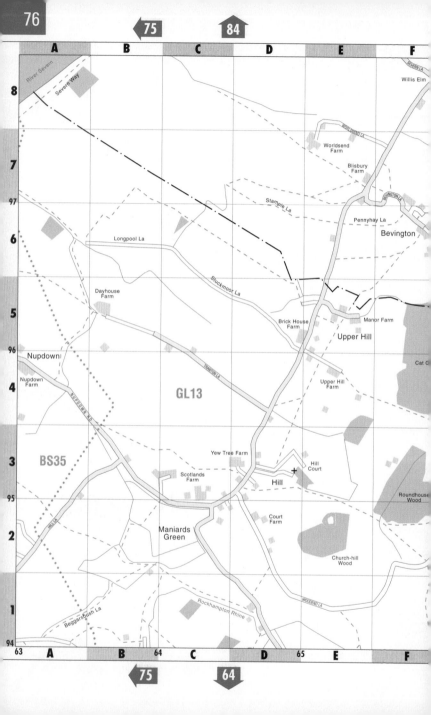

8

7

97

6

5

96

4

3

95

2

1

94

A B C D E F

Bluegates
Farm

Park
House

Whitcliff Park
(Deer Park)

Comeley
Farm

Park
Farm

Tanhouse
Farm

Doverte Brook

Lobthorn
Covert

Pedington
Elm Farm

Pedington
Elm

Matford
Bridge

Little Avon River

Pedington
Manor Farm

Pedington
Farm

The
Quarries

Hystfield

Hystfield
Farm

Appleridge
Farm

GL13

Dog-gate Lane

APPLERIDGE LA

Westend
House

Stone with
Woodford
CE Sch

A38

WOTFORD

DAMERY LA.

Newpark
Farm

Lowerstone
Farm

COURT MEW

COURT VIEW

SCHOOL MEWS

COLING MEAD

PH

Stone

DAMERY LA

GLOUCESTER
RD

95

Manor
Farm

Stone
Bridge

Lowerstone
Wood

WOODEND LA

Lower
Stone

MOORSLADE LA

Glen
Farm

Moorslade

The
Mount

Green
Farm

A38

Chestnut
Farm

GL12

A B 67 C D 68 E F

A B C D E F

8

Newport

Greenways

Goldwick
Farm

Crossw

HIGH VIEW
CHURCH VIEW

Hotel

Baynhamcourt
Farm

7

Oakleaze
Farm

Doverte Brook

Hogsdown
Farm

97

6

GL13

Lower
Wick

GL11

HERDERS LA

Swanley
Farm

Swanley

Lowerwick
Farm

Midd
Wick

5

SWANLEY LA

Woodfordgreen
Farm

Middlewick
Farm

96

Whitehall
Farm

4

A38

Woodford

PH

Wick
Bridge

Michaelwood
Farm

Harold's
Brake

DAMERY LA

MULE ST

Michael Wood
Service Area

Sweetbri
Brake

3

Woodford
Farm

Middle Mill
Farm

95

DAMERY LA

Furzeground
Wood

2

DAMERY LA

Micheal Wood

Michaelwood Lodge
Farm

Little Avon River

GL12

Damery

1

Crockley's
Farm

Damery
Bridge

Iron Mill Grove

M5

Daniel's Wood

94

69 A B 70 C D 71 E F

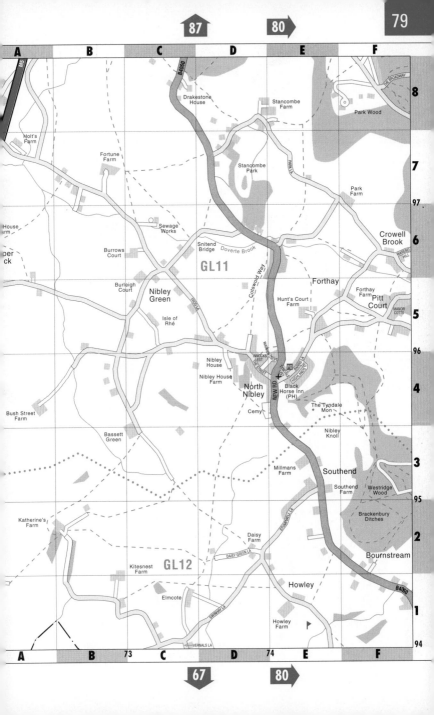

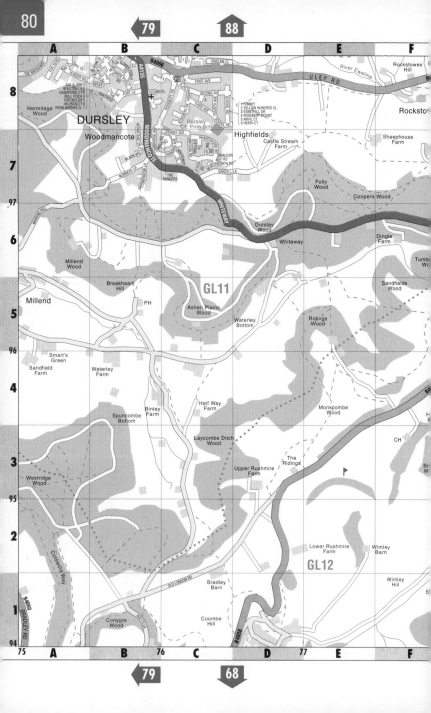

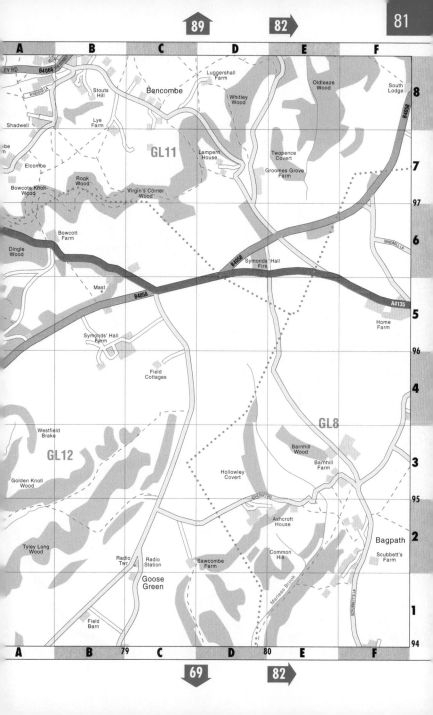

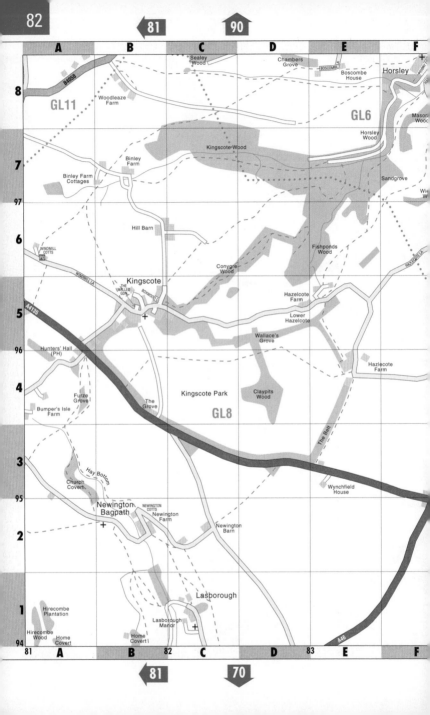

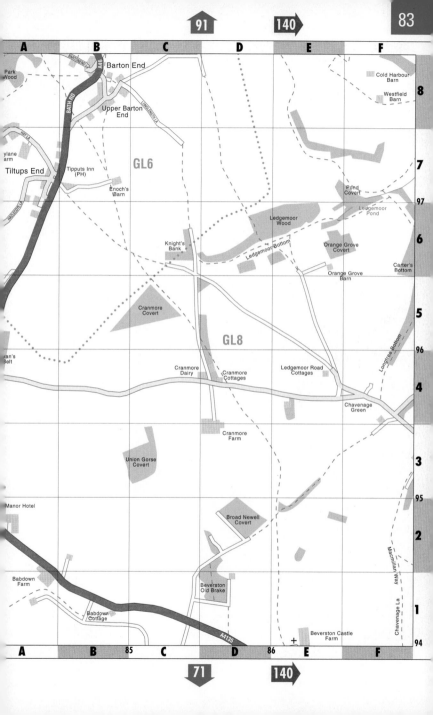

A   B   C   D   E   F

Park Wood

Barton End

8 Cold Harbour Barn

Westfield Barn

Upper Barton End

BATH RD

A46

LONGTREE LA

GL6

ylane arm

Tiltups End

Tipputs Inn (PH)

7

HAZEL LA

Enoch's Barn

Pond Covert

97

Ledgemoor Pond

Ledgemoor Wood

6

Knight's Bank

Ledgemoor Bottom

Orange Grove Covert

Carter's Bottom

Orange Grove Barn

Cranmore Covert

5

GL8

96

Longtree Bottom

an's Belt

Cranmore Dairy

Cranmore Cottages

Ledgemoor Road Cottages

4

Chavenage Green

Cranmore Farm

3

Union Gorse Covert

95

Manor Hotel

2

Broad Newell Covert

Macmillan Way

Babdown Farm

Chavenage La

Babdown Cottage

Beverston Old Brake

1

A4135

Beverston Castle Farm

94

A   B   85   C   D   86   E   F

GL15

Lydney
COOKSON
TERR
LC
RAILWAY
TERR
THE MARINA
HARBOUR RD
Lydney Harbour
Lydney Marsh
Lydney
Ind Est
Naas
House
HARBOUR RD

New Grounds

Saniger Sands

River Severn

Black
Rock

Bull
Rock

Lydney Sand

Hayward
Rock

Severn Way

GL13

Severn House
Farm
SEVERN LA

63   64   65

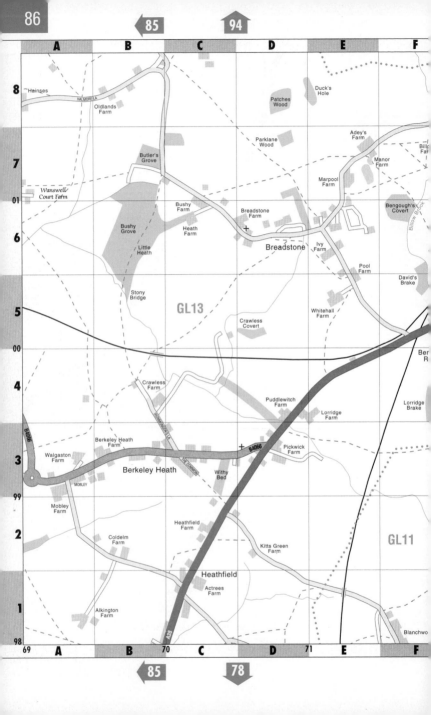

8

7

01

6

5

00

4

3

99

2

1

98

75   A   B   76   C   D   77   E   F

Halmore Mill

River Cam

Draycott Farm

Meadbridge's Grove

The Elms

Church Farm

Coaley CE Prim Sch

Coaley

Pinnells End Farm

Betworthy Farm

FIELD LA

Field Farm

Hamshill

Trenley House

Sil Str Hou

HAM ST

Upthorpe

Pear Orchard Farm

Upper Upthorpe Farm

UPTHORPE LA

GREEN LA

Upthorpe Farm

Green Street

Ashmead Covert

Ashmead Farm

GL11

Ashmead House

Myles House

ROWLEY MEWS

GLEBELANDS

STATION RD

Cam

Cam Everlands Prim Sch

Cam Hopton CE Prim Sch

Dulkin Brook

Ashmead Green

Everlands

Upper Cam

Cam Long Down

Nature Reserve

Cotswold Way

Norman Hill

Church Farm

ROWAN GR

MAPLE LA

ST GEORGE'S RD

CHURCH RD

HILL SQ

Downhouse Farm

P

Springhill

Peaked Down

SPRINGHILL

PRIORY CT

Redbrook Sch

Kingshill

KINGSHILL RD

A4135

SPRINGHILL

Farfield

The Grove

Uleyfield

Hydega

DURSLEY

Sports Ctr

Cam House Sch

DRAKE LA

Coldharbour Farm

Downham Hill

WINDSOR RD

DURSLEY CT

THE BROADWAY 1
FIVE ACRES 2?

Liby

CASTLE ST

PARSONAGE ST

SILVER ST

LONG ST

CHESTAL

A4135

Home Farm

Chestal

Newbrook Farm

HILL RD

PROSPECT PL

Ferney Hill

Wresden Farm

1 BOULTON LA
2 BULL PITCH
3 BROADWELL TERR
4 YELLOW HUNDRED CL
5 FERNEY

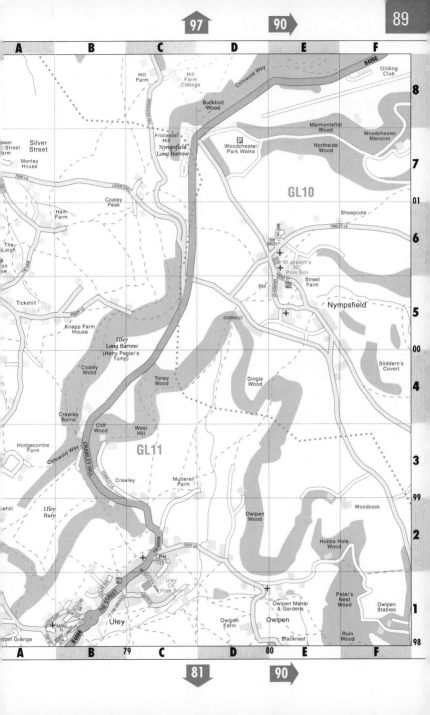

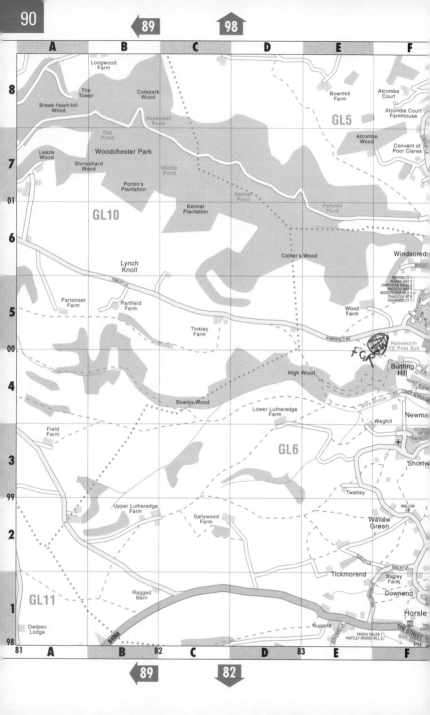

8

7

01

6

5

00

4

3

99

2

1

98

81   **A**   **B**   82   **C**   **D**   83   **E**   **F**

Longwood
Farm

The
Tower

Colepark
Wood

Break-heart-hill
Wood

Honeywell
Pond

Old
Pond

Bownhill
Farm

GL5

Atcombe
Court

Atcombe Court
Farmhouse

Atcombe
Wood

Convent of
Poor Clares

Leaze
Wood

Woodchester Park

Stoneshard
Wood

Pontin's
Plantation

Middle
Pond

GL10

Kennel
Pond

Kennel
Plantation

Parkmill
Pond

Windsored

WINDSO

Lynch
Knoll

TINKLEY LA

Collier's Wood

NORTON CT 1
ROWAN WAY 2
HAWTHORN RIDGE 3
BADGERS WAY 4
WOODPECKER WLK 5
CRADDOCK CT 6
HIGHWOOD CT 7

Partstreet
Farm

Partfield
Farm

Tinkley
Farm

Wood
Farm

NYMPSFIELD RD

Nailsworth
CE Prim Sch

FGR

Bunting
Hill

High Wood

Bowlas Wood

Lower Lutheredge
Farm

Miry Brook

LOWER NEWMA

HIGHER NEWM

Newma

Field
Farm

Waghill

COTSW
COTT
NORTHWOOD

GL6

Shortw

Upper Lutheredge
Farm

Sallywood
Farm

Twatley

WALLOW
GR

Wallow
Green

SUGLEY LA

GL11

Ragged
Barn

SUGLEY LA

Tickmorend

Sugley
Farm

Downend

Horsle

Owlpen
Lodge

B4058

Nupend

B4058

PRIORY FIELDS 1
HARTLEY BRIDGE HILL 2

THE STREET

PH 1

THE

Sch

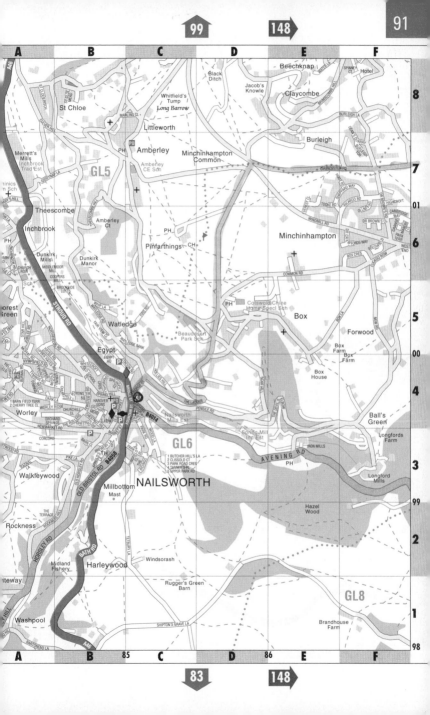

147 156

| A | B | C | D | E | F |

8
Shaphouse Farm

Oldcroft
1 BRIERLEY WAY
2 CHURCH WLK

Little Purlieu

Hulks Farm

Soilwell Farm

Needs Top

7
Ten Acre Wood

Soilwell Manor

Allaston Meend

Tingley Wood

Purlieu End Farm

The Purlieu

05

6
NEW MILLS

Allaston

Little Allaston

Billings Barn

5
Millrough Wood

Allaston Court
Primrose Hill
CE Prim Sch

Driffield Farm

Mast

Nursehill Wood

Nursehill

04

PH

Primrose Hill

Cross Hands

GL15

4
Middle Forge

Highfield

1 NODENS WAY
2 NERO CL
3 CAESARS CL

Rodley Manor

Hurst Farm

Warren

Well Ga

THE SPRINGS

Newerne

3
Lydney
CE Prim Sch

Lydney

Severnbanks
Prim Sch

Warren Grove

TUTHILL RISE 1
THE FOLDERS 2
HAWTHORN CT 3

Lydney
Tower

HAMPTON MEWS
FAIRFIELD MEWS

03

Crump Farm

Kears Wood

Dean Forest Rly

1 WYNTOUR'S PAR
2 DARTERS CL
3 HERBERT HOWELL'S CL
4 STEEPLE VW
5 VICARAGE CL

2
Bathurst Park

Whitecross Sch

St Mary's

Tutnalls

Mount Pleasant Cl

Plummer's Farm

Cliff Farm

Iron Foundry

CH

Naas Crossing
(LC)

1
A48

LC
Lydney
Junc

Naas Court

Naas

02

| 63 | A | B | 64 | C | D | 65 | E | F |

A   B   C   D   E   F

8

Middle Point

River Severn

7

Frampton Sand

05

6

Tites Point

The Dumbles

PH

The Trumps

Twr

The Royal Drift

PH
Swing
Bridge

Purton

Oldmoor
Cliff

5

Swing
Bridge

Severn Way

04

The Gloucester and Sharpness Canal

Pockington
Farm

Decoy
Pool

4

Decoy Pool
House

GL2

Water Treatment
Works

Gilgal Brook

RIDDLE
ST

3

Ironwells
New Covert

GL13

Red
Wood

03

Halmore
Farm

2

The
Plantation

Priorswood
Farm

Hurst
Farm

Halmore

PH

Pool Farm

Gilgal
Bridge

TYNDALE RD

Wards
Grove

Oxenbrook

1

Howes's
Grove

Acton
Hall

02

69   A   B   70   C   D   71   E   F

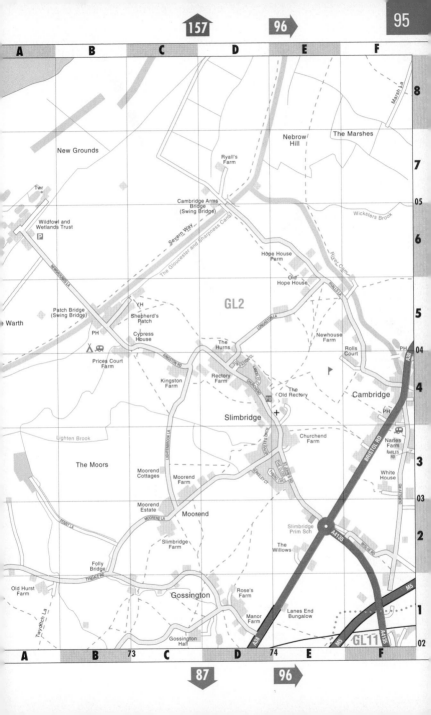

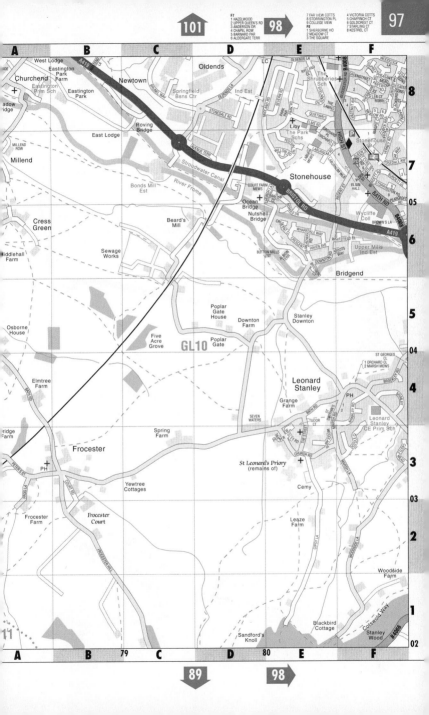

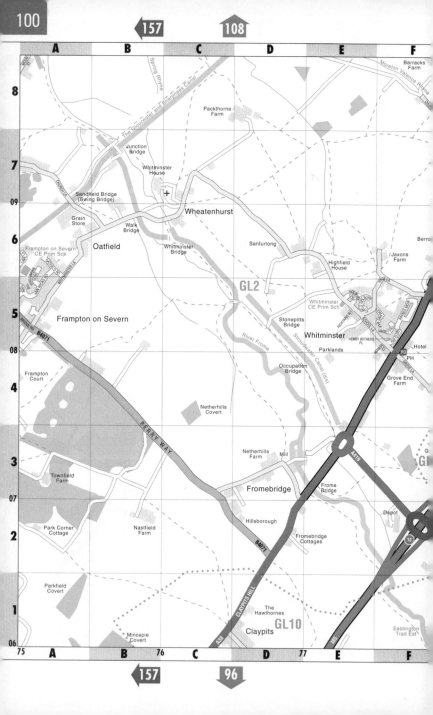

157
108

A B C D E F

8

Barracks
Farm

Moreton Valence Rifle

Packthorne
Farm

Junction
Bridge

7

Whitminster
House

09

Sandfield Bridge
(Swing Bridge)

Wheatenhurst

Grain
Store

Walk
Bridge

6

Oatfield

Whitminster
Bridge

Sanfurlong

Berro

Frampton on Severn
CE Prim Sch

Highfield
House

Jaxons
Farm

GL2

Whitminster
CE Prim Sch

5

Frampton on Severn

Stonepitts
Bridge

Whitminster

Henry Withers

Hotel

River Frome

PO
PH

08

B4071

Parklands

Grove End
Farm

Frampton
Court

Occupation
Bridge

4

Netherhills
Covert

PERRY WAY

Netherhills
Farm

Mill

A419

G
GI

3

Townfield
Farm

Frome
Bridge

Fromebridge

07

Depot

2

Park Corner
Cottage

Nastfield
Farm

Hillsborough

B4071

Fromebridge
Cottages

13

Parkfield
Covert

CLAYPITS HILL

The
Hawthornes

GL10

1

Claypits

A38

Eastington
Trad Est

06

Mincepie
Covert

M5

75 **A** **B** 76 **C** **D** 77 **E** **F**

157
96

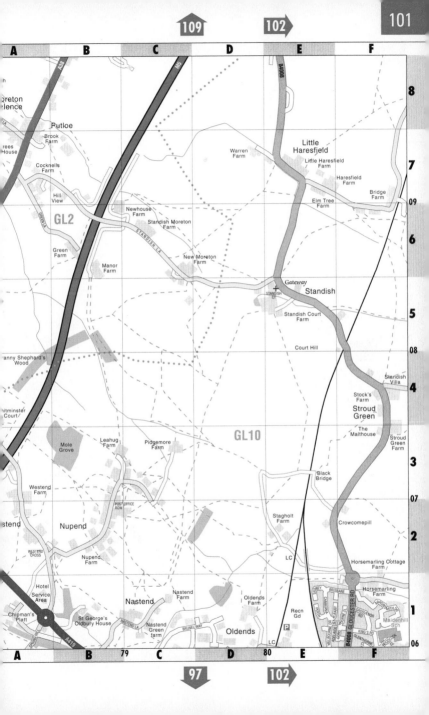

109
102

A   B   C   D   E   F

8

Putloe

Little
Haresfield

7

09

Brook
Farm

Warren
Farm

Little Haresfield
Farm

Haresfield
Farm

Bridge
Farm

Cocknells
Farm

Elm Tree
Farm

oreton
lence

rees
House

Hill
View

GL2

Newhouse
Farm

Standish Moreton
Farm

6

Green
Farm

Manor
Farm

New Moreton
Farm

Gateway

Standish

STANDISH

5

Standish Court
Farm

Court Hill

08

anny Shephard's
Wood

Standish
Villa

4

hitminster
Court

Stock's
Farm

Stroud
Green

Mole
Grove

Leahug
Farm

Pidgemore
Farm

GL10

The
Malthouse

Stroud
Green
Farm

3

Westend
Farm

Black
Bridge

07

POST OFFICE
ROW

Stagholt
Farm

stend

Nupend

Crowcomepill

2

WESTEND
CROSS

Nupend
Farm

LC

Horsemarling Cottage
Farm

Hotel
Service
Area

Horsemarling
Farm

Chipman's
Platt

St George's
Oldbury House

Nastend

MASTEND LA

Nastend
Farm

Oldends
Farm

BRUNEL WAY

Recn
Gd

Maidenhill
Sch

1

Nastend
Green
farm

Oldends

P

B4008 GLOUCESTER RD

KING'S RD

06

A   B   79   C   D   80   E   F

102

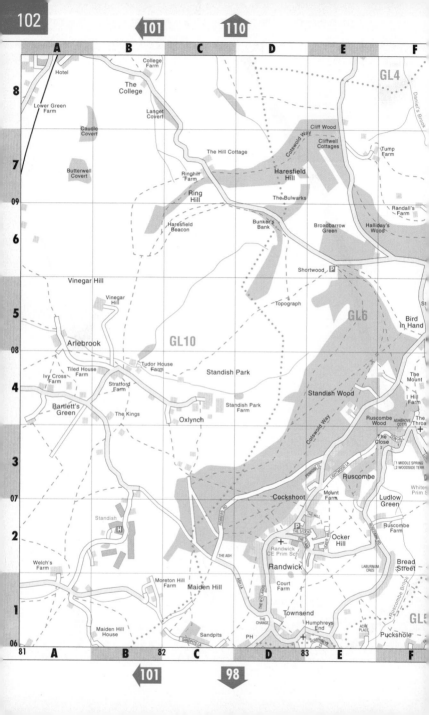

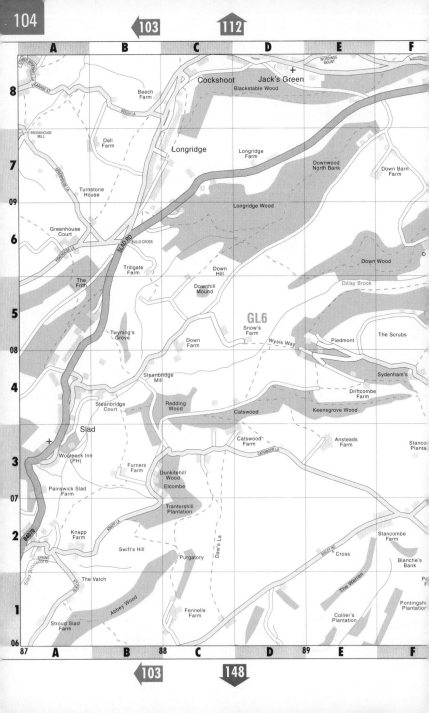

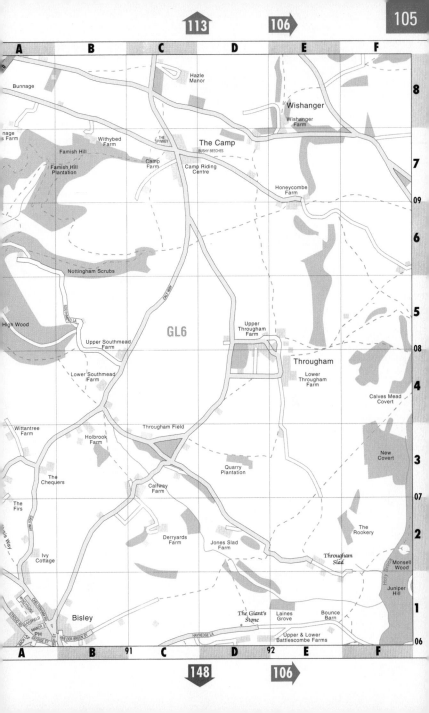

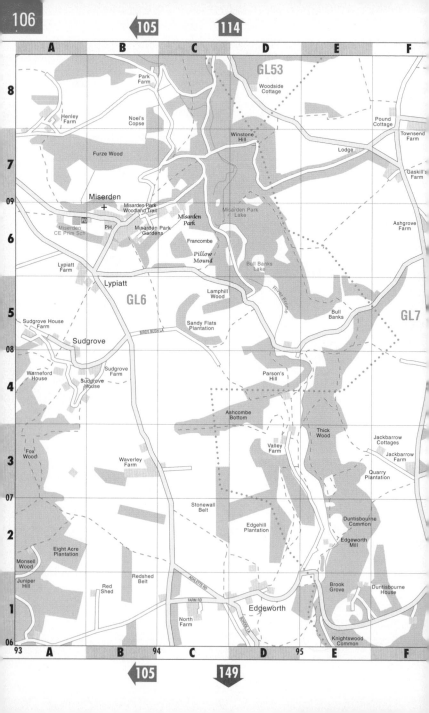

105
114

GL53

A B C D E F

8

Park
Farm

Woodside
Cottage

Henley
Farm

Noel's
Copse

Pound
Cottage

Townsend
Farm

Winstone
Hill

Lodge

Furze Wood

7

Gaskill's
Farm

Miserden

09

Misarden Park
Woodland Trail

Misarden Park
Lake

Ashgrove
Farm

Miserden
CE Prim Sch

PH

Misarden Park
Gardens

Misarden
Park

6

Francombe

Lypiatt
Farm

Pillow
Mound

Bull Banks
Lake

Lypiatt

GL6

Lamphill
Wood

River Frome

5

Sudgrove House
Farm

Sandy Flats
Plantation

Bull
Banks

GL7

Sudgrove

BIRDS BUSH LA

08

Warneford
House

Sudgrove
Farm

Parson's
Hill

Sudgrove
House

4

Ashcombe
Bottom

Thick
Wood

Jackbarrow
Cottages

Fox
Wood

Waverley
Farm

Valley
Farm

Jackbarrow
Farm

3

Quarry
Plantation

07

Stonewall
Belt

Duntisbourne
Common

Edgehill
Plantation

2

Eight Acre
Plantation

Edgeworth
Mill

Monsell
Wood

Juniper
Hill

Redshed
Belt

ASH FLATS RD

Brook
Grove

Duntisbourne
House

Red
Shed

FARM RD

Edgeworth

1

North
Farm

SCHOOL LA

Knightswood
Common

06

93 A 94 B C 94 D 95 E F

105
149

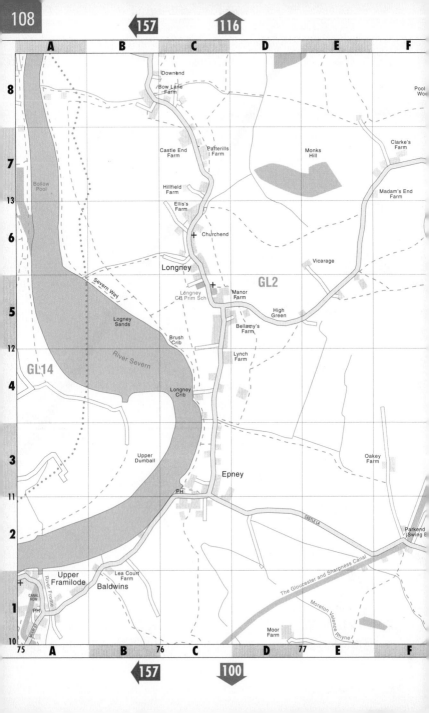

A   B   C   D   E   F

8
Downend
Bow Lane
Farm
Pool
Woo

7
Castle End
Farm
Patterills
Farm
Monks
Hill
Clarke's
Farm

Bollow
Pool
13
Hillfield
Farm
Madam's End
Farm

6
Ellis's
Farm
Churchend

Longney
Vicarage

GL2
Longney
C& Prim Sch
Manor
Farm

5
Logney
Sands
High
Green

Severn Way
Bellamy's
Farm

12
Brush
Crib
Lynch
Farm

River Severn

GL14
4
Longney
Crib

3
Upper
Dumball
Oakey
Farm

Epney

11
PH

2
CASTLE A
Parkend
(Swing B

The Gloucester and Sharpness Canal

Upper
Framilode
Lea Court
Farm
Baldwins

CANAL
ROW
Moreton Valence Rhyne

1
PH

River Frome

Moor
Farm

10
75   A   B   76   C   D   77   E   F

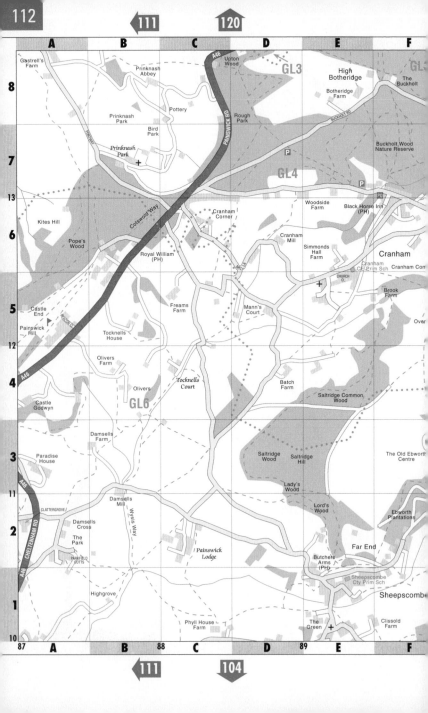

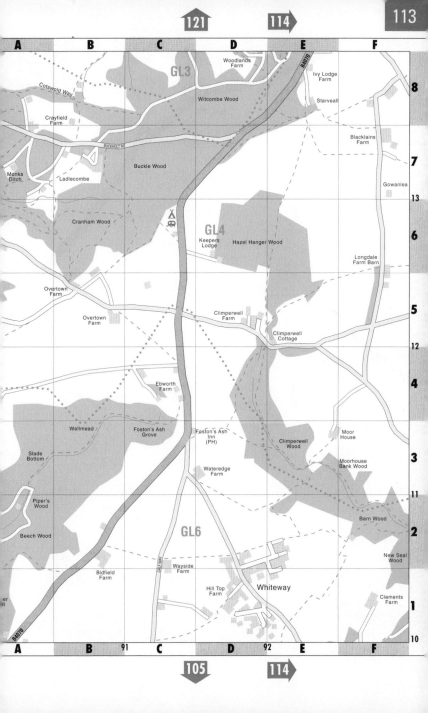

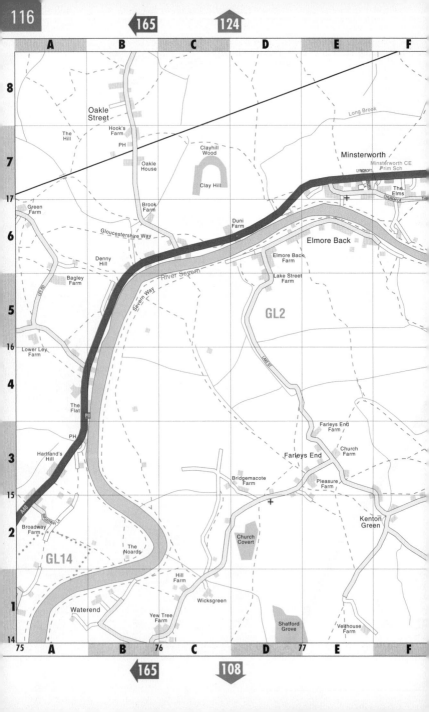

8

Oakle
Street

The
Hill

Hook's
Farm

PH

Oakle
House

Clayhill
Wood

Clay Hill

Long Brook

7

Minsterworth

Minsterworth CE
Prim Sch

LYNCROFT

The
Elms

CHURCH LA

17

Green
Farm

Brook
Farm

Gloucestershire Way

Duni
Farm

Elmore Back

6

Denny
Hill

River Severn

Elmore Back
Farm

Bagley
Farm

Severn Way

Lake Street
Farm

5

GL2

16

Lower Ley
Farm

LAKE ST

4

The
Flat

PO

3

PH

Hartland's
Hill

Farleys End
Farm

Farleys End

Church
Farm

15

Bridgemacote
Farm

Pleasure
Farm

2

Broadway
Farm

The
Noards

Church
Covert

Kenton
Green

GL14

1

Waterend

Hill
Farm

Yew Tree
Farm

Wicksgreen

Shatford
Grove

Velthouse
Farm

14

A B C D E F

8

The Redlands

Moorcroft House Farm

7

Clark's Cottage

Hampton Farm

PH

WEIR LA

A38

17

Highcross Farm

Gloucestershire Way

6

Minsterworth Ham

Upper Rea Farm

5

Ash Covert

Groundless Pool

GL2

idge art

Middle Rea

16

Windmill Hill

River Severn

Severn Way

4

Works

Corn Ham

Riversmead Farm

SIMS LA

Elmore Court

Weir Green

Highley Farm

Elmore

Weir Farm

VICTORIA COTTS

Lower Rea

3

Hanging Covert

Stonebench House

LONGFIELD 1
CAMELLIA WLK 2
ELDERSFIELD CL 3
MAGNOLIA WLK 4

Prim Sch

15

Severn Farm

Gloucester and Sharpness Canal

2

Brookfield House

COPPERS ELM

Dimore Brook

ELMORE LA

Prim Sch

Libv

Hockley Wood

Hollow Farm

MALLARD CL 1
SANDPIPER CL 2
THE CAUSEWAY 3
WATERMANS CT 4
MERCHANTS MEAD 5
WATERWHEEL CL 6
KINGFISHER RISE 7

THE WILLOWS

COPPER BEECH GR

PO

Martin's Wood

Quedgeley

Sch

1

14

A B C D E F

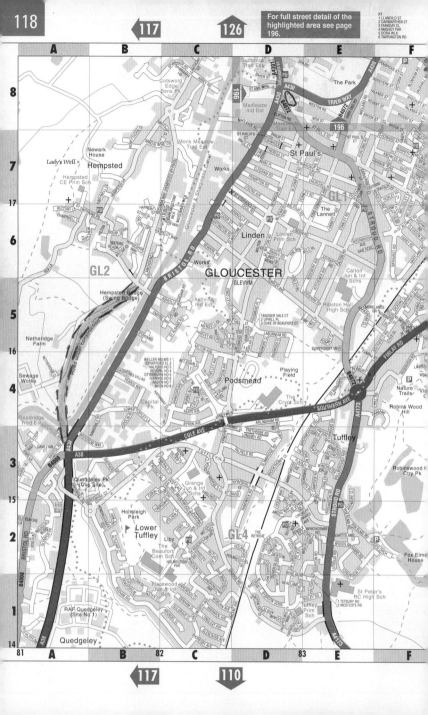

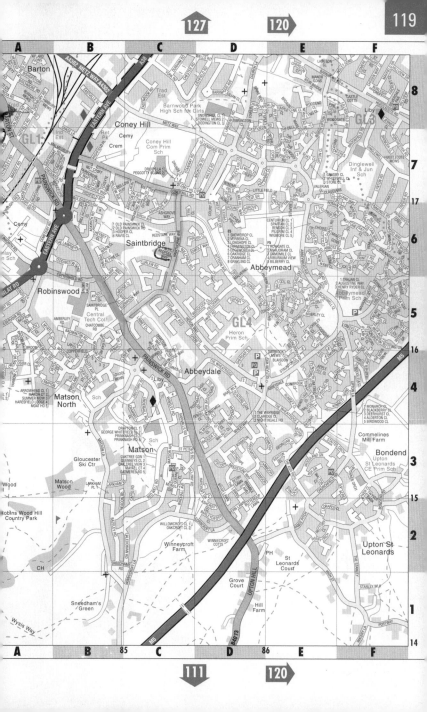

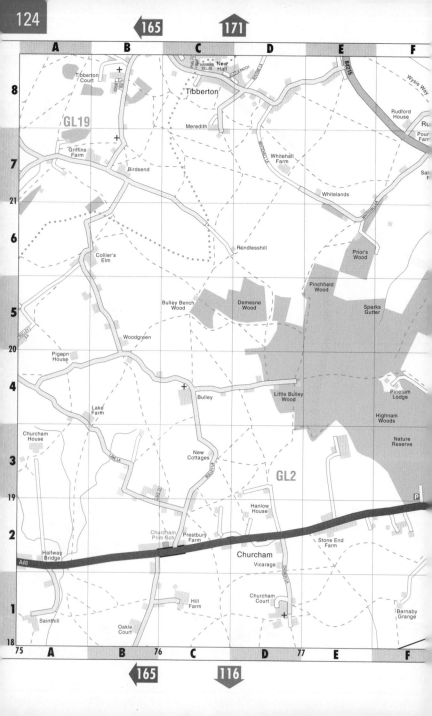

125 172

A B C D E F

8

White House
Abbot's Lodge
The Steadings Bsns Ctr
Maisemore Court
Upper Parting
Works
Gloucestershire Way

Maisemore
CHURCH RISE
PH
Maisemore Bridge Cross
7

21

Rectory Farm
West Channel
Maisemore Ham
Alney Island
PH
Queen's Dyke
Longford
CHESTERTON CT 1
LONSFORD MEWS 2
FINCHMOOR MEWS 3
TAURUS, CL 4
AUSTIN DR
LEWIS AV

6

Persh Farm
East Channel
Severn Way
Caravan Site
Walham
Frogcastle Fram
TEWKESBURY RD

Pla Fi

5

20

GL2
Alney Island

Over
Wysis Way
PH
A40
Over Bridge
A417
Town Ham
WALHAM LA
LAWRENCE WAY
River Twyver
GL1
Livestock Market
Ind Est
ESTCOURT RD
A430
A417
196
Girls High Sch
Kingsholm
RFC Ground
Kingsholm CE Prim Sch

4

River Severn
Port Ham
Lower Parting
OVER CSWY
Richard's Wood
WESTEND TERR
ALNEY TERR
Pool Meadow I
P&R
Mean Ham
L Ctr
A417
Works
GL1

3

19

GL1
Oxlease
196
A38
Shire Hall
Cath
Mus
B4063 LONDON RD
GL

2

Severn Way
Sud Meadow
GLOUCESTER
GLEVVM
Castle Meads
Prison
50 Ct
Mus
BARRACK
Mus
THE QUAY
WESTGATE ST
The King's Sch
Mkt Mus & Art Gal
The Docks
Mus
Mus
SOUTHGATE ST
Coll
Coll
The Forum
L Ctr
METZ WAY
A430 BRUTON WAY
Glouce

1

18

Lanthony Rd Est
Severnside Trad Est
Llanthony Priory (rems of)
High Orchard
Sports Gd
COMMERCIAL RD

81 A B 82 C D 83 E F

125 118

For full street detail of highlighted area see page 196.

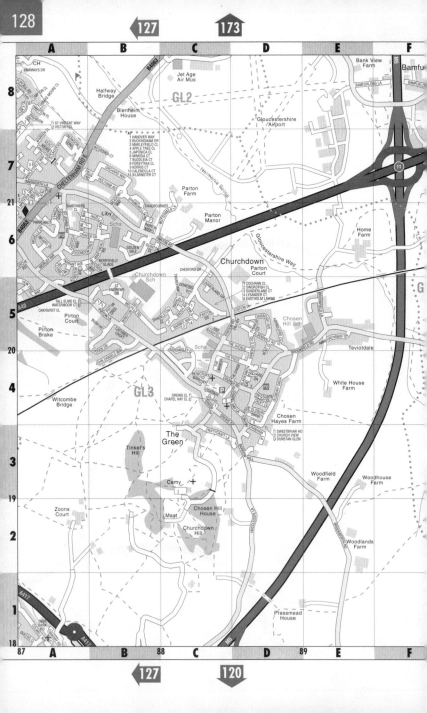

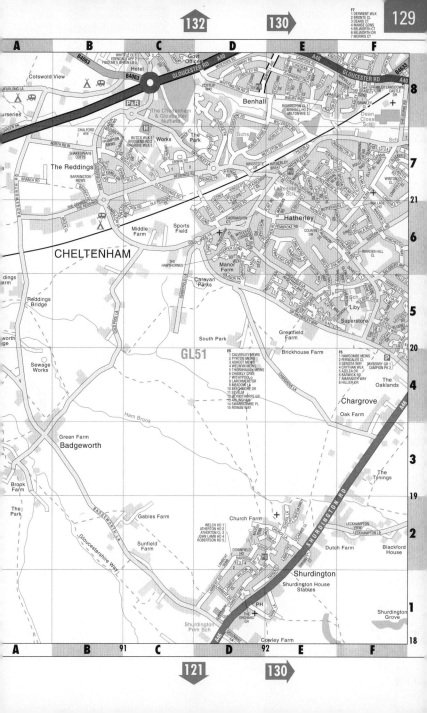

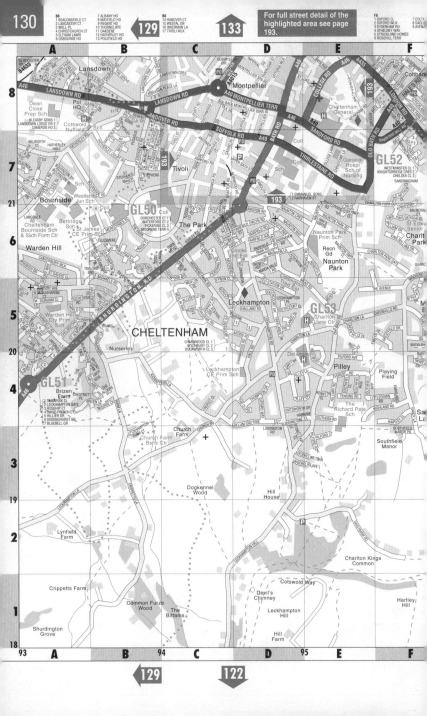

8

Nurseries

A4019

M5

Church Lane Farm

Church Farm

Chosen View Farm

WITHYBRIDGE LANE

M10

7

Fairoaks

Chestnut Farm

Dog Bark Lane (Track)

THE ORCHARD

25

Butler's Court

Uckington Farm

Uckington

6

Withy Bridge

Millhouse Farm

Old Hall

MOAT LN

River Chelt

TEWKESBURY RD

Swindon

M5

WITHYBRIDGE LANE

5

Pilgrove Farm

Pilgrove Bridge

Nursery

CORNMEADOW DR 1
HALLMEAD CL 2
HARVEST GR 3

B4634

24

OLD GLOUCESTER RD

Hayden Hill

FULBROOK CL 4
SHEPHERDS CL 5
WATERMOOR CL 6
WHITEMARSH CL 7
THISTLEDOWN CL 8
MAYTHORN DR 9
HONEYBOURNE DR 10

PILGROVE WAY

1 PETER PENNELL CL 1
2 SPRINGFIELD HO

Sch

Wks

PATTERDALE CL 1
SUMMERFIELD CL 2
KEIRLE WLK 3

WALDRIST

RHYATTIELD

PH

4

Orchard House

Hope Farm

GL51

Arthur Dye Prim Sch

LIPSON VILLAS

Arle

B4634

Hayden Farm

PARK VIEW

Sch

Hayden

3

Hayden Green

Springbank Club

HAMILTON

Hester's Way

PRINCESS ELIZABETH WAY

23

Sewage Works

Tanks

Fiddler's Green

Pates Gram Sch

Rowan Inf & Jun

2

Hayden Knoll

ALMOND CT 1
JUNIPER CT 2
LABURNUM CT 3

ACACIA

ALDER

MARSLAND RD

Sch

Playing Field

1

Golden Valley

Hotel

PH

Fiddlers Green Farm

B4063

Govt Offices

AUSTRALIA HO 1
CANBERRA HO 2

A4013

Monkscroft Com Prim Sch

St Mark's

JESSE MARY CHAMBERS ALMSHOUSES

Works

22

B4063

WHITTLE CL 1
EDENDALE APP 2
BARNWELL CL 3

A40 GLOUCESTER RD A40

90 A **91** B **91** C **92** D E F

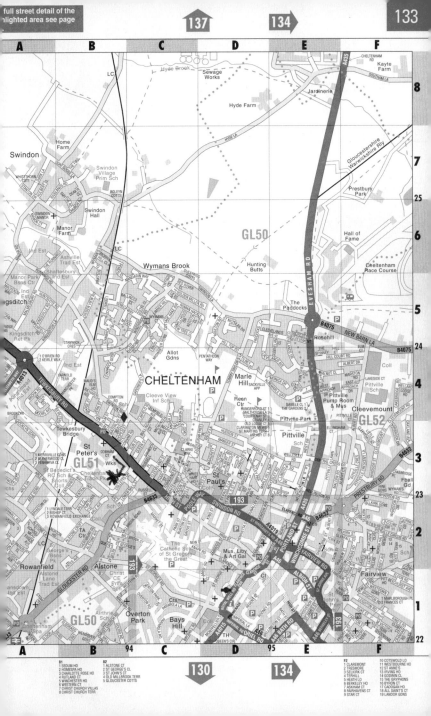

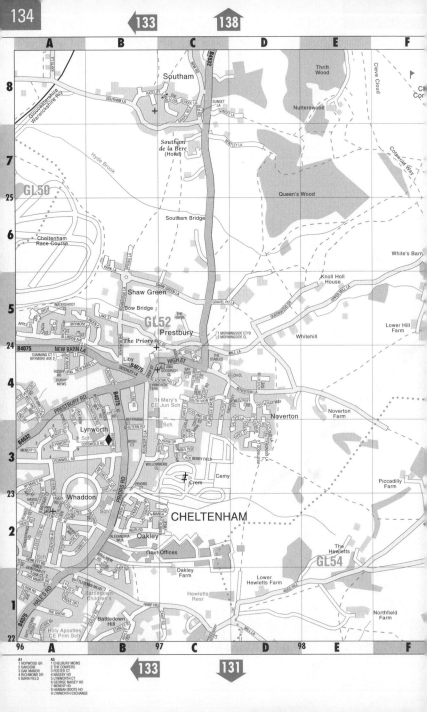

A B C D E F

8
7
25
6
5
24
4
3
23
2
1
22

96 97 98

Southam
Thrift Wood
Nutterswood
Southam de la Bere (Hotel)
GL50
Hyde Brook
Queen's Wood
Cheltenham Race Course
Southam Bridge
Cotswold Way
White's Barn
Knoll Holl House
Shaw Green
Bow Bridge
GL52
Prestbury
The Priory
Whitehill
Lower Hill Farm
The Hayes
1 MORNINGSIDE CTYD
2 MORNINGSIDE CL
New Barn La
B4075
Liby
HIGH ST
The Stables
Noverton
Noverton Farm
St Mary's CE Jun Sch
Lynworth
Sch
Whaddon
Piccadilly Farm
Crem
Cemy
CHELTENHAM
Oakley
Govt Offices
The Hewletts
GL54
Oakley Farm
Lower Hewletts Farm
Hewletts Resr
Hales Rd
Battledown Children's Ctr
Battledown Hill
Holy Apostles CE Prim Sch
Harp Hill
Northfield Farm

A1
1 HOPWOOD GR
2 OAKDENE
3 OAK MANOR
4 RICHMOND DR
5 BARN FIELD

A3
1 CHELBURY MEWS
2 THE CONIFERS
3 FOSTER CT
4 NAISBY RD
5 LYNWORTH CT
6 GEORGE NAISEY HO
7 MENDIP HO
8 HANNAH BOOTE HO
9 LYNWORTH EXCHANGE

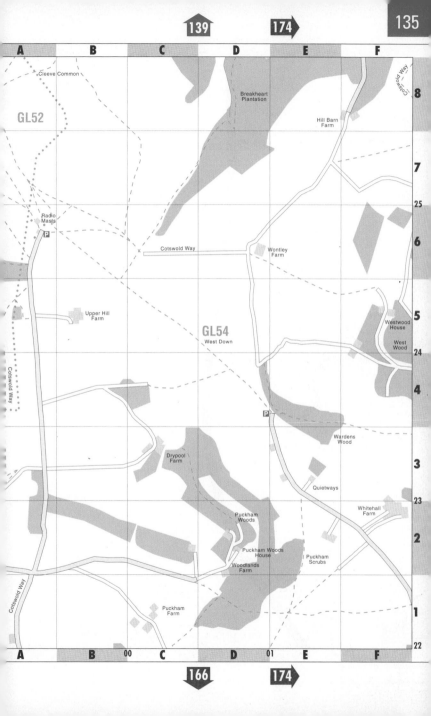

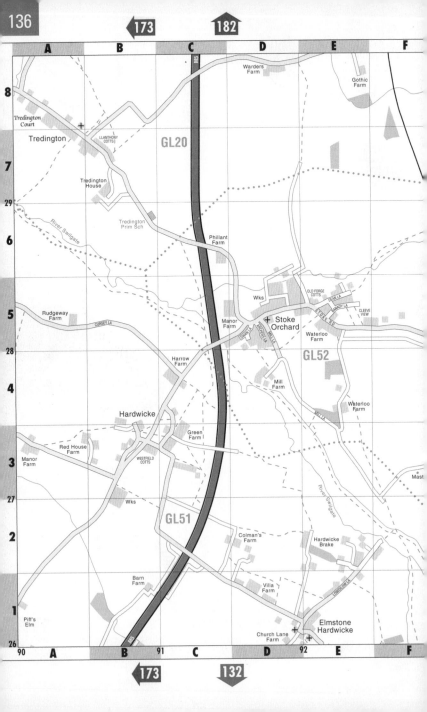

182
138
133
138

Springfield Kennels

Clayden Farm

GOTHERINGTON FIELDS

Ruddles Farm

Gotherington Field Farm

MALLESON RD

WOODBINE LA

The Shutter (PH)

SHUTTER

LONG FURLONG

Dean Brook

GL52

Farmers' Arms (PH)

Court Farm

Glebe Farm

Dean Farm

CHERRY BLOSSOM CL 1
HONEYSUCKLE WAY 2

Tom Bridge

BISHOPS MDW 5
YARLINGTON CL 6
STONECROFT CL 7

STREAMSIDE

HARVESTERS VIEW 1
BEECHURST WAY 2
WHEATSHEAF DR 3
NORTENHAM CL 4

Malvern View Bsns Pk

Irish Butts

WHITEFIELDS

STOKE RD

Wingmoor Lodge

STOKE RD

TRILLA WAY

CLEEVE LAKE STOKE
PARK CT

PULLAR CT

PH

CHURCH RD

Liby

Bishop's Cleeve Prim Sch

GREEN MEADOW BANK 8
STANWAY WOOD DR 9
LAVENDER MEWS 10
MIDDLEHAY CT 11
GATCOMBE CL 12
MARLBOROUGH CL 13
LITTLECOTE CL 14
CHARLECOTE CNR 15

GREENHILL HO
THE GREEN

BISHOPS CP

The Park

Wingmoor Farm

Bishop's Cleeve

The Grange

Grangefield Sch

TWO HEDGES RD

READ WAY

Lower Farm

THE HOLT

MEADWAY

1 ABBOTS MEWS
2 CHANTRY GATE
3 DEACONS PL
4 CANTORS CT

Home Farm

GL51

Brockhampton

Longacre Farm

GL50

Wks

CHELTENHAM RD

A435

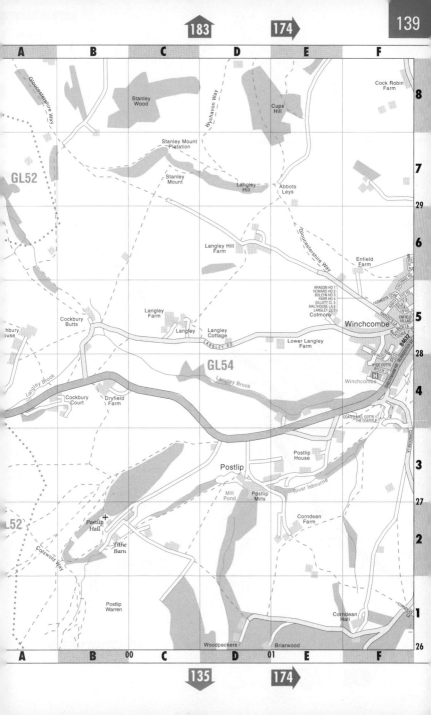

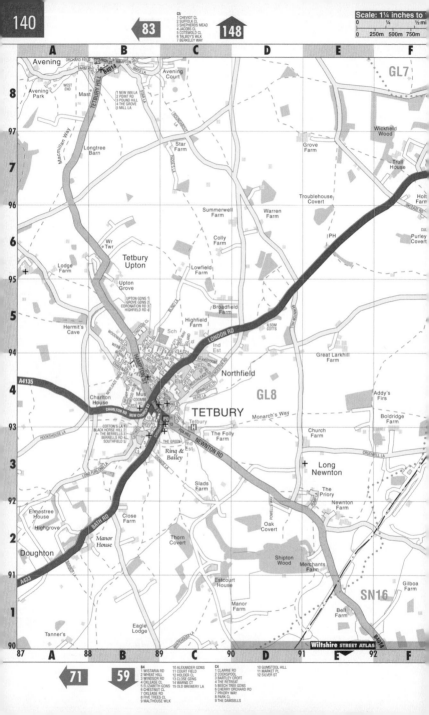

← 83   148 ↑

Scale: 1¼ inches to

| 0 | ¼ | ½ mi |
| 0 | 250m | 500m | 750m |

C5
1 CHEVIOT CL
2 SUFFOLK CL
3 SHEPHERDS MEAD
4 JACOBS CL
5 COTSWOLD CL
6 TALBOY'S WLK
7 BERKELEY WAY

Avening   GL7

ORCHARD FIELD   HAMPTON LA
FARM RYD

Avening Court

WEST END
Avening Park   Mast

Wickfield Wood

B4014

1 NEW INN LA
2 POINT RD
3 POUND HILL
4 THE GROVE
5 MILL LA

Star Farm   Grove Farm   Trull House

Longtree Barn

Holt Farm

Troublehouse Covert   OZLEA RD   Purley Covert

Summerwell Farm   Warren Farm   PH   CUL

Wr Twr   Colly Farm

Tetbury Upton

Lodge Farm

Lowfield Farm   ILSOM COTTS

Upton Grove

Hermit's Cave   Highfield Farm   Broadfield Farm   LONDON RD

UPTON GDNS 1
GROVE GDNS 2
CORONATION RD 3
HIGHFIELD RD 4

Sch   Ind Est   Great Larkhill Farm

HAMPTON ST   Northfield   GL8

A4135   Charlton House   Mus   Addy's Firs

CHARLTON RD   NEW CHURCH   Boldridge Farm

COTTON'S LA 1
BLACK HORSE HILL 2
THE BERRELLS 3
BERRELLS RD 4
SOUTHFIELD 5

HOOKSHOUSE LA   TETBURY   Monarch's Way   Church Farm   CRUDWELL LA

PO   Tetbury   The Folly Farm

THE GREEN   NEWNTON RD

Ring & Bailey   Ind Est   Long Newnton

Slads Farm   The Priory

Elmestree House   Close Farm   Newnton Farm

Highgrove   Thorn Covert   Oak Covert

BATH RD   Manor House

Doughton   Merchants Farm   Gilboa Farm

A433   Shipton Wood

Estcourt House   SN16

Tanner's   Manor Farm   Bell Farm

Eagle Lodge   B4040

Wiltshire STREET ATLAS

← 71   59 ↑

B4
1 WISTARIA RD
2 WHEAT HILL
3 WINDSOR RD
4 OXLEASE CL
5 ELIZABETH GDNS
6 CHESTNUT CL
7 OXLEASE RD
8 FIVE TREES CL
9 MALTHOUSE WLK
10 ALEXANDER GDNS
11 COURT FIELD
12 HOLDER CL
13 CLOSE GDNS
14 WARNS CT
15 OLD BREWERY LA

C4
1 CLARRIE RD
2 COOKSPOOL
3 BARTLEY CROFT
4 THE RETREAT
5 BEECH TREE GDNS
6 CHERRY ORCHARD RD
7 PRIORY WAY
8 PARK CL
9 THE DAMSELLS
10 GUMSTOOL HILL
11 MARKET PL
12 SILVER ST

Scale: 1¼ inches to 1
0   ¼   ½ mil
0 250m 500m 750m

141

Ewen

South Leaze
Farm

Point-to-Point
Course

River
Churn

TIMBRELLS CL 1
CHURCH LA 2
CLARK'S HAY 3
THE LAURELS 4
CHURN CL 5
RIVER WAY 6

EDWARDS
COLL

Upper
Up

Sch

GL7

Works

Gravel
Pit

Shorncote

Ashton
Down

BROADWAY CT 7
PAYMANS TERR 8
THE PADDOCK 9
SUDELEY DR 10
OAK WAY 11
THE LEAZE 12
BEVERSTONE CL 13
BEVERSTONE RD 14

Pool Keynes
Glebe
Farm

Upper Mill
Farm

CHURCH
ROW

ELM VIEW

Keynes
Country Park

COTSWOLD
COMMUNITY

Works

Poole
Keynes

River Thames or Isis

Thames Path

PH

Somerford
Keynes

North
End

SN6

Neigh Bridge
Country Park

Cotswold Water
Park

Ind
Est

Ash
Keyr

CHURCH LA

Lowfield
Farm

Moor Farm
Cottage

CH

Derry
Fields

THE STREET

Oaksey

Lower Moor
Farm

Swill Brook

Pike
Corner

THE DERRY

1 STREET COTTS
2 COURT FARM

Sch

Clattinger
Farm

Swillbrook
Farm

Glebe
Farm

Park
Airstrip

Stert
Farm

Cooles
Farm

RISBY'S LA

Derry Brook

Grove
Farm

Lyngrove
Farm

TIDLING
CNR

Telling's
Farm

Flistering
Wood

Brandier

LC

Lower
Moor

Flowers
Farm

SN16

Field
Farm

ST LEONARDS CL 1
ST LEONARD'S ROW 2

TELLINGS GRN

Sawyers
Hill

Upper
Minety

Sch

PO

COPPENACRE 1
ELM FARM CL 2

The
Elms

SAWYERS RISE 1
HORNSBURY CL 2
CHANDLER CL 3

Minety

STATION
APP

Gryphon Lodge
Farm

Cloatley
End

PH

Braydon
Hall

Wiltshire Street Atlas

F5
1 RICHMOND CT
2 THE LEAZE
3 COVE HOUSE GDNS
4 SADLERS FIELD
5 PARK PL
6 THE LOTTS

F4
1 PAR
2 THA
3 THE
4 BIR

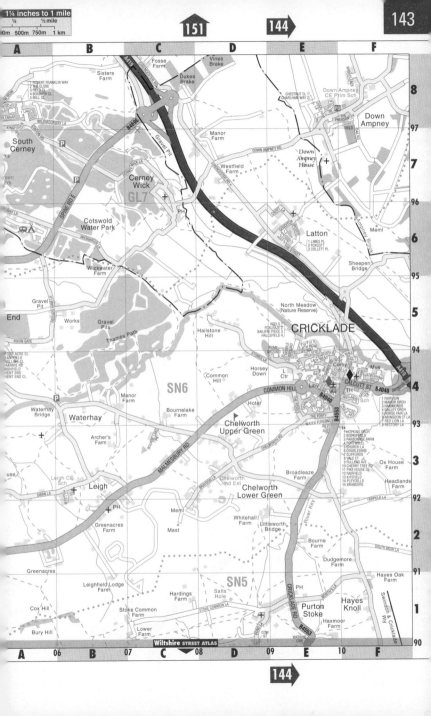

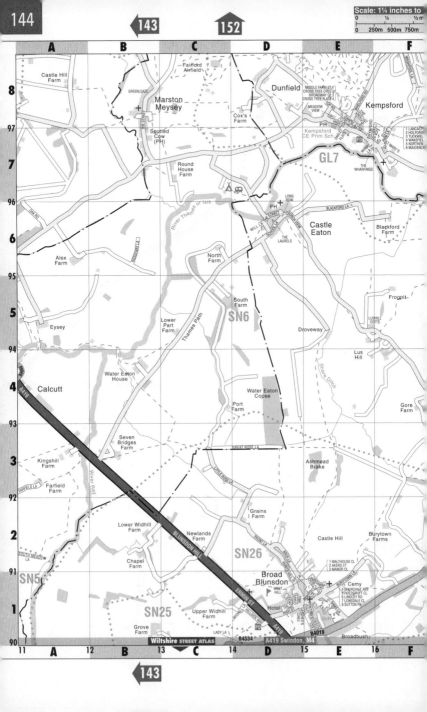

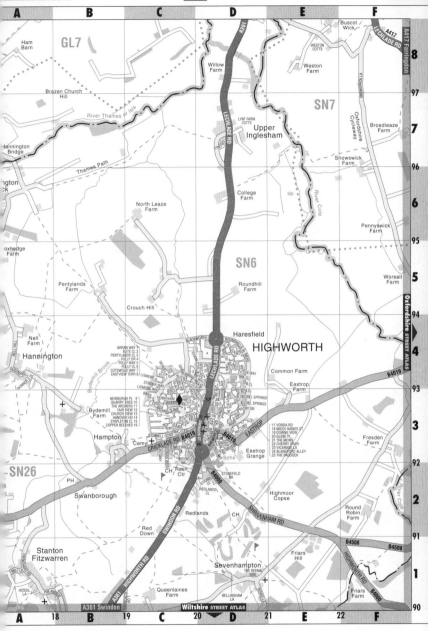

1¼ inches to 1 mile

¼   ½ mile

0m 500m 750m 1 km

GL7
Ham Barn
Brazen Church Hill
River Thames or Isis
Hannington Bridge
Thames Path
ington ck
oxhedge Farm
Nell Farm
Hannington
BELL HILL
Bydemill Brook
Bydemill Farm
Hampton
Cemy
CRICKLADE RD
B4019
SN26
PH
Swanborough
Stanton Fitzwarren
HOSSIL LA
THE AVENUE
A361 HIGHWORTH RD
Queenlaines Farm
Red Down
Redlands
CH
SWINDON RD

Willow Farm
LECHLADE RD
LYNT FARM COTTS
LYNT
Upper Inglesham
College Farm
North Leaze Farm
Pentylands Farm
Crouch Hill
Roundhill Farm
SN6
Haresfield
BLACKWORTH RD
HIGHWORTH
LECHLADE RD
ARRAN WAY 1
BUTE CL 2
PENTYLANDS CL 3
FOLLY DR 4
FOLLY WAY 5
FOLLY CL 6
COTSWOLD WAY 7
EASTVIEW TERR 8
NEWBURGH PL 9
QUARRY CRES 10
THE ARCHERS 11
FAIR VIEW 12
CHURCH VIEW 13
HANOVER HO 14
STAPLETON CL 15
COPPER BEECHES 16
17 VORDA RD
18 MIDDI HAINES CT
19 DOWNS VIEW
20 GLEBE PL
21 THE MEWS
22 CHERRY ORCH
23 VICARAGE LA
24 BLANDFORD ALLEY
25 THE PADDOCK
STROMA
LISMORE
Schs
EASTROP
Eastrop Grange
Rec Ctr
STONEFIELD DR
B4000
REDLANDS CL
SHRIVENHAM RD
Highmoor Copse
Sevenhampton
THE REEMA HOS
BELLINGHAM RD
Wiltshire STREET ATLAS
Friars Hill
Friars Farm
B4508
B4508
HIGHWORTH RD
River Cole

Buscot Wick
LECHLADE RD
A417 Faringdon
Weston Cotts
Weston Farm
SN7
Oxfordshire Cycleway
Broadleaze Farm
Snowswick Farm
Pennyswick Farm
Worsall Farm
B4019
Common Farm
Eastrop Farm
Fresden Farm
Round Robin Farm
River Cole

Oxfordshire STREET ATLAS

A361 Swindon

A B C D E F
18   19   20   21   22

Scale: 1¼ inches to
0   ¼   ½ m
0   250m 500m 750m

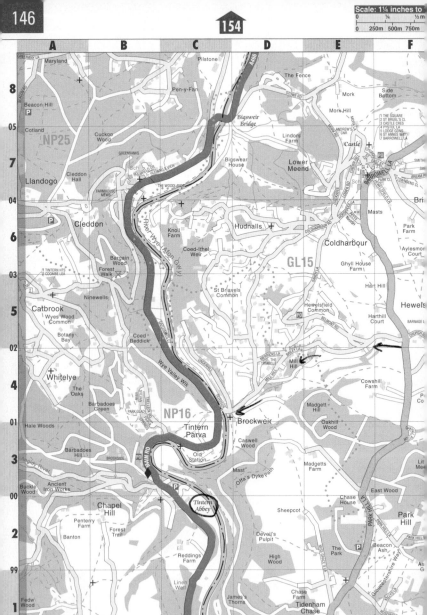

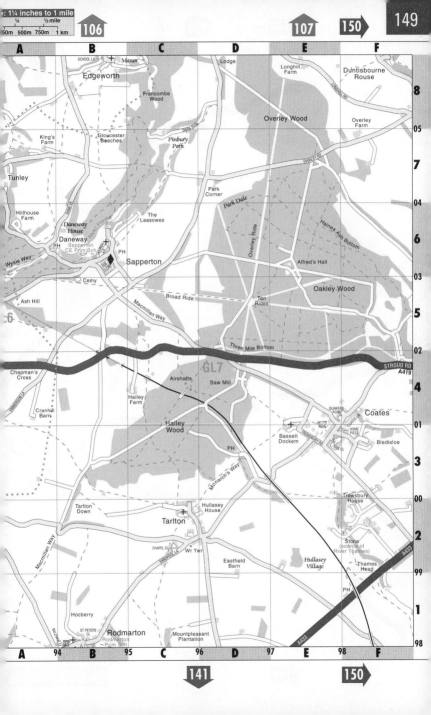

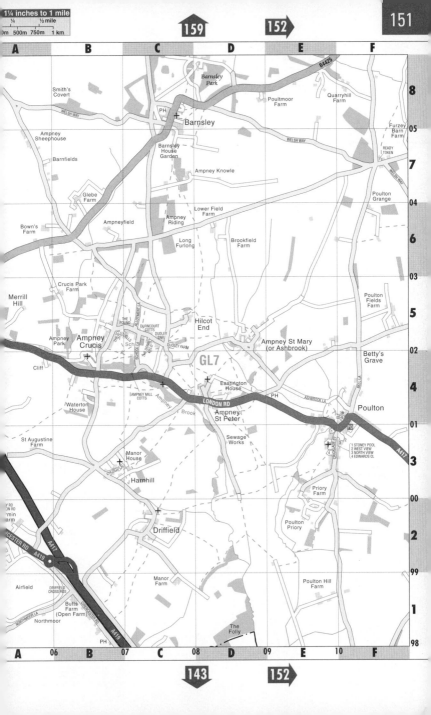

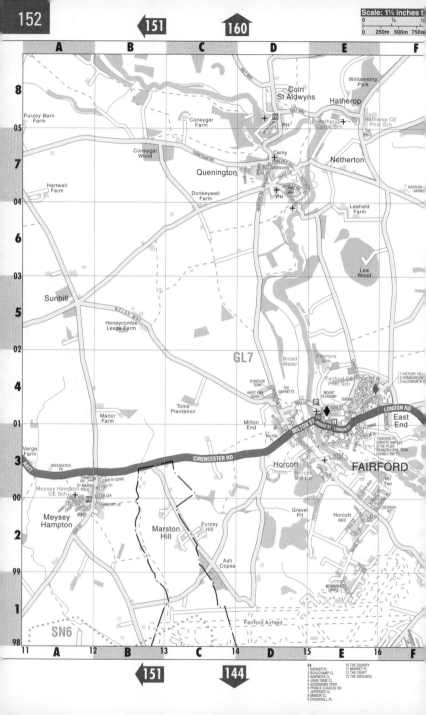

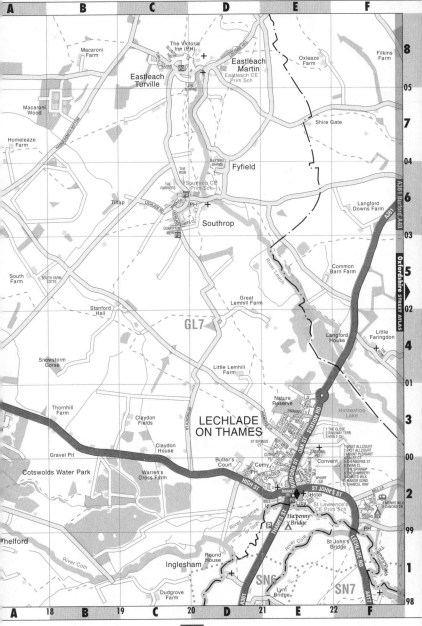

¼ inches to 1 mile
¼   ½ mile
500m 750m 1 km

A361 Burford A40

A361

Oxfordshire STREET ATLAS

Macaroni Farm

The Victoria Inn (PH)

Eastleach Martin

Eastleach CE Prim Sch

Oxleaze Farm

Filkins Farm

Eastleach Turville

Macaroni Wood

Shire Gate

Homeleaze Farm

BAXTERS BARNS

Fyfield

THE ROW

S Southrop CE Prim Sch

THE FARRIERS

Tiltup

LECHLADE RD

PH

Southrop

QUARRY VIEW

Langford Downs Farm

South Farm

SOUTH FARM COTTS

River Leach

Common Barn Farm

Stanford Hall

Great Lemhill Farm

GL7

Langford House

Little Faringdon

Snowstorm Gorse

Little Lemhill Farm

Thornhill Farm

Claydon Fields

Nature Reserve

SWANSFIELD

BRIAR

STATION RD

Horseshoe Lake

Gravel Pit

Claydon House

LECHLADE ON THAMES

ST BIRINUS CT

CUTHWINE

1 THE CLOSE
2 RAILWAY TERR
3 KEBLE CL

1 WEST ALLCOURT
2 EAST ALLCOURT
3 MOUNT PLEASANT
4 GALES CT
5 SHERBORNE ST
6 SWAN CL
7 THE SPINNERY
8 THE SHRUBBERY
9 ABBOTS WLK
10 MANOR GDNS
11 CHANCEL WAY

Cotswolds Water Park

Warren's Cross Farm

Butler's Court

Cemy

Convent

helford

Gravel Pit

BURFORD ST

OAK ST

HIGH ST

PH

MARKET PL

PO

ST JOHN'S ST

Hotel

LIDL

BELL

WHARF LA

St Lawrence's CE Prim Sch

MILL LA

LECHLADE RD

1 MONKS WLK
2 CANONS DR

PRIORS WLK

PH

River Coln

River Thames or Isis

THAMES ST

Ha'penny Bridge

River Cole

St John's Bridge

A417

Thames Path

Inglesham

Round House

SN6

Lynt Bridge

SN7

Dudgrove Farm

A   B   C   D   E   F

8

Dixton

NEWTON COURT LA.

1 MONKSWELL RD
2 MONKSWELL CL
3 JONES HO
4 BURGAGE

Haberdashers
Sch for Girls

Fiddler's
Elbow

HR9

Mailscot Wood

Braceland
Adventure Centre

Christchu

13

May Hill

The
Garth
Ind Est

MONMOUTH

Redding's Inclosure

Highmeadow Woods

Coalpit
Hill

Forest
Trail

7

Kymin
Naval
Temple

Wysis Way

STAUNTON RD

Beaulieu
Farm

Buck
Stone

PH

STAUNTON HO 1
TILLIS VIEW 2

Staunton

Marian
Inclosure

WAPPINGTON'S CNR

12

Wyesham

HAMMETT CT

UNDERWOOD

Sewage
Works

NEWLAND WAY   1
CHURCH FARM   2
CLWYDIAN RD   3
CHESTNUT TERR   4
LIMETREE AVE   5
HEATH ST   6
READE ST   7
BLAKE ST   8
THE DOWNHAMS   10
OAK LCREST ST   11
GREENFIELD CL   12
WYTERIDGE ST 13
ST JAMES 14
GARTH CRES 15
ST JAMES SQ 16
WHITECROSS ST 17

Lord's
Grove

Ollie's Dyke Path

Bunjups
Wood

Birchen
Wood

Knockalls
Inclosure

GL16

Stowfield
Quarry

6

11

Troypark
Wood

Wye Valley Walk

RUTTER CT

**Upper
Redbrook**

BREWERY
COTTS

High Meadow
Farm

Scowles

Whitec

5

Penallt

Glyn
Farm

Redbrook
CE Prim Sch

WYE VIEW
TERR

PH

WYES
GN

**Lower
Redbrook**

Bell's Old
Gram Sch

ALMSHOUSES RD

The Ostrich
(PH)

Whitec

10

Peny-garn
Farm

HIGHBURY
TERR

Highbury
Farm

AUNDRY RD

SAVAGE HILL

Newland

Mil

4

Pen-twyn

NP25

Bush Inn
(PH)

REDBROOK RD

LONE LA

Sewage
Works

Scatterford
Farm

Moorcroft

Glyn
Farm

09

Common
Farm

GREEN
PASTURES

CROSS
VANE

Inwood
Farm

COUNCIL
VILLAS

WAINLAND
PL

3

Lower Meend
Farm

The
Argoed

The
Grove

08

Hoop

Tre-gagle

Coxbury
Farm

Lodges
Farm

Caudwell
Farm

GL15

2

Newmills

Hael Woods

Lodges Barn
Farm

Clee
Qua

07

Trelleck
Common

FOREST
VIEW

CLEARWELL ST

SCHOOL LA

Wyeseal
Farm

OVER-ROSS AND WYE FOOTPATH

STOWE LA

The
Traveller's
Rest
(PH)

1

The Narth

Trekkers
(PH)

ROCK LA

Whitebrook

Wyegate
Green

Wyegate
Hill

STOWE RD

Quarr

Stowe

Vicar's
Allotment

Manor Wood

Forest
Walks

06

51   A   52   B   53   C   54   D   55   E   56   F

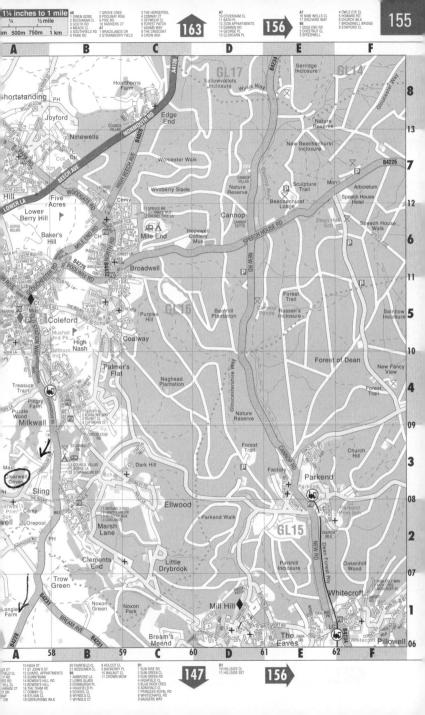

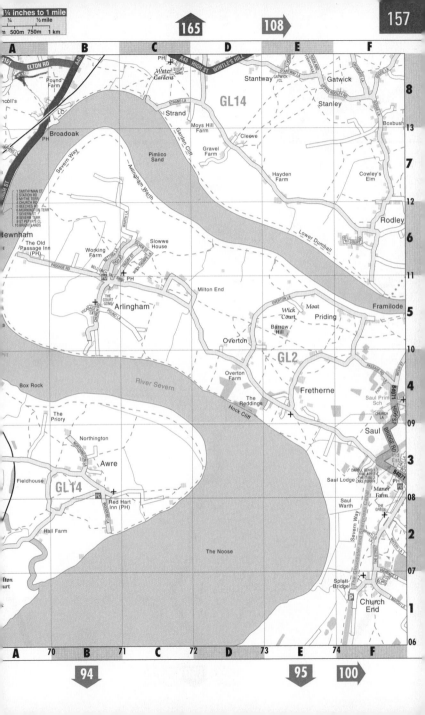

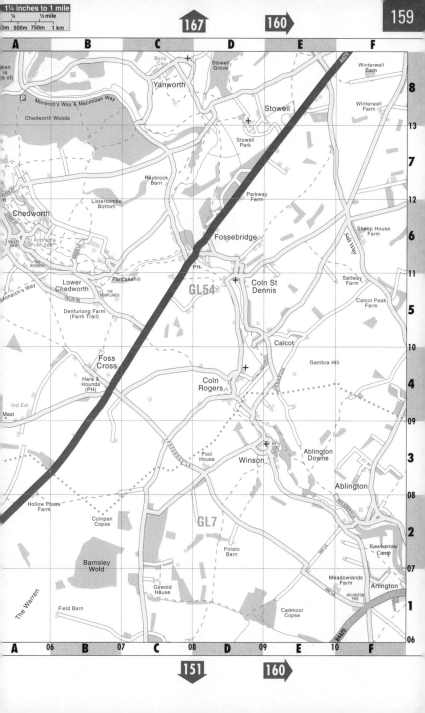

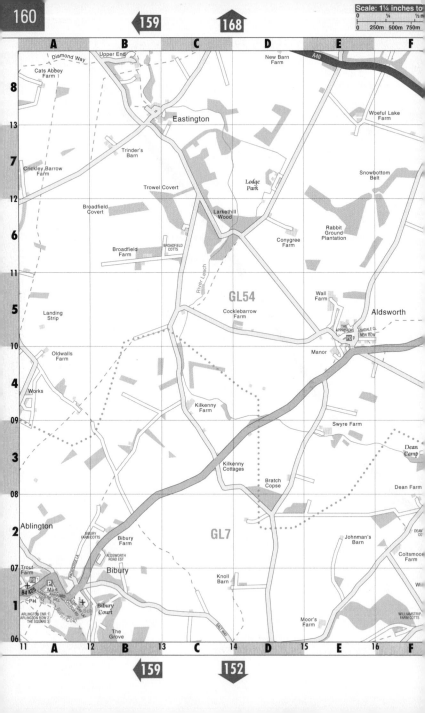

1¼ inches to 1 mile

¼ ½ mile
0m 500m 750m 1 km

A B C D E F

Great
Barrington

Deer Park

Barrington Park

River Windrush

PH

PAPER MILL
COTTS

Windrush

CHURCH LA

Little
Barrington

MINNOW LA

MIDDLE RD

Home
Farm

A40 Oxford

Camp
Barn

Budgehill
Wood

Windrush
Camp

Hurst
Barn Farm

B4425

Landing
Strip

Hill
Barn

Leyes
Farm

ckpits
opse

GL54

OX18

THE HILL

Westwell

Downs
Farm

Oxfordshire STREET ATLAS

Ladbarrow
Farm

Barrington Downs
Farm

Westwell
Copse

Holwell
Downs Farm

No Man's Land
Plantation

Eastleach
Downs Farm

Macaroni
Downs Farm

GL7

Lappingwell
Wood

River Leach

Broughtondowns
Plantation

Filkins Down
Farm

Tyning
Wood

Sheephouse
Farm

College
Farm

Eastleach
Folly

Beer Furlong
Buildings

A 18 B 19 C 20 D 21 E 22 F

8
13
7
12
6
11
5
10
4
09
3
08
2
07
1
06

Scale: 1¼ inches to

HR2

Kilreague

Upper Field

Tredunnock

Trereece

Treworgan

Welsh Newton Common

St Wolstan's Farm

Callow Hill

Pyefinch Wood

NP25

Orles Wood

Cannes Farm

CH

Priory Farm

Newton Court

Llangarron Court

Herbert's Hill

Herbert's Hill

Llangarron

Garren View

The Grove

Llangrove CE Prim Sch

Llangrove

Chapelfields 1 Westfield 2

Llanwithy

Trewarne

Lewstone

Ganarew

Hayes Coppice

Hadnock Court

Bernithan Court

Thatch Close

Treverven

Trewen

Greenway Farm

Crocker's Ash

Little Doward

Wyastone Leys

Wye Valley Walk

King Arthur's Cave

Far Hearkening Rock

Suck Stone

A4137 Hereford (A49)

The Thorn

Whitfield

Trebandy House Farm

Ruxton Green

HR9

Hill Farm

The Tump Farm

Whitchurch

Grange Pk 4 Norton Cl 2

PH

Stoneyhills Ind Est

Great Doward

Symonds Yat

Lady Park Wood

Lord's Wood

The Biblins

A40 Ross-on-Wye

Mast

Mount Craig Hall

Pencraig

Brelston Green

Marstow

Old Forge

Queen Stone

River Wye

Whitchurch Sch

Jubilee Park

Maze

Hotel

Hotel

Huntsham Ct

Huntsham Hill

Ferry

Ferry

Hotel

WYE RAPIDS COTTS

Rapids

Seven Sisters Rocks

Mailscot Wood

154

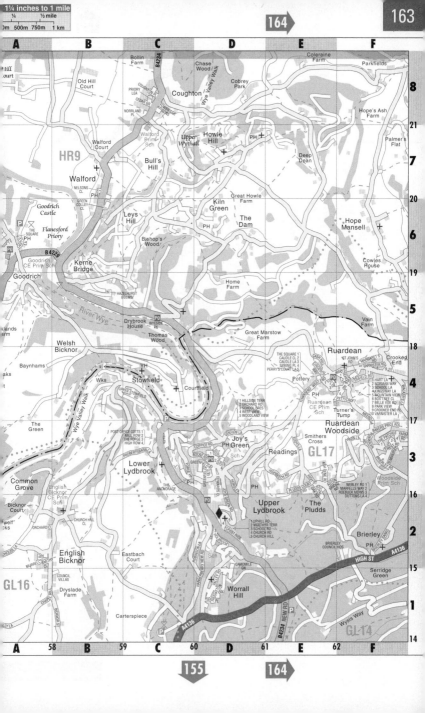

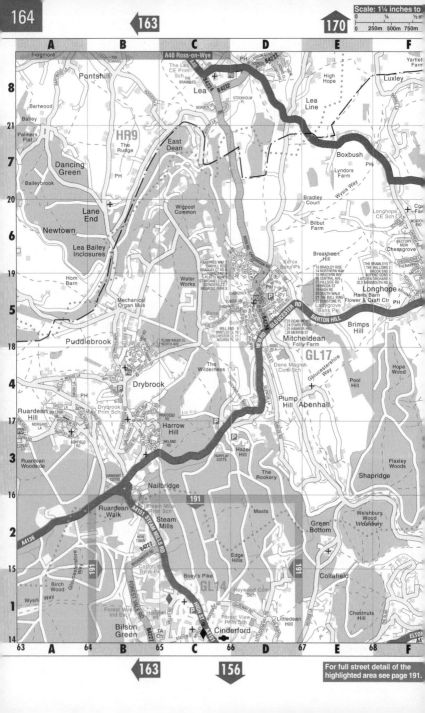

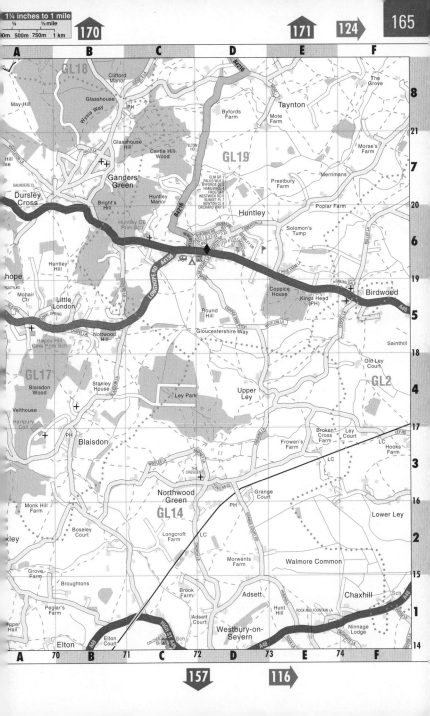

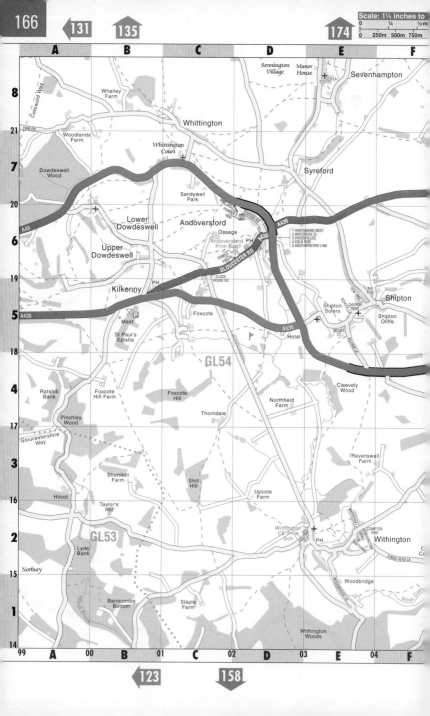

Scale: 1¼ inches to
0   ¼   ½ m
0   250m 500m 750m

A   B   C   D   E   F

8

21

Sennington
Village

Manor
House

CHURCH LA

Sevenhampton

Whalley
Farm

Whittington

Woodlands
Farm

HAM RD

Cotswold Way

Whittington
Court

7

20

Dowdeswell
Wood

Sandywell
Park

Syreford

A40

Lower
Dowdeswell

Andoversford

PREBEN

HUNTERS
WAY

PO

STATION RD

A436

A436

1 HUNTSMANS MEET
2 WATERSIDE CL
3 CROSSFIELDS
4 COLN RISE
5 ANDOVERSFORD LINK

6

19

Upper
Dowdeswell

Ossage

Andoversford PH
Prim Sch

TEMPLE
FIELD

GLOUCESTER RD

CLOCK
HOUSE SQ

PH

Kilkenny

THE RISE

Shipton

5

18

A436

Mast

P

St Paul's
Epistle

Foxcote

A436

Hotel

Shipton
Solers

SCHOOL LA

CHURCH
ROW

WYATT
CL

AVENUE LA

Shipton
Oliffe

GL54

4

17

Ratshill
Bank

Foxcote
Hill Farm

Foxcote
Hill

Thorndale

Northfield
Farm

Cleevely
Wood

Pinchley
Wood

Gloucestershire
Way

3

16

Shornhill
Farm

Shill
Hill

Upcote
Farm

Ravenswell
Farm

Hilcot

Taylor's
Hill

2

15

GL53

Lyde
Bank

Withington
CE Prim Sch

SCHOOL RD

PH

NETHERCOTE

COMPTON
RISE

Withington

KINGS HEAD LA

Norbury

Woodbridge

River Coln

1

14

Hilcot Brook

Barncombe
Bottom

Staple
Farm

Withington
Woods

WOODBRIDGE LA

99   00   01   02   03   04
A   B   C   D   E   F

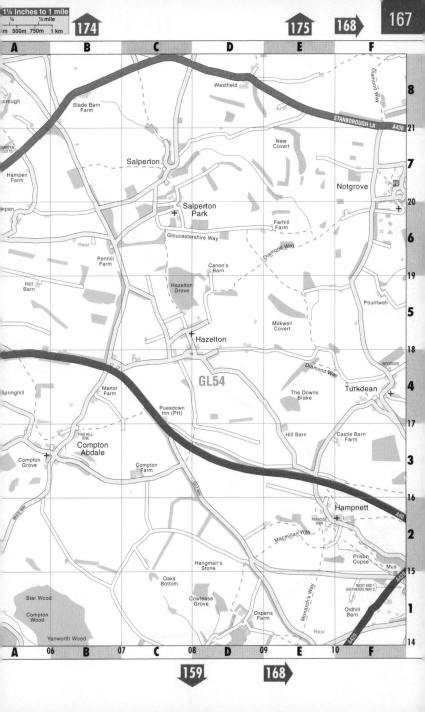

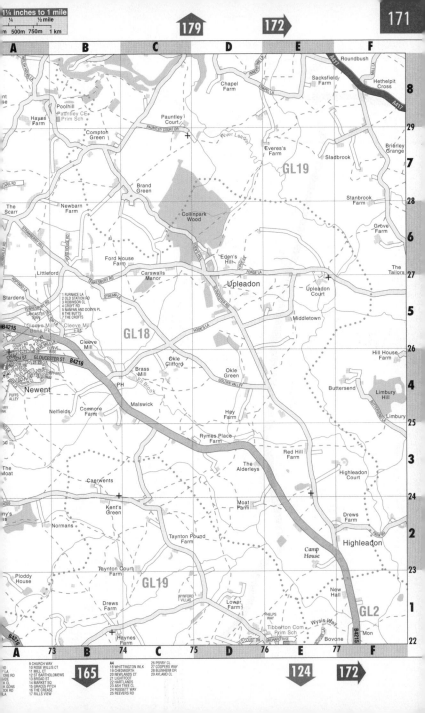

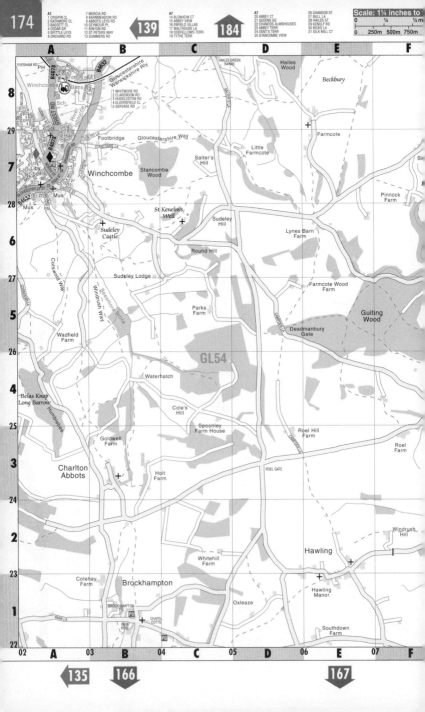

Scale: 1¼ inches to
0   ¼   ½ m
0 250m 500m 750m

A B C D E F

Hans Hill Farm

THE FOLLY
CHANCEL WAY
PH

GANBOROUGH RD
OLD RECTORY GDNS 1
ORCHARD RISE 2
CHURCH CL 3

Longborough

GL56

Hinchwick Manor Farm

Ganborough PH

Banks Fee

Luckley Farm

Donnington

Condicote

Banks Fee Farm

THE ROW

B4077

Fox Farm

Gloucestershire Way

Flagstone Farm

Donnington Brewery

Duncombe House

Upper Swell

THE ROW

Swell Hill Farm

Swell Buildings Farm

Heart of England Way

NEWLANDS CT 1
WALTER REYNOLDS HOMES 2
FOSSE LA 3
FOSSE LA 4
COUNCIL HOS 5

6 THE STABLES
7 FOSSEWAY HO
8 THE COURTYARD
9 HIGH ST
Stow Well

Abbotswood

TEWKESBURY RD

B4077

Bowl Farm

Library

GL54

Lower Swell

St MARY'S
PH

Hotel

PH

STOW-ON-THE-WOLD

SHEEP ST
PARK ST
BACK WALL

A436
POST

1 RECTORY COTTS
2 STONEHOUSE CT
3 FOX DR
4 WHITTLESTONE CL
5 WHITTLESTONE HOLLOW
6 PEAR TREE CL

Eyford Park

Rockcliffe

RECTORY CL

Sch

RECTORY BARNS

Nether Swell Manor

Manor

BARTLETTS
PK
FISHER HO
CHAMBERLAYNE HO

Macmillan Way

St Edward's Well

Eyford Knoll

EYFORD COTTS

Swiss Farm House

Fir Farm

Hyde Mill

Hotel

PH

A424

B4068

Kirkham Farm

Upper Slaughter

Copse Hill

Gloucester Way
Monarch Way
Macmillan Way &
Heart of England Way

River Dikler

Meadow Way

Wyck Hill

BAGHOTS SQ

Hotel
Manor House

RICKY HILL

River Eye

CHURCH FURLONG

Stow Bridge

Heath Hill

Hill Farm

Manor Farm

Mus
THE SQUARE 1
MALTHOUSE LA 2
MILL LA 3

Hotel

FOX LA

Lower Slaughter

KINGS DEFT

A429

Diamond Way

14 A 15 B 16 C 17 D 18 E 19 F

F4
1 CAMP GDNS
2 LANDGATE YARD
3 ODDFELLOWS ROW
4 SHEPHERDS ROW
5 CHAPEL ST
6 ABBEYFIELD HO
7 FOX LA
8 CHURCH WLK
9 CHURCH ST

10 DIGBETH ST
11 GLEBE CL
12 JUBILEE CL
13 WHITE HART LA
14 CLIFTON CL
15 STOW GR
16 YEW TREE COTTS
17 MOUNT PLEASANT CL
18 CONDURROW CT
19 SHEPHERDS WAY

F4
20 OAKEYS CL
21 BAILEY CL
22 WRAGGS ROW
23 TAYLORS ROW
24 FLEECE ALLEY
25 BREWERY YARD
26 PARKLAND MEWS
27 LOWER PARK ST
28 CHAMBERLAYNE HO

F4
29 CHAMR
30 FISHER

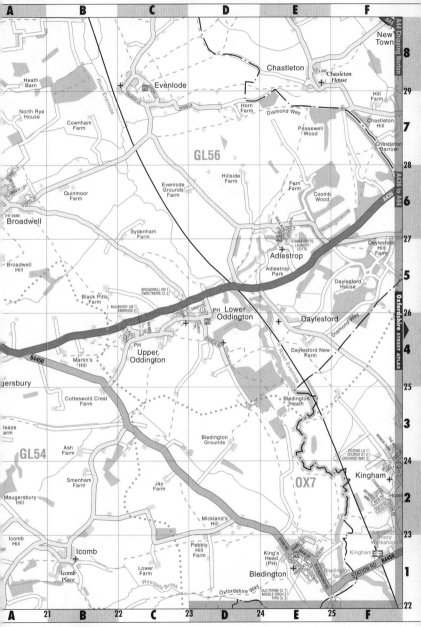

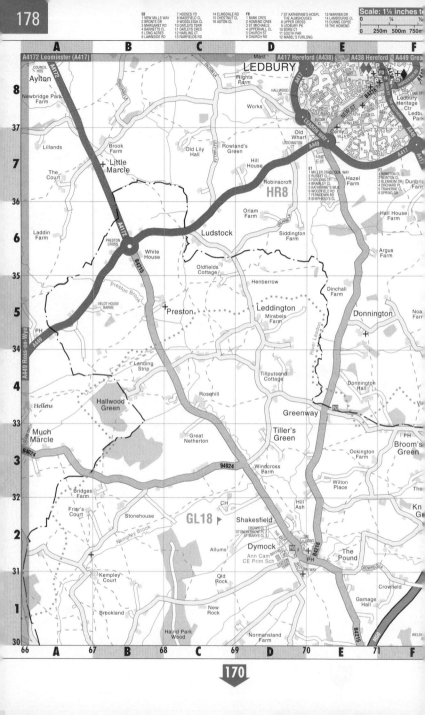

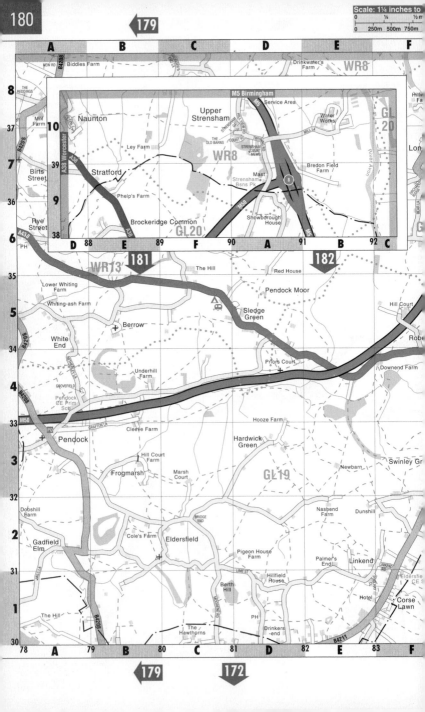

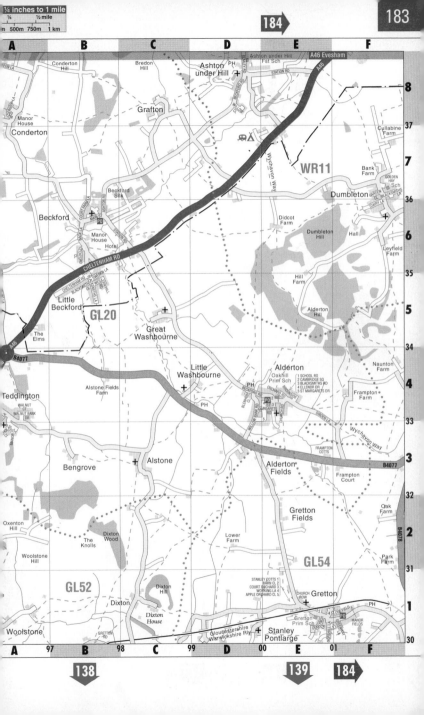

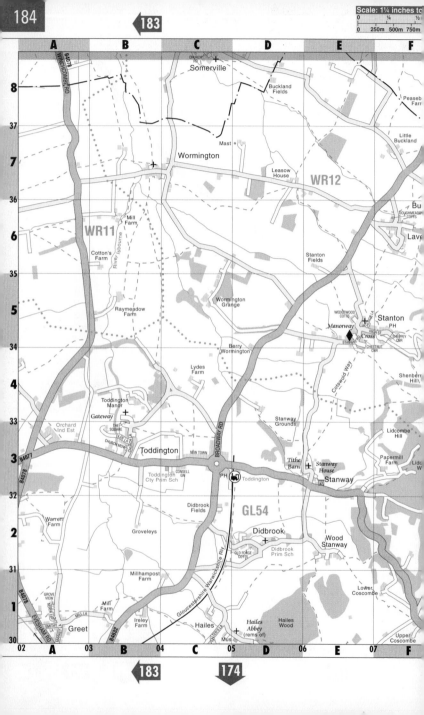

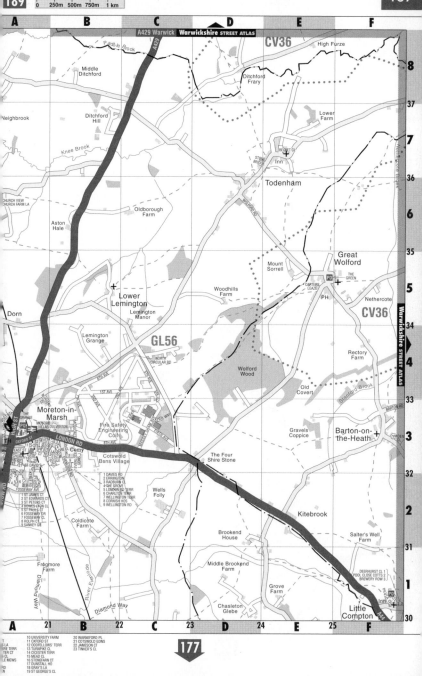

189

187

Scale: 1¼ inches to 1 mile

0   ¼   ½ mile
0   250m 500m 750m 1 km

A429 Warwick **Warwickshire** STREET ATLAS

A B C D E F

Peeble Brook

CV36

High Furze

Middle
Ditchford

Ditchford
Frary

8

37

Neighbrook

Ditchford
Hill

Lower
Farm

Church View
Church Farm La

Knee Brook

Aston
Hale

Oldborough
Farm

7

36

Todenham

Inn

STONE
BRIDGE

BECKET CL

Woodhills
Farm

Mount
Sorrell

Great
Wolford

THE
GREEN

CARTERS
LEAZE

PH

Nethercote

CV36

Dorn

Lower
Lemington

Lemington
Manor

Lemington
Grange

GL56

NORTH
CIRCULAR RD

Woodhills
Farm

Wolford
Wood

Rectory
Farm

Old
Covert

Stanford Brook

5

34

4

33

Moreton-in-
Marsh

6TH AVE

1ST AVE

5TH AVE

FARR AVE

LONDON RD

Fire Safety
Engineering
Coll

Cotswold
Bsns Village

Gravels
Coppice

Barton-on-
the-Heath

BARTON RD

3

OXFORD ST

FOSSEWAY AVE

1 DAVIES RD
2 ERRINGTON
3 RADBURN CL
4 THE GROVE
5 LONDON RD TERR
6 CHARLTON TERR
7 WELLINGTON TERR
8 CORNISH HOS
9 WELLINGTON RD

The Four
Shire Stone

Wells
Folly

Kitebrook

Salter's Well
Farm

32

2

Coldicote
Farm

Brookend
House

DEERHURST CL 1
POOL CLOSE COTTS 2
BREWERY ROW 3

Fremore
Farm

Middle Brookend
Farm

River Evenlode

Grove
Farm

31

1

Diamond Way

Chaselton
Glebe

Little
Compton

Inn

30

A 21 B 22 C 23 D 24 E 25 F

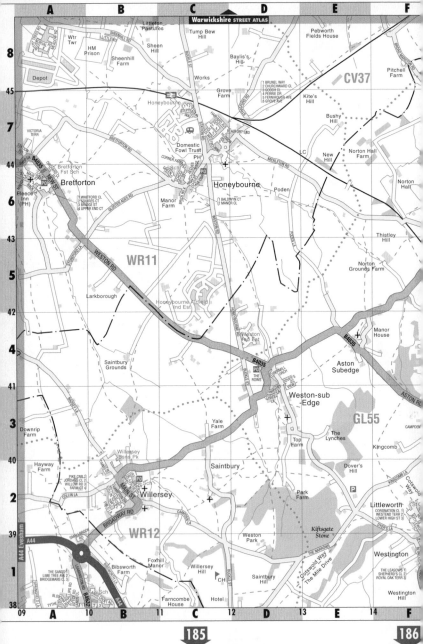

Scale: 1¼ inches to
0   ¼   ½ π
0   250m   500m   750m

Warwickshire STREET ATLAS

8

Littleton
Pastures

Tump Bew
Hill

Pebworth
Fields House

Wtr
Twr

HM
Prison

Sheenhill
Farm

Sheen
Hill

Baylis's
Hill

Pitchell
Farm

CV37

Depot

Works

Grove
Farm

Kite's
Hill

45

Honeybourne

1 BRUNEL WAY
2 CHURCHWARD CL
3 GOODH CL
4 PERRIE DR
5 FERNIHOUGH AVE
6 GROVE AVE

New
Hill

Bushy
Hill

Norton Hall
Farm

7

Domestic
Fowl Trust

PH

Seaport End

MICKLETON RD

LC

New
Hill

Norton
Hall

44

Bretforton
Fst Sch

Bretforton

PO

Honeybourne

Poden

Thistley
Hill

Fleece
Inn
(PH)

1 WHITFORD CL
2 SQUIRES CT
3 BRIDGE ST
4 UPPER END CT

Manor
Farm

1 BALDWIN CT
2 MANOR CL

6

43

WESTON RD

WR11

Norton
Grounds Farm

5

Larkborough

Honeybourne
Ind Est

42

Weston
Ind Est

B4035

Manor
House

4

Saintbury
Grounds

B4035

PO
THE
ROWS

Aston
Subedge

ASTON RD

41

Weston-sub
-Edge

Downrip
Farm

Yale
Farm

GL55

CAMPDEN

3

Hayway
Farm

Willersey
Bsns Pk

The
Lynches

Kingcomb

40

PIKE CNR 1
JORDANS CL 2
WILLOW RD 3
FARM CT 4

Top
Farm

Dover's
Hill

Cotswold
Way

Saintbury

2

PO

Willersey

Park
Farm

Littleworth

CORONATION CL 1
WESTEND TERR 2
LOWER HIGH ST 3

BROADWAY RD

Kiftsgate
Stone

Westington

39

A44 Evesham

A44

WR12

Weston
Park

Cotswold Way
The Mile Drive

THE LEASOWS 1
SHEPHERD'S CL 2
ROYAL OAK TERR 3

1

THE SANDS 1
LIME TREE AV 2
BRIDGEMANS CL 3

Bibsworth
Farm

Foxhill
Manor

Willersey
Hill

Saintbury
Hill

Westington
Hill

B4632

Sch

CH

Farncombe
House

Hotel

38

09   A   10   B   11   C   12   D   13   E   14   F

¼ inches to 1 mile

¼ ½ mile
500m 750m 1 km

A B C D E F

CV37

Lower
Meon

Admington
Hall

Lower
Clopton

Meon
Hall

Meon
Hill

Top
Farm

York
Farm

Admington Lane
Units

ADMINGTON LA

Upper
Clopton
Farm

Coleman's
Hill

Lower
Lark Stoke

Centenary Way

PARK LA

MICKLETON RD

Lark Stoke

CV36

Ilmington
CE Prim
Sch

Ilmington

FRONT ST

Mickleton

Hidcote
Combe

Mickleton Wood
Farm

Monarch's Way

Hidcote
Manor
Garden

Hidcote
Bartrim

Mast

CAMPDEN PITCH

CAMPDEN HILL

PARK LA

Woodmeadow
Farm

Nebsworth

Kiftsgate Court
Gardens

Nineveh
Farm

BAKER'S HILL

Baker's
Hill

Hidcote
House

Masts
The
Downs House

HIDCOTE BOYCE

NEBSWORTH LA

Foxcote
Farm

Windmill
Hill

Longlands
Farm

Ebrington
Hill

CAMPDEN RD

GL55

Diamond Way

TURKEL LA

Mickleton Hills
Farm

Hoarston

Longmoor
House

1 BARRELS PITCH
2 WOLDS END CL
3 GRIGGS CL
4 ROLLING STONES
5 SEYMOUR GATE
6 COLDICOTTS CL
7 NOEL CT
8 THE OLD GRAMMAR SCHOOL MEWS
9 ALMSHOUSES
10 VICARAGE COTTS
11 CHURCH COTTS

Heart of England Way

The Old Orchard 1
Church Cl 2
Keytes Acre 3

Ebrington

Ebrington

CAMPDEN RD

12   13
PH

Goose
Hill

ping Campden
Sch

Sports
Ctr

LC

Battledene
Farm

Charingworth
Manor
(Hotel)

Charingworth

Braxfield
House

B4035

STATION RD

THE CAM

Diamond Way

B4035

Chipping
Campden

St James' &
Ebrington
CE Prim Sch

PUDLICOTT LA

Marfurlong
Farm

B4479

1 HAYSUM'S CL
2 PEAR TREE CL
3 GAINSBOROUGH TERR
4 SHEEP ST
5 CHERRY ORCHARD CL
6 CATBROOK

GL56

Briar Hill
Farm

GL56

B4479

Black Downs

8
45
7
44
6
43
5
42
4
41
3
40
2
39
1
38

A 16 B 17 C 18 D 19 E 20 F

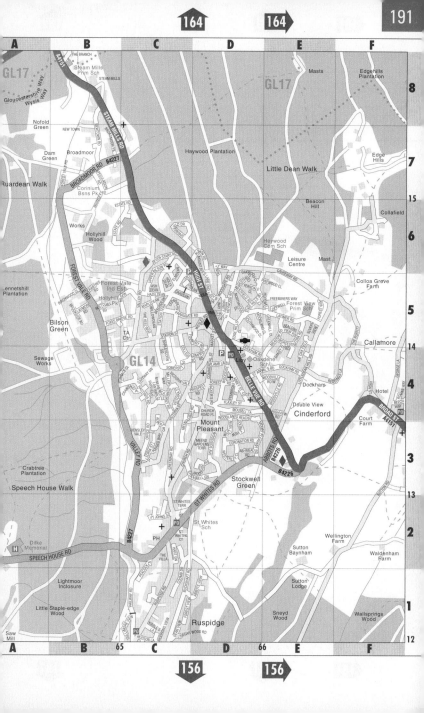

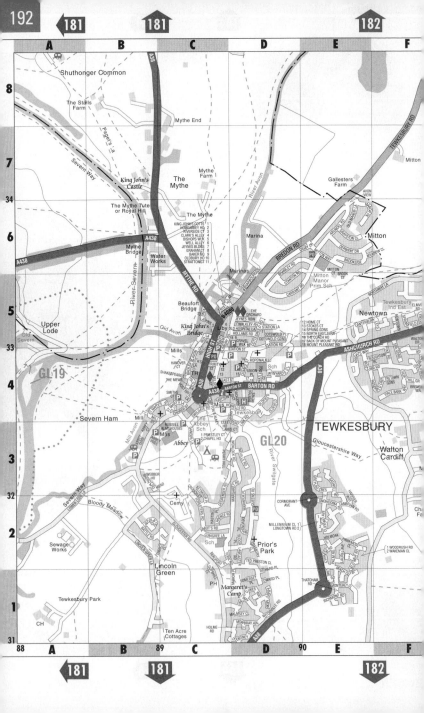

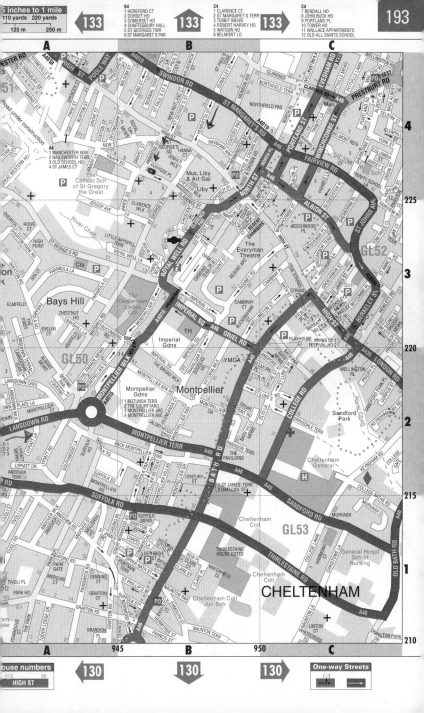

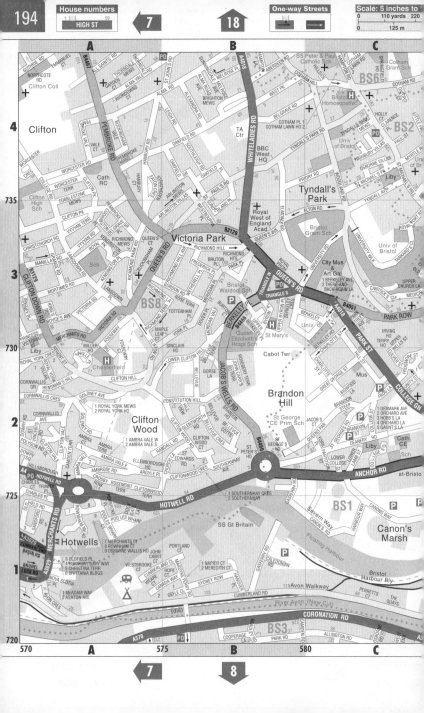

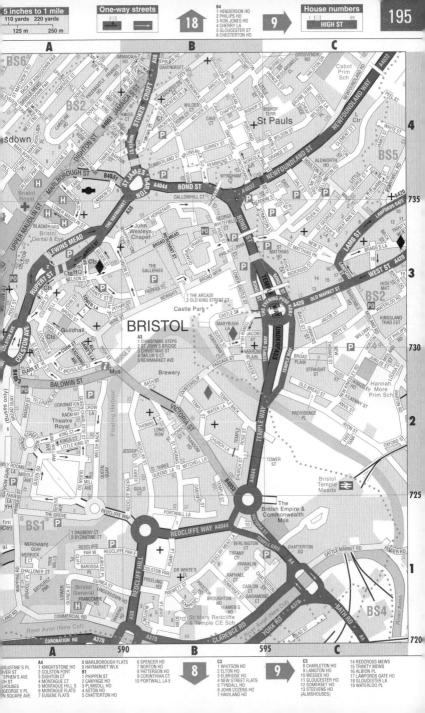

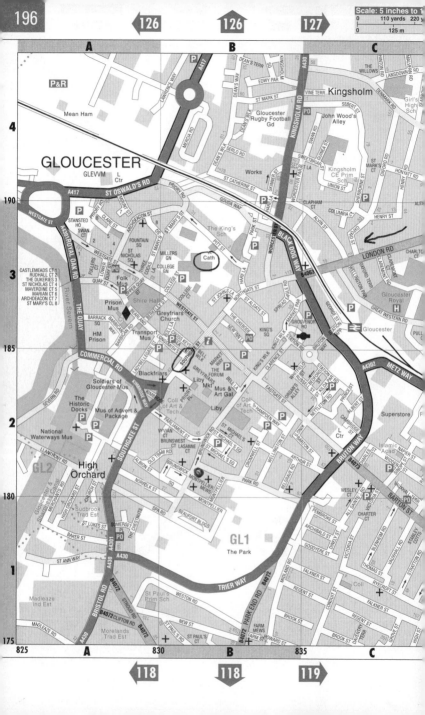

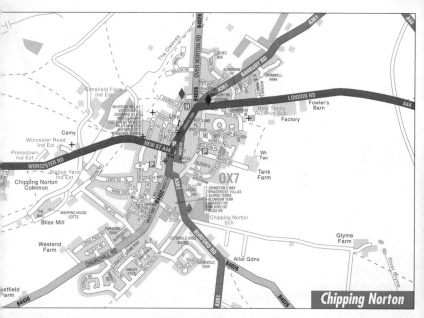

Chipping Norton

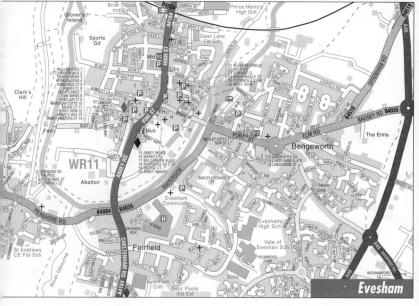

Evesham

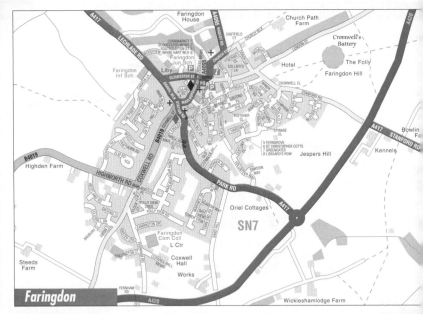

Faringdon

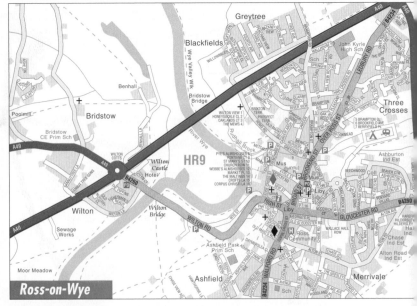

Ross-on-Wye

urch Rd **6** Beckenham BR2..........**53** C6

...ce ...ne y be abbreviated .. the map	Location number	Locality, town or village	Postcode district	Page and grid square
	Present when a number indicates the place's position in a crowded area of mapping	Shown when more than one place has the same name	District for the indexed place	Page number and grid reference for the standard mapping

blic and commercial buildings are highlighted in magenta. **Places of interest** are highlighted in blue with a star★

Abbreviations used in the index

	Academy	Comm	**Common**	Gd	**Ground**	L	**Leisure**	Prom	**Prom**
	Approach	Cott	**Cottage**	Gdn	**Garden**	La	**Lane**	Rd	Road
	Arcade	Cres	**Crescent**	Gn	**Green**	Liby	**Library**	Recn	**Recreation**
	Avenue	Cswy	**Causeway**	Gr	**Grove**	Mdw	**Meadow**	Ret	**Retail**
	Bungalow	Ct	**Court**	H	**Hall**	Meml	**Memorial**	Sh	**Shopping**
	Building	Ctr	**Centre**	Ho	**House**	Mkt	**Market**	Sq	**Square**
, Bus	**Business**	Ctry	**Country**	Hospl	**Hospital**	Mus	**Museum**	St	**Street**
	Boulevard	Cty	**County**	HQ	**Headquarters**	Orch	**Orchard**	Sta	**Station**
	Cathedral	Dr	**Drive**	Hts	**Heights**	Pal	**Palace**	Terr	**Terrace**
	Circus	Dro	**Drove**	Ind	**Industrial**	Par	**Parade**	TH	**Town Hall**
	Close	Ed	**Education**	Inst	**Institute**	Pas	**Passage**	Univ	**University**
	Corner	Emb	**Embankment**	Int	**International**	Pk	**Park**	Wk, Wlk	**Walk**
	College	Est	**Estate**	Intc	**Interchange**	Pl	**Place**	Wr	**Water**
	Community	Ex	**Exhibition**	Junc	**Junction**	Prec	**Precinct**	Yd	**Yard**

Index of localities, towns and villages

s Leigh 7 A8	
...ton 159 F3	
Turville 35 F6	
trop 177 E5	
on 183 E4	
orth 160 E5	
idsbury 40 B5	
ton 51 B4	
rley 91 C7	
ey Crucis 151 B5	
ersford 166 C6	
ley 173 C7	
ham 157 B5	
urch 182 C4	
worth 172 C4	
n Keynes 142 F5	
n under Hill 183 D8	
Magna 186 F6	
.......................49 A6	
ng 140 A8	
nouth 26 D2	
.......................157 B3	
rton 147 E4	

B
Badminton 46 F2	
Bagendon 158 C1	
Bamfurlong 128 F8	
Barnsley 151 C8	
Barton End 83 B8	
Barton-on-the-Heath .187 F3	
Bath 6 F1	
Beachley 61 C3	
Beckford 183 B6	
Berkeley 85 F3	
Berkeley Heath 86 B3	
Berry Hill 155 A7	
Bevington 76 F6	
Bibury 160 B1	
Birdwood 165 F5	
Bishop's Cleeve 137 E3	
Bisley 105 B1	
Bitton 5 E8	
Blakeney 156 E2	
Bledington 177 E1	
Blockley 186 C6	
Boughspring 73 C7	
Bourton-on-the-Hill .186 D3	
Bourton-on-the-Water .169 A7	
Bream 147 D8	

Bredon 182 C8	
Brentry 28 B2	
Bretforton 188 A6	
Brierley 163 F2	
Brimpsfield 114 C6	
Brimscombe 99 E2	
Bristol 8 E7	
Bristol 195 B3	
Broad Blunsdon 144 D1	
Broadway 185 C8	
Broadwell 177 A6	
Brockworth 120 F6	
Bromberrow Heath .179 B3	
Brookthorpe 110 F5	
Burton 36 B3	
Bushley 181 D5	
Bussage 148 B6	

C
Cam 87 F4	
Cambridge 95 F4	
Castle Eaton 144 E6	
Chalford 148 D5	
Charfield 67 B4	
Charlton Abbots ...174 A3	
Charlton Kings 131 C6	

Chastleton 177 E8	
Chedworth 159 A6	
Chedworth Laines ..158 F6	
Cheltenham 133 C4	
Cheltenham 193 C1	
Chelworth 141 E5	
Chepstow 60 D6	
Chipping Campden .189 A2	
Chipping Sodbury ...44 D1	
Churcham 124 D2	
Churchdown 128 D6	
Cinderford 164 C1	
Cinderford 191 E4	
Cirencester 150 C4	
Cirencester 190 F3	
Clapton-on-the-Hill .168 F4	
Clearwell 155 A2	
Cleeve Hill 138 E2	
Clifford's Mesne ...170 E1	
Coaley 88 E8	
Coalpit Heath 31 D6	
Coates 149 F4	
Codrington 33 C2	
Cold Ashton 13 F6	
Coln Rogers 159 D4	
Coln St Aldwyns ...152 D8	
Compton Abdale ...167 B3	
Condicote 176 A7	
Cranham 112 F6	
Cricklade 143 E5	
Cromhall 66 A1	
Crudwell 141 C3	
Culkerton 141 A1	

Coleford 168 B6	
Coleford 155 B5	
Colerne 15 F6	
Colesbourne 158 A8	

D
Daglingworth 150 A8	
Didbrook 184 D2	
Didmarton 57 C4	
Doughton 140 A2	
Down Ampney 143 F8	
Down Hatherley 173 C1	
Doynton 23 A1	
Draycott (nr Dursley) .87 F8	
Draycott (nr Moreton-in-Marsh) .186 E6	
Drybrook 164 B4	
Dumbleton 183 F7	
Dundry 1 D2	
Duntisbourne Abbots .107 C4	
Dursley 88 B2	

Acacia Cl continued
Prestbury GL52 . . . . .134 A5
Acacia Ct
Cheltenham GL51 . . . . .132 C2
Gloucester GL2 . . . . .126 C1
Acacia Dr GL11 . . . . .88 A3
Acacia Mews 4 BS16 . . . . . . .20 D4
Acacia Pk GL52 . . . . .137 D4
Acacia Rd BS16 . . . . .20 D4
Acer Gr GL2 . . . . .127 E4
Acid Rd BS11 . . . . .26 C4
Acomb Cres GL52 . . . . .131 B6
Acorn Gr BS13 . . . . .1 E6
Acraman's Rd 7 BS3 . . . . .8 C4
Acre Pl GL6 . . . . .102 G1
Acre St GL5 . . . . .99 C7
Acresbush Cl BS13 . . . . .2 A5
Acton Rd BS16 . . . . .20 A3
Adams Ct 5 BS8 . . . . .7 F6
Adams Hay 8 BS4 . . . . .9 D1
Adam's La GL6 . . . . .155 A7
Adderly Gate BS16 . . . . .21 B7
Addis Rd BS11 . . . . .133 B3
Addiscombe Rd BS14 . . . . . . .3 B5
Addison Rd BS3 . . . . .8 E3
Addymore GL11 . . . . .87 F5
Adelaide Gdns GL10 . . . . . . .101 F1
Adelaide Pl
Bristol, Fishponds BS16 . . . . . . .19 F4
12 Bristol, Upper Easton BS5 . .9 B8
Adelaide St GL1 . . . . .119 A7
Adelaide Terr 1 BS16 . . . . . . .20 A4
Adey's La GL12 . . . . .68 B8
Admington Lane Units
CV36 . . . . .189 E7
Admiral Cl GL51 . . . . .132 D2
Admirals Cl 6 GL11 . . . . . . .155 D1
Adryen Ct 6 BS5 . . . . .9 C7
Aesops Orch GL52 . . . . .138 C3
Agate St BS3 . . . . .8 B2
Aggs Hill GL54 . . . . .134 D1
Aggs La GL52 . . . . .138 A8
Aiken St BS5 . . . . .9 B6
Aintree Dr BS16 . . . . .30 F1
Air Balloon Ct 1 BS5 . . . . . . .10 A7
Air Balloon Hill Jun & Inf
Schs BS5 . . . . .10 A7
Air Balloon Rd BS5 . . . . .10 A7
Airport Rd BS14 . . . . .3 A8
Airthrie Sch GL50 . . . . .133 B1
Aisne Rd BS16 . . . . .19 D4
Akeman Rd GL7 . . . . .190 E4
Akeman Way BS11 . . . . .16 C8
Akermans Orch GL18 . . . . . .170 F4
Akers Cl SN26 . . . . .144 E1
Alanscourt BS30 . . . . .11 B5
Aland Rd BS4 . . . . .2 F7
Alaska Ave GL4 . . . . .152 E1
Albany Cl
Cheltenham GL51 . . . . .130 B7
Albany St Bristol BS15 . . . . . . .10 C8
Gloucester GL1 . . . . .119 A8
Albany Rd
1 Bristol, Bedminster BS3 . . . .8 D3
Bristol, Eastfield BS8 . . . . . . .18 A7
Cheltenham GL52 . . . . .193 C4
Albert Rd Brimscombe GL5 . . .99 F1
Bristol, Hanham BS15 . . . . . . .10 D5
Bristol, St Philip's Marsh
BS2 . . . . .9 A4
Bristol, Staple Hill BS16 . . . . . .20 E4
Cinderford GL14 . . . . .191 E4
Gloucester GL7 . . . . .190 E4
Keynsham BS31 . . . . .4 E5
Ledbury HR8 . . . . .178 E8
Severn Beach BS35 . . . . .38 A6
Albert St Bristol BS5 . . . . . . .9 C8
Cheltenham GL50 . . . . .133 D3
Gloucester GL1 . . . . .196 C2
Lydney GL15 . . . . .92 B3
Albert Terr BS16 . . . . .19 F4
Alberton Rd BS16 . . . . .19 F4
Albion Cl BS16 . . . . .20 F5
Albion Pl 10 Bristol BS2 . . . .195 C3
Cheltenham GL52 . . . . .193 C4
Cinderford GL14 . . . . .191 D6
Albion St 5 Bristol BS2 . . . .9 C8
Cheltenham GL52 . . . . .193 C3
Cirencester GL7 . . . . .190 B7
Gloucester GL1 . . . . .196 A2
Albion Terr Bristol BS34 . . . . .40 B1
Stonehouse GL10 . . . . .97 E6
Albion Wlk GL50 . . . . .193 C4
Albright La HR8 . . . . .179 D4
Alcotts Gn GL22 . . . . .172 F2
Alcove Rd BS16 . . . . .19 F3
Alder Cl GL2 . . . . .127 C4
Alder Ct GL51 . . . . .132 C2
Alder Dr BS5 . . . . .19 E1
Alder Way 7 GL6 . . . . .148 C6

Acacia Cl
Prestbury GL52 . . . . .134 A5
Aldercombe Rd BS9 . . . . .17 C8
Alderdale GL15 . . . . .92 B4
Alderdown Cl BS11 . . . . .17 A8
Aldergate St GL10 . . . . .97 F7
Aldergate Terr 6 GL10 . . . . .97 F7
Alderley Rd BS7 . . . . .68 D1
Alderman Knight Sch
GL20 . . . . .182 B4
Aldermoor Way BS30 . . . . . . .10 E4
Alderney Ave BS4 . . . . .9 H3
Alderney Flats 1 GL22 . . . . .127 B2
Alders The Bristol BS16 . . . . . .30 B1
Cheltenham GL33 . . . . .130 B4
Alderton Cl GL51 . . . . .129 D6
Alderton Cl GL4 . . . . .119 E4
Alderton Rd Bristol BS7 . . . . .18 E8
Burton SN14 . . . . .36 D6
Cheltenham GL51 . . . . .129 E8
Aldridge Cl GL50 . . . . .133 C3
Aldsworth Cl GL7 . . . . .152 F4
Aldsworth Road Est
GL7 .160 B2
Aldworth No Rd BS2 . . . . . . .195 C4
Alexander Ave GL51 . . . . . . .129 D6
Alexander Croft GL51 . . . . . .133 B2
Alexander Gdns 10 GL8 . . . .140 B4
Alexander Hosea Prim Sch
The GL12 . . . . .54 B5
Alexandra Cl BS16 . . . . .20 D4
Alexandra Gdns BS16 . . . . . .20 D4
Alexandra Park Ctr BS16 . . .19 F4
Alexandra Pk
Bristol, Cotham BS6 . . . . .18 C2
Bristol, Ridgeway BS16 . . . . . .19 E3
Alexandra Rd Bristol BS8 . . .194 B4
Bristol, Hanham BS15 . . . . . . .10 D5
Bristol, Highridge BS13 . . . . . . .1 F7
Coalpit Heath BS36 . . . . .37 B7
Gloucester GL1 . . . . .127 A3
Alexandra St GL50 . . . . .130 B7
Alexandra Way
Northway GL2 . . . . .182 B4
Thornbury BS35 . . . . .64 B3
Alexandra Wlk GL52 . . . . . . .134 B2
Alford Rd BS4 . . . . .9 C2
Alfred Hill BS2 . . . . .195 A4
Alfred Lovell Gdns 7
BS30 . . . . .11 A4
Alfred Par BS2 . . . . .195 A4
Alfred Pl BS2 . . . . .194 C4
Alfred Rd
Bristol, Bedminster BS3 . . . . . . .8 D3
Bristol, Newton BS2 . . . . .9 A6
Gloucester GL1 . . . . .119 A8
Alfred St
Bristol, Moorfields BS5 . . . . . . .9 D8
Bristol, St Pauls BS2 . . . . .195 C4
Ambleside Ave BS10 . . . . .28 B2
Alfred St
Bristol, Redfield BS5 . . . . .9 F6
Bristol, Windmill Hill BS3 . . . . . . .8 E3
Alfred St
Blakeney GL15 . . . . .156 E2
Stroud GL5 . . . . .99 D8
All Saint's La 1 BS1 . . . . .195 A2
All Saints' Rd Bristol BS8 . . .194 A4
Cheltenham GL52 . . . . .193 F2
All Saints' St BS1 . . . . .195 A3
All Saints' Terr GL52 . . . . . . .133 F1
All Saints' Villas Rd
GL52 . . . . .133 F2
Allanmead Rd BS14 . . . . .3 B8
Allaston Rd GL15 . . . . .92 B6
Allen Dr GL5 . . . . .99 A8
Allen's Almshouses The 12
GL54 . . . . .168 A1
Allendale Cl GL7 . . . . .3 B8
Allenfield Rd GL53 . . . . .130 C5
Allengrove La SN14 . . . . .47 C3
Allerton Cres BS14 . . . . .3 B4
Allerton Gdns BS14 . . . . .3 B5
Allerton Rd BS14 . . . . .3 A4
Allerton Rd BS7 . . . . .19 A3
Allington Dr BS30 . . . . .10 F4
Allington Rd BS3 . . . . .194 C1
Allison Ave BS4 . . . . .9 E3
Allison Rd BS4 . . . . .9 E3
Alma Cl Bristol BS14 . . . . . . .151 C5
Alcosp Cl GL14 . . . . .156 F6
Alma Ct BS8 . . . . .18 B1
Cheltenham GL51 . . . . .129 F7
Alma Dr NP16 . . . . .61 A4
Alma Pl GL11 . . . . .118 D7
Alma Rd
Bristol, Clifton BS8 . . . . .194 B4
Bristol, Kingswood BS15 . . . . . .20 E1
Cheltenham GL51 . . . . .129 E8
Alma Road Ave BS8 . . . . . . .194 B4
Alma St BS8 . . . . .18 B1
Alma Terr
Gloucester GL1 . . . . .118 C3
Stroud GL5 . . . . .98 F8
Alma Vale Rd BS8 . . . . .194 A4
Almeda Rd BS5 . . . . .10 A6
Almhouses GL7 . . . . .190 C4
Almond Cl GL4 . . . . .119 D3

Almond Cl GL51 . . . . .132 C2
Almond Way BS16 . . . . .20 F5
Almond Wlk GL15 . . . . .92 B4
Almondsbury Bsns Ctr
BS32 . . . . .40 D3
Almondsbury CE Prim Sch
BS32 . . . . .40 A4
Almondsbury Intc BS32 . . . . .40 A4
Almondsbury Rdbt BS32 . . . .40 B3
Almorah Rd BS3 . . . . .8 E3
Almshouses
5 Bristol BS1 . . . . .195 A2
Chipping Campden GL55 . . . .189 A2
Marshfield SN14 . . . . .14 E8
Wooton-u-E GL12 . . . . .68 B7
Almshouses Rd GL16 . . . . . . .136 E4
Alney Terr GL1 . . . . .126 C3
Alpha Cl GL20 . . . . .182 B4
Alpha Ctr The BS37 . . . . .43 C3
Alpha Rd Bristol BS3 . . . . .8 D4
Chepstow NP16 . . . . .60 F6
Alpine Ct GL4 . . . . .119 B6
Alpine Rd BS5 . . . . .19 C1
Alsop Rd 4 BS15 . . . . .20 D1
Alstone Ave GL51 . . . . .133 B2
Alstone Croft GL51 . . . . .133 B2
Alstone Ct 5 GL51 . . . . .133 B2
Alstone La GL51 . . . . .133 A2
Alstone Lane Trad Est
GL51 .133 A1
Althorp Cl GL4 . . . . .118 B2
Alton Rd BS7 . . . . .18 F5
Altrringham Rd 8 BS5 . . . . . . .9 C8
Alverstoke BS14 . . . . .2 F7
Alverton Dr GL52 . . . . .137 E2
Alveston Grange GL55 . . . . .189 A6
Alveston Hill GL55 . . . . .51 A6
Alveston Rd BS32 . . . . .50 D3
Alveston Wlk BS9 . . . . .17 B7
Alvin St GL1 . . . . .196 C3
Alvins Ct 2 BS30 . . . . .10 F4
Amaranth Way 7 GL51 . . . . .129 F5
Amberley CE Sch GL5 . . . . . .91 C7
Amberley Cl Bristol BS16 . . . .20 D7
Keynsham BS31 . . . . .4 E4
Amberley Ct 10 GL51 . . . . . .132 C2
Amberley House Sch
BS8 . . . . .18 A1
Amberley Rd
Bristol, Kingswood BS15 . . . . . .20 D7
Bristol, Patchway BS34 . . . . . .29 B8
Cheltenham GL51 . . . . .132 E2
Gloucester GL4 . . . . .119 A2
Amberley Ridge Specl Sch
GL5 . . . . .99 C1
Amberley Way GL12 . . . . .54 B4
Amble Cl BS15 . . . . .10 F7
Ambleside Ave BS10 . . . . . . .28 B2
Ambra Ct BS8 . . . . .194 A2
Ambra Terr BS8 . . . . .194 A2
Ambra Vale BS8 . . . . .194 A2
Ambra Vale E BS8 . . . . .194 A2
Ambra Vale S BS8 . . . . .194 A2
Ambra Vale W BS8 . . . . .194 A2
Ambrose La 1 GL16 . . . . .155 B5
Ambrose Rd BS8 . . . . .193 B4
Ambrose St GL50 . . . . .193 B4
Amercombe Wlk BS14 . . . . . . .3 D7
America Gdns GL18 . . . . .171 A4
Amos Cl GL50 . . . . .193 A4
Ampney Crucis CE Prim Sch
GL7 . . . . .151 C5
Ampney La GL14 . . . . .165 D3
Ampney Mill Cotts GL7 . . . .151 C4
Anbrook Cres GL4 . . . . .119 E7
Anchor Cl BS5 . . . . .9 F6
Anchor Rd
Bristol, Canon's Marsh
BS1 .194 C2
Bristol, Kingswood BS15 . . . . . .21 A2
Anchor Way BS20 . . . . .16 D4
Anchorage The
Gloucester GL2 . . . . .118 B6
Lower Lydbrook GL17 . . . . . . .163 C3
Ancient Rd GL16 . . . . .162 F1
Andereach Cl BS14 . . . . .3 B8
Anderson Cl GL2 . . . . .127 C4
Anderson Dr 1 GL10 . . . . . . .97 F7
Andorra Way GL3 . . . . .128 B6
Andover Ct GL50 . . . . .193 A1
Andover Rd Bristol BS4 . . . . . . .8 F2
Cheltenham GL50 . . . . .193 A1
Andover Terr GL50 . . . . .193 A2
Andover Wlk GL50 . . . . .193 A1
Andoversford Link
GL54 . . . . .166 D6
Andoversford Prim Sch
GL54 . . . . .166 D6
Andrew Millman Ct BS37 . . .43 F1
Andrew's Cl GL4 . . . . .110 F5
Andrew's Cnr GL15 . . . . .146 E7
Andruss Dr BS41 . . . . .1 D2
Angel Field GL4 . . . . .155 A5
Angelica Way GL4 . . . . .119 F5
Angels Gd BS4 . . . . .9 F6
Angers Rd BS4 . . . . .9 A4
Anglesea Pl BS8 . . . . .18 A2
Anlaby Ct GL52 . . . . .133 E2
Ann Cam CE Prim Sch
GL18 . . . . .178 D2
Ann Edwards Prim Sch
GL7 . . . . .142 F7
Ann Goodrich Cl GL52 . . . . .134 C4
Ann Wicks Rd GL52 . . . . .100 A5
Anne Hathaway Dr GL3 . . . .128 E5
Anns Wlk GL17 . . . . .164 D4

Ansdell Dr GL3 . . . . .120 E6
Ansell Cl GL51 . . . . .129 F6
Anson Bsns Pk GL51 . . . . . . .173 E1
Anson Ct BS31 . . . . .5 D2
Anstey St BS5 . . . . .19 B1
Anstey's Rd BS15 . . . . .10 C5
Ansteys Cl BS15 . . . . .10 B5
Antelope Paddock 11
GL54 . . . . .168 A1
Anthea Rd BS5 . . . . .19 E2
Anthony Cl SN16 . . . . .58 C1
Anthony Ct GL6 . . . . .148 C5
Anthony's Cross GL18,
GL19 . . . . .171 A2
Antona Ct BS11 . . . . .16 D7
Antona Dr BS11 . . . . .16 D7
Antrim Rd BS9 . . . . .18 B6
Anvil St BS2 . . . . .195 C2
Apex Ct BS32 . . . . .40 D3
Apperley Cl BS37 . . . . .32 E8
Apperley Dr GL2 . . . . .117 E1
Apperley Pk GL19 . . . . .173 C7
Apple Cl GL52 . . . . .134 D4
Apple Orch GL52 . . . . .134 A5
Apple Orch The GL20 . . . . . .182 C5
Apple Orchard Cl GL54 . . . .183 E1
Apple Tree Cl
4 Churchdown GL3 . . . . .128 A7
Gloucester GL4 . . . . .119 E4
Woodmancote GL52 . . . . .138 C2
Apple Yd The GL15 . . . . .156 A2
Appleby Wlk BS4 . . . . .2 D7
Appledore Cl BS14 . . . . .3 B8
Applegate BS10 . . . . .28 B3
Appleridge La GL13 . . . . .77 C4
Appleton Ave GL51 . . . . .129 B6
Appleton Way GL3 . . . . .120 A6
Applin Gn BS16 . . . . .21 C6
Apprentice Cl NP16 . . . . .61 B4
Approach The GL54 . . . . .160 E5
April Cl GL11 . . . . .80 A8
Apseleys Mead BS32 . . . . . . .40 C2
Apsley Cl GL7 . . . . .190 B3
Apsley Rd Bristol BS8 . . . . . . .18 A1
Cirencester GL7 . . . . .190 B2
Aragon Ho GL54 . . . . .139 F5
Aragon Way GL3 . . . . .127 F7
Arbour Cl GL55 . . . . .189 A6
Arbutus Dr BS9 . . . . .17 C8
Arcade The BS1 . . . . .195 B3
Archdeacon Ct GL1 . . . . .196 A3
Archdeacon St GL1 . . . . .196 A3
Archer Cl BS30 . . . . .11 C7
Archer Wlk BS14 . . . . .3 E6
Archers La GL52 . . . . .136 D5
Archers The BS5 . . . . .145 C3
Archery Rd GL7 . . . . .190 E4
Arches The 1 BS5 . . . . .9 B7
Archfield Ct BS6 . . . . .18 C1
Archfield Rd BS6 . . . . .18 C1
Archibald St GL1 . . . . .196 C1
Archway Cl GL14 . . . . .155 C5
Archway Gdns GL5 . . . . .99 A8
Archway Sch GL5 . . . . .98 F8
Ardea Cl GL2 . . . . .117 D1
Arden Cl BS32 . . . . .29 E6
Arden Ho GL2 . . . . .118 C4
Arden Rd GL53 . . . . .130 D5
Ardenton Wlk BS10 . . . . .28 A3
Arden Cl GL99 . . . . .17 B8
Ardmore BS8 . . . . .7 D7
Ardmore Cl GL4 . . . . .118 E2
Argus Gr BS3 . . . . .8 C2
Argus Rd BS3 . . . . .8 C2
Argyle Ave BS5 . . . . .19 C2
Argyle Pl BS8 . . . . .194 A2
Argyle Rd
Bristol, Chester Park BS16 . . .20 B2
Bristol, St Pauls BS2 . . . . . . .195 B4
Argyle St
5 Bristol, Eastville BS5 . . . . . .19 C2
6 Bristol, Southville BS3 . . . . .8 C4
Argyll Pl GL2 . . . . .127 B2
Argyll Rd
Cheltenham GL53 . . . . .130 F8
Gloucester GL2 . . . . .127 B2
Ariel Lodge Rd GL52 . . . . . . .133 F2
Arkells Ct GL12 . . . . .54 A6
Arkendale Dr GL2 . . . . .109 D8
Arkle Cl GL50 . . . . .133 C5
Arle Ave GL51 . . . . .133 B2
Arle Cl GL51 . . . . .133 B2
Arle Cotts GL51 . . . . .132 F4
Arle Dr GL51 . . . . .133 A3
Arle Gdns GL51 . . . . .133 A3
Arle Rd GL51 . . . . .133 A3
Arley Cotts 4 BS6 . . . . .18 D1
Arley Hill BS6 . . . . .18 D1
Arley Pk BS6 . . . . .18 D1
Arley Terr BS5 . . . . .9 E1
Arlingham GL51 . . . . .129 E5
Arlingham Rd GL2 . . . . .118 D4
Arlington Cnr GL7 . . . . .160 B2
Arlington Ct NP16 . . . . .61 B8
Arlington Mans GL52 . . . . . .194 B4
Arlington Mill Mus* GL7 . . .160 A1
Arlington Pike GL7 . . . . .159 F1
Arlington Rd GL7 . . . . .159 F1
Arlington Row* GL7 . . . . . . .160 A1
Arlington Terr 3 GL56 . . . . .186 C5
Arlington Villas BS8 . . . . . . .194 B3
Armada Cl GL3 . . . . .127 F7

Armada Ho BS2 . . . . .195 B4
Armada Pl BS11 . . . . .195 B4
Armada Rd BS14 . . . . .3 A6
Armidale Ave 2 BS6 . . . . .18 E1
Armidale Cotts 5 BS6 . . .18 E1
Armoury Sq BS5 . . . . .9 A8
Armscroft Ct GL2 . . . . . .127 B1
Armscroft Cres GL2 . . . . .127 C1
Armscroft Gdns GL2 . . . .127 B1
Armscroft Pl GL2 . . . . . . .127 B1
Armscroft Rd GL2 . . . . . .127 C1
Armscroft Way GL2 . . . . .127 B1
Armstrong Cl BS35 . . . . . .51 D7
Armstrong Ct BS37 . . . . . .43 C3
Armstrong Dr BS30 . . . . . .11 B5
Armstrong Way BS37 . . . . .43 B3
Arnall Dr BS10 . . . . .27 F1
Arncliffe EPD BS10 . . . . . .18 A8
Arneside Rd BS10 . . . . . . .28 C1
Arno's St BS4 . . . . .9 A3
Arnold St BS37 . . . . .44 B1
Arnold's La GL6 . . . . .91 B3
Arnolds Field Trad Est
  GL12 . . . . .54 A5
Arnolds Way GL7 . . . . . .190 E5
Arreton Ave SN6 . . . . . . .145 C4
Arreton Ave GL4 . . . . . . .119 C6
Arrowfield Cl BS14 . . . . . .3 A2
Arrowhead Cl GL4 . . . . . .119 B4
Arrowsmith Dr GL10 . . . .101 F1
Arthur Cooper Way
  GL16 . . . . .155 A4
Arthur Dye Prim Sch
  GL51 . . . . .132 D4
Arthur Skemp Cl BS5 . . . . .9 B7
Arthur St
  7 Bristol, Moorfields BS5 . .9 C8
  Bristol, St Philip's Marsh
  BS2 . . . . .64 A6
  Gloucester GL1 . . . . . . .196 B2
Arthurs Cl BS16 . . . . .21 C6
Arthurswood Rd BS13 . . . . .2 B5
Charlton Kings GL53 . . . .131 C4
  Gloucester GL4 . . . . .118 C1
Arundel Ct BS7 . . . . .18 D3
Arundel Dr GL5 . . . . .99 B6
Arundel Ho 1 GL51 . . . . .132 E2
Arundel Rd BS31 . . . . .4 D5
  Tewkesbury GL20 . . . . . .192 E6
Arundel Wlk BS31 . . . . .4 D5
Arundell Mill La GL5 . . . . .99 D6
Ascot Cl BS16 . . . . .30 F1
Ascot Ct GL1 . . . . .119 A8
Ascot Rd BS10 . . . . .28 E2
Ash Cl
  Bristol, Hillfields BS16 . . . .20 C3
  Bristol, Little Stoke BS34 . .29 D7
  Bristol, Stoke Gifford GL53 .131 C4
  Chepstow NP16 . . . . .60 E5
  Dursley GL11 . . . . .88 A4
  Lydney GL15 . . . . .92 B4
  Yate BS37 . . . . .43 D3
Ash Ct BS34 . . . . .3 A6
Ash Dene Rd GL1 . . . . . . .163 E3
Ash Gr Bristol BS16 . . . . . .20 D3
  Mitcheldean GL17 . . . . . .164 D6
  Upton St Leonards GL4 . . . .119 E3
Ash Grove Pl GL15 . . . . . .156 B1
Ash La Almondsbury BS32 . .39 D2
  Down Hatherley GL2 . . . .173 B1
  Randwick GL6 . . . . .102 D1
Ash Path The GL4 . . . . . . .119 E3
Ash Rd Bristol BS7 . . . . . . .18 E5
  Northway GL20 . . . . .227 C6
  Stroud GL5 . . . . .99 A4
Ash Ridge Rd BS32 . . . . . . .40 B3
Ash Tree Cl 2 BS16 . . . . . .20 F5
Ash Wlk BS10 . . . . .18 B1
Ashbourne Cl 2 BS30 . . . .11 C6
Ashbrook La GL7 . . . . . . .151 F4
Ashburton Rd BS10 . . . . . .28 C1
Ashchurch Ind Est GL20 . .182 C4
Ashchurch Prim Sch
  GL20 . . . . .182 C4
Ashchurch Rd GL20 . . . . .182 B4
Ashchurch Sta GL20 . . . . .182 C4
Ashcombe Cl 1 BS30 . . . .11 C6
Ashcombe Cres BS30 . . . . .11 D6
Ashcot Mews 3 GL51 . . . .129 E5
Ashcott BS14 . . . . .2 E8
Ashcroft Ave BS31 . . . . .4 D5
Ashcroft Cl GL4 . . . . .119 D2
Ashcroft Gdns GL7 . . . . .190 C4
Ashcroft Ho GL5 . . . . .99 D5
Ashcroft Rd BS9 . . . . .17 C7
  Cirencester GL7 . . . . .190 C4
  Wooton-u-E GL8,GL12 . . . .81 D3
Ashdale Cl GL4 . . . . .191 C5
Ashdale Rd BS13 . . . . .1 A5
Ashdene Ave BS5 . . . . .19 D3
Ashdown Ct BS9 . . . . .17 F8
Asher La BS2 . . . . .195 C3
Ashes La HR9 . . . . .162 E4
Ashfield Cl GL52 . . . . .138 A3
Ashfield Cl GL52 . . . . .138 A3
Ashfield Ho GL50 . . . . . . .193 A3
Ashfield Pl BS2 . . . . .18 F1
Ashfield Rd Bristol BS3 . . . . .8 A3
  Ruardean RB GL17 . . . . . .164 A8
Ashfield Terr 8 BS3 . . . . . .8 A3
Ashford Rd BS34 . . . . .29 A7
  Cheltenham GL50 . . . . . .193 A1
Ashford Way BS37 . . . . . . .11 A7

Ashgrove
  Charlton Kings GL53 . . . .131 C4
  Thornbury BS35 . . . . .64 C1
Ashgrove Ave
  Abbots Leigh BS8 . . . . .7 B7
  Bristol BS7 . . . . .18 F4
  Gloucester GL4 . . . . .119 C6
Ashgrove Cl Bristol BS7 . . . .18 F4
  Hardwicke GL2 . . . . .109 E7
Ashgrove Cotts GL6 . . . . .102 F4
Ashgrove Rd
  Bristol, Ashley Down BS7 . .18 F4
  Bristol, Bedminster BS3 . . . .8 B3
Ashgrove Way GL4 . . . . . .119 C6
Ashland Rd BS13 . . . . .2 A4
Ashlands Cl GL51 . . . . . . .132 E3
Ashlands Rd GL51 . . . . . . .132 E3
Ashlea Mdws GL52 . . . . . .137 D4
Ashleigh La GL52 . . . . . . .138 D1
Ashletts Rd GL16 . . . . . . .154 F7
Ashlesworth CE Prim Sch
  GL19 . . . . .172 D4
Ashleworth Gdns GL2 . . .109 E8
Ashley Cl Bristol BS7 . . . . .18 E3
  Charlton Kings GL52 . . . .131 B7
Ashley Court Rd 2 BS7 . . .18 E2
Ashley Down Jun & Inf Schs
  BS7 . . . . .18 F5
Ashley Down Rd BS7 . . . . .18 F4
Ashley Grove Rd
  7 Bristol BS2 . . . . .18 F2
  1 Bristol BS2 . . . . .19 A1
Ashley Hill BS6,BS7 . . . . . .18 F2
Ashley Ho BS34 . . . . .39 F1
Ashley La GL53 . . . . .130 C6
Ashley Pk BS6 . . . . .18 F3
Ashley Rd Bristol BS6 . . . . .18 E1
  Cheltenham GL52 . . . . . .131 B8
Ashley St BS2 . . . . .8 A4
Ashley Trad Est 8 BS2 . . . .18 F2
Ashman Cl 5 BS5 . . . . .9 A8
Ashman Ct 1 BS16 . . . . . . .19 E3
Ashmead GL52 . . . . .127 B5
Ashmead Dr GL52 . . . . . .138 A8
Ashmead Rd
  Cinderford GL14 . . . . .191 D3
  Keynsham BS31 . . . . .5 B5
Ashmead Road Ind Est
  BS31 . . . . .5 B5
Ashmead Way 6 BS1 . . . . . .7 B5
Ashmore Rd GL4 . . . . . . .118 F4
Ashton BS16 . . . . .30 C1
Ashton Ave BS1 . . . . .7 A4
Ashton Cl GL4 . . . . .119 E3
Ashton Court Est* BS41 . . . . .7 C2
Ashton Gate Prim Sch
  BS3 . . . . .7 F2
Ashton Gate Rd 8 BS3 . . . .8 A4
Ashton Gate Terr 8 BS3 . . . .8 A4
Ashton Gate Trad Est BS3 . . .7 F3
Ashton Underpass
  Ashton Keynes CE Prim Sch
  SN6 . . . . .142 F5
  Ashton Rd Beckford BL20 .183 B6
  Bristol, Ashton Gate BS3 . . . .7 F3
  Bristol, Bower Ashton BS3 . . .7 D3
  Minety SN6 . . . . .142 D7
  Siddington GL7 . . . . .150 E1
Ashton under Hill Fst Sch
  WR11 . . . . .183 D8
Ashton Vale Prim Sch BS3 . . .7 F2
Ashton Vale Rd BS3 . . . . . . .7 F3
Ashton Vale Trad Est BS3 . . .7 F1
Ashton Way BS31 . . . . .4 E6
Ashville Bsns Pk GL2 . . . .173 E1
Ashville Ind Est GL2 . . . . .118 C5
Ashville Rd Bristol BS3 . . . .8 A4
  Gloucester GL2 . . . . .118 C5
Ashville Trad Est GL51 . . .133 A6
Ashway Netherend GL15 . .147 C3
  17 Northleach GL54 . . . . .168 A1
Ashwell Cl BS14 . . . . .3 A5
Ashwell Gr BS14 . . . . .3 A5
Ashwicke BS14 . . . . .2 E8
Ashwicke Rd SN14 . . . . . . .15 B3
Ashwood Way GL3 . . . . . .119 F6
Askham Ct 7 GL52 . . . . . .133 E7
Askwith Rd GL4 . . . . .119 B6
Aspen Cl SN14 . . . . .15 F6
Aspen Dr GL2 . . . . .117 E2
Asquith Rd GL53 . . . . .130 E6
Assembly Rooms La 1
  BS1 . . . . .195 A2
Aster Cl GL4 . . . . .118 C3
Aston Bank HR9 . . . . .170 C2
Aston Cl Berry Hill GL16 . . .155 A7
  11 Ledbury HR8 . . . . .178 E8
Aston Gr
  Cheltenham GL51 . . . . . .132 D2
  Cold Aston GL54 . . . . . . .168 B6
Aston Ho 4 BS5 . . . . .195 B1
Aston Rd GL55 . . . . .188 F3
Aston View GL4 . . . . .148 C6
Astor Cl GL3 . . . . .120 D6
Astridge Rd GL1 . . . . .121 A4
Astry Cl GL1 . . . . .27 A1
Atchley St 11 BS5 . . . . .9 B7
Atcombe Rd GL6 . . . . .90 F8
Athelney Way 4 GL2 . . . .130 F8
Atherston BS30 . . . . .11 D5
Atherstone Cl GL51 . . . . . .132 C3

Atherton Cl GL51 . . . . . . .129 D2
Atherton Ho GL51 . . . . . .129 D2
Athlone Wlk BS4 . . . . .8 E1
Atkins Cl BS14 . . . . .3 E6
Atlantic Rd BS11 . . . . .16 C8
Atlas Cl BS5 . . . . .20 A2
Atlas Rd BS3 . . . . .8 E3
Atlas St BS2 . . . . .9 B5
Attwood Cl GL51 . . . . . . .132 F5
Aubrey Ho 9 BS3 . . . . .8 B3
Aubrey Meads BS30 . . . . . .5 E8
Aubrey Rd BS3 . . . . .8 B3
Auburn Ave BS30 . . . . .11 C2
Auburn Rd BS6 . . . . .18 B1
Auckland Ho 1 GL51 . . . .132 F3
Audley Cl BS37 . . . . .43 A8
Audrey Wlk BS9 . . . . .18 D7
Augustine Way GL4 . . . . . .119 F6
Augustus Ho GL15 . . . . . . .18 B6
Augustus Way GL15 . . . . . .92 B4
Aust Cres NP16 . . . . .60 F5
Aust La BS9 . . . . .18 A8
Aust Rd Olveston BS35 . . . .49 F5
  Pilning BS35 . . . . .48 D3
Austen Gr BS7 . . . . .18 D3
Austen Ho BS7 . . . . .18 A8
Austin Dr GL2 . . . . .126 F6
Austin Rd
  Ashchurch GL20 . . . . .182 D4
  Cirencester GL7 . . . . .190 E4
Australia Ho GL51 . . . . . .132 E1
Avalon Rd BS5 . . . . .10 B6
Avebury Cl GL4 . . . . .118 B1
Avebury Rd BS3 . . . . .7 E2
Avenall Cl 4 GL52 . . . . . .130 F8
Avenall Par GL53 . . . . . . .130 C8
Avening Rd Bristol BS15 . . .10 A8
  Gloucester GL4 . . . . .118 F5
  Nailsworth GL6 . . . . .91 E3
Avenue Terr GL10 . . . . .97 D7
Avenue The
  Bourton-on-t-W GL54 . . . .168 F8
  Brimscombe GL5 . . . . .148 B5
  Bristol, Ashley Down BS7 . .18 F3
  Bristol, Clifton BS8 . . . . . .18 A1
  Bristol, Frenchay BS16 . . . .29 E1
  Bristol, Little Stoke BS34 . . .29 C6
  Bristol, Patchway BS34 . . . .40 B2
  Bristol, Shirehampton BS9 . .17 E3
  Bristol, St George BS5 . . . . .9 F8
  Cheltenham GL53 . . . . . .130 F5
  Churchdown GL3 . . . . .128 D5
  Cirencester GL7 . . . . .190 D4
  Dursley GL11 . . . . .87 D3
  Keynsham BS31 . . . . .4 E6
  Leighterton GL8 . . . . .70 C3
  Lower Oddington GL56 . . .177 C4
  Marshfield SN14 . . . . .14 F8
  Mickleton GL55 . . . . .189 A6
  Pill BS20 . . . . .16 C5
  Pucklechurch BS16 . . . . . . .22 C4
  Wickwar GL12 . . . . .54 A5
  Winchcombe GL54 . . . . . .174 A7
  Winstone GL7 . . . . .107 A8
Back Montpellier Terr
  GL50 . . . . .193 B2
Back Of Avon GL2 . . . . . . .192 C4
Back Of Kingsdown Par
  BS6 . . . . .195 A4
Back Of Mount Pleasant
  GL20 . . . . .192 C4
Back Rd BS3 . . . . .8 A4
Back Row GL1 . . . . .177 B6
Back St
  Ashton Keynes SN6 . . . . .142 F5
  Hawkesbury Upton GL9 . . . .56 A3
  Ilmington CV36 . . . . .189 E6
  Newnham GL14 . . . . .157 A6
Back Stoke La BS9 . . . . .17 F6
Back The 72 F1
Back Walls GL54 . . . . .176 F4
Backfields BS2 . . . . .195 B4
Backfields Ct BS2 . . . . . . .195 B4
Backfields La BS2 . . . . . . .195 B4
Backwell Wlk BS13 . . . . .1 F8
Baden Hill Rd GL12 . . . . . . .37 E5
Baden Rd
  Bristol, Kingswood BS15 . . .11 A7
  Bristol, Redfield BS5 . . . . . .9 C7
Badenham Gr BS11 . . . . . . .16 F8
Bader Ave GL3 . . . . .128 C5
Bader Cl BS37 . . . . .43 D3
Baders Dean NP25 . . . . . .154 B1
Badger Cl Bristol BS30 . . . .10 F3
  Gloucester GL4 . . . . .119 D3
Badger Vale Ct GL2 . . . . . .118 C5
Badger's La GL52 . . . . .39 C3
Badgers Cl BS32 . . . . .24 C4
Badgers Dene HR2 . . . . . . .60 D8
Badgers Field GL55 . . . . . .189 A2
Badgers Mdw NP16 . . . . . . .60 B6
Badgers Rise BS30 . . . . . . .28 E4
Badgers Way
  8 Bristol GL5 . . . . .155 D1
  Nailsworth GL6 . . . . .90 F5
Badgers Wlk BS4 . . . . .9 D1
Badgeworth Cl GL51 . . . . .129 B7
Badgeworth La GL51 . . . . .129 B7
Badgeworth Rd GL51 . . . . .129 A7
Badhams The GL20 . . . . . .180 F7
Badminton BS16 . . . . .38 C1
Badminton CE Sch GL53 . . .130 D6
Badminton Ct BS37 . . . . . . .43 C2
Badminton Rd
  Bristol, Downend BS16 . . . .20 E7
  Bristol, Montpelier BS2 . . . .18 F1

Badminton Rd continued
  Chipping Sodbury BS37 3
  Frampton Cotterell BS36,
  BS37 . . . .
  Gloucester GL4 . . . .
Badminton Road Trad Est
  BS37 . . . .
Badminton Sch BS9 . . . .
Badminton Wlk BS16 . . . .
Badock's Wood Prim Sch
  BS10 . . . .
Badsey La WR12 18
Bafford App GL53 13
Bafford Farm GL53 1
Bafford Gr GL53 . . . .
Bafford La GL53 . . . .
Baglyn Ave BS15 . . . .
Bagnell Cl BS14 . . . .
Bagnell Rd BS14 . . . .
Bagpath Ho GL54 . . . .
Bagshots Sq GL54 1
Bagstone Rd BS37,GL12 1
Bagworth Dr BS30 . . . .
Bailey Cl 21 GL54 17
Bailey Ct BS32 . . . .
Bailey La NP16,GL15 . . . . . .
Bailey's Court Prim Sch
  BS32 . . . .
Bailey's Hay NP16 . . . .
Baileys Court Rd BS32 . . . . .
Bailey's Mead Rd BS16 . . . . .
Bailiffe Piece SN6 1
Baines Cl 1 GL54 17
Bakehouse La GL50 1
Baker Sq GL20 19
Baker St
  Cheltenham GL51 1
  Gloucester GL2 1
Baker's Hill GL55 1
Baker's La GL19 . . . .
Bakers Ground BS34 . . . .
Bakers Hill GL16 1
Bakers Piece Rd GL17 1
Bakersfield BS30 . . . .
Bala Rd GL51 . . . .
Balaclava Rd BS16 . . . .
Balcarras GL53 1
Balcarras Gdns GL53 1
Balcarras Rd GL53 1
Balcarras Retreat GL53 1
Balcarras Sch GL53 1
Baldwin Cl GL7 1
Baldwin St BS1 1
Baldwyn St WR11 1
Balfour Rd Bristol BS3 . . . . .
Ball La GL19 . . . .
Ballards Cl GL55 1
Ballast La BS11 . . . .
Ballinode Cl GL50 1
Ballinska Mews GL2 1
Balmain St BS4 . . . .
Balmoral Cl BS34 . . . .
Balmoral Ct Bristol BS16 . . . .
  Cheltenham GL53 1
Balmoral Mans 3 BS7 . . . . .
Balmoral Rd
  Bristol, Longwell Green
  BS30 . . . .
  Bristol, Montpelier BS7 . . . .
  Keynsham BS31 . . . .
Baltic Pl BS20 . . . .
Bamfield BS14 . . . .
Bamfurlong Ind Pk
  GL51 1
Bamfurlong La
  Bamfurlong GL51 1
  Cheltenham GL51 1
Bampton Cl
  Bristol, Emerson's Green
  BS16 . . . .
  Bristol, Headley Park BS13 . .
Bampton Croft BS16 . . . . . .
Bampton Dr BS16 . . . .
Banady La GL52 1
Baneberry Rd GL4 1
Banfield Cl BS11 . . . .
Bangor Gr BS4 . . . .
Bangrove Wlk BS11 . . . .
Bangup La GL54 1
Banister Gr BS4 . . . .
Bank Cres 1 HR8 1
Bank Leaze Prim Sch
  BS11 . . . .
Bank Pl BS20 . . . .
Bank Rd Avonmouth BS11 . . .
  Bristol BS15 . . . .
  Pilning BS35 . . . .
Bank Side SN16 . . . .
Bank St Chepstow NP16 . . . .
  Coleford GL16 1
Bank The Broadwell GL56 . . .1
  Prestbury GL52 1
Banks Fee La GL56 1
Bankside Bristol BS16 . . . . .
  North Cerney GL7 1
Bankside Rd BS4 . . . .
Banner Rd BS6 . . . .
Bannerleigh La BS8 . . . .
Bannerleigh Rd BS8 . . . .
Bannerman Rd BS5 . . . .
Bannerman Road Prim Sch
  BS5 . . . .
Bannetts Tree Cres BS35 . . .
Bantock Cl BS7 . . . .
Bantry Rd BS4 . . . .
Banwell Cl Bristol BS13 . . . .
  Keynsham BS31 . . . .

Rd BS3 .....8 A3
CI GL4 .....119 F6
ans BS5 .....19 A1
Way GL17 .....164 A3
La GL8 .....140 A2
y CI GL50 .....130 B6
d Rd GL7 .....196 A3
n Way GL1 .....196 A3
r Gdns BS13 .....2 D3
r Rd BS3 .....8 A3
ge Rd GL1 .....132 E3
t CI BS15 .....10 C8
ans La HR8 .....178 B8
s BS5 .....9 C7
PI ▪ GL7 .....152 E4
Wlk BS5 .....19 A1
s Leys GL52 .....138 B4
s Mead BS37 .....43 F4
s Hill BS16 .....19 C5
La GL4 .....139 F5
is Ho BS10 .....27 F3
s La GL50 .....194 C6
CI Bristol BS16 .....21 A6
nan GL51 .....132 D5
on Cotterell BS36 .....35 C8
cke GL2 .....109 E6
Close Prim Sch 21 A6
Croft BS9 .....
orn Sq GL14 .....191 C4
roft GL4 .....119 D2
CI GL10 .....97 E7
Rd GL51 .....132 F4
round GL2 .....125 D5
ill Rd GL16 .....155 C6
a GL17 .....163 F3
wl Way BS34 .....29 F5
hay GL7 .....196 A2
as St ▪ BS2 .....18 E1
y CI GL1 .....118 F7
rk Trad Est BS3 .....8 C1
re Dr GL3 .....127 F4
e La GL15 .....147 A4
ad Par ▪ GL10 .....97 F7
d Wlk BS31 .....4 B8
Ho GL7 .....190 D5
... St ▪ BS5 .....9 B7
s Wallis Way GL3 .....128 C5
t Ave HR8 .....178 E8
t CI GL51 .....132 E5
t Way 127 D1
thleach La GL4 .....168 A1
wns GL4 HR8 .....178 E8
alds GL4 .....113 A5
ay GL3 .....128 C4
d CI BS37 .....44 A4
ll Rd BS37 .....44 B1
eadow Rd ▪ 174 A7
ey House Gdn* 151 C7
aple Ct BS4 .....2 E8
ple Rd BS4 .....2 E8
aple Wlk BS4 .....2 F8
ood Gr GL4 .....119 D8
ood CE Prim Sch 127 D1
ood Park Sch for Girls 119 D8
ood Rd .....
ester GL2 .....127 C2
S37 .....32 C7
sa PI BS1 .....195 A1
CI SN6 .....145 C3
ck Sg GL1 .....196 A3
ck's La BS11 .....16 A3
cks The GL15 .....156 A4
st BS5 .....19 C1
ct's Mill La GL53 .....193 C3
La GL17 .....164 F8
s Pitch GL55 .....189 A2
gton Ave GL51 .....129 B3
gton CI BS15 .....20 F2
gton Ct .....
stol, Knowle BS2 .....8 F4
l, New Cheltenham 20 B1
gton Dr GL3 .....129 F8
gton Mews GL51 .....129 F8
w CI GL2 .....109 F8
w Elm Barns GL7 .....152 F7
w Hill .....
hdown GL3 .....128 D3
BS30 .....12 B5
w Hill Cres BS11 .....16 C7
w Hill Rd BS11 .....16 D6
w Hospl BS48 .....1 A6
w Rd BS2 .....9 A7
well La GL15 .....146 F7
wfield Rd GL51 .....133 A1
wmead Dr BS11 .....16 F7
Court Ave BS30 .....11 A5
Court Prim Sch 10 F5
Court Rd BS30 .....11 A5
La GL11 .....79 E4
t BS30 .....11 C1

Barry Rd BS30 .....11 C2
Barstable Ho BS2 .....195 C3
Bartholomew CI GL19 .....172 D4
Bartlett's Rd BS3 .....8 C2
Bartletts Ho GL14 .....176 F4
Bartley Croft ▪ GL8 .....140 C4
Bartley St BS3 .....8 C4
Barton CI Alveston BS35 .....51 A5
Bristol BS4 .....
Charlton Kings GL53 .....131 A4
Winterbourne BS36 .....30 E5
Barton Ct
Bristol BS5 .....9 A8
Bayleys Dr BS15 .....10 C6
Barton Gn BS15 .....85 D8
Barton Hill GL17 .....164 E5
Barton Hill Inf Sch BS5 .....9 B6
Barton Hill Prim Sch BS5 .....9 B6
Barton Hill Rd BS5 .....9 B7
Barton Hill Trad Est ▪
BS5 .....
Barton La GL7 .....190 B5
Barton Manor BS2 .....9 A6
Barton Mews GL20 .....192 D4
Barton Vill
Bristol BS1 .....195 B4
Tewkesbury GL20 .....192 D4
Barton St Bristol BS1 .....195 A4
Gloucester GL1 .....119 A8
Tewkesbury GL20 .....192 C4
Barton Vale ▪ BS2 .....9 A6
Bartonend La GL6 .....129 E6
Bartonend La GL6 .....91 A1
Bartonia Gr BS4 .....9 D1
Bartwood La HR9 .....164 A8
Barwick Ho BS1 .....16 E7
Barwick Rd BS15 .....129 F5
Barwood CI BS3 .....10 F5
Base La GL17 .....172 F1
Basil CI GL4 .....119 D4
Bassett CI ▪ GL54 .....174 A7
Bassett CI BS31 .....4 E4
Bassetts The GL55 .....98 D8
Batch The BS31 .....
Batchfield La BS16,BS37 .....22 D8
Bateman CI GL4 .....118 D1
Bates CI BS5 .....9 A8
Bath Bldgs BS6 .....18 E1
Bath Cres GL51 .....155 F1
Bath Ho GL11 .....
Bath Mews GL53 .....193 C2
Bath Par GL53 .....193 C2
Bath PI
▪ Berry Hill GL7 .....155 A7
Lydney GL15 .....92 B3
Bath Race Course* BA1 .....6 F6
Bath Rd Bitton BA1,BA2,BS30 .....5 F7
Bristol,Brislington BS4 .....9 D2
Bristol,Brislington BS4,BS31 .....9 F1
Bristol,Longwell Green
BS30 .....10 F3
Bristol,North Common BS30 .....11 D6
Bristol,Willsbridge BS30 .....11 C1
Cheltenham GL50,GL53 .....193 B2
Chipping Sodbury BS37,GL9 .....34 C4
Colerne SN14 .....15 E2
Cricklade SN6 .....143 E4
Eastington GL10 .....96 F6
Leighterton GL8 .....70 B2
Leonard Stanley GL10 .....97 F2
Nailsworth GL6 .....91 B2
Stonehouse GL10 .....97 F7
Tetbury GL8 .....140 B2
Thornbury BS35 .....
Wick BS30 .....12 E4
Woodchester GL5 .....99 A3
Bath St Bristol BS1 .....195 B2
Bath Vale Mews GL53 .....193 B2
Bathams CI GL17 .....164 F5
Bathings The ▪ BS5 .....51 C8
Bathleaze GL10 .....98 A3
Bathurst Par BS1 .....195 A1
Bathurst Park Rd GL15 .....92 A3
Bathurst Rd
Cirencester GL7 .....190 D3
Gloucester GL1 .....118 F6
Bathwell Rd BS4 .....9 B3
Batley CI GL52 .....131 D4
Batsford Arboretum*
GL56 .....186 E5
Batten CI BS37 .....44 C1
Batten's La BS5 .....10 A6
Battenburg Rd BS5 .....10 A8
Battens Rd BS5 .....10 B7
Battersby Way BS10 .....27 E2
Battersea Rd BS5 .....9 C8
Battle Rd GL52 .....192 B2
Battledown App GL52 .....134 A8
Battledown Dr GL52 .....131 A8
Battledown Grange
GL52 .....131 A8
Battledown Mead GL52 .....134 A8
Battledown Priors GL52 .....134 A1
Battledown Trad Est
GL52 .....131 A8
Batts La GL17 .....164 A4
Battson Rd BS14 .....3 E4
Baugh Gdns BS16 .....30 E1
Baugh Rd BS16 .....30 E1

Baunton La GL7 .....150 C7
Baxter CI BS15 .....10 F8
Baxters Barns GL12 .....153 D6
Bay Gdns BS15 .....19 C2
Bay Tree CI BS34 .....28 F7
Bay Tree Ct GL52 .....134 C4
Bay Tree Rd GL4 .....119 F5
Bayberry PI ▪ GL16 .....155 B5
Bayfield Gdns GL18 .....178 D2
Bayham Rd BS4 .....9 A3
Bayham's Wlk GL16 .....155 B5
Baylands GL13 .....85 D8
Bayleys Dr BS15 .....10 C6
Bayliss Ho GL51 .....132 E4
Bayliss Rd GL20 .....188 D5
Baynham Ct ▪ BS15 .....10 B5
Baynham Rd GL17 .....164 D5
Baynham Way GL50 .....193 B4
Baynham's Wlk GL16 .....155 B5
Baynton Ho ▪ BS5 .....9 B7
Bays Gdns BS5 .....8 A4
Bays Hill GL13 .....85 C8
Bayshill GL50 .....193 A3
Bayshill Rd GL50 .....193 A3
Bayswater Ave BS6 .....18 B7
Bayswater Rd BS7 .....18 C5
Bazeley Rd GL4 .....119 B2
Beach Ave BS35 .....38 A7
Beach Hill BS30 .....11 F3
Beach La BS30 .....12 C2
Beachgrove Gdns BS16 .....20 C4
Beachgrove Rd BS16 .....20 C4
Beachley Rd
Beachley NP16 .....61 B4
Tutshill NP16 .....73 A1
Beachley Wlk BS11 .....16 D7
Beacon CI GL4 .....112 A5
Beacon La BS16 .....30 C6
Beacon Rd
Gloucester GL4 .....119 B2
Llandogo NP25 .....146 A8
Beacon Rise Prim Sch
BS15 .....10 D6
Beaconlea BS15 .....10 D6
Beacons View Rd GL14 .....191 E5
Beaconsfield Ct ▪
GL50 .....130 B8
Beaconsfield Rd
Bristol, Clifton BS8 .....18 A1
Bristol, Knowle BS4 .....9 B3
Bristol, St George BS5 .....9 F8
Beaconsfield St ▪ BS5 .....9 B6
Beagles The GL5 .....98 D7
Beale CI Bristol BS14 .....3 E6
Bussage GL6 .....148 B6
Beale Rd GL51 .....132 D3
Beam St BS5 .....9 C7
Bean Acre The BS11 .....16 D8
Bean St GL16 .....155 A1
Beanhill Cres BS15 .....99 B2
Bear CI GL20 .....180 F6
Bear La GL12 .....68 B7
Bearbridge Rd BS13 .....1 F4
Bearcroft Gdn GL55 .....189 B4
Bearcroft Gdns GL55 .....189 B7
Beard's La GL5 .....99 A2
Bearland GL1 .....196 A3
Bearlands GL12 .....80 B3
Bearpacker Almshouses
GL12 .....68 C8
Baarsfield GL6 .....133 C3
Beauchamp CI 2 GL7 .....152 E4
Beauchamp Mdw GL15 .....92 C4
Beauchamp Rd BS7 .....18 C5
Beaudesert Park Sch
.....91 C5
Beaufort Bristol BS16 .....
Chepstow NP16 .....60 E8
Beaufort Ave BS37 .....43 D2
Beaufort Bldgs
▪ Gloucester GL7 .....7 F1
Gloucester GL1 .....196 B1
Beaufort CI BS5 .....19 B1
Beaufort Com Sch The
GL4 .....118 B2
Beaufort Cres BS34 .....29 E4
Beaufort Ct Bristol BS16 .....21 A8
Cirencester GL7 .....190 C3
Beaufort Dr GL15 .....92 B2
Beaufort End WR11 .....188 D7
Beaufort Hts ▪ BS5 .....9 B7
Beaufort Hts BS5 .....9 E7
Beaufort Mws BS37 .....44 B1
Beaufort PI
Bristol, Frenchay BS16 .....30 B1
Bristol, Upper Easton BS5 .....9 A8
Chepstow NP16 .....60 E8
Beaufort Rd
Bristol, Clifton BS8 .....18 A1
Bristol, Horfield BS7 .....18 F6
Bristol, Kingswood BS15 .....20 C1
Bristol, St George BS5 .....9 E7
Bristol, Staple Hill BS16 .....20 B3
Bristol, Vinney Green BS16 .....21 A8
Charlton Kings GL53 .....131 A8
Frampton Cotterell BS36 .....31 A8
Gloucester GL4 .....117 F8
Yate BS37 .....43 D2
Beaufort St
Bristol, Bedminster BS3 .....8 C2
Bristol, Upper Easton BS5 .....9 A8
Beaufort Way BS10 .....18 D8
Beauley Rd BS3 .....8 B4

Beaumont CI BS30 .....11 A3
Beaumont Dr GL51 .....132 D4
Beaumont PI GL15 .....92 A2
Beaumont Rd
Cheltenham GL51 .....132 D3
Gloucester GL2 .....127 C5
Beaumont St BS5 .....9 B8
Beaumont Terr ▪ BS5 .....9 A8
Beaumoor Rd GL7 .....152 E3
Beaver CI BS36 .....30 F7
Beazer CI ▪ BS16 .....20 D3
Beck CI BS16 .....21 C7
Beck Ho BS34 .....29 A8
Becket CI GL56 .....187 E7
Becket Ho BS34 .....22 B5
Becketts La GL54 .....174 A8
Beckfield Farm BS37 .....42 F5
Beckford CI GL20 .....183 B6
Beckford Gdns BS14 .....3 A3
Beckford Rd
Alderton GL20 .....183 D8
Ashton under Hill WR11 .....183 D8
Beckford Silk* GL20 .....183 E4
Beckington Rd BS3 .....8 D1
Beckington Wlk BS3 .....8 D1
Beckside Ct ▪ GL1 .....127 A1
Beckspool Rd BS16 .....30 C1
Becky Hill GL54 .....176 B1
Beddome Way GL54 .....168 F8
Bedford Ave GL51 .....133 A2
Bedford Cres BS7 .....18 F5
Bedford St
Gloucester GL1 .....196 C2
▪ Stroud GL5 .....99 C7
Bedminster Down Rd
BS13 .....8 B1
Bedminster Down Sch
BS13 .....1 F3
Bedminster Par ▪ BS3 .....8 C4
Bedminster PI ▪ BS3 .....8 C4
Bedminster Rd BS3 .....8 C2
Bedminster Sta BS3 .....8 C3
Beech Ave GL16 .....155 B7
Beech CI Alveston BS35 .....51 A5
Bristol BS30 .....11 A5
Hardwicke GL2 .....107 E8
Highnam GL2 .....125 D4
Prestbury GL52 .....134 C4
Beech Ct BS14 .....3 A6
Beech Gr Chepstow NP16 .....60 D7
Cirencester GL7 .....190 E5
Highworth SN6 .....145 C3
Woodchester GL5 .....80 E2
Beech Green Prim Sch
GL2 .....117 F1
Beech Grove Ct GL7 .....190 E5
Beech Ho BS16 .....19 C5
Beech La GL4 .....140 B6
Beech Lea
Broad Blunsdon SN26 .....144 E1
Meysey Hampton GL7 .....152 B3
Beech Leaze BS35 .....51 A5
Salford BS35 .....5 E3
Yorkley GL15 .....156 A2
Beech Rd
Bristol, Bradley Stoke BS30 .....29 D8
Bristol, Frenchay BS16 .....30 B1
Bristol, Oldland Common
BS30 .....11 C2
Bristol, St Anne's Park BS4 .....9 E5
King's Stanley GL10 .....96 E3
Beechfield CI BS41 .....7 C2
Beechfield Gr BS9 .....17 C8
Beechmore Dr ▪ GL51 .....129 E5
Beechmount CI BS14 .....3 B8
Beechurst Ave GL52 .....193 C3
Beechurst Way GL52 .....137 D4
Beechwood Ave GL15 .....10 D5
Beechwood CI Bristol BS14 .....3 B8
Cheltenham GL52 .....131 B8
Beechwood Gr
Gloucester GL4 .....118 G3
Wooton-u-E GL12 .....68 D8
Beechwood PI GL50 .....193 C3
Beechwood Rd
Bristol BS16 .....20 D6
Easton-in-G BS20 .....16 A4
Beechwood Rise GL11 .....87 F2
Beehive Trad Est BS5 .....9 E7
Beeks La SN14,BA1 .....14 D5
Beesmoor Rd BS36 .....31 B6
Begbrook Dr BS16 .....19 F6
Begbrook La BS16 .....19 F6

Begbrook Pk BS16 .....20 A7
Begbrook Prim Sch BS16 .....19 F6
Beggar Bush La BS8 .....7 C5
Beggarswell CI GL2 .....195 C4
Bekdale CI GL2 .....109 D8
Belas Knap Long Barrow*
GL54 .....174 A4
Belfast Wlk BS4 .....2 E8
Belfrey The NP16 .....61 C7
Belfry BS30 .....10 A8
Belfry Ave BS5 .....10 B4
Belfry CI GL4 .....119 E8
Belgrave Hill ▪ BS8 .....18 A2
Belgrave PI BS8 .....194 A3
Belgrave Rd Bristol BS8 .....194 A3
Gloucester GL1 .....196 B2
Bell Bank ▪ GL56 .....186 C5
Bell Barn Rd BS9 .....17 D6
Bell CI BS10 .....18 C7
Bell Hill BS16 .....19 C4
Bell Hill Rd BS5 .....9 F8
Bell La Blockley GL56 .....186 C5
Bristol BS1 .....195 A3
Bromberrow Heath GL18 .....179 B4
Gloucester GL1 .....196 B2
Lechlade on T GL7 .....153 E2
Minchinhampton GL6 .....148 A3
Poulton GL7 .....151 F4
Stroud GL5 .....98 C4
Bell Orch GL2 .....157 B6
Bell Pitch GL6 .....102 F3
Bell Rd BS36 .....31 C6
Bell Sq SN14 .....15 A8
Bell Wlk GL1 .....196 B2
Bell's Old Gram Sch
GL16 .....154 E4
Bella Vista GL52 .....138 B3
Bellamy Ave BS13 .....2 C4
Bellamy CI BS15 .....10 A5
Belland Dr Bristol BS14 .....2 C4
Charlton Kings GL53 .....131 A4
Belle CI 7 BS2 .....9 C7
Belle Vue CI BS15 .....99 C7
Belle Vue Cotts BS9 .....18 A7
Belle Vue Rd Bristol BS5 .....9 C8
Cinderford GL14 .....191 C4
Ruardean GL17 .....163 F4
Stroud GL5 .....99 C7
Belle Vue Terr GL6 .....148 C5
Bellevue BS8 .....194 E2
Bellevue CI BS15 .....10 E2
Bellevue Cotts BS8 .....194 B2
Bellevue Ct BS8 .....194 B2
Bellevue Pk BS4 .....9 D2
Bellevue Rd
Bristol, Kingswood BS15 .....10 F7
Bristol, St George BS5 .....10 A8
▪ Bristol, Totterdown BS2 .....8 F4
Bellevue Terr
Bristol, Brislington BS4 .....9 D2
Bristol, Clifton Wood BS8 .....194 B2
Bristol, Totterdown BS4 .....8 F4
Bellfields La BS16 .....30 C1
Bellflower Rd GL20 .....192 E2
Bellhouse Wlk BS11 .....27 B1
Bellingham La SN6 .....145 D1
Bells PI Cinderford GL14 .....136 C6
Coleford GL16 .....155 A5
Belluton Rd BS4 .....9 A3
Belmont Ave GL3 .....120 B7
Belmont Dr BS34 .....24 C8
Belmont La GL16 .....155 A8
Belmont Lo GL52 .....193 C4
Belmont PI BS4 .....28 F1
Belmont Rd
Bristol, Brislington BS4 .....18 C3
Bristol, Montpelier BS6 .....18 C3
Cheltenham GL52 .....193 C4
Hewelsfield GL15 .....146 E5
Stroud GL5 .....99 E6
Belmont St BS5 .....19 B1
Belmore PI GL53 .....193 B2
Beloe Rd BS7 .....18 E5
Belroyal Ave BS4 .....9 F3
Belsher Dr BS15 .....11 A6
Belstone Wlk BS4 .....2 C8
Belton Rd BS5 .....9 B8
Belvedere Mews GL6 .....148 C5
Belvedere Rd BS6 .....18 B3
Belworth Ct ▪ GL51 .....129 F7
Belworth Dr GL51 .....130 A7
Bence Ct 2 BS15 .....10 B5
Bences CI SN14 .....14 F8
Bendall Ho ▪ GL52 .....193 C4
Bendy Bow SN16 .....141 F4
Benford CI GL52 .....134 D4
Benhall Ave GL51 .....129 E8
Benhall Gdns GL51 .....132 E1
Benhall Ho GL51 .....129 D8
Benhall Inf Sch GL51 .....129 D7
Bennett PI GL5 .....9 F7
Bennett Way BS1,BS8 .....7 F5
Bennett's Ct BS37 .....44 B1
Bennington St GL50 .....193 B4
Bensaunt Gr BS10 .....28 D4
Benson CI GL14 .....119 C6
Bentley CI Bristol BS14 .....2 F3
Quedgeley GL2 .....117 F2
Bentley La GL52 .....134 D7
Benton CI GL10 .....89 E6
Benville Ave BS9 .....17 C8
Berchel Ho ▪ BS3 .....8 D4

Berenda Dr BS30 ....11 B3
Beresford Cl BS31 ....5 E2
Beresford Ho GL7 ....190 C6
Berkeley Ave Bristol BS8 .194 C3
Bristol, Bishopston BS7 ...18 D3
Berkeley Castle & Butterfly
Ho* GL13 ....85 F2
Berkeley Cl Bristol BS16 ..21 A8
Charfield GL12 ....67 A5
Gloucester GL3 ....120 C6
South Cerney GL7 ....142 F7
Stroud GL5 ....98 D7
Berkeley Cres
Bristol BS8 ....194 B3
Lydney GL15 ....92 B5
Berkeley Ct
Bristol, Bishopston BS7 ...18 D3
Bristol, Upper Easton BS5 .9 B7
Cheltenham GL52 ....193 C3
Slimbridge GL2 ....95 D3
Berkeley Gdns BS31 ....4 E4
Berkeley Ho
Bristol, Eastville BS5 ....19 D2
Bristol, Frenchay BS16 ....30 B1
Berkeley Gr BS5 ....19 C2
Berkeley Ho Bristol BS1 .194 C3
[7] Berkeley, Staple Hill BS20 D5
[6] Cheltenham, Fairview
GL52 ....133 F2
[6] Cheltenham, Hester's Way
GL51 ....132 B3
Berkeley Hospl GL13 ....85 E3
Berkeley Mews GL52 ......193 C3
Berkeley Rd Bristol BS7 ...18 D3
Cheltenham GL52 ....193 C3
Berkeley Prim Sch GL13 ..85 E3
Berkeley Rd
Bristol, Bishopston BS7 ...18 D3
Bristol, Kingswood BS15 ..20 B2
Bristol, Mayfield Park BS16 20 B2
Bristol, Staple Hill BS16 ..20 D5
Bristol, Westbury Park BS6 .18 B4
Cirencester GL7 ....190 C1
Berkeley Sq BS8 ....194 B3
Berkeley St Bristol BS5 ...19 C3
Cheltenham GL52 ....193 C3
Gloucester GL1 ....196 A3
Berkeley Vale Com Sch
GL13 ....85 E7
Berkeley Way Bristol BS16 .21 B7
[7] Tetbury GL8 ....140 C5
Berkeleys Mead BS34 .....30 A6
Berkhampstead Sch
GL52 ....134 A2
Berkley Ave BS8 ....194 B3
Berkshire Rd BS7 ....18 D3
Berlington Ct BS1 ....195 B1
Bernard Ct BS4 ....2 D7
Berrells Rd GL8 ....140 B3
Berrells The GL8 ....140 B3
Berrington Rd GL55 ....189 B2
Berrow Wlk BS3 ....8 E2
Berrows Mead BS37 ....43 A8
Berry Cl GL6 ....103 F8
Berry Croft BS3 ....8 D4
Berry Hill Cres GL7 ....190 C7
Berry Hill Prim Sch
GL16 ....155 A7
Berry Hill Rd GL7 ....190 D7
Berry La BS7 ....18 F6
Berry Lawn GL4 ....119 D3
Berrycroft GL13 ....85 E4
Berryfield GL5 ....98 F2
Berryfield Glade GL2 ......128 A6
Berrymore Rd GL5 ....98 F2
Bertha's Field GL9 ....57 B4
Berton Cl BS16 ....32 D5
Berwick Cl BS10 ....27 E8
Berwick Cl BS10 ....27 B5
Berwick La BS10 ....27 D7
Berwick Rd
Bishop's Cleeve GL52 .....137 F5
Bristol BS5 ....19 B2
Beryl Gr BS14 ....3 C8
Beryl Rd BS3 ....8 B3
Besbury Pk GL6 ....148 A4
Besford Ct GL52 ....138 E3
Besom La BS37 ....32 D5
Bessemer Cl [21] GL16 ...155 A5
Bestal Cl GL20 ....182 B4
Bethel Rd BS5 ....9 B8
Bethesda St GL50 ....193 B1
Betjeman Cl GL2 ....118 C4
Betjeman Ct [2] BS30 ......11 A5
Bettenson Rise [17] GL54 .168 A1
Bettertons Cl GL7 ....152 D3
Bettridge Ct GL52 ....134 B3
Bettridge Sch GL51 ....130 A6
Betts Gn BS16 ....21 C7
Betworthy Est GL11 ....88 E8
Beuchamp Mdw GL55 .....92 C4
Bevan Cotts GL20 ....181 F8
Bevan Ct BS34 ....28 F2
Bevan Gdns GL20 ....182 C5
Beverley Ave BS16 ....30 F1
Beverley Cl BS5 ....10 B6
Beverley Croft GL51 ....132 C2
Beverley Gdns Bristol BS9 .17 C7
Woodmancote GL52 ....138 C3
Beverley Rd BS7 ....18 F8
Beverly Ct [8] BS14 ....3 B8
Beverston Gdns BS11 ....27 B2
Beverstone GL5 ....10 C8
Beverstone Cl GL7 ....142 F7

Beverstone Rd GL7 ....142 F7
Bevin Cl [5] BS2 ....18 F1
Bevington Cl BS34 ....39 E1
Bevington La GL13 ....76 F7
Bevington Wlk BS34 ....39 E1
Bewley Way GL3 ....128 A6
Bexley Rd BS16 ....20 B3
Beyon Dr GL11 ....87 F6
Beyon Dr GL11 ....87 F6
Bglws The GL16 ....155 B5
Bhirraff Ct [14] BS6 ....18 B1
Bibstone BS15 ....11 A8
Bibsworth Ave [4] WR12 .185 C8
Bibsworth La
Broadway WR12 ....185 C8
Broadway WR12 ....188 B1
Bibury Ave BS34 ....29 B8
Bibury CE Prim Sch
GL7 ....160 A1
Bibury Cl BS9 ....18 D7
Bibury Cres
Bristol, Hanham BS15 .....10 C5
Tewkesbury GL20 ....182 C5
Bibury Rd
Cheltenham GL51 ....129 E8
Gloucester GL4 ....119 A6
Bibury Trout Farm*
GL7 ....160 A1
Bickerton Cl BS10 ....27 F3
Bickford Cl BS30 ....11 A6
Bickley Cl BS15 ....10 C2
Bicknor St GL16 ....155 A8
Bicks La [30] GL54 ....174 A7
Biddel Springs SN6 ....145 D3
Biddestone Rd GL2 ....28 E1
Biddulph Way HR8 ....178 E7
Bideford Cres BS4 ....2 F8
Bidwell Cl BS10 ....28 B3
Bifield Cl BS14 ....3 F5
Bifield Gdns BS14 ....3 E5
Bifield Rd BS14 ....3 F5
Bigstone Cl GL4 ....119 C6
Bigstone Gr NP16 ....73 A2
Bigwood La BS1 ....194 C2
Bijou Ct GL1 ....126 F4
Bilberry [7] Bristol BS9 ....17 C8
[5] Gloucester GL4 ....119 F5
Bilbie Cl BS10 ....18 E7
Billand Cl BS13 ....1 E3
Billbrook Rd GL3 ....120 A7
Billingham Cl GL4 ....119 B6
Billimas Way GL50 ....130 B6
Bilson GL14 ....191 C5
Binbury Gr BS14 ....3 D5
Binmead Gdns BS13 ....8 A2
Binyon Rd GL4 ....139 F5
Birbeck Rd BS9 ....17 E5
Birch Ave GL14 ....119 C6
Birch Cl Bristol BS34 ....28 E7
Charlton Kings GL53 ....131 C4
Ledbury HR8 ....178 E8
Birch Croft BS14 ....3 A3
Birch Ct BS31 ....4 C4
Birch Dr Alveston BS35 ....50 F4
Pucklechurch BS20 ....32 E7
Birch Glade [4] SN6 ....142 F4
Birch Ho BS16 ....20 B5
Birch Pk GL16 ....155 C5
Birch Rd
Bristol, Kingswood BS15 ..20 D8
Bristol, Southville BS3 .....8 B4
Dursley GL11 ....88 A4
Mile End GL16 ....155 C6
Woodchester GL5 ....99 A3
Yate BS37 ....43 D2
Birchall Cl GL4 ....119 C3
Birchall Rd BS6 ....18 C4
Birchdale BS30 ....11 B6
Birches Cl GL5 ....99 C8
Birches Cl GL5 ....99 C8
Birches La GL18 ....170 F7
Birches Rd NP25 ....154 B5
Birches The GL5 ....99 C8
Birchill Rd GL4 ....139 F4
Birchills Trad Est BS4 ....9 F1
Birchley Rd GL52 ....131 B8
Birchmore Rd GL1 ....119 A8
Birchwood Cl GL14 ....191 B5
Birchwood Ct BS14 ....3 A4
Birchwood Fields GL4 ....118 E3
Birchwood Rd Bristol BS4 .9 F4
Netherend GL15 ....147 C3
Bird Rd GL3 ....120 B6
Birdale Cl BS10 ....27 E3
Birdland* GL54 ....168 F7
Birdlip Cl BS48 ....20 C2
Birdlip Ho GL1 ....127 A2
Birdlip Prim Sch GL4 .....121 F1
Birds Bush La GL6 ....106 B5
Birdwell Prim Sch BS41 ...1 A8
Birdwood BS15 ....10 D6
Birdwood Cl GL14 ....119 E4
Birdwood Gdns NP16 ....60 C4
Birgage Rd GL9 ....55 F2
Birkdale Bristol BS30 ....11 B6
Yate BS37 ....32 E8
Birkin St [5] BS2 ....9 A6
Bishop Cl GL51 ....133 A2
Bishop Manor Rd BS10 ...18 D7
Bishop Rd
Bristol, Bishopston BS7 ...18 D4
Bristol, Emerson's Green
BS16 ....21 C6
Shurdington GL51 ....129 E2

Bishop Road Prim Sch
BS7 ....18 D4
Bishop St BS2 ....195 B4
Bishop Terr BS2 ....195 C4
Bishop's Cl GL15 ....99 D6
Bishop's Cleeve Prim Sch
GL52 ....137 F3
Bishop's Wlk GL19 ....181 C3
Bishop's Wood BS32 ....40 C6
Bishops Cl
Bishop's Cleeve GL52 .....138 A3
Bristol BS9 ....17 E3
Chepstow NP16 ....60 F4
Bishops Cove BS13 ....1 F5
Bishops Dr GL52 ....137 F3
Bishops Gate GL15 ....92 A2
Bishops Knoll BS9 ....17 C3
Bishops Mdw GL52 ....137 E4
Bishops Mead NP16 ....60 B4
Bishops Rd GL4 ....119 E6
Bishops Wlk
Cirencester GL7 ....190 C4
Tewkesbury GL20 ....182 C5
Bishopsfield [2] SN6 ......143 E4
Bishopstone CE GL51 ....132 C1
Bishopstone Rd GL1 ......119 A8
Bishopstone CE Jun Sch
BS13 ....1 F6
Bishopsworth Rd BS13 .....2 A7
Bishopthorpe Rd BS10 ...18 E7
Bishport Ave BS13 ....2 C3
Bishport Cl BS13 ....2 B4
Bishport Gn BS13 ....2 C3
Bishton La NP16 ....73 B3
Bisley BS37 ....32 C7
Bisley Bluecoat CE Prim Sch
GL6 ....148 D8
Bisley Old Rd GL5 ....99 C7
Bisley Rd Bisley GL6 ......104 E2
Cheltenham GL51 ....129 E8
Bisley St GL6 ....103 F8
Bissex Mead BS16 ....21 B5
Bittern Ave GL4 ....119 C6
Bitterwell Cl BS36 ....31 D3
Bittlemead BS13 ....2 F4
Bitton Sta BS30 ....11 B1
Bixhead Wlk GL16 ....155 C5
Blaby Cl GL4 ....119 F5
Black Berry Field GL52 ..134 C3
Black Dog Way GL1 ....196 B3
Black Horse Hill GL8 ......140 B3
Black Jack Mews GL7 ....190 C5
Black Jack St GL7 ....190 C5
Black Stone Kilns La
HR9 ....162 D3
Black Wells GL11 ....80 B7
Blackacre BS14 ....3 C4
Blackberry Ave [5] BS16 ...19 C5
Blackberry Cl GL4 ....119 E4
Blackberry Dr BS36 ....31 C6
Blackberry Gr GL52 ....137 E4
Blackberry Hill BS16 ......20 A8
Blackberry Hill Hospl
BS16 ....20 A8
Blackbird Ave GL3 ....127 D6
Blackbird Ct GL10 ....90 F7
Blackboy [15] BS15 ....99 C7
Blackboy Rd BS13 ....8 B3
Blackdown Cr BS14 ....3 B5
Blackford La GL7 ....144 E6
Blackfriars BS1 ....194 C3
Blackfriars La BA1 ....6 B3
Blackhorse Cty Prim Sch
BS16 ....21 A8
Blackhorse Hill BS35,
BS10 ....28 B8
Blackhorse La BS16 ....21 A8
Blackhorse Pl BS16 ....21 A6
Blackhorse Rd
Bristol, Kingswood BS15 .10 D8
Bristol, Mangotsfield BS16 .21 A7
Blackhorse Rd BS15 ....10 D8
Blackmoor Rd BS8 ....16 E2
Blackmoors La BS3 ....7 F4
Blackquarries Hill GL12 ...68 E7
Blackrock La BS14 ....3 D1
Blacksmith Cl GL20 ....183 B5
Blacksmith Hill GL7 ....69 C7
Blacksmith La
Churchdown GL3 ....128 D4
Leigh The GL19 ....173 D5
Blacksmith's La BA1 ....6 B3
Blacksmiths Ground
GL2 ....125 D5
Blacksmiths La
Beckford GL20 ....183 B5
Dumbleton WR11 ....183 F7
Highnam GL2 ....125 F7
Blackthorn Cl GL51 ....134 C4
Blackthorn Dr BS20 ....183 D4
Blackthorn End GL53 .....130 A4
Blackthorn Gdns GL4 .....117 F1
Blackthorn Rd BS3 ....9 B3
Blackthorn Wlk BS15 .....20 D2
Blackwater Way GL2 ......127 C5
Blackworth SN6 ....145 D4
Bladon Mews GL3 ....129 B7
Blagdon Cl BS3 ....8 E2
Blagrove Cl BS13 ....2 C3
Blagrove Cres BS13 ....2 C3
Blaisdon GL37 ....32 E7
Blaisdon Cl Bristol BS10 ..28 A1

Blaisdon Cl continued
Gloucester GL4 ....119 E4
Blaisdon La GL17 ....165 B4
Blaisdon Way GL51 ....132 E5
Blaise Castle Mus* BS10 .27 E2
Blaise Hamlet BS11 ....27 D2
Blaise Prim Sch BS10 .....27 F2
Blaise Wlk BS9 ....17 C6
Blake Croft GL51 ....132 E4
Blake Hill Way GL4 ....119 D7
Blake Rd Bristol BS7 ....19 B6
Cirencester GL7 ....190 C5
Blake St NP25 ....154 A7
Blakeley Ct GL3 ....127 F6
Blakeney Cl GL4 ....118 D3
Blakeney Hill Rd GL15 ....156 D2
Blakeney Mills BS37 ....43 C1
Blakeney Prim Sch
GL15 ....156 D3
Blakeney Rd
Bristol, Horfield BS7 ....19 A7
Bristol, Patchway BS34 ...39 E1
Blakes St BS3 ....64 B1
Blakewell Mead GL6 ......103 E8
Blanchards BS37 ....33 D8
Blanchards Cotts BS37 ...33 D8
Blandford Alley SN6 ....145 D3
Blandford Cl [2] BS9 ....18 B6
Bleasby Gdns GL50 ....130 A8
Bledington Sch OX7 ......177 C1
Blenheim Cl
Alderton GL20 ....183 E4
Upper Rissington GL54 ..169 D6
[14] Winchcombe GL54 ...40 D3
[14] Winchcombe GL54 ...174 A7
Blenheim Dr
Bredon GL20 ....182 C7
Bristol BS34 ....29 B4
[3] Ledbury HR8 ....178 F7
[2] Newent GL18 ....171 A4
Yate BS37 ....43 D3
Blenheim Ho GL3 ....120 A7
Blenheim Orch GL51 ......129 E2
Blenheim Rd Bristol BS6 ..18 B3
Blenheim Sq GL51 ....132 E3
Blenheim St BS5 ....19 A1
Blenman Cl BS16 ....20 A7
Bleriot Rd GL54 ....169 D6
Blethwin Cl BS10 ....27 F1
Blineshire GL15 ....156 C3
Blind La
Chipping Campden GL55 .188 F1
Tetbull GL6 ....140 C5
Blinkhorns Bridge La
GL2 ....127 B1
Blockley CE Sch GL56 ...186 C6
Bloomfield Rd Bristol BS4 .9 C4
Gloucester GL1 ....118 C7
Bloomfield Road Link BS4 .9 C4
Bloomfield Terr GL11 ......118 D6
Bloomsbury St GL51 ......193 A4
Bloxham Rd WR12 ....188 A1
Bloxhams Orch GL19 .....172 D4
Bloy Sq BS5 ....19 C1
Bloy St BS5 ....19 C1
Blue Boys' Pk GL6 ....148 A4
Blue Coat CE Prim Sch
GL12 ....68 B6
Blue La GL15 ....170 D4
Blue Quarry Rd GL7 ....190 E5
Blue Rock Cres [5] GL15 .155 D7
Bluebell Chase GL6 ....148 C6
Bluebell Cl Bristol BS9 ....17 B6
Thornbury BS35 ....64 D2
Bluebell Dr NP16 ....60 F5
Bluebell Gr GL51 ....130 A5
Bluebell Rise GL6 ....148 C6
Bluebells The BS32 ....29 F7
Blundson Hill SN26 ....144 C2
Blunts Hay GL7 ....152 C8
Boakes Dr GL10 ....97 E6
Bobbie Cl GL54 ....169 C6
Bockenem Cl BS35 ....51 D7
Bodey Cl BS30 ....11 A5
Bodiam Ave GL4 ....118 B1
Bodmin Wlk BS4 ....2 F8
Bodnam Rd GL51 ....132 E4
Bodyce Rd [4] BS35 ....51 A5
Boiling Wells La BS2 ....19 A3
Boleyn Cl GL3 ....127 F7
Boleyn Cotts GL51 ....133 B7
Boleyn Ho GL54 ....139 F5
Bolton Rd BS7 ....18 E3
Bond St BS1 ....195 B3
Bond's La SN14 ....24 E1
Bondend Rd GL4 ....119 F2
Bonds Mill Est GL10 ....97 C2
Bonnington Wlk BS7 ....19 A4
Bonville Bsns Ctr BS4 ......9 F2
Bonville Rd BS4 ....9 F2
Book End GL17 ....164 F5
Boot La BS3 ....8 A4
Bootenhay Rd GL2 ....138 A4
Booth Rd BS3 ....8 A4
Borage Cl GL4 ....119 F5
Bordesley Rd BS14 ....3 A3
Borleyton Wlk BS13 ....1 H4
Born Ct [10] HR8 ....178 F8
Borough Cl GL10 ....98 A3
Borver Gr BS13 ....8 A4
Boscombe Cres BS16 ......20 F7
Boscombe La GL6 ....90 E1
Bospin La GL5 ....98 F1

Boston Rd BS7 ....18 F8
Boswell St [4] BS5 ....19 C1
Botany SN6 ....145 C3
Botham Dr BS4 ....3 D1
Boucher Pl [2] BS2 ....19 C1
Boulters Rd BS13 ....2 B5
Boulton La GL11 ....87 D8
Boulton Rd GL50 ....193 B6
Boulton's La [1] BS15 ....10 A1
Boulton's Rd [5] BS15 ......10 A1
Bouncer's La GL52 ....133 F2
Boundary Cotts GL3 ....120 A7
Boundary Pl GL19 ....172 D2
Boundary Rd
Avonmouth BS11 ....15 A2
Coalpit Heath BS36 ....31 F7
Bourchier Gdns BS13 ....8 A4
Bourne Cl Bristol BS15 ....20 D8
Winterbourne BS36 ....31 A6
Bourne La
Brimscombe GL5 ....101 A5
Bristol BS5 ....19 D2
Bourne Lake Pk SN6 ......170 A2
Bourne Rd BS15 ....20 D8
Bourne The BS15 ....20 D8
Bournside Cl GL51 ....132 E2
Bournside Dr GL51 ....132 E2
Bournside Rd GL51 ....132 E2
Boursland Cl BS32 ....29 C1
Bourton Ave BS34 ....29 A7
Bourton Cl BS34 ....29 A7
Bourton Mead BS41 ....16 A1
Bourton Rd
Gloucester GL4 ....119 F1
Moreton-in-M GL56 ....187 A6
Bourton-on-the-Water Prim
Sch GL54 ....168 A6
Bouverie St BS5 ....19 C1
Boverton Ave GL3 ....120 A7
Boverton Dr GL3 ....120 A7
Boverton Rd GL3 ....120 A7
Bovone La GL2 ....127 A4
Bow La
[5] Bourton-on-t-W GL54 .168 A6
Ripple GL20 ....182 C7
Bow Wow GL7 ....144 E1
Bowbridge Lock GL5 ......101 A6
Bowden Cl BS9 ....16 D5
Bowden Pl BS16 ....21 F7
Bowden Rd BS5 ....19 E8
Bowen Cl GL52 ....133 E4
Bowen's Hill [1] GL16 .....155 C6
Bowen's Hill Rd [4]
GL16 ....155 C6
Bower Ashton Terr BS3 .....7 F4
Bower Ct BS3 ....7 F4
Bower Rd BS3 ....8 A4
Bower Wlk BS3 ....8 B4
Bowerleaze BS9 ....16 C7
Bowes Lyon Cl GL56 ......187 A5
Bowl Hill GL5 ....101 A5
Bowldown Cotts GL8 ......140 C5
Bowldown Rd GL8 ....140 C5
Bowler Rd GL20 ....182 A1
Bowlers Lea GL11 ....88 C8
Bowling Green Ave GL7 ..190 D5
Bowling Green Cres
GL7 ....190 D5
Bowling Green Ct GL56 ..187 A5
Bowling Green La GL7 ....190 D5
Bowling Green Rd GL7 ...190 D5
Bowling Hill Bsns Pk
BS37 ....27 B1
Bowling Hill BS37 ....27 B1
Bowly Rd GL7 ....190 C4
Bowly Cres GL7 ....190 C4
Bowmead [7] BS4 ....9 F2
Bownham Mead GL5 ......148 F2
Bownham Park Sch GL5 ..148 F2
Bownham Pk GL5 ....148 F2
Bowood GL54 ....169 C6
Bowring Cl BS13 ....2 B4
Bowsland GL2 ....125 D5
Bowsland Green Sch
BS32 ....29 C2
Bowsland Way BS32 ....29 D2
Bowstreet La BS35 ....38 D1
Box Cres GL6 ....90 D2
Box La GL6 ....90 D2
Box Rd GL11 ....88 B8
Box Tree CV GL17 ....22 E1
Box Wlk BS31 ....4 C4
Boxbush Cl GL17 ....164 F5
Boxbush Rd
Coleford GL16 ....155 C4
South Cerney GL7 ....142 F7
Boxhedge Farm La BS36 ..37 F5
Boxwell Rd GL8 ....140 B4
Boxwood Cl GL8 ....140 B4
Boyce Cl GL4 ....119 C3
Boyce Dr BS2 ....9 C7
Boyce's Ave BS8 ....194 A3
Boyd Cl BS30 ....11 F6
Boyd Rd BS31 ....5 A5
Brabazon Rd BS34 ....29 F4
Bracelands GL6 ....101 A5
Bracelands Dr [1] GL16 ..155 C6
Bracewell Gdns BS10 ......28 A4
Bracey Dr BS16 ....20 F7

n Cl GL15 92 C3
n Dr GL15 92 B3
nbury Dr BS34 29 F5
ndene BS32 40 C1
n Dr BS14 3 A5
ton Gr BS16 20 A7
rd Rd 5 GL2 127 B2
rds Cl GL18 170 F4
rds Ct GL18 170 F4
rds La GL18 170 F4
irst St 7 BS5 9 B6
y Ave Bristol BS11 16 E6
bourne BS36 30 E5
y Cl GL2 127 C4
y Court Rd GL17 164 D6
y Cres BS11 16 E6
y Ct BS16 20 C5
y Pavilions BS32 40 C2
y Rd Bristol BS34 39 F1
n Kings GL53 131 A4
n-u-E GL12 68 A8
y Rise GL17 164 D6
y St GL12 68 A7
y Stoke Way BS32 29 E7
aw Cl GL2 127 E5
one Rd BS36 30 D5
ell Gr BS10 18 C8
Vlk GL4 119 D4
ar Ave BS7 28 F1
ar Cres BS7 28 F1
or Ct BS9 18 A8
s La BS2 195 C3
nridge Rd BS4 9 D4
field BS9 17 F6
Cl
, Bradley Stoke BS32 29 E7
, Warmley Hill BS15 10 F7
The
Heath BS36 31 C5
S37 43 E5
vell Gdns BS14 3 A4
le Chase GL52 137 F4
le Dr Bristol BS9 17 D3
y GL11 88 A3
le La Bristol BS9 17 C3
house GL10 97 F8
le Lawn GL4 119 D3
le Rd GL16 155 B4
le Rise GL52 134 C3
les The
ey GL13 85 E4
ham BS31 4 D3
R9 164 C8
ling Wlk BS16 19 F6
ey Cl
wood GL12 67 F4
dbury HR8 178 E7
ton BS35 50 A3
20 16 C4
ey Ct 6 BS30 10 F4
ey Dr GL19 165 D6
ey Mews GL4 120 A6
ey Rd
nham GL51 132 F3
sbury GL20 192 D6
eys The GL17 164 F5
h Hill Rise GL53 131 A4
h Rd
rlong GL51 129 A7
nham GL51 129 B7
h The GL17 164 B3
he Gr BS13 2 D3
ash Rd BS37 44 C1
ers 15 SN6 143 E4
on Cl GL3 128 A8
on Ho BS8 194 B2
on Pl GL50 193 A1
on St BS1 194 C2
on Steep BS1 194 C2
wyn Gr BS7 19 B6
some Cres BS34 29 B3
some Dr
l BS34 29 B3
rbourne BS36 30 E6
some Rd BS6 18 B3
igan Ct GL20 182 C5
La GL56 177 C4
combe Ct BS3 8 D2
combe Rd BS9 17 C4
down Hill SN16 59 A3
wood Rd GL6 148 C6
hite Cl BS7 19 B7
nose Rd GL20 182 C7
ington Gdns GL54 166 E2
nes The GL55 189 A3
on Rd BS4 2 D7
ton Rd BS3 8 C3
nder Ho GL7 190 D4
Ave HR8 178 F8
rooke Cl GL8 140 C4
on Ave BS32 29 D7
on La SN6 143 D3
e Ct BS30 10 F3
h Rd BS3 8 A3
hes Gate BS32 29 F6
hes The BS20 16 B5
n Ave GL15 155 B1
n CE Prim Sch
155 D1
n Rd Bream GL15 147 E7
avels GL15 147 B7
Down Ave BS9 18 B5
knock Rd BS4 9 A3
on Cl Bristol BS9 18 B6
geley GL2 109 E8
on Rd BS9 18 B6
on Way GL16 155 C8
on BS37 32 D7

Bredon Cl BS15 10 F7
Bredon Hancocks Endowed Fst Sch GL20 182 C8
Bredon Lodge GL20 182 C7
Bredon Nook Rd BS10 18 C7
Bredon Rd GL20 192 D6
Bredon Sch (Pull Court) GL20 181 C7
Bredon View WR12 185 C8
Bregawn Cl GL52 137 E2
Breinton Way GL2 127 D5
Brendon Cl BS30 11 C4
Brendon Rd BS3 8 D3
Brenner St BS5 19 B2
Brensham Ct GL3 120 A7
Brent Rd BS7 18 F5
Brentry Ave 5 BS5 9 B7
Brentry Hospl BS10 28 B2
Brentry La BS10 28 B3
Brentry Lo BS10 28 A3
Brentry Prim Sch BS10 28 B4
Brentry Rd BS16 19 F3
Brereton Way BS30 11 B4
Bretforton Fst Sch WR11 188 A6
Bretforton Rd WR11 188 B7
Brewerton Cl BS10 28 C3
Brewery Cotts NP25 154 C5
Brewery Hill BS30 5 F7
Brewery La
Nailsworth GL6 91 B3
Thrupp GL5 99 E2
Brewery Row GL56 187 F1
Brewery St SN6 145 D3
Brewery Yd 25 GL54 176 F4
Briar Cl GL5 103 D1
Briar Ct BS20 16 C4
Briar Lawn GL4 119 D3
Briar Way BS16 20 C3
Briar Wlk Bristol BS16 20 C3
Prestbury GL52 134 C3
Briarbank Rise GL52 131 C7
Briarfield Ave BS15 10 C5
Briarleaze BS35 50 F2
Briars Cl GL3 128 A6
Briarside Ho BS10 28 D3
Briarside Rd BS10 28 D3
Briarwood BS9 17 F6
Briarwood Sch BS16 20 B3
Briary Rd GL7 153 E3
Briavels Gr BS6 18 F2
Brick Cotts BS35 62 E1
Brick St BS2 195 C3
Brick Wlk WR11 188 C6
Brickfield Terr GL5 99 A6
Brickfields GL12 68 B6
Bricknell Ave GL20 182 C7
Brickrow GL5 99 C7
Bridewell St BS1 195 A3
Bridge Cl
Cirencester GL7 190 D2
Gloucester GL2 118 B6
Whitchurch BS14 3 C4
Bridge End
Cirencester GL7 190 D3
Staunton GL19 180 C2
Bridge Farm GL2 126 B7
Bridge Farm Cl BS14 3 A3
Bridge Farm Inf Sch BS14 3 A4
Bridge Farm Jun Sch BS14 3 A4
Bridge Rd
Bristol, Eastville BS5 19 B3
Bristol, Lower Soundwell BS15 21 A3
Bristol, Shortwood BS16 21 C4
Cirencester GL7 190 D2
Frampton on Severn GL2 157 F3
Harrow Hill GL17 164 B3
Leigh Woods BS8 7 E6
Sharpness GL13 93 C1
Stroud GL5 98 D6
Yate BS37 43 A2
Bridge St Blakeney GL15 156 D1
Bretforton WR11 188 A6
Bristol BS1 195 A2
Bristol, Eastville BS5 19 D2
Cheltenham GL51 133 B4
Chepstow NP16 72 F1
Fairford GL7 152 E4
Ledbury HR8 178 E8
Nailsworth GL6 91 C4
Newent GL18 171 A5
Stroud GL5 98 E6
Bridge Valley Rd BS8 7 E8
Bridge Way BS36 31 B8
Bridge Wlk BS7 19 A8
Bridge-Side GL5 98 F6
Bridgeleap Rd BS16 20 F8
Bridgemans Cl WR12 188 B1
Bridgend Ct GL10 97 E6
Bridgend Rd GL51 129 C7
Bridges Ct 2 BS16 20 B4
Bridges Dr BS16 20 C6
Bridget Dr NP16 61 A7
Bridgman Gr BS34 29 B3
Bridgwater Rd BS41,BS13, BS48 1 D6
Bridle The GL5 98 D7
Bridle Way BS35 50 F4
Briercliffe Rd BS9 17 D7
Brierley Banks GL17 163 F2
Brierley Cl GL4 119 E5
Brierley Council Hos GL17 163 F2
Brierley Rd GL17 163 F3
Brierley Way GL15 156 B1
Brierly Furlong BS34 29 D3

Briery Leaze Rd BS14 3 A4
Bright St
Bristol, Barton Hill BS5 9 B7
Bristol, Kingswood BS15 10 D8
Brightlands GL14 157 A6
Brighton Cres BS3 8 B2
Brighton Mews BS8 194 B4
Brighton Pk 16 BS5 9 B8
Brighton Pl BS15 20 D1
Brighton Rd
Bristol, Patchway BS34 28 F8
Bristol, Redland BS6 18 C1
Cheltenham GL52 133 F1
Brighton St 13 BS2 18 E1
Brighton Terr 9 BS3 8 B2
Brigstocke Rd BS2 195 B4
Brimbles BS7 29 B2
Brimley GL10 97 F4
Brimscombe CE Prim Sch GL5 99 F1
Brimscombe Hill GL5 91 E8
Brimscombe La GL5 99 F1
Brimsham Green Sec Sch BS37 43 D4
Brimsome Mdw GL2 125 D5
Brindle Cl GL4 119 C4
Brinkmarsh La GL12 65 D2
Brinkworthy Rd BS16 19 E6
Brinmead Wlk BS13 1 F3
Brins Cl BS34 29 F4
Brinsham La BS37 44 A6
Brionne Way GL2 127 B5
Brisbane GL10 101 F1
Briscoes Ave BS13 2 D4
Brislington Hill BS4 9 E2
Brislington Ret Pk BS4 9 E1
Brislington Sch BS4 3 F8
Brislington Trad Est BS4 9 F2
Bristol & Anchor Ho 7 BS5 9 D8
Bristol Bsns Pk BS16 29 E1
Bristol Cathedral* BS1 194 C2
Bristol Cathedral Sch BS1 194 C2
Bristol City Coll Brunel Ctr BS7 18 F4
Bristol City Fball Gd BS3 7 F3
Bristol City Mus & Art Gal* BS8 194 C3
Bristol Dental Hospl BS1 195 A3
Bristol Eye Hospl BS1 195 A3
Bristol Gate 1 BS8 7 F5
Bristol General Hospl BS1 195 A1
Bristol Gram Sch BS8 194 C3
Bristol Harbour Rly* BS1 194 C1
Bristol Hill BS4 9 D2
Bristol Homeopathic Hospl BS8 194 C4
Bristol Ind Mus* BS1 195 A1
Bristol Old Vic Theatre Sch BS8 18 A1
Bristol Parkway N BS34 30 A5
Bristol Parkway Sta BS34 29 E4
Bristol Rd Bristol BS16 30 C2
Cambridge GL2 95 F3
Cirencester GL7 190 D3
Cromhall GL12 53 B7
Frampton Cotterell BS36 42 B3
Gloucester GL1,GL2 118 C6
Keynsham BS31 4 E6
Luckington SN14 47 E3
Stonehouse GL10 97 E7
Thornbury BS35 51 B8
Upper Rissington GL54 169 D7
Whitchurch BS14 3 D3
Winterbourne BS16 30 D4
Bristol Royal Infmy BS2 195 A4
Bristol Vale Ctr For Ind BS3 8 B1
Bristol Waldorf Sch BS8 194 B3
Bristol Zoo Gdns* BS8 17 F1
Bristow Broadway BS11 26 C1
Bristowe Ho BS16 20 B5
Britannia Cres BS34 29 D5
Britannia Ct 1 BS16 20 D5
Britannia Rd
Bristol, Kingswood BS15 10 C8
Bristol, Lower Easton BS5 19 C1
Bristol, Patchway BS34 28 E7
Britannia Way GL52 138 B3
British Rd BS3 8 C3
British Sch The GL12 68 C6
Briton Cl NP16 61 A4
Brittania Bldgs BS8 194 A1
Britten Ct 10 BS30 10 F4
Britten Pl GL51 132 E2
Brittons Pass SN14 14 F8
Brixham Rd BS3 8 C1
Brixton Rd BS5 9 B8
Brixton Road Mews 22 BS5 9 B8
Brizen La GL53 130 B4
Broad Croft BS32 40 C2
Broad La
Coalpit Heath BS36 31 D5
Westerleigh BS37 32 A4
Yate BS37 43 C4
Broad Leys Rd GL4 119 D7
Broad Marston Rd GL55 189 A7
Broad Oak Rd BS13 1 F4
Broad Oak Way GL51 129 F6
Broad Oaks BS8 7 E6
Broad Plain BS2 195 C2
Broad Quay BS1 195 A2

Broad Rd BS15 20 C1
Broad St Bristol BS1 195 A3
Bristol, Staple Hill BS16 20 F4
Chipping Sodbury BS37 44 B1
Hartpury GL19 172 C4
King's Stanley GL10 98 A3
13 Newent GL18 171 A4
Stroud GL5 98 D3
Broad Weir BS1 195 B3
Broad Wlk BS4 9 A2
Broad Wlk The GL50 193 B2
Broadacre Cl GL20 182 C7
Broadbury Rd BS4 2 E8
Broadclose Rd GL2 173 B2
Broadfield Ave BS15 20 C1
Broadfield Cotts GL54 160 C6
Broadfield Rd Bristol BS4 9 B1
Eastington GL10 96 F8
Broadlands Ave BS31 4 D6
Broadlands Ct GL54 168 F7
Broadlands Dr BS11 27 A1
Broadlands Sch BS31 4 D6
Broadleas BS13 2 C7
Broadleaze Bristol BS11 16 E7
Down Ampney GL7 143 F8
Broadleys Ave BS9 18 C7
Broadmead BS1 195 B3
Broadmead La BS31 5 A6
Broadmere GL11 87 E4
Broadmere Cl GL11 87 E3
Broadmoor La BA1 6 F4
Broadmoor Pk GL14 191 B7
Broadmoor Rd GL14 191 B7
Broadoak Hill BS41 1 F2
Broadoak Wlk BS16 20 B4
Broadstone Cl GL4 119 E8
Broadstone Wlk BS13 2 D5
Broadwalk Sh Ctr BS4 9 B2
Broadway Gloucester GL4 118 F5
Saltford BS31 5 D3
Yate BS37 43 F2
Broadway Ave BS9 18 D6
Broadway Bears & Dolls Mus* WR12 185 C8
Broadway Cl
Kempsford GL7 144 E8
Prestbury GL52 134 A5
Broadway Fst Sch WR12 188 B1
Broadway Inf Sch BS37 43 F2
Broadway La
Minsterworth GL2 116 A2
South Cerney GL7 143 A6
Broadway Rd
Bristol, Bishopston BS7 18 D3
Bristol, Bishopsworth BS13 1 F5
Mickleton GL55 189 A6
Toddington GL54 184 C3
Willersey WR12 188 B2
Winchcombe GL54 174 A7
Broadway The
Chalford GL6 148 E6
Dursley GL11 80 A8
North Nibley GL11 79 F8
Broadway Tower Ctry Pk* WR12 185 D4
Broadways Dr BS16 19 F7
Broadwell Bridge 7 GL16 155 B6
Broadwell Cl GL4 119 E5
Broadwell Rd GL56 177 C5
Broadwell Terr GL11 88 B1
Brock Cl GL51 129 B6
Brockeridge Cl GL2 117 E2
Brockeridge Inf Sch BS36 31 C7
Brockeridge Rd GL20 181 F7
Brockhampton Pk GL54 174 B1
Brockhollands Rd GL15 147 D8
Brockhurst Gdns BS15 10 A8
Brockhurst Rd BS15 10 A8
Brockley Acres GL6 148 C7
Brockley Cl BS34 29 C7
Brockley Ct GL56 186 C6
Brockley Rd
Leonard Stanley GL10 97 F4
Saltford BS31 5 D3
Brockley Wlk BS13 2 A8
Brockmoor La HR9 170 C4
Brockridge La BS36 31 C7
Brocks 4 BS4 9 D1
Brocks Rd BS13 2 C3
Brockworth BS37 32 C6
Brockworth Comp Sch GL3 120 F6
Brockworth Cotts GL3 120 F4
Brockworth Cres BS16 19 F6
Brockworth Prim Sch GL3 120 E5
Brockworth Rd GL3 128 E2
Brome Rd GL4 119 F5
Bromfield Wlk BS16 21 B7
Bromley Dr BS16 20 D8
Bromley Heath Ave BS16 20 D8
Bromley Heath Jun & Inf Schs BS16 20 E8
Bromley Heath Rd BS16 20 D8
Bromley Rd Bristol BS7 18 F5
Ellwood GL16 155 C3
Brompton Cl BS15 11 A8
Broncksea Rd BS7 28 F1
Bronte Cl 2 GL51 129 F7
Bronte Dr 2 HR8 178 E8
Brook Cl Long Ashton BS41 7 B1
15 Northleach GL54 168 A1
Winchcombe GL54 139 F4
Brook Ct
Cheltenham GL50 130 B6

Brook Ct continued
Tewkesbury GL20 192 E5
Brook Gate BS3 7 E1
Brook Hill BS6 18 F1
Brook Ho Bristol BS34 29 C8
3 Thornbury BS35 51 C8
Brook House (Dean Close Sch) GL51 129 F7
Brook La
1 Blockley GL56 186 C5
Bristol, Montpelier BS6 18 F1
Bristol, Stapleton BS16 19 E6
Down Hatherley GL2 173 B1
Brook Lintons BS4 9 D3
Brook Rd
Bristol, Montpelier BS6 18 F1
Bristol, Southville BS3 8 D4
Bristol, Speedwell BS5 19 F1
Bristol, Warmley BS15 11 B8
Bristol,Hillfields BS16 20 B4
Bristol,Mangotsfield BS16 20 F6
Cheltenham GL51 133 A4
Brook St Bristol BS5 9 C7
Chipping Sodbury BS37 33 A8
Gloucester GL1 196 B1
Mitcheldean GL17 164 D5
Brook Vale GL52 131 A7
Brook Way BS32 29 D8
Brookcote Dr BS34 29 D6
Brookdale Rd BS13 2 B6
Brooke Rd GL7 190 B2
Brookfield SN6 145 C3
Brookfield Ave BS7 18 D3
Brookfield Cl BS37 44 C2
Brookfield La
2 Bristol BS6 18 D2
Churchdown GL3 128 E5
Brookfield Rd
3 Bristol, Montpelier BS6 18 D2
Bristol, Patchway BS34 29 B8
Churchdown GL3 128 D5
Gloucester GL3 119 F7
Brookfield Senior Sch GL51 130 A7
Brookfield Wlk BS30 11 C3
Brookhouse La SN14 24 D1
Brookhouse Mill GL6 104 A7
Brookland Rd BS6 18 D5
Brooklands Pk GL2 127 D5
Brooklea BS30 11 B3
Brookleaze BS9 17 C5
Brooklyn Cl 4 GL51 132 F3
Brooklyn Ct GL51 133 A4
Brooklyn Gdns GL51 133 A3
Brooklyn Rd Bristol BS13 2 B8
Cheltenham GL51 132 F2
Brookmead BS35 51 D7
Brookridge Ct 5 BS16 20 D4
Brookridge Ho BS10 27 F3
Brooksdale La GL53 130 C6
Brookside Alderton GL20 183 E4
Crudwell SN16 141 C3
4 Newent GL18 171 A4
Paxford GL55 186 E8
Pill BS20 16 D3
Tewkesbury GL20 192 E6
Tintern Parva NP16 146 B3
Brookside Cotts GL5 91 B5
Brookside Dr BS36 31 B8
Brookside Rd Bristol BS4 9 E2
Cinderford GL14 191 B5
Brookside Villas GL2 127 B2
Brookthorpe BS37 32 D8
Brookthorpe Ave BS11 27 A1
Brookthorpe Cl GL4 118 D3
Brookview Wlk BS13 2 B7
Brookway Dr GL53 131 A6
Brookway Rd GL53 131 A6
Broom Bglws GL4 119 A5
Broom Hill Bristol BS16 19 E5
Coleford GL16 154 F7
Broom Ho GL4 119 A5
Broomhill Jun & Inf Schs BS4 9 F3
Broomhill Rd BS4 10 A2
Brooms The BS16 31 A1
Brotherswood Ct BS32 40 D4
Broughton Ho BS1 195 B1
Brown Cl GL51 132 E3
Brown's End Cotts HR8 179 C5
Brown's La GL10 98 A4
Brown's Piece GL12 68 B7
Browne Ct 4 BS8 7 F6
Browning Ct BS7 19 B8
Browning Mews GL51 129 F7
Browns Hill GL6 148 B5
Brownshill Rd GL6 148 B5
Broxholme Wlk BS11 16 F8
Bruce Ave BS5 19 C1
Bruce Rd BS5 19 C1
Brummels Dr GL16 155 A7
Brunel Cl BS30 11 C7
Brunel Ct BS37 43 C2
Brunel Lock Rd BS1 7 F5
Brunel Rd Bristol BS13 2 A8
Chepstow NP16 60 E6
Brunel Way Bristol BS1,BS3 7 F4
Honeybourne WR11 188 C7
Stonehouse GL10 101 C1
Thornbury BS35 51 B7
Brunswest Ct GL1 196 B2
Brunswick Pl 10 BS1 7 F5
Brunswick Rd GL1 196 B2
Brunswick Sq
Bristol BS2 195 B4

Brunswick Sq *continued*
Gloucester GL1 196 B2
Brunswick St Bristol BS2 195 B4
Bristol, Redfield BS5 9 C7
Cheltenham GL50 133 D3
Brush The GL5 98 D8
Bruton Cl BS5 9 F8
Bruton Pl BS8 194 B3
Bruton Way GL1 196 C2
Bryansons Cl BS16 19 D6
Bryant's Hill BS5 10 B6
Bryants Cl BS16 30 C1
Bryaston Cl GL51 133 A2
Bryerland Rd GL3 121 A4
Brymore Ave GL52 134 A5
Brymore Cl GL52 134 A5
Brynland Ave BS7 18 E4
Bryony Bank GL53 130 B4
Bryworth La GL7 153 C3
Buchan Ho 7 GL56 186 C5
Buchanan Ave GL16 155 A6
Buchanan Cl 2 GL16 155 A6
Buckholt Rd GL4 112 E8
Buckholt Way GL3 120 E5
Buckholt Wood Nature Reserve* GL4 112 F7
Buckingham Ave GL51 132 F2
Buckingham Cl GL10 96 E8
Buckingham Ct
Bristol BS32 40 D3
Cheltenham GL50 193 B3
Buckingham Dr
Bristol BS34 29 D5
2 Churchdown GL3 128 A7
Buckingham Gdns BS16 20 E6
Buckingham Ho BS34 28 F2
Buckingham Pl
Bristol BS8 194 A3
Bristol, Mangotsfield BS16 20 E6
Buckingham Rd BS4 9 D5
Buckingham St BS3 8 C2
Buckingham Vale BS8 194 A4
Buckland Cl GL52 137 F3
Buckle St
Broadway WR12,GL54, GL56 185 D5
Honeybourne WR11 188 C8
Weston-s-E GL55 188 D4
Buckle's Row GL53 131 B5
Bucklehaven GL53 130 F5
Buckles Cl GL53 131 B5
Buckshaft Rd GL14 191 C1
Buckstone Cl GL16 155 B7
Budd Ho 1 BS2 18 F1
Budding Rd GL10 96 E8
Budding The GL5 103 E1
Buddleia Cl GL4 119 F4
Buddleia Ct 7 GL3 128 A7
Bude Ave BS5 10 A8
Bude Rd BS34 29 B4
Buildings The GL11 87 D3
Bull La Bristol BS5 9 F6
Gloucester GL1 196 B3
Pill BS20 16 C4
27 Winchcombe GL54 174 A7
Bull Pitch GL11 88 B1
Bull Ring The GL17 164 D5
Bullens Cl BS32 40 D2
Buller Rd BS4 9 C2
Bulley La Birdwood GL2 165 F6
Churcham GL2 124 C3
Bullfinch Rd GL4 119 C6
Bullfinch Way GL3 127 D7
Bullingham Ct GL51 133 C3
Bulls Cross GL6 104 B6
Bully La BS37 53 D1
Bulwark Ave NP16 60 F5
Bulwark Rd NP16 60 E7
Bulwarks The GL6 148 A3
Bunting Hill GL6 91 A4
Bunting Way GL6 90 F4
Burbank Cl BS30 11 A3
Burchells Ave BS15 20 B1
Burchells Green Cl BS15 20 B1
Burchells Green Rd BS15 20 B1
Burcombe Cl BS36 31 D6
Burcombe La GL7 158 A3
Burcombe Rd GL6 148 C6
Burcombe Way GL6 148 C6
Burcott Rd BS11 26 D5
Burden Cl BS32 29 F6
Burdett Cl GL10 97 F7
Burdett Rd GL10 97 F7
Burfoot Rd BS14 3 E4
Burfoote Gdns BS14 3 E4
Burford Dr GL5 99 A7
Burford Gr BS11 16 F5
Burford Mews GL1 119 A8
Burford St GL7 153 E2
Burgage NP25 154 A8
Burgage Cl BS37 33 B8
Burgage The GL52 134 B5
Burge Ct GL7 190 D3
Burgess Green Cl BS4 9 E7
Burghill Rd BS10 28 A1
Burghley Ct BS36 30 E5
Burghley Rd BS6 18 E2
Burgis Rd BS14 3 D6
Burleigh Croft GL3 119 F8
Burleigh La GL5 91 F8
Burleigh Tor GL5 91 F7
Burleigh View 7 GL6 148 B6
Burleigh Way GL12 54 B5
Burley Ave BS16 20 F5
Burley Crest BS16 20 F5
Burley Gr BS16 20 F5
Burlington Ct 9 BS6 18 B2
Burlington Rd BS6 18 B2
Burltons The GL12 66 B2
Burma Ave GL52 134 B2
Burma Rd GL6 91 A4
Burnbush Cl BS14 3 E6
Burnbush Prim Sch BS14 3 D5
Burnell Dr BS2 195 C4
Burneside Cl BS10 28 C2
Burnet Cl GL4 119 A4
Burnett Bsns Pk BS31 5 B1
Burney Way BS30 11 A3
Burnham Cl BS15 20 F1
Burnham Dr BS15 20 F1
Burnham Rd BS11 16 D6
Burns Ave GL2 118 C4
Burnt Barn Rd NP16 60 F4
Burnt Oak GL11 88 A2
Burrington Wlk BS13 2 A8
Burrough Way BS36 30 E6
Burrups La HR9 170 B5
Burton Cl BS1 195 B1
Burton Ct Bristol BS8 194 B3
2 Bristol, Upper Eastville BS16 19 E3
Burton Rd GL9 35 F6
Burton St GL50 193 A4
Burtons Bank OX7 169 F7
Burwalls Rd BS8 7 E6
Bury Bar La GL18 171 A4
Bury Court Rd GL14 157 F6
Bury Hill BS36 30 F3
Bury Hill La BS37 44 A8
Bury Hill View BS16 30 E1
Bury La Doynton BS30 12 F7
Minsterworth GL2 116 E7
Burycourt Cl BS11 27 A1
Burytown La SN26 144 E1
Buscombe Gdns GL3 120 B7
Bush Ave BS34 29 D5
Bush Cl GL10 96 F8
Bush Ct Alveston BS32 50 F5
10 Bristol BS4 8 F4
Prestbury GL52 134 B3
Bush Hay GL3 128 B5
Bush Ind Est BS5 9 D8
Bushcombe Cl GL52 138 C3
Bushcombe La GL52 138 D4
Bushes La BS37 45 A6
Bushy Beeches GL6 105 D7
Bushy Ho BS2 8 F3
Bushy Pk BS4 8 F3
Bushy Way GL51 132 D5
Business Pk The BS13 2 E3
Bussage CE Prim Sch GL6 148 B6
Bussage Hill GL6 148 B6
Butcher Hill's La GL6 91 B3
Butcombe Wlk BS14 3 B5
Bute Cl SN6 145 C4
Butler Ho 5 BS5 9 F8
Butler's Field GL7 153 E3
Butlers Cl Bristol BS5 9 F7
Sherston SN16 58 C1
Butlers Mead GL15 156 E1
Butlers Wlk 3 BS5 9 F6
Butt Gn GL6 111 F1
Butt La BS35 64 C3
Butt St GL6 148 A3
Butt's La Dyrham SN14 24 B4
Woodmancote GL52 138 C4
Butt's Wlk GL51 129 C7
Buttercliffe Rise BS41 7 C3
Buttercross La GL52 134 D3
Buttercup Lawn GL4 119 D2
Butterfield Cl BS10 18 E7
Butterfield Rd BS10 18 E7
Butterfield Cl BS36 31 B6
Buttermere Cl GL51 129 F6
Buttermilk La GL3 128 C6
Butterow W GL5 99 B5
Butterow Hill GL5 99 C4
Butterow La GL5 99 D4
Buttersend La GL19 171 F4
Butterworth Ct BS4 2 D7
Buttington GL4 119 F5
Buttington Hill NP16 61 B7
Buttington Rd NP16 61 A7
Buttington Terr NP16 61 B6
Button Cl BS14 3 A6
Button Mills Est GL10 97 E6
Butts Farm (Open Farm)* GL7 151 A1
Butts La GL15 156 E2
Butts The Crudwell SN16 141 C3
Gloucester GL4 119 A4
Newent GL18 171 A5
Buxton Wlk BS7 19 A8
Byard Rd GL2 118 B5
Bybrook Gdns GL4 118 D1
Bybrook Rd GL4 118 D1
Bydemill Gdns SN6 145 C3
Bye Mead BS16 21 B8
Bye St HR8 178 E8
Byfield Cl GL52 138 C2
Byfords Cl GL19 165 D6
Byfords Rd GL19 165 D6
Byron Ave GL2 118 C4
Byron Ct 16 GL52 133 F2
Byron Pl Bristol BS8 194 B3
Bristol, Staple Hill BS16 20 E4
Byron Rd
Cheltenham GL51 132 F1
Dursley GL11 80 C7
Byron St
Bristol, Redfield BS5 9 C7
5 Bristol, St Pauls BS2 19 A1
Byzantine Ct BS1 195 A1

C

Cabot Cl Bristol BS15 10 C7
Chipping Sodbury BS37 43 F1
Saltford BS31 5 D2
Cabot Ct BS7 28 F1
Cabot Gn BS5 9 B7
Cabot Ho 6 BS35 51 C8
Cabot Pk BS11 26 E5
Cabot Prim Sch BS2 195 C4
Cabot Twr* BS8 194 B2
Cabot Way Bristol BS8 7 F5
Pill BS20 16 D3
Cadbury Heath Cty Prim Sch BS30 11 B6
Cadbury Heath Rd BS30 11 B5
Cadbury Rd BS31 5 A2
Caddick Cl BS15 20 F2
Cade Cl
Bristol, Kingswood BS15 10 F6
Bristol, Stoke Gifford BS34 29 E5
Cadmium Rd BS11 26 C4
Cadogan Ho 17 GL52 133 F2
Cadogan Rd BS14 3 A8
Caen Rd BS3 8 E3
Caernarvon Cl GL51 129 E6
Caernarvon Ct GL51 129 D6
Caernarvon Rd
Cheltenham GL51 129 F6
Keynsham BS31 4 C4
Caerwent La NP16 60 F4
Caesar Rd GL2 118 C5
Caesars Cl GL15 92 C4
Caine Rd BS7 18 F7
Cains Cl BS15 10 E6
Cainscross Rd GL5 98 F7
Caird St NP16 60 E7
Cairn Gdns BS36 30 E4
Cairns Ct BS6 18 C4
Cairns Rd BS6 18 C4
Cairns' Cres 12 BS2 18 F1
Cakebridge Pl GL52 133 F3
Cakebridge Rd GL52 133 F4
Cala Trad Est BS3 7 F3
Calcott Rd BS4 9 A3
Calcutt St SN6 143 F4
Caldbeck Cl BS10 28 D2
Calder Cl BS31 5 A4
Calderdale GL4 119 F5
Calderwood Ct GL50 193 B2
Caldicot Cl
Bristol, Lawrence Weston BS11 27 C2
Bristol, Willsbridge BS30 11 B2
Caledonia Mews BS8 7 F6
Caledonia Pl BS8 7 F7
Caledonian Rd
Bristol BS1 194 B1
Gloucester GL4 119 C2
Calendula Ct 10 GL3 128 A7
Calf Way GL6 105 C5
Calf's La GL55 189 A2
California Rd BS30 11 B3
Callicroft Inf Sch BS34 28 F8
Callicroft Jun Sch BS34 28 F8
Callicroft Rd BS34 29 A7
Callington Rd BS4 9 D1
Callowell GL6 103 A1
Callowell Prim Sch GL5 103 A1
Callowhill Ct BS1 195 B3
Calspick Way GL2 127 D5
Calton Jun & Inf Schs GL1 118 E5
Calton Rd GL1 118 E6
Calverley Mews 1 GL51 129 E5
Cam & Dursley Sta GL10 96 A1
Cam Everlands Prim Sch GL11 88 A4
Cam Gn GL11 88 C5
Cam Hopton CE Prim Sch GL11 88 B4
Cam House Sch GL11 88 C2
Cam Pitch GL11 87 F5
Cam Rd GL52 134 B3
Cam The GL55 189 B2
Camberley Cl GL3 120 A8
Camberley Dr BS36 30 F8
Camberley Rd BS4 2 D8
Camberwell Rd GL51 132 D2
Camborne Rd BS7 19 A7
Cambourne Pl GL15 92 B2
Cambray Ct
Cheltenham GL50 193 B3
Cirencester GL7 190 D4
Cambray Pl GL50 193 C3
Cambrian Dr BS37 43 E3
Cambrian Rd GL20 192 E2
Cambridge Ave
Cheltenham GL51 132 F1
Dursley GL11 80 B7
Cambridge Cres BS9 18 A7
Cambridge Pk BS6 18 B3
Cambridge Rd BS7 18 E4
Cambridge Sq GL20 183 E4
Cambridge St
8 Bristol, Redfield BS5 9 C7
Bristol, Totterdown BS3 8 F4
Gloucester GL1 196 C2
Cambridge Way GL6 91 F6
Camden Cl GL56 187 F3
Camden Rd BS3 194 B1
Camden Terr BS8 194 A2
Camelford Rd BS5 19 D1
Camellia Ct GL51 130 A5
Camellia Wlk GL2 117 E2
Cameron Ho GL50 130 A8
Cameron Wlk BS7 19 C6
Camerons Cl BS31 4 E4
Camerton Cl BS31 5 E3
Camerton Rd BS5 19 D1
Camomile Cl 3 GL4 119 F5
Camomile Gn GL17 163 D2
Camp Gdns 1 GL54 176 F4
Camp La SN14 24 C4
Camp Rd Bristol BS8 7 F7
Charlton Kings GL52 134 C1
Chepstow NP16 60 F6
Thornbury BS35 63 B6
Camp View BS36 30 E4
Campbell Cl GL3 127 E7
Campbell Ct BS11 26 F1
Campbell Farm BS11 26 F1
Campbell Farm Dr BS11 26 F1
Campbell Rd GL16 155 B6
Campbell St BS2 18 E1
Campden Ave CV36 189 E5
Campden Hill CV36 189 F6
Campden La
Hawling GL54 174 D5
Willersey WR12 188 C2
Campden Pitch CV36 189 F6
Campden Rd
Cheltenham GL51 129 E8
Chipping Campden GL55 189 A4
Ebrington GL55 189 C3
Gloucester GL4 118 E3
Mickleton GL55 189 B8
Campion Cl
Gloucester GL4 119 B4
Thornbury BS35 64 D2
Campion Dr BS32 40 D2
Campion Pk GL51 130 A4
Campion Wlk BS4 2 D6
Cams Ground GL2 125 D6
Camwal Ind Est BS2 9 A5
Camwal Rd BS2 9 A5
Canada Ho GL51 132 E3
Canada Way BS1 194 B1
Canal Row GL2 108 A1
Canal Way GL2 126 B4
Canberra GL10 101 E1
Canberra Gr BS34 29 B4
Canberra Ho GL51 132 E1
Candy Ct BS4 9 D5
Canford La BS9 17 E8
Canford Rd BS9 17 F8
Cann La BS30 11 E6
Cannans Cl BS36 30 E7
Canning Rd GL2 127 E5
Cannon St Bristol BS1 195 A4
Bristol, Bedminster BS3 8 C4
Cannop Cotts GL16 155 D6
Cannop Rd GL15 155 E3
Cannop Villas GL16 155 D7
Canon Pk GL13 85 F4
Canon St BS5 9 C8
Canon's Rd BS1 194 C1
Canon's Wlk BS15 20 F2
Canonbury St GL13 85 F3
Canons Dr GL7 153 F2
Canons Rd BS1 194 C2
Canons Way BS1 194 C1
Canowie Rd BS6 18 B3
Cantell Gr BS14 3 F5
Canterbury Cl BS37 43 E3
Canterbury Ct BS16 19 E6
Canterbury Leys GL20 192 E5
Canterbury St 5 BS5 9 B6
Canterbury Wlk GL51 130 A6
Canters Leaze GL12 54 B4
Cantock's Cl BS8 194 C3
Canton Acre GL6 111 F1
Cantors Ct GL52 137 F2
Cantors Dr GL52 137 E2
Cantors Way SN16 142 E1
Canvey Cl BS10 18 E7
Canynge Ho 2 BS1 195 B1
Canynge Rd BS8 7 F8
Canynge Sq BS8 7 F8
Canynge St BS1 195 B2
Capel Cl BS15 11 B8
Capel Ct GL5 99 D8
Capel Rd Bristol BS11 27 B1
Gloucester GL4 119 C2
Capgrave Cl BS4 10 A3
Capgrave Cres BS4 10 A3
Capital Pk GL2 118 B4
Captain Barton Cl GL5 99 E8
Captains Green Rd GL15 156 A2
Caraway Gdns BS5 19 C2
Cardigan Rd BS9 18 B6
Cardill Cl BS13 2 A8
Cares Cl GL52 138 A4
Carfax Ct BS6 18 A3
Carisbrook Rd GL17 164 D6
Carisbrooke Dr GL52 131 C6
Carisbrooke Rd Bristol BS4 2 D7
Gloucester GL3 120 A7
Carlow Rd BS4 2 E8
Carlton Ct 3 BS9 18 A7
Carlton Gdns GL5 99 C6
Carlton Ho 2 BS9 18 A7
Carlton Pk BS5 9 C8
Carlton Pl GL50,GL51 133 C3
Carlton St GL52 133 F1
Carlyle Gr GL51 132 D4
Carlyle Rd BS5 19 C1
Carmarthen Cl BS37 43 F4
Carmarthen Gr BS30 11 B1
Carmarthen Rd
Bristol BS9 18 A5
Carmarthen Rd *continued*
Cheltenham GL51
Carmarthen St 2 GL1
Carnarvon Rd BS6
Carne Pl GL4
Caroline Cl
Chipping Sodbury BS37
Keynsham BS31
Caroline Ho BS2
Carpenter Cotts GL16
Carpenters Cl SN16
Carpenters La
Cirencester GL7
Keynsham BS31
Carr Ho 3 BS2
Carrant Brook Jun Sch GL20
Carrant Rd GL20
Carrick Ho 7 BS8
Carrington Rd BS3
Carrol Gr GL51
Carroll Ct BS16
Carsons Rd BS16
Carter Rd GL51
Carter Wlk BS32
Carters Leaze CV36
Carters Orch GL2
Carters Way GL6
Cartledge Rd 6 BS5
Cartway Gn GL14
Cary Ct 2 BS2
Casey Cl GL1
Cash Hill GL17
Cashes Green Hospl GL5
Cashes Green Prim Sch GL5
Cashes Green Rd GL5
Cashmore Ho 8 BS5
Casino Pl GL50
Casion Ct BS1
Cassell Rd BS16
Cassey Bottom La BS5
Casson Dr BS16
Castle Cl Bristol BS10
Painswick GL6
Castle Coombe BS35
Castle Cotts GL3
Castle Cres GL15
Castle Ct Bristol BS4
Thornbury BS35
Castle End GL6
Castle Farm Cl GL8
Castle Farm La BS41
Castle Farm Rd BS15
Castle Gdns
Chepstow NP16
Chipping Campden GL55
Castle Hill Dr GL3
Castle Hill Prim Sch GL3
Castle La Goodrich HR9
Marshfield SN14
Moreton Valence GL2
Castle Mead GL10
Castle Nurseries GL55
Castle Pitch GL5
Castle Prim Sch BS31
Castle Rd
Bristol, Kingswood BS15
Bristol, Oldland Common BS30
Pucklechurch BS16
Castle Rise GL5
Castle Sch The BS35
Castle Sixth Form Ctr BS35
Castle St Bristol BS1
Cirencester GL7
Dursley GL11
King's Stanley GL10
Stroud GL5
Thornbury BS35
Winchcombe GL54
Castle The GL5
Castle View NP16
Castle Villas 19 GL5
Castlefields Ave GL52
Castlefields Dr GL52
Castlefields Rd GL52
Castleford Gdns NP16
Castleford Hill NP16
Castlegate Ho BS4
Castlemaine Dr GL51
Castlemead Rd GL5
Castlemeads Ct GL1
Castleton Rd GL4
Castlett St GL54
Catbrain Hill BS10
Catbrain La BS10
Catbrook GL55
Catbrook Cl GL55
Catchmays Ct NP16, NP25
Catchpot La BS37
Cater Rd BS13
Cathedral Church of St Pe[ter] & the Holy Family* GL1
Cathedral Church of The H[oly] & Undivided Trinity BS1
Cathedral Gram Sch BS1
Catherine Ct GL1
Catherine Hill BS35
Catherine Mead St BS3
Catherine St BS11
Catherine's Cl GL5

Sch of St Gregory
reat The GL50 .....193 A4
ol GL2 .....109 E7
S4 .....7 B2
BS41 .....19 B2
od Ct GL5 .....103 E1
d La GL6 .....104 D3
ck Dr BS5 .....10 B6
arket Rd BS1 .....195 C1
ook Rd BS16 .....21 C5
ook St
ol GL5 .....6 E7
BS5 .....9 B8
d GL17 .....163 E4
a GL17 .....163 E4
ay Rd GL4 .....191 E5
ot St
Heath BS36 .....31 D7
er GL2 .....117 D1
Dr BS30 .....11 A5
Wlk BS4 .....8 D1
BS2 .....195 B4
BS16 .....21 D6
BS2 .....195 B4
sh Ave GL3 .....128 D5
sh Cl BS31 .....5 A2
sh Gdns BS9 .....17 C4
sh Rd
Henleaze BS9 .....43 D6
Patchway BS34 .....28 F8
otts BS16 .....20 D2
er BS5 .....19 F1
Bristol, Clifton BS8 .....7 B8
Kingswood BS15 .....10 D5
ster GL1 .....118 D6
Hill GL7 .....190 B5
l
Oldland BS30 .....11 A4
Patchway BS34 .....28 F7
h Kings GL53 .....131 B5
wn NP16 .....60 E5
GL5 .....98 D6
ourt Rd GL3 .....193 B2
st
Mangotsfield BS16 .....20 E6
Westbury on Trym 17 F8
Combe Dingle BS9 .....17 D7
Sneyd Park BS9 .....22 C5
HR8 .....178 F8
Dr Dursley GL11 .....88 A1
am BS51 .....19 B2
La GL6 .....97 F8
Dr Bristol BS9 .....17 D5
HR9 .....163 C8
chcombe GL54 .....174 A7
Hall BS16 .....20 C8
Pk BS9 .....17 C5
Rd
orth GL3 .....120 D7
ion GL55 .....189 B6
ay GL20 .....182 C4
Row BS51 .....6 F7
Way Mile End GL16 .....155 B6
church BS16 .....22 C5
ourne BS36 .....30 D5
ean GL14 .....191 C5
The
ster GL2 .....120 A8
r-t-E GL12 .....68 C8
wood Dr GL4 .....119 E6
ine Bank GL52 .....138 B4
ine Cl GL7 .....64 D2
ine Ct NP16 .....60 F5
ne Rd BS37 .....43 C3
ourne BS36 .....30 C6
ry La Bibury GL7 .....160 A1
n-on-t-W GL54 .....169 A7
y Rd Bristol BS4 .....9 A3
ester GL4 .....119 A6
k Ave BS15 .....20 E1
rus Rd BS34 .....28 D7
Ave Bristol BS15 .....10 C5
nham GL17 .....164 D5
Beach BS10 .....38 A4
I Cross Dr GL50 .....133 C3
I Pk BS14 .....3 B7
l GL7 .....118 E7
GL5 .....98 F7
l Tech Coll GL4 .....119 F5
l Trad Est BS4 .....9 A4
l Way Bristol BS10 .....18 E8
l Way GL11 .....133 B3
le The BS31 .....4 F5
rion Cl GL4 .....119 E6
rion Rd GL15 .....92 B4
rions Wlk 10 GL16 .....155 A5
y Cl GL7 .....193 D5
y Ct GL50 .....193 D5
Cl BS30 .....10 F2
on Gate BS34 .....39 F2
er House Gdns*
y La BS11 .....16 E5
y Wick La GL7 .....143 C7
n Cl BS37 .....33 A3
n Ho GL51 .....132 F4
er GL4 .....109 E8
eley GL2 .....128 E5
Rd GL51 .....132 F1
ournes GL3 .....128 B6
igh Gr BS4 .....2 D7
rick Cl GL4 .....118 D2
nch Cl GL3 .....127 D7

Chaffinch Ct 5 GL10 .....97 F8
Chaingate La BS37 .....43 B6
Chakeshill Cl BS10 .....28 C1
Chakeshill Dr BS10 .....28 C4
Chalcombe Cl BS34 .....29 C8
Chalcroft Ho 1 BS8 .....7 A6
Chalcroft Wlk BS13 .....1 L4
Chalet The BS10 .....28 A1
Chalfield Cl BS31 .....5 A2
Chalford Ave GL51 .....129 B7
Chalford GL37 .....32 D8
Chalford Hill Prim Sch
GL6 .....148 C5
Chalford Rd GL4 .....118 E1
Chalks Rd BS5 .....19 E2
Challender Ave BS10 .....27 F2
Challoner Ct BS1 .....5 A1
Chamberlayne Ho 29
GL54 .....176 F4
Chambon Cl SN16 .....142 D1
Champion Rd BS15 .....21 A2
Champneys Ave BS10 .....27 F3
Chamwell Sch GL2 .....127 B5
Chamwells Ave GL2 .....127 B4
Chamwells Wlk GL2 .....127 B4
Chance St GL20 .....192 D4
Chancel Cl Bristol BS9 .....17 D3
Gloucester GL4 .....127 C1
Chancel Pk GL53 .....130 F6
Chancel Way
Charlton Kings GL53 .....131 A6
Lechlade on T GL7 .....153 E2
Chancery St BS5 .....9 B7
Chandag Inf Sch BS31 .....5 A4
Chandag Jun Sch BS31 .....5 A4
Chandag Rd BS31 .....5 A4
Chandler Rd GL52 .....137 F2
Chandos Almshouses 22
GL54 .....174 A7
Chandos Dr GL3 .....120 E5
Chandos Rd Bristol BS6 .....18 C1
Keynsham BS31 .....5 A4
Stroud GL5 .....99 A4
Chandos St 28 GL54 .....174 A7
Chandos Trad Est BS2 .....9 A5
Change The GL4 .....163 C8
Changue View NP16 .....60 E5
Channell's Hill BS9 .....18 A8
Channon's Hill BS16 .....19 F4
Chantry Cl
Cirencester GL7 .....190 C5
Lydney GL15 .....92 A1
Chantry Ct GL8 .....140 C4
Chantry Gate GL52 .....137 E2
Chantry Gdns GL6 .....186 D3
Chantry Gr BS11 .....27 C2
Chantry La BS51 .....30 E1
Chantry Rd Bristol BS8 .....18 B1
Thornbury BS35 .....51 B8
Chapel Appartments 12
GL16 .....155 A5
Chapel Barton 7 BS3 .....8 B2
Chapel Cl Bristol BS15 .....11 B8
Chepstow NP16 .....60 F6
Kempsford GL7 .....144 E8
Minchinhampton MP25 .....154 A7
Tarlton GL7 .....149 C2
Chapel Cotts GL54 .....174 F1
Chapel Ct
Bristol, Brentry BS10 .....28 D3
Bristol, St Philip's Marsh
BS2 .....9 A5
Chapel Gdns Bristol GL2 .....109 F7
Quedgeley GL2 .....109 F7
Chapel Green La BS6 .....18 B2
Chapel Hay Cl GL3 .....128 C4
Chapel Hay La GL3 .....128 D4
Chapel Ho
Aylburton GL15 .....71 E4
Broad Blunsdon SN26 .....144 D1
English Bicknor GL16 .....163 A1
Newport NP13 .....78 B7
Chapel Ho GL20 .....192 C4
Chapel La
Acton Turville GL9 .....36 A6
Blockley GL56 .....186 C5
Bristol, Clay Hill BS5 .....19 E2
Bristol, Lawrence Weston
BS11 .....27 C2
Bristol, Warmley BS15 .....11 B8
Bristol, Fishponds BS16 .....20 A4
Cheltenham GL50 .....193 B1
Chepstow NP16 .....60 E5
Chipping Sodbury BS37 .....34 A1
Churcham GL2 .....165 F5
Cold Aston GL54 .....168 B6
Gorsley HR9 .....170 B4
Hankerton SN16 .....141 E1
Hillesley GL12 .....55 E8
Hinton SN14 .....23 C3
Kinsham GL20 .....182 D6
Longhope GL17 .....165 A8
Mickleton GL55 .....189 A6
Minchinhampton GL6 .....148 A3
Minety SN16 .....142 D1
North Cerney GL7 .....158 D3
Oaksey SN16 .....141 F4
Staunton GL8 .....171 E8
Stroud GL5 .....98 D6
Thornbury BS35 .....65 A1
Westmancote GL20 .....182 D8
Weston-s-E GL55 .....188 D3
Woodmancote GL52 .....138 C3
Chapel Pitch GL18 .....170 D2

Chapel Rd
Berry Hill GL16 .....155 A7
Bristol, Bishopsworth BS13 .....2 A6
Bristol, Hanham BS15 .....10 C5
2 Bristol, Lower Easton
BS5 .....19 B1
Kempsford GL7 .....144 E8
Thornbury BS35 .....63 C5
Viney Hill GL15 .....156 C1
Chapel Row
5 Blockley GL56 .....186 C5
Luckington SN14 .....47 E4
Pill BS20 .....4 D4
2 Stonehouse GL10 .....97 F7
Chapel St
Bledington OX7 .....177 E1
Bristol BS2 .....9 A5
Broadwell GL56 .....177 A6
Cheltenham GL50 .....193 B4
Dursley GL11 .....88 A5
5 Stow-to-W GL54 .....176 F4
Stroud GL5 .....99 D7
Thornbury BS35 .....51 B8
Chapel Way BS41 .....2 A1
Chapel Wlk
Cheltenham GL50 .....193 B3
Didmarton GL9 .....57 B3
Edge End GL16 .....155 C2
Chapelfields HR9 .....162 B6
Chaplin Rd BS5 .....19 B1
Chapman Way GL51 .....129 F7
Chapter St BS2 .....195 B4
Charborough Gate BS34 .....29 F5
Charborough Ho BS34 .....29 A2
Charborough Rd BS34 .....28 F2
Charborough Road Prim Sch
BS34 .....28 F2
Charbury Wlk BS11 .....16 E5
Chard Cl BS14 .....3 B6
Chardstock Ave BS9 .....17 D8
Chardwar Gdns GL54 .....168 F7
Charfield 4 BS15 .....11 A8
Charfield Prim Sch GL12 .....66 F5
Charfield Rd Bristol BS10 .....28 D1
Chargrove 3 Bristol BS30 .....11 C5
Yate BS37 .....32 D7
Chargrove La GL51 .....129 B1
Charis Ave BS10 .....18 C7
Charlcombe Ct BS9 .....17 F6
Charlcote Ave GL4 .....118 D7
Charlcote Cnr GL2 .....137 E3
Charlecote Cnr GL4 .....110 D8
Charles Ave BS34 .....29 A4
Charles Cl BS35 .....64 C3
Charles Ct BS8 .....194 A2
Charles England Ho
BS34 .....28 F2
Charles Pl BS8 .....194 A2
Charles St
Bristol BS1 .....195 A4
Cheltenham GL51 .....133 C3
Gloucester GL1 .....196 C2
Charlesway GL56 .....186 C5
Charleswood Rd GL55 .....155 F1
Charleston Ho 6 BS15 .....21 B4
Charlham La GL7 .....143 E8
Charlock Cl GL4 .....147 A4
Charlotte Rose Ho 3 BS2 .....133 B1
Charlotte St
Bristol, Brandon Hill BS1 .....194 A2
Bristol, St Pauls BS2 .....195 C4
Charlotte St S BS1 .....194 C2
Charlton Ave BS4 .....28 F2
Charlton Common BS10 .....28 D3
Charlton Court Rd GL52 .....131 A2
Charlton Ct Bristol BS34 .....39 F1
Gloucester GL1 .....196 C3
Charlton Down Cotts
GL8 .....71 E4
Charlton Dr GL20 .....180 C8
Charlton Gdns BS10 .....28 D4
Charlton Kings Cty Jun Sch
GL53 .....131 A6
Charlton Kings Inf Sch
GL53 .....131 B6
Charlton La GL53 .....28 A1
Charlton Lane Ct GL53 .....131 A7
Charlton Lawn GL52 .....131 A7
Charlton Mead Ct BS10 .....28 D3
Charlton Mead Dr BS10 .....28 D3
Charlton Park Dr GL53 .....130 F6
Charlton Park Gate
GL53 .....130 F6
Charlton Pk BS31 .....4 D8
Charlton Pl BS10 .....28 D4
Charlton Rd
Bristol, Kingswood BS15 .....21 B4
Keynsham BS31,BS14 .....4 F3
Tetbury GL8 .....140 B4
Charlton St 11 BS5 .....9 B7
Charlton Terr GL54 .....187 B3
Charlton Way GL52 .....127 C6
Charminster Rd BS16 .....20 B3
Charmouth Ct GL54 .....174 A8
Charnell Rd BS16 .....20 F4
Charnhill Brow BS16 .....21 A4
Charnhill Cres BS16 .....20 F4
Charnhill Dr BS16 .....20 F4
Charnhill Ridge BS16 .....21 A4
Charnhill Vale BS16 .....20 F4
Charnwood BS16 .....21 A4
Charnwood Rd BS13 .....130 D5

Charnwood Ct GL15 .....92 B5
Charnwood Rd Bristol BS14 .....3 B4
Cheltenham GL53 .....130 D5
Charter Cl GL1 .....196 C1
Charter Wlk BS14 .....3 A6
Charterhouse Rd 5 BS5 .....9 D8
Chartist La GL19 .....179 F2
Chartist Piece GL19 .....172 B8
Chartist Way GL19 .....172 A8
Chartists Way NP16 .....60 E5
Chartley BS9 .....17 D2
Chase Ave GL52 .....131 C6
Chase La Gloucester GL4 .....119 B7
Wickwar GL12 .....54 C6
Chase Rd BS15 .....20 D2
Chase The Weston BS16 .....20 C3
Churchdown GL3 .....128 D4
Gloucester GL4 .....119 D5
Stroud GL5 .....98 E7
Chasefield La 1 BS16 .....20 E6
Chasely Cres 6 GL51 .....129 C5
Chasewood Cnr 3 GL6 .....148 B6
Chatcombe GL52 .....32 E7
Chatcombe Cl GL53 .....131 B4
Chatcombe Rd GL4 .....119 B5
Chatsworth Ave GL4 .....118 C1
Chatsworth Dr GL53 .....130 D4
Chatsworth Pk BS16 .....20 F4
Chatsworth Rd
Bristol, Arno's Vale BS4 .....9 C4
Bristol, Hillfields BS16 .....20 D2
Chatterton Gn BS14 .....2 A8
Chatterton Ho 8 BS1 .....195 B1
Chatterton Rd BS37 .....43 D1
Chatterton Sq BS1 .....195 B1
Chatterton St BS1 .....195 C1
Chaucer Cl GL1 .....196 A4
Chaucer Rd BS7 .....18 A4
Chaundey Gr BS13 .....2 B5
Chavenage BS15 .....21 A1
Chavenage La GL8 .....140 B4
Cheap St GL54 .....159 A6
Cheapside Bristol BS2 .....195 C4
Stroud GL5 .....99 B7
Cheapside St 8 BS3 .....9 A5
Cheddar Gr BS13 .....2 A8
Cheddar Grove Sch BS13 .....2 A8
Chedworth BS15 .....20 F3
16 Newent GL18 .....171 A4
Chedworth Rd Bristol BS7 .....19 A6
Gloucester GL4 .....119 C8
Chedworth Way GL51 .....129 B7
Cheese La BS2 .....195 B3
Chelbury Mews 1 GL52 .....134 A3
Chelford Gr BS34 .....29 B8
Chelmer Gr BS31 .....4 F4
Chelmsford Wlk BS4 .....9 F5
Chelsea Cl
Keynsham BS31 .....5 A4
Bristol BS5 .....19 B1
Chelsea Pk BS5 .....9 C8
Chelsea Rd BS5 .....19 B1
Chelston Rd BS4 .....2 D4
Chelt Rd GL52 .....134 B3
Cheltenham & Gloucester
Coll of H Ed
Cheltenham, Cleevemount
GL52 .....133 F4
Cheltenham, The Park
GL53 .....130 C6
Cheltenham & Gloucester
Coll of H Ed (Francis College
Hall) GL50 .....133 D3
Cheltenham & Gloucester
Nuffield Hospl The
GL51 .....129 C7
Cheltenham Bournside Sch &
Sixth Form Ctr GL51 .....130 A6
Cheltenham Coll Jun Sch
GL53 .....193 B1
Cheltenham Coll 2 BS56 .....130 D1
Cheltenham Cres 2 BS56 .....28 D1
Cheltenham General Hospl
GL53 .....193 C2
Cheltenham Kingsmead Sch
GL51 .....132 F4
Cheltenham La GL18 .....170 D2
Cheltenham Ladies Coll The
GL50 .....193 B3
Cheltenham Mus & Art Gal*
GL50 .....193 B4
Cheltenham Race Course
GL50,GL52 .....133 B6
Cheltenham Racecourse Hall
of Fame* GL50 .....133 F6
Cheltenham Rd
Bagendon GL7 .....150 D7
Beckford GL20 .....183 B6
Bishop's Cleeve GL52 .....137 F3
Bisley GL6 .....105 A1
Bredon GL20 .....182 D7
Bristol BS6 .....18 C2
Broadway WR12 .....185 A8
Chedworth GL7 .....124 E8
Gloucester GL2 .....127 D3
Painswick GL6 .....112 A2
Pitchcombe GL6 .....103 C4
Winchcombe GL54 .....139 F4
Cheltenham Spa Sta
GL53 .....133 A1
Cheltenham Trade Pk
GL51 .....133 B3
Cheltey Cl BS13 .....2 D3
Chelwood Rd Bristol BS11 .....16 D7
Saltford BS31 .....5 E4

Chelworth Ind Est SN6 .....143 D3
Chelworth Rd SN6 .....143 E3
Chepstow Bulwark*
NP16 .....60 F6
Chepstow Castle* NP16 .....72 E1
Chepstow Comm Hospl
NP16 .....72 D2
Chepstow Ho 18 GL51 .....132 E2
Chepstow Mus* NP16 .....72 E1
Chepstow Pk BS16 .....30 F1
Chepstow Race Course*
NP16 .....72 C3
Chepstow Rd BS4 .....2 08
Chepstow Sta NP16 .....60 F8
Chepstow Wlk BS31 .....4 F5
Chequers Cl BS30 .....11 C3
Chequers Ct BS30 .....30 A6
Chequers Rd GL4 .....119 B7
Cherington Bristol BS15 .....10 B5
Yate BS37 .....32 D6
Cherington Rd BS10 .....18 D7
Cheriton Cl GL51 .....129 F5
Cheriton Pl
Bristol, Eastfield BS9 .....18 B7
Bristol, Warmley BS30 .....11 C6
Cherrington Dr GL4 .....119 E5
Cherry Ave GL53 .....131 C4
Cherry Bank GL18 .....171 A4
Cherry Blossom Cl GL52 .....137 F5
Cherry Cl GL2 .....109 E7
Cherry Garden La BS15 .....11 B2
Cherry Garden Prim Sch
BS30 .....11 C2
Cherry Garden Rd BS30 .....11 C1
Cherry Gdns Bristol BS30 .....11 C1
Gloucester GL3 .....120 A8
Cherry Gr BS16 .....21 A6
Cherry La BS1 .....195 B4
Cherry Orch
Bredon GL20 .....182 C7
Highworth SN6 .....145 D3
Wooton-u-E GL12 .....68 C7
Cherry Orch The GL51 .....173 F2
Cherry Orchard CI GL55 .....189 A1
Cherry Orchard La
3 Bristol BS9 .....9 F8
Luckington SN14 .....47 C5
Twyning GL20 .....181 F7
Cherry Orchard Rd GL8 .....140 C4
Cherry Tree Cl GL8 .....44 A1
Cherry Tree Cl
Bristol BS16 .....20 C2
Keynsham BS31 .....4 C4
Nailsworth GL6 .....91 A4
Cherry Tree La GL16 .....155 C4
Cherry Tree Rd 10 SN6 .....143 F5
Cherry Wlk GL51 .....92 A4
Cherry Wood BS30 .....11 B2
Cherrytree Ct BS16 .....20 C5
Cherrytree La GL7 .....150 F5
Cherrytree Rd BS16 .....20 C2
Cherrywood Gdns GL4 .....118 E3
Chertsey Rd BS6 .....18 B1
Chervil Cl BS14 .....119 B4
Cherwell Cl BS35 .....51 C7
Cherwell Rd BS31 .....5 A4
Chesford Dr GL3 .....128 C6
Chesham Way GL51 .....20 D1
Cheshire Cl BS37 .....43 E3
Cheshire Rd BS3 .....127 E6
Chesils The GL54 .....174 A8
Chesley Hill BS30 .....11 F7
Chesmann Ct GL1 .....126 F4
Chessel Cl BS32 .....40 C2
Chessel Ct 6 BS3 .....8 B2
Chessel St BS3 .....8 B2
Chessell Ave BS35 .....38 B7
Chessgrove La GL17 .....164 F6
Chessington Ave BS14 .....3 B5
Chestal GL11 .....88 B1
Chester Cl GL19 .....173 C7
Chester Cres GL7 .....190 D4
Chester Ct 8 BS16 .....20 A3
Chester Park Jun & Inf Sch
BS16 .....20 A3
Chester Park Rd BS16 .....20 B2
Chester Pk BS5 .....19 E1
Chester Rd BS5 .....19 E1
Chester St Bristol BS5 .....19 C8
Cirencester GL7 .....190 D4
Chester Wlk GL50 .....193 B4
Chesterfield Ave BS16 .....18 E2
Chesterfield Hospl BS8 .....194 B4
Chesterfield Rd
Bristol, Mangotsfield BS16 .....20 E5
Bristol, Montpelier BS6 .....18 C2
Chestermaster Cl BS32 .....40 A5
Chesters BS30 .....11 A4
Chesterton Cl GL2 .....126 F5
Chesterton Gr GL7 .....190 C3
Chesterton Ho 8 BS2 .....195 B4
Chesterton La GL7 .....190 C3
Chesterton Pk GL7 .....190 B4
Chesterton Prim Sch
GL7 .....190 C2
Chestnut Ave GL10 .....97 F8
Chestnut Cl Bristol BS14 .....3 F5
Down Ampney GL7 .....143 E8
18 Ledbury HR8 .....178 E8

Ian Sq GL51 ....133 A2
on Terr BS6 ....195 A4
and Cl BS35 ....51 E8
m Rise BS14 ....2 F3
urt Dr BS16 ....20 B7
lew NP16 ....62 A2
le GL20 ....192 E2
d Gdns BS11 ....16 D6
Rd BS16 ....20 C4
a SN6 ....143 E4
use Rd BS3 ....8 A4
use Spur BS3 ....7 F4
BS1 ....195 A1
C1 Bristol BS8 ....7 F7
-on-t-W GL54 ....176 F4
Coll BS8 ....194 A4
College Prep Sch

....................................17 F1
Down Sh St 7 F7
Down Rd BS8 ....194 A3
Down Sh Ctr 18 B1

Down Sta GL20 ....18 B1
High Gr BS9 ....17 E5
High Sch BS8 ....194 A4
Hill BS8 ....194 A2
Metro BS10 ....18 B1
Park Rd BS8 ....7 F8
Pk BS5 ....194 A3
Bristol BS8 ....194 A2
ster GL1 ....196 A1
St

Bedminster BS23 ....3 C3
Upper Easton BS5 ....9 A8
Suspension Bridge*

....................................7 E7
Vale BS8 ....194 A4
Vale Cl BS8 ....194 A2
View BS3 ....194 A4
Wood Ct BS8 ....194 B2
Wood Rd BS8 ....194 A3
wood Cres BS8 ....194 B2
wood Terr BS8 ....194 A2
Ho GL7 ....190 D5
Down GL11 ....87 C4
La GL11 ....87 C4
Rd BS3 ....8 C2
Ct GL6 ....91 B3
d BS14 ....3 F6
Rd SN16 ....141 E1
ouse Sq GL54 ....166 C6
es Rd BS36 ....30 F6
ney Way GL2 ....127 D5
r Rd BS4 ....8 D1
dns

le GL54 ....176 B7
ury GL8 ....140 B4
St

Henbury BS10 ....28 A5
Little Stoke BS34 ....29 C6
Patchway BS32 ....40 C1
Upper Soundwell

....................................20 D3
ham BS13 ....130 D4
GL11 ....86 E7
Heath BS36 ....31 C6
GL16 ....155 C6
GL11 ....87 E4
ter Cl GL7 ....153 E3
dge GL2 ....95 E3
nge GL2 ....143 A8
m GL52 ....134 C8
ter GL2 ....100 F5
d BS4 ....7 F2
he GL12 ....68 B7
Hill Ave BS5 ....9 F8
Hill Rd BS5 ....9 F8
y Rd BS5 ....9 F8

ord

ord GL14 ....156 C6
GL16 ....155 B4
Dr GL2 ....109 E6
Ground BS9 ....18 B7
Leaze GL2 ....29 C6
Piece GL4 ....119 D6
ale Dr BS30 ....11 A3
ea Bsns Ctr BS36 ....31 C3
ea Rd BS30 ....11 C5
ve BS31 ....4 A5
res GL52 ....134 A2
GL53 ....8 C3
Gdns BS5 ....10 B6
r BS34 ....28 F2
Ho BS7 ....35 A2
a BS6 ....18 C2
Mews BS6 ....18 C2

CE Prim Sch

....................................88 E8
Rd BS11 ....16 D5
ck La BS36 ....31 B3

Coalville Rd BS36 ....31 D7
Coalway Ind Sch GL16 ....155 B5
Coalway Prim Sch GL16 ....155 B5
Coalway Rd GL16 ....155 B5
Coape Rd BS14 ....3 B1
Coates Gdns GL10 ....97 F8
Coates Ho GL21 ....132 E2
Coates La GL7 ....149 F4
Coates Mill Cotts BS14 ....139 F4
Coates The GL14 ....139 F4
Coates Wlk BS4 ....9 B8
Cobbler's Cl The GL52 ....138 A7
Cobblestone Mews BS8 ....194 A4
Cobden St GL1 ....9 C7
Coberley BS15 ....10 C6
Coberley CE Prim Sch

....................................123 A5
Coberley Rd

Cheltenham GL51 ....129 D8
Gloucester GL4 ....118 E3
Cobham Ct GL53 ....133 B3
Cobham Rd GL51 ....133 B3
Cobhorn Dr BS13 ....1 F4
Cobourg Rd BS6 ....18 F2
Cochran Cl GL3 ....128 C5
Cock La SN14 ....23 D5
Cock's Hill GL15 ....10 F6
Cockadilly GL10 ....89 D5
Cockatoos La HR9 ....170 B5
Codrington Pl BS8 ....194 A3
Codrington Rd BS7 ....18 D3
Cody Ct BS15 ....10 B5
Cogan Rd BS16 ....20 E3
Cogsall Rd BS14 ....3 F6
Coker Street Cl

Mitcheldean GL17 ....164 D5
Northwood Green GL14 ....165 C1
Coldharbour Cres BS4 ....2 D7
Cold Pool La

Bamfurlong GL51 ....129 B5
Cheltenham GL51 ....129 D6
Coldharbour La

Bristol BS16 ....19 E8
Newent GL18 ....170 F6
Coldharbour Rd

Bristol BS6 ....18 B4
St Briavels GL15 ....146 E4
Coldicotts Cl GL55 ....189 A2
Coldpark Gdns BS13 ....1 E5
Coldpark Rd BS13 ....1 E5
Coldray Cl GL1 ....127 B1
Coldrick Cl BS14 ....2 D7
Coldwell Gl10 ....98 B3
Coldwell Cl GL10 ....98 B3
Coldwell La BS10 ....17 A1
Cole Ave GL2 ....118 C3
Cole Rd BS2 ....9 B6
Colebridge Ave GL2 ....127 C3
Colebrook Rd BS15 ....10 C8
Coleford Rd Bream GL15 ....147 E5
Bristol BS10 ....28 D1
Tutshill NP16 ....72 F2
Colemead BS13 ....1 C3
Coleridge Ho BS34 ....40 A1
Coleridge Rd BS5 ....19 C7
Colerne Dr GL3 ....120 B7
Colesborne CE BS37 ....32 E8
Colesbourne Rd GL51 ....129 D8
Coleshill Dr BS13 ....1 C3
Colin Cl BS35 ....64 C1
Colin Rd GL4 ....127 D1
Coll of St Matthias Inf Sch

....................................20 A5
Collard Ho BS2 ....20 A5
Collard Ho Ave GL16 ....20 A5
College Baths Rd GL53 ....193 C2
College Ct Bristol BS1 ....20 A5
Gloucester GL1 ....196 B3
College Fields BS8 ....7 F8
Gloucester GL1 ....127 D4
College Gate Bristol BS1 ....20 A5
College Gn Bristol BS1 ....195 C7
Gloucester GL1 ....196 B3
College Lawn GL53 ....193 C1
College Park Dr BS10 ....27 F1
College Rd Bredon GL20 ....182 B7
Bristol, Clifton BS8 ....7 F8
Bristol, Fishponds BS16 ....20 A5
Bristol, Westbury on Trym

....................................18 A3
Cheltenham GL52 ....193 C2
Cinderford GL14 ....191 C4
Stroud GL5 ....99 A8
College St Bristol BS1 ....194 C2
Gloucester GL1 ....196 B3
College View

Cirencester GL7 ....190 B1
Stonehouse GL10 ....97 F7
Collett Cl BS35 ....10 B5
Collett Pl SN6 ....143 E6
Collett Way BS37 ....43 C3
Colletts Dr GL51 ....133 B3
Colletts Fields WR12 ....185 C8
Colletts Gdns WR12 ....185 C8
Colliers Break BS16 ....21 B5
Colliers Pitch GL15 ....147 F5
Colliers Wood GL6 ....91 A5
Collin Cl WR12 ....188 B2
Collin La WR12 ....188 A2
Collin Rd BS4 ....9 D4
Collingbourne Rd GL4 ....119 A2
Collingwood Ave BS15 ....29 C6
Collingwood Cl

Chepstow NP16 ....61 A5
Salford BS31 ....5 E2
Collingwood Rd BS6 ....18 B1
Collins Ave BS34 ....29 C6

Collins Cl GL19 ....172 A8
Collins St BS11 ....16 B8
Collinson Rd BS13 ....2 B5
Collister Cres BS3 ....8 B2
Coln End Rise GL53 ....130 C4
Coln House Specl Sch

GL7 ....152 D3
Coln Rise GL54 ....166 D6
Coln Sq BS35 ....51 E8
Colne Ave GL52 ....134 A3
Colne Gn BS31 ....195 A2
Colston Ave Bristol BS1 ....195 A2
Colston Cl Bristol BS16 ....20 E4
Winterbourne BS36 ....30 E4
Colston Dale BS16 ....19 D3
Colston Dr BS31 ....5 A3
Colston Fort B2 BS2 ....195 A4
Colston Mews BS6 ....18 E1
Colston Par BS1 ....195 A1
Colston St BS1 ....195 A3
Colston St Bristol BS1 ....195 A3
Bristol, Upper Soundwell

....................................20 D3
Colston Yd BS1 ....195 A3
Colston's Girls Sch BS6 ....18 E1
Colston's Prep Sch BS6 ....18 D1
Colston's Sch BS6 ....19 C4
Colstone Ct BS16 ....19 E3
Colsty Mdw GL51 ....130 F8
Coltham Ct GL52 ....130 F8
Coltham Fields GL52 ....130 F8
Coltham Rd GL52 ....130 F8
Colthurst Dr BS15 ....10 E5
Coltman Cl GL17 ....164 D5
Colts Gn BS37 ....33 E8
Columbia Cl GL12 ....196 C3
Columbia St GL52 ....193 C4
Colville Ho GL7 ....190 D5
Colwell Ave BS14 ....1 A1
Colwyn Dr GL51 ....129 E6
Colwyn Rd B3 BS5 ....19 B8
Colyton GL3 ....8 D1
Comb Paddock BS9 ....18 B7
Combe Cross Wlk BS13 ....2 B3
Combe Gdns GL11 ....87 C3
Combermere BS35 ....51 D8
Combfactory La B3 BS5 ....9 B8
Combrook Cl GL4 ....119 F4
Commercial Rd

Bristol BS1 ....195 A1
Chalford GL6 ....148 C5
Gloucester GL1 ....196 A2
Commercial St

Cheltenham GL50 ....193 B1
Gloucester GL14 ....191 D4
Common (East) The

BS32 ....40 C1
Common Hill SN26 ....143 E4
Common Mead La BS36 ....16 B2
Common Rd Bristol BS15 ....10 B3
Minchinhampton GL6 ....91 E6
Winterbourne BS36 ....30 F7
Common The

Berkeley Heath GL13 ....86 C3
Bristol, Frenchay BS16 ....30 D3
Bristol, Patchway BS32 ....40 C1
Minety SN16 ....142 E1
Siddington GL7 ....150 E2
Commonfield Rd BS11 ....27 B1
Commonwead La BS37 ....33 F8
Compton Cl

Churchdown GL3 ....128 A8
Staunton GL19 ....172 A7
Compton Dr BS9 ....17 C7
Compton Gn BS31 ....4 E4
Compton Lodge B3 BS6 ....18 B1
Compton Rd GL51 ....133 B4
Compton Rise GL54 ....166 E2
Compton St BS5 ....9 C7
Compton's Alley GL20 ....192 C4
Comyn Wlk BS16 ....20 A8
Concord Cl GL6 ....91 A3
Concord Dr BS10 ....28 B1
Concord Rd BS16 ....28 E7
Concord Way GL12 ....119 B7
Condicote La GL54 ....176 B5
Condor Ho BS7 ....19 C2
Condover Rd GL4 ....10 D3
Conduit Hill GL55 ....188 F1
Conduit Pl BS2 ....19 C4
Conduit Rd BS2 ....19 C4
Conduit St GL1 ....196 C2
Condurrow Ct BS16 ....176 F4
Cone The BS16 ....20 A8
Coney Hill Com Prim Sch

GL4 ....119 C7
Coney Hill Par GL4 ....119 C7
Coney Hill Rd GL4 ....119 C7
Coneygar Rd GL7 ....152 C7
Coneygre GL20 ....192 C2
Coneygre Ave BS9 ....17 E6
Coneygree La WR12 ....185 A3
Coneygreen Cotts GL56 ....186 C6
Congleton Rd BS5 ....9 D8
Conham Hill BS15 ....10 A5
Conham Rd BS4,BS5,BS15 ....9 F5
Conifer Cl Bristol BS16 ....20 D6
Frampton Cotterell BS36 ....42 A1
Conifers The

Cheltenham GL52 ....134 A3
Gloucester GL4 ....119 A7
Conigre La GL20 ....172 C2
Coniston Ave BS9 ....17 E6
Coniston Cl BS30 ....11 D6
Coniston Prim Sch BS34 ....39 F1

Coniston Rd Bristol BS34 ....39 F1
Cheltenham GL51 ....129 E7
Gloucester GL2 ....127 C4
Connaught Rd BS4 ....2 E8
Consell Gn BS14 ....184 C3
Constable Cl BS31 ....4 F6
Constable Rd BS7 ....19 B6
Constance Cl BS15 ....98 F5
Constantine Ave BS34 ....29 E5
Constitution Hill BS8 ....194 B2
Convent Cl BS10 ....27 D2
Convent La GL15 ....90 F7
Convent The OX7 ....169 A7
Conway Ct BS14 ....165 A7
Conway Gn BS31 ....5 A3
Conway Rd Bristol BS4 ....7 F1
Gloucester GL3 ....120 A8
Conygar BS8 GL8 ....140 C4
Conygre Gr BS34 ....29 C3
Conygre Rd BS34 ....29 B3
Cook Cl BS30 ....11 A5
Cook St BS11 ....16 C8
Cook's Folly Rd BS9 ....17 D2
Cook's La GL19 ....172 C4
Cook's Dr BS35 ....39 A1
Cooke's Dr BS35 ....118 D4
Cooks Cl BS32 ....40 D3
Cooks La BS36 ....31 D3
Cooks Orch GL7 ....127 A3
Cooksley Rd BS5 ....9 C8
Cookson Terr GL11 ....86 F6
Cookspool BS GL8 ....140 C4
Cookworthy Cl B2 BS5 ....9 B6
Coomb Dr GL14 ....191 C1
Coomb Rocke BS9 ....17 D6
Coombe Bridge Ave BS9 ....17 D6
Coombe Cl BS10 ....27 D6
Coombe Dale BS9 ....17 C6
Coombe Gdns BS9 ....17 E6
Coombe Glen La GL51 ....129 D6
Coombe Ho GL8 ....140 C4
Coombe La Bristol BS9 ....17 C6
Easton-in-G BS8 ....16 A1
King's Stanley GL10 ....98 C2
Wootton-u-E GL12 ....68 D8
Coombe Meade BS9 ....17 E6
Coombe Meade GL52 ....138 B3
Coombe Rd Bristol BS5 ....19 C2
Wootton-u-E GL12 ....68 C8
Coombe Terr GL12 ....68 C8
Coombes Way BS30 ....11 F1
Coombs Rd GL16 ....155 A6
Cooper Rd BS9 ....17 F8
Cooper's Ct

Brockworth GL3 ....120 E5
Charlton Kings GL53 ....131 B5
Cooper's Hill* GL3 ....120 E5
Cooper's View 120 E5
Cooperage La BS3 ....194 B1
Cooperage Rd BS5 ....9 D7
Coopers Dr BS37 ....43 E5
Coopers Elm GL2 ....117 F2
Coopers Mill GL51 ....91 A6
Coopers Rd GL16 ....155 A8
Coopers Way BS27 ....171 A4
Cope Pk BS32 ....40 C5
Copeland Dr BS14 ....3 A5
Copford La BS41 ....7 A1
Copley Ct BS15 ....10 E5
Copley Gdns BS7 ....19 B6
Copper Beech Gr GL2 ....117 E7
Copper Beeches SN6 ....145 C3
Copperfield Cl GL4 ....119 E5
Coppice Daw Pitch

GL19 ....165 D3
Coppice Gate BS51 ....132 F5
Coppice Hill GL6 ....148 D5
Coppice The

Bristol, Bradley Stoke BS32 .....29 E7
Bristol, Highridge BS13 ....1 E4
Keynsham BS31 ....5 C4
Copse The BS14 ....4 A5
Copsehill Rd GL54 ....176 C1
Copt Elm Cl GL53 ....131 A6
Copt Elm Rd GL53 ....131 A6
Copthorne Ct BS14 ....2 B3
Coral Cl GL4 ....118 B3
Corbett Ct BS11 ....27 C2
Corbett Ho BS11 BS5 ....9 F8
Corder's La BS37 ....187 A3
Corders Cl BS16 ....32 E7
Cordingley Cl GL3 ....128 C5
Cordwell Wlk BS10 ....18 D7
Corey Cl GL52 ....134 C4
Corfe Cres BS31 ....4 A4
Corfe Ho GL2 ....117 E8
Corfe Pl BS30 ....11 B1
Corfe Rd BS4 ....8 C3
Coriander Dr Bristol BS34 ....29 F7
Innsworth GL3 ....127 F7
Coriander Wlk BS5 ....19 C2
Corinium Bsns Pk GL14 ....191 A7
Corinium Cntr GL7 ....190 C3
Corinium Gate GL7 ....190 B3
Corinium Ho GL7 ....190 B3
Corinium Mus* GL7 ....190 C3
Corinth Rd GL53 ....195 B1
Corker's Hill BS5 ....9 F6
Cormorant Ave GL20 ....192 E2
Corn St BS1 ....195 A3

Corncroft La GL4 ....119 D2
Corndean La GL54 ....174 A5
Corner Farm Dr WR11 ....188 C6
Corner Rd GL13 ....155 F1
Cornfield Cl BS22 ....40 C1
Cornfield Dr

Bishop's Cleeve GL52 ....137 E4
Hardwicke GL2 ....109 E7
Cornfields The GL52 ....137 E4
Cornflower Rd GL4 ....119 E5
Cornhill GL1 ....99 C7
Cornhill Dr BS14 ....3 A7
Cornhill Gr BS14 ....3 E6
Cornish Hos

Cinderford GL14 ....156 C6
Moreton-in-M GL56 ....187 B3
Cornish Rd BS14 ....3 E6
Cornish Wlk BS14 ....3 E6
Cornleaze BS13 ....2 A5
Cornmeadow Dr GL51 ....132 D5
Cornwall Ave GL51 ....133 A2
Cornwall Dr BS37 ....43 F3
Cornwall Rd BS7 ....18 D4
Cornwallis Ave BS8 ....194 A2
Cornwallis Cres BS8 ....194 A2
Cornwallis Gr BS8 ....194 A2
Corolin Rd GL2 ....118 B4
Coronation Ave

Bristol BS16 ....20 A4
Keynsham BS31 ....4 D3
Coronation Cl

Bristol BS30 ....11 A5
Chipping Campden GL55 ....188 F2
Coronation Flats GL52 ....131 A4
Coronation Gr GL2 ....127 B2
Coronation Pl BS1 ....195 A2
Coronation Rd

Bristol BS3 ....194 B3
Bristol, Cadbury Heath

BS30 ....11 B5
Bristol, Mangotsfield BS16 ......21 B5
Bristol, Warmley BS15 ....11 A7
Cinderford GL14 ....191 D3
Prestbury GL52 ....134 B4
Stroud GL5 ....99 B6
Tetbury GL8 ....140 B5
Coronation Sq GL51 ....132 E2
Coronation St GL7 ....152 D4
Corpus St GL52 ....131 A4
Corriett The GL11 ....88 A5
Corsend Rd GL19 ....172 B4
Corsley Wlk BS4 ....2 F8
Corston Wlk BS11 ....16 D7
Cossham Cl BS35 ....64 C2
Cossham Meml Hospl

BS16 ....20 C3
Cossham Rd Bristol BS5 ....9 D7
Pucklechurch BS16 ....22 C4
Cossham St BS16 ....21 B5
Cossham Wlk BS5 ....20 A1
Cossington Rd BS4 ....2 F8
Cossins Rd BS6 ....18 B3
Costers Cl BS35 ....51 A5
Costiland Dr BS13 ....1 F6
Cote Dr BS9 ....18 A4
Cote House La BS9 ....18 A5
Cote La BS9 ....18 A5
Cote Lea Pk BS9 ....18 B5
Cote Paddock BS9 ....17 F4
Cote Pk BS9 ....17 E6
Cote Rd BS9 ....18 A4
Cotham Brow BS6 ....18 D1
Cotham Gdns B2 BS6 ....18 C1
Cotham Gr BS6 ....18 D1
Cotham Hill BS6 ....18 C1
Cotham Lawn Ho BS6 ....194 C4
Cotham Lawn Rd BS6 ....18 C1
Cotham Pk BS6 ....18 C1
Cotham Pk N BS6 ....18 C1
Cotham Pl BS6 ....18 C1
Cotham Rd BS6 ....195 A4
Cotham Rd S BS6 ....18 D1
Cotham Sch BS6 ....18 D1
Cotham Vale BS6 ....18 C1
Cothar's Pitch HR9 ....170 A5
Cothers Ct GL56 ....186 C6
Cotman Wlk BS7 ....19 B6
Cotrith Gr BS10 ....27 E3
Cotsmore Cl GL56 ....187 B3
Cotswold

Cirencester GL7 ....190 C3
Eastington GL10 ....96 F7
Cotswold Bsns Village

GL56 ....91 A5
Cotswold Chine Home Specl

Sch GL6 ....91 B5
Cotswold Cl

Breston G20 ....182 C7
Brimscombe GL5 ....148 A5
Cirencester GL7 ....190 B3
Tetbury GL8 ....140 C5
Cotswold Ct BS37 ....44 B1
Cotswold Cotts GL8 ....90 F3
Cotswold Edge GL55 ....189 A6
Cotswold Edge Bsns Pk

GL2 ....118 C8
Cotswold Falconry Ctr* 186 E4
Cotswold Farm Pk*

GL54 ....175 D5

Cotswold Gdns
Gloucester GL2 . . . . .127 D5
🞵 Moreton-in-M GL56 . . .187 A3
Tewkesbury GL20 . . . . .192 D5
Wooton-u-E GL12 . . . . .68 C7
Cotswold Gn GL10 . . . . .98 A8
Cotswold La GL37 . . . . .34 A6
Cotswold Lo GL52 . . . . .133 F2
Cotswold Mead GL6 . . . . . .103 E7
Cotswold Mill GL7 . . . . .190 C4
Cotswold Nuffield Hospl
GL51 .130 A8
Cotswold Pl GL20 . . . . .192 D5
Cotswold Rd Bristol BS3 . . . .8 D3
Cheltenham GL52 . . . . .33 B8
Chipping Sodbury BS37 . . . .33 B8
Stroud GL5 . . . . .9 B8
Cotswold Sch The GL54 . .168 F8
Cotswold View
Bristol, Filton BS34 . . . . . . .29 A3
Bristol, Kingswood BS15 . .20 D2
Charfield GL12 . . . . .67 B5
Tirley GL19 . . . . .172 F7
Wickwar GL12 . . . . .54 B6
Woodmancote GL52 . . . . . .138 B3
Cotswold Water Pk*
GL7 . . . . .142 D5
Cotswold Way SN6 . . . . . . .145 C3
Cotswolds Countryside Mus*
GL54 .167 F2
Cotswolds Motoring Mus
The* GL54 . . . . .168 F7
Cotswolds Water Pk*
GL7 . . . . .153 A2
Cottage Field GL12 . . . . . . .125 D5
Cottage Pitch GL18 . . . . . . .171 A5
Cottage Pl BS2 . . . . .195 A4
Cottage Rake Ave GL50 . . .133 C5
Cottage The GL5 . . . . .98 C7
Cotteswold Rd
Gloucester GL4 . . . . .119 B5
Tewkesbury GL20 . . . . .192 D5
Cotteswold Rise GL7 . . . . . . .99 D7
Cottington Ct BS15 . . . . . . .10 E5
Cottisford Rd BS5 . . . . .19 B4
Cottle Gdns BS14 . . . . .3 F6
Cottle Rd BS14 . . . . .3 F6
Cotton Cl GL4 . . . . .119 F5
Cotton's La GL8 . . . . .140 B3
Cottonwood Dr BS30 . . . . .11 A3
Cottrell Ave BS15 . . . . .20 C2
Cottrell Rd BS5 . . . . .19 C3
Cotts The GL56 . . . . .186 F6
Coughton PI HR9 . . . . .163 C8
Coulson Wlk BS15 . . . . .20 C2
Coulson's Cl BS14 . . . . .3 A3
Coulson's Rd BS14 . . . . .3 A3
Council Hos
Cold Aston GL54 . . . . .168 B6
Eastnor HR8 . . . . .179 C7
Ledbury HR8 . . . . .178 A8
Stow-on-t-W GL54 . . . . . . .176 F5
Council Villas
Clearwell GL16 . . . . .154 F3
Edge End GL16 . . . . .155 C8
English Bicknor GL16 . . . .163 B1
Sling GL16 . . . . .155 D3
Counterpool Rd BS15 . . . . .10 C7
Countership GL51 . . . . .130 A2
Countership Gdns BS14 . . . .3 C6
Countess Lilias Rd GL7 . . .190 C2
Countess Wlk BS16 . . . . . . .19 D6
County Court Rd GL50 . . . .193 B3
County Cres 🞵 GL1 . . . . . .127 A1
County St BS4 . . . . .9 A4
Court Ave BS34 . . . . .29 F5
Court Cl BS7 . . . . .18 E2
Court Dr GL19 . . . . .173 B6
Court Farm Oaksey SN16 .142 A4
Tibberton GL19 . . . . .124 B8
Court Farm La
Beckford GL20 . . . . .183 B6
Mitcheldean GL17 . . . . . . .164 D5
Court Farm Mews GL10 . . .97 D7
Court Farm Rd
Bristol, Longwell Green
BS30 .10 E2
Bristol, Whitchurch BS14 . . .2 F3
Court Field 🞱 GL8 . . . . . . .140 B4
Court Gdn GL11 . . . . .89 B1
Court Gdns
Gloucester GL2 . . . . .118 B6
St Arvans NP16 . . . . .72 B6
Strand GL14 . . . . .77 C7
Court Gdns The GL2 . . . . . .193 B5
Court La Netherend GL15 .147 D3
🞱 Randwick GL18 . . . . . . .171 A4
Wick BS30 . . . . .12 B6
Court Mdw Stone GL13 . . . .77 E3
Wooton-u-E GL12 . . . . .68 C7
Court Mead GL13 . . . . .77 E3
Court Mews The GL52 . . . .131 A2
Court Orch Gretton GL54 .183 E1
Wooton-u-E GL12 . . . . .68 A3
Court Pl GL4 . . . . .119 D7
Court Rd
Bristol, Horfield BS7 . . . . . .18 F6
Bristol, Kingswood BS15 . .10 D7
Bristol, Oldland Common
BS30 .11 C3
Brockworth GL3 . . . . .120 E6
Frampton Cotterell BS36 . .30 F8
Frocester GL10 . . . . .97 B3
Lydney GL15 . . . . .92 B5
Newent GL18 . . . . .171 A5

Court Rd continued
Prestbury GL52 . . . . .134 C4
Upper Strensham WR8 . . .180 D7
Court St SN16 . . . . .58 C1
Court View GL6 . . . . .148 D6
Court View Cl BS32 . . . . .40 A5
Court Way Cl BS32 . . . . .40 A5
Courtbrook GL7 . . . . .152 E3
Courtenay Rd BS31 . . . . .5 B2
Courtenay St GL50 . . . . . . .133 D3
Courtenay Cres BS4 . . . . .2 C7
Courtfield Dr 🞱 GL52 . . . .131 B6
Courtfield Gr BS16 . . . . .20 A4
Courtfield Rd GL2 . . . . .109 F8
Courthouse Gdns GL11 . . . .87 F6
Courtis Gate GL52 . . . . .138 A3
Courtlands Bristol BS32 . . .40 C1
Keynsham BS31 . . . . .4 E5
Courtlands La BS3 . . . . .7 E4
Courtlands Unit BS4 . . . . . . .2 D8
Courtney Cl GL20 . . . . .192 D1
Courtney Prim Sch BS15 . .10 F7
Courtney Rd BS15 . . . . .10 F7
Courtney Way BS15 . . . . . . .11 A7
Courtside Mews BS6 . . . . . .18 C1
Courtyard The
Bourton-on-t-W GL54 . . . .168 F8
Cheltenham GL50 . . . . .193 A2
Stow-on-t-W GL54 . . . . . . .176 F5
Courville Cl BS35 . . . . .51 A4
Cousins Cl BS10 . . . . .27 D3
Cousins La BS5 . . . . .9 F8
Cousins Mews BS4 . . . . .9 F6
Cousins Way BS16 . . . . .21 D8
Cousley Cl GL3 . . . . .120 A7
Couzens Cl BS37 . . . . .44 B2
Couzens Pl BS34 . . . . .29 F5
Cove House Gdns 🞳
SN6 . . . . .142 F5
Coventry Cl GL20 . . . . .192 D2
Coventry Wlk BS4 . . . . .9 F6
Coverham Cl 🞵 GL16 . . .155 A7
Coverham Rd GL16 . . . . . . .155 A7
Cow La GL5 . . . . .91 A6
Cowcombe Hill GL6 . . . . . .148 C5
Cowdray Rd BS4 . . . . .2 D7
Cowhorn Hill BS30 . . . . .11 C4
Cowle La GL14 . . . . .174 A7
Cowler Wlk BS13 . . . . .1 F4
Cowley Cl GL51 . . . . .129 E7
Cowley La HR9 . . . . .170 C2
Cowley Rd GL4 . . . . .118 E3
Cowling Dr BS14 . . . . .3 C5
Cowling Rd BS14 . . . . .3 D5
Cowlsmead GL51 . . . . .129 E7
Cowper Rd Bristol BS6 . . . .18 C1
Cheltenham GL51 . . . . .132 E1
Cowship La GL12 . . . . .53 D6
Cowslip Mdw GL52 . . . . . . .138 B3
Cowswell La GL6 . . . . .148 B6
Cox Cl BS30 . . . . .10 F4
Cox's Hill SN6 . . . . .142 F5
Cox's Way Bream GL15 . . .155 D1
Gloucester GL4 . . . . .118 C2
Coxbury & Wyegate La
GL16 .154 D2
Coxgrove Hill BS16 . . . . . . .21 F7
Coxmoor Cl OX7 . . . . .177 F2
Coxwell Cl GL7 . . . . .190 C5
Coxwell St GL7 . . . . .190 C5
Cozens La OX7 . . . . .177 F2
Crab Tree Pl GL50 . . . . .133 C3
Crabtree Cl BS41 . . . . .1 D1
Crabtree La
Cirencester GL7 . . . . .190 F3
Dundry BS41 . . . . .1 D2
Duntisbourne Abbots GL7 .187 B3
Crabtree Pk GL7 . . . . .152 E4
Crabtree Rd GL14 . . . . .191 B5
Crabtree Wlk BS16 . . . . . . .19 D2
Craddock Cl GL6 . . . . .9 E7
Craddock Rd 🞱 GL18 . . . .174 A1
Cradock Cl BS30 . . . . .11 B4
Craftes Ct BS5 . . . . .19 A4
Craig Yr Afon NP16 . . . . . . .60 E7
Crail View GL54 . . . . .168 A1
Cranberry Wlk BS9 . . . . .17 C8
Cranbourne Rd BS34 . . . . . .28 F7
Cranbrook Rd BS6 . . . . .18 C3
Crandell Cl BS10 . . . . .27 F4
Crane Cl BS15 . . . . .11 B8
Crane Furlong GL6 . . . . . . .148 B8
Cranford Cl GL52 . . . . .138 C3
Cranford Ct 🞵 BS9 . . . . . . .18 B6
Cranham GL37 . . . . .32 C7
Cranham CE Prim Sch
GL4 . . . . .112 G6
Cranham Cl Bristol BS15 . .20 F2
🞵 Gloucester GL4 . . . . . . .119 E5
Cranham Dr BS34 . . . . .40 C1
Cranham La GL3 . . . . .128 B3
Cranham Rd Bristol BS10 . .18 C8
Paswick GL6 . . . . .112 F5
Cranhams La GL7 . . . . .190 B2
Cranleigh Court Inf Sch
BS37 . . . . .43 D2
Cranleigh Court Rd BS37 . .43 D2
Cranleigh Gdns BS9 . . . . . .17 E4
Cranleigh Rd BS14 . . . . .3 A4
Cranley GL50 . . . . .133 E3
Cranmoor Gn BS35 . . . . . . .38 D7
Cranmore Ave BS31 . . . . .4 E6
Cranmore Cres BS10 . . . . . .28 D1
Cranside Ave BS6 . . . . .18 C4
Cransley Cres BS9 . . . . .18 C7
Crantock Ave BS13 . . . . .2 B8
Crantock Dr BS32 . . . . .40 B5

Crantock Rd BS37 . . . . .43 D1
Cranwell Cl GL4 . . . . .119 C4
Cranwell Gr BS14 . . . . .3 A5
Crapen The GL11 . . . . .87 E4
Crashmore La GL20 . . . . . .182 F7
Crates Cl BS15 . . . . .10 E8
Craven Cl BS30 . . . . .10 F5
Craven Dr GL3 . . . . .128 B6
Cravenly Hill GL11 . . . . .89 B3
Crawley La GL11 . . . . .89 B3
Crawshay Pl GL14 . . . . .191 C4
Craydon Gr BS14 . . . . .3 D4
Craydon Rd BS14 . . . . .3 D4
Craydon Wlk BS14 . . . . .3 D4
Crease The 🞱 GL18 . . . . . .171 A4
Crediton Cres BS13 . . . . .2 C6
Crescent Cl
Coleford GL16 . . . . .155 A6
Stonehouse GL10 . . . . .97 E6
Crescent Rd Bristol BS16 . .20 C6
Stonehouse GL10 . . . . .97 E6
Crescent Terr GL50 . . . . . . .193 B3
Crescent The
🞱 Berry Hill GL16 . . . . . . .155 A7
Bristol, Frenchay BS16 . . . .29 F1
Bristol, Henleaze BS9 . . . . .18 C5
Bristol, Sea Mills BS9 . . . . .17 C6
Bristol, Upper Soundwell
BS16 .20 D3
Brockworth GL3 . . . . .120 D6
Chalford GL6 . . . . .148 E6
Coleford GL16 . . . . .155 A5
Coleford GL16 . . . . .155 A6
Dursley GL11 . . . . .87 F4
Mitcheldean GL17 . . . . .164 D6
Northwood Green GL14 . .165 D3
Olveston BS35 . . . . .50 D4
Sharpness GL13 . . . . .85 D8
Wick BS30 . . . . .12 C7
Crescendale GL7 . . . . .127 A5
Crest The Bristol BS4 . . . . . . .9 C2
West Kington SN14 . . . . . . .25 F3
Crest Way GL4 . . . . .127 F1
Creswicke Ave BS15 . . . . . .10 C5
Creswicke Rd BS4 . . . . .2 E7
Crew's Hole Rd BS5 . . . . .9 E7
Cribbs Causeway Ctr
BS34 . . . . .28 A6
Cribbs Cswy BS10 . . . . .28 A6
Cricklade Rd Bristol BS7 . .18 C8
Cirencester GL7 . . . . .190 E2
Cricklade SN5 . . . . .143 E1
Highworth SN6 . . . . .145 C3
Cricklade St
Cirencester GL7 . . . . .190 C4
Poulton GL7 . . . . .151 E3
Crickley Hill Ctry Pk*
GL3 . . . . .122 A5
Criftycraft La GL3 . . . . .128 C3
Crippetts La GL51 . . . . .130 B3
Cripps Rd Bristol BS3 . . . . . .8 C3
Cirencester GL7 . . . . .190 C4
Crispin Cl Gloucester GL2 .127 C5
🞱 Winchcombe GL54 . . . .174 A7
Crispin La BS35 . . . . .64 B1
Crispin Rd GL54 . . . . .174 A7
Crispin Way BS15 . . . . .20 F2
Critchford La BS37 . . . . .175 A5
Crockerne CE Prim Sch
BS20 . . . . .16 C4
Crockerne Dr BS20 . . . . . . .16 C4
Crockerne Ho BS20 . . . . . . .16 C4
Croft Ave BS16 . . . . .19 C4
Charlton Kings GL53 . . . . .131 B5
Croft Cl Bitton BS30 . . . . .5 D8
Churchdown GL3 . . . . .128 D4
Newent GL18 . . . . .171 A5
Croft Cty Prim Sch The
GL6 . . . . .103 E8
Croft Dr GL53 . . . . .131 A5
Croft Farm Leisure & Water
Pk* GL20 . . . . .182 A6
Croft Gdns
🞵 Broadway WR12 . . . . . .185 B8
Charlton Kings GL53 . . . . .131 B5
Croft Hall Sch GL7 . . . . . . .152 E4
Croft Holm GL56 . . . . .187 B3
Croft La Latton GL56 . . . . .143 E6
Winstone GL7 . . . . .107 A7
Croft Par GL53 . . . . .131 B5
Croft Rd
Charlton Kings GL53 . . . . .131 A5
Newent GL18 . . . . .171 A5
Croft St GL53 . . . . .131 A5
Croft The
Bristol, Mangotsfield BS16 . .20 F5
Bristol, Oldland Common
BS30 .11 C3
Dursley GL11 . . . . .88 A4
🞵 Fairford GL7 . . . . .152 E4
Painswick GL6 . . . . .112 F5
Croft Thorne Cl GL51 . . . .129 F5
Croft View BS9 . . . . .18 C6
Crofters Wlk BS32 . . . . .29 D8
Croftlands The GL20 . . . . . .182 C7
Crofton Ave BS7 . . . . .18 F6
Crofton Fields BS36 . . . . . . .30 E6
Crofts End Ind Est BS5 . . . .19 F1
Crofts End Rd BS5 . . . . .19 F1
Crofts Field GL20 . . . . .181 D5
Crokeswood Wlk BS11 . . . .27 A1
Crome Rd BS7 . . . . .19 A7
Cromer Rd BS5 . . . . .19 C2
Cromers Cl GL20 . . . . .182 C5

Cromhall La GL12 . . . . .65 D1
Cromwell Ct BS15 . . . . .10 E5
Cromwell Rd
Bristol, Montpelier BS6 . . .18 E2
Bristol, St George BS5 . . . .10 A8
Cheltenham GL52 . . . . .130 E7
Chepstow NP16 . . . . .60 E5
Cromwell St Bristol BS3 . . . .8 D3
Gloucester GL1 . . . . .196 B2
Cromwell Way BS16 . . . . . . .18 E2
Cromwells Hide BS16 . . . . .19 E5
Crooked End PI GL17 . . . . .163 F4
Crooks Ind Est GL53 . . . . .130 D6
Croomes Hill BS16 . . . . .20 D6
Cropthorne Rd BS7 . . . . . . .29 A1
Cropthorne Rd S BS7 . . . . .19 A8
Crosby Row BS8 . . . . .194 A2
Cross Elms La BS9 . . . . .17 E5
Cross Farm GL15 . . . . .147 E4
Cross Hands Rd BS35 . . . . .38 D7
Cross Keys La GL11 . . . . . . .196 B3
Cross Lanes BS20 . . . . .16 C4
Cross St Bristol BS15 . . . . . .20 D1
Keynsham BS31 . . . . .4 E5
Cross The Horsley GL6 . . . .90 F1
Nympsfield GL10 . . . . .89 E6
Ripple GL20 . . . . .181 D8
Cross Tree Cres GL7 . . . . . .144 F7
Cross Tree Flats GL7 . . . . .144 E7
Cross Tree Gr BS32 . . . . .29 D8
Cross Vane NP25 . . . . .154 F3
Cross Wlk BS14 . . . . .3 A6
Crosscombe Dr BS13 . . . . . . .2 C3
Crossfield Rd BS16 . . . . .20 E3
Crossfields GL54 . . . . .166 C3
Crossleaze Rd BS15 . . . . . . .10 C3
Crossley Cl BS36 . . . . .30 F7
Crossman Ave BS36 . . . . . . .30 E5
Crossways GL16 . . . . .154 F6
Crossways Jun & Inf Sch
BS35 . . . . .64 D1
Crossways Rd Bristol BS4 . . .9 A1
Thornbury BS35 . . . . .64 D1
Crouch Cl GL20 . . . . .192 C3
Crow Ash Rd GL11 . . . . . . .155 A7
Crow Ash Rd GL16 . . . . . . .155 A7
Crow La Bristol BS1 . . . . . . .195 A2
Henbury BS10 . . . . .27 E2
Crow Mdw GL12 . . . . .67 F4
Crowfield GL52 . . . . .138 B4
Crowfield La GL18 . . . . .178 E2
Crowgate La GL14 . . . . .157 F8
Crowgate Way BS11 . . . . . . .26 B1
Crown Cl
Bishop's Cleeve GL52 . . . .137 F3
Dymock GL18 . . . . .178 D2
Crown Cotts GL5 . . . . .98 A8
Crown Cl GL10 . . . . .98 A4
Crown Dr GL52 . . . . .137 F2
Crown Gdns BS30 . . . . .11 A7
Crown Hill BS5 . . . . .9 F8
Crown Hill Wlk BS5 . . . . . . .19 F2
Crown Ind Est BS30 . . . . . . .12 A7
Crown La Bristol BS16 . . . . .20 D4
Parkend GL15 . . . . .155 E2
Yorkley GL15 . . . . .156 A1
Crown Mdw 🞱 GL16 . . . .155 B5
Crown Rd
Bristol, Upper Soundwell
BS15 .20 D2
Bristol, Warmley BS30 . . . .11 C6
Crowndale Rd BS4 . . . . .9 B2
Crownleaze BS16 . . . . .20 D3
Crows Gr BS32 . . . . .40 D3
Crowther Pk BS7 . . . . .19 A4
Crowther Rd BS7 . . . . .19 A4
Crowther St 🞱 BS3 . . . . .8 D3
Crowthers Ave BS37 . . . . . . .43 C3
Croydon Rd 🞱 BS5 . . . . .9 B8
Croydon St BS5 . . . . .9 B8
Crucible Cl GL16 . . . . .155 A5
Crucible Rd GL16 . . . . .155 A5
Crudwell CE Prim Sch
SN16 .141 C2
Crudwell La GL8 . . . . .140 F3
Crump Pl GL15 . . . . .92 C2
Crunnis The BS32 . . . . .29 E6
Crusty La BS20 . . . . .16 E4
Crypt Ct GL4 . . . . .118 C3
Crypt Sch The GL2 . . . . . . .118 D4
Crypt The GL18 . . . . .178 D2
Crythan Wlk 🞵 GL51 . . . .129 F5
Cuckoo Cl 🞵 GL6 . . . . . . .148 C6
Cuckoo La BS36 . . . . .30 F3
Cuckoo Row GL6 . . . . .91 F6
Cud La GL6 . . . . .103 B8
Cudnall St GL53 . . . . .131 A7
Cuffington Ave BS4 . . . . .9 D4
Culkerton GL8 . . . . .140 F6
Cullerns The SN6 . . . . .145 D3
Culleysgate La BS30 . . . . . . .12 F6
Cullimore View GL14 . . . . .191 C1
Cullingham GL19 . . . . .172 A8
Cullis La GL16 . . . . .155 B6
Culross Cl GL50 . . . . .133 E4
Culver Hall GL15 . . . . .91 A8
Culver St Bristol BS1 . . . . . .194 C2
Newent GL18 . . . . .171 A4
Culverhay GL17 . . . . .163 B2
Culverhill Rd BS37 . . . . .44 A1
Culverhill Sch BS37 . . . . . . .32 D7
Culvers Rd BS31 . . . . .4 E5
Culvert The BS32 . . . . .29 D8
Culverwell Rd BS13 . . . . .2 A5
Cumberland Basin Rd BS8 . .7 F5
Cumberland Cl BS1 . . . . . . .194 A1
Cumberland Gr 🞵 BS6 . . . .18 F2

Cumberland Pl 🞲 BS8 . . . . .
Cumberland Rd BS1 . . . .
Cumberland St BS2 . . . .
Cumbria Cl BS35 . . . .
Cumming Ct GL52 . . . .
Cunningham Gdns BS16 . .
Cupola Cl GL16 . . . .
Curland Gr BS14 . . . .
Curlew Cl BS16 . . . .
Northway GL20 . . . .
Cursey La GL51 . . . .
Cursey Lane Cvn Pk
GL51 . . . .
Cursus The GL7 . . . .
Curtis Hayward Dr GL2 . . .
Curtis La BS34 . . . .
Custom Cl BS14 . . . .
Cut & Fry Rd GL15 . . . .
Cut Throat La HR9 . . . .
Cutham La GL7 . . . .
Cuthwine Pl GL7 . . . .
Cutler Rd Bristol BS13 . . . . .
Stroud GL5 . . . .
Cutlers Brook Jun Sch
BS2 . . . .
Cutsdean Cl GL52 . . . .
Cutsheath Rd GL12 . . . .
Cutters Row BS3 . . . .
Cutwell GL8 . . . .
Cylde Pk BS6 . . . .
Cynder Way BS16 . . . .
Cypress Ct BS9 . . . .
Cypress Gdns BS8 . . . .
Cypress Gr BS9 . . . .
Cypress Rd GL20 . . . .
Cypress Wlk SN14 . . . .
Cyrus Ct BS10 . . . .

D

Daffodil Cl GL4 . . . .
Daffodil Leaze GL10 . . . .
Daffodil St GL50 . . . .
Daffodils The GL10 . . . .
Dagmar Rd GL50 . . . .
Daines Cl 🞰 BS16 . . . .
Dainty St GL1 . . . .
Dairy Farm SN6 . . . .
Dairy La WR11 . . . .
Dairycroft BS2 . . . .
Daisy Bank GL5 . . . .
Daisy Green La GL12 . . . . . .
Daisy Rd BS5 . . . .
Daisybank Rd GL53 . . . .
Dakin Cl BS4 . . . .
Dakota Dr BS14 . . . .
Dalby Ave BS3 . . . .
Daldry Gdns BS35 . . . .
Dale Cl GL4 . . . .
Dale St Bristol BS2 . . . .
Bristol, St George BS5 . . . . .
Dale Wlk GL52 . . . .
Dalebrook HR9 . . . .
Dalkeith Ave BS15 . . . .
Dallaway GL5 . . . .
Dalrymple Rd 🞸 BS2 . . . . . .
Dalston Rd BS3 . . . .
Dalton Sq BS2 . . . .
Damery La Stone GL13 . . . .
Woodford GL13 . . . .
Dampier Rd BS3 . . . .
Damsells The 🞹 GL8 . . . . . .
Damson Cl GL4 . . . .
Danbury Cres BS10 . . . .
Danbury Wlk BS10 . . . .
Danby Cl Cinderford GL14 .
Yorkley GL15 . . . .
Danby Ho BS2 . . . .
Danby Rd GL15 . . . .
Dancey Mead BS13 . . . .
Dancey Rd GL3 . . . .
Dane Cl GL12 . . . .
Dane La GL7 . . . .
Danes Cl NP16 . . . .
Danes Hill NP16 . . . .
Danford La GL19 . . . .
Danford Villas GL19 . . . .
Dangerfield Ave BS13 . . . . .
Daniels Ind Est GL5 . . . .
Daniels Rd GL2 . . . .
Dapps Hill BS31 . . . .
Dapwell La BS14,BS31 . . . . .
Darell Cl GL2 . . . .
Darell Gdns GL2 . . . .
Dark La Chalford GL6 . . . . .
Nailsworth GL6 . . . .
North Cerney GL7 . . . .
Stroud GL5 . . . .
Swindon GL51 . . . .
Dark Ride GL7 . . . .
Darken La GL15 . . . .
Darks Rd GL18 . . . .
Darley Cl BS10 . . . .
Darleydale Cl GL2 . . . .
Darnell's La HR9 . . . .
Darnley Ave BS7 . . . .
Darren Rd 🞲 GL15 . . . .
Dart Cl Quedgeley GL2 . . . .
Thornbury BS35 . . . .
Dart Rd GL52 . . . .
Darters Cl GL15 . . . .
Dartmoor St BS3 . . . .
Dartmouth Wlk BS31 . . . . . .
Darwin Cl GL51 . . . .
Darwin Rd GL4 . . . .

n Cl C2 WR12 .....185 C8
eny Cl BS16 .....20 B5
eny Ct BS1 .....195 A1
sia Dr GL51 .....129 F5
atry Rd BS4 .....9 F5
try Terr GL1 .....196 C1
St BS2 .....18 F1
Terr BS12 .....18 F1
French Ct GL51 .....130 A5
St BS2 .....195 C3
s La BS35 .....51 A4
s Rd BS14 .....3 C6
s Cl BS35 .....51 A4
s Dr BS4 .....9 F5
s Rd BS6 .....187 B3
ian Cl GL2 .....118 A3
Cres BS20 .....16 C3
Cl BS30 .....30 D5
Cl BS35 .....64 C2
St BS11 .....18 E5
t BS3 .....18 E4
Cl GL2 .....109 F6
t Cl GL2 .....153 C6
s Ct BS8 .....7 F6
s The GL2 .....109 F8
Cr BS36 .....30 E7
sh Rd BS3 .....8 D2
Rise BS15 .....21 A1
leys The SN16 .....141 C3
BS16 .....20 B4
use La GL12 .....55 C8
La GL56 .....186 C5
Rd BS2 .....9 A6
sford Cl GL51 .....129 D8
Ct SN16 .....141 C3
Road Commercial Ctr 9 A7
fford Rd BS11 .....27 C2
rrieres Wlk
 .....132 D2
Warre Ct BS4 .....9 F6
rose Ct BS15 .....10 E4
St
enham BS31 .....129 F7
bourne BS36 .....30 E5
m Cl GL52 .....137 E2
n Cl GL51 .....133 B7
Ave BS35 .....64 C2
Cl BS15 .....10 B4
Close Prep Sch 130 A8
Close
enham GL51 .....129 F8
Rd GL11 .....130 A8
Cres Bristol BS3 .....8 C4
istol BS3 .....8 A2
Mdws GL17 .....164 D5
Rd avonmouth BS11 .....26 C5
ham GL14 .....156 F6
BS37 .....43 C3
St
l, Bedminster BS3 .....8 C4
l, St Pauls BS2 .....195 B4
Swift Cl HR9 .....114 A2
View GL14 .....191 C1
er BS5 .....20 A2
n Quarry GL5 .....91 F7
s Terr GL1 .....196 B4
s Way GL1 .....196 B4
s Wlk GL17 .....164 B4
s Wlk GL17 .....164 B4
ery Cl BS15 .....11 B8
n, Warmley BS15 .....11 B8
hill La BA1 .....6 F2
na Ct BS16 .....20 E6
s Cl BS16 .....20 A1
s Terr GL1 .....196 B4
s Way GL1 .....196 B4
s Wlk GL17 .....164 B4
s Wood City Prim Sch
 .....21 A2
swood BS11 .....21 A2
ere Ave GL52 .....138 A2
ere Rd GL52 .....138 A2
eye Hospl GL53 .....130 D4
ale Rd GL54 .....174 A7
ware Rd GL7 .....152 E2

Delius Gr BS4 .....2 D7
Delkin Rd GL11 .....87 F4
Delkin Rd GL11 .....87 F4
Dell Ave GL51 .....132 E4
Dell Prim Sch The NP16 .....72 E1
Dell The Blockley GL56 .....186 C6
  Bredon GL20 .....182 C8
  Bristol, Bradley Stoke BS32 .....36 E7
  Bristol, Oldland Common
   BS30 .....11 C5
  Bristol, Westbury on Trym
   .....17 F5
  Gloucester GL4 .....119 E7
Dell View NP16 .....60 E8
Delmont Gr GL5 .....99 C8
Delphinium Dr GL52 .....137 E3
Delta Dr GL20 .....182 B4
Delta Way GL3 .....120 C6
Delvin Rd BS10 .....18 C8
Denbigh Dr NP16 .....61 A5
Denbigh Rd GL51 .....132 B6
Denbigh St BS2 .....18 F1
Dene Magna Com Sch
 .....164 D4
Dene Rd BS14 .....3 C4
Denehurst GL17 .....163 F3
Denfurlong Farm (Farm
  Trail)* GL54 .....159 B5
Denham Cl
  Gloucester GL4 .....118 C1
  Woodmancote GL52 .....138 C3
Denleigh GL8 .....3 A4
Denley Cl GL52 .....137 F2
Denmark Ave BS1 .....194 C2
Denmark Ct GL51 .....127 A3
Denmark Dr NP16 .....61 B7
Denmark Pl BS7 .....18 E3
Denmark Rd GL51 .....132 B6
Denmark St BS1 .....194 C2
Denning Cl GL50 .....193 A1
Dennisworth BS16 .....22 B5
Dennor Pk BS14 .....3 B7
Denny Isle Dr BS35 .....38 A6
Denston Wlk BS13 .....2 A7
Dent's La GL19 .....172 B2
Dent's Terr BS4 .....9 E7
Denton Patch BS16 .....21 B7
Dentwood Gr BS9 .....17 B8
Denvale Trad Pk BS4 .....2 E7
Denys Ct BS35 .....50 A3
Derby Cl GL1 .....127 A1
Derby Rd Bristol BS7 .....18 E3
  Gloucester GL1 .....127 A1
Derby St BS5 .....9 D7
Derham Rd BS13 .....2 A5
Dermot St BS1 .....18 F1
Derrick Rd BS15 .....186 C6
Derricke Rd BS14 .....3 F6
Derry Rd SN16 .....142 E1
Derry Rd BS3 .....8 B2
Derry Rd SN6 .....142 F4
Derwent Cl Bristol BS34 .....29 A8
  Brockworth GL3 .....120 E5
Derwent Ct BS35 .....51 D8
Derwent Dr GL20 .....192 E6
Derwent Rd BS5 .....5 A5
Derwent Rd BS15 .....186 C6
Derwent Wlk GL51 .....129 F7
Desford Cl GL4 .....119 F5
Despenser Rd GL20 .....192 C2
Detmore Cl GL53 .....131 D5
Devaney Cl BS4 .....9 C8
Devauden Rd NP16 .....72 B7
Devereaux Cres GL1 .....98 C7
Devereaux Rd GL5 .....98 C7
Devereon Gr BS31 .....5 A4
Devil's Chy* GL53 .....130 D1
Devil's Elbow The GL6 .....91 F6
Devil's La GL12 .....67 A2
Devon Ave BS5 .....133 A2
Devon Gr BS5 .....9 C8
Devon Road Trad Est
  BS5 .....19 C1
Devonshire Bldgs BS3 .....8 E4
Devonshire Dr GL20 .....192 D5
Devonshire Rd BS6 .....18 B4
Devonshire St GL50 .....193 A4
Devonshire Terr
  GL56 .....187 A3
Dewey Cl GL52 .....138 B3
Dewfalls Dr BS32 .....40 D1
Dial La BS16 .....20 D6
Diamond Rd BS5 .....19 F7
Diamond St BS3 .....8 C3
Diamonite Ind Pk BS16 .....20 A3
Dibden Cl BS16 .....20 A1
Dibden Ct BS16 .....21 A8
Dibden La
  Alderton GL20,GL54 .....183 L4
  Bristol BS16 .....21 B7
Dibden Rd BS16 .....21 A7
Dickens Cl Bristol BS7 .....18 A8
Dickens Mews GL1 .....118 F5
Didbrook Prim Sch
  GL54 .....184 D2
Didsbury Cl BS10 .....27 F1
Digbeth St GL54 .....176 H4
Digby Pk GL20 .....192 E6
Dighton Ct BS2 .....195 A4
Dighton Gate BS34 .....29 E5
Dighton St BS2 .....195 A4
Dikler Cl GL54 .....169 A6
Dilke Meml Hospl
  Cinderford GL14 .....191 A2

Dilke Meml Hospl continued
  Ruspidge GL14 .....156 H2
Dill Ave GL51 .....132 E4
Dillon Cl BS5 .....9 D7
Dimore Cl GL2 .....109 E7
Dinas Cl GL51 .....129 F6
Dinas Rd GL51 .....129 F6
Dinely St GL1 .....196 C1
Dingle Bglws GL51 .....158 A8
Dingle Cl BS9 .....17 C6
Dingle Ct BS13 .....1 F7
Dingle La GL20 .....182 A8
Dingle Rd BS9 .....17 D7
Dingle The Bristol BS9 .....17 D7
  Winterbourne BS36 .....37 E6
Dingle View BS9 .....17 C7
Dinglevale Dr GL4 .....119 F6
Dinglewell Inf & Jun Sch
  GL3 .....119 F7
Dinglewood Cl BS9 .....17 D7
Dingly Wlk BS2 .....9 A6
Dinglywood Dr GL4 .....119 F6
Distel Cl GL50 .....133 C5
District Ctr BS32 .....29 E8
Ditch La GL7 .....147 F3
Ditchford BS4 .....9 F2
Dixton Cl NP25 .....154 A8
Dixton Rd NP25 .....154 A8
Dock Gate La BS8 .....194 A1
Dock La GL20 .....182 C8
Dock Rd GL13 .....93 B1
Dockham Rd GL14 .....191 D4
Dockins Hill Way GL17 .....164 D4
Docks Ind Est BS11 .....26 E7
Dodd Dr GL54 .....119 D7
Doddington La GL54 .....174 A3
Dodington La BS37 .....33 C5
Dodington Rd BS37 .....33 B7
Dog La GL3 .....121 B6
Dog Trap La SN16 .....142 C1
Dollar St GL7 .....190 C5
Dolman Cl BS10 .....27 F3
Domby Cl GL16 .....155 A5
Domestic Fowl Trust*
  WR11 .....188 C7
Dominion Rd BS16 .....19 F3
Dominion Rd BS13 .....1 F7
Doncaster Rd BS10 .....18 C8
Doncombe Hill SN14 .....15 F7
Doncombe La SN14 .....15 F7
Donegal Rd BS4 .....8 D1
Dongola Ave BS7 .....18 E4
Dongola Rd BS7 .....18 E4
Donkey Field The GL7 .....151 C5
Donnington Ave BS6 .....186 C5
Donnington Wlk BS31 .....4 D4
Donside GL7 .....190 A7
Doone Rd BS7 .....18 F4
Dora Wlk BS5 .....118 F7
Dorcas Ave BS34 .....29 F5
Dorchester Cl BS10 .....27 F1
Dorchester Rd GL51 .....130 C6
Dorchester St BS1 .....19 A7
Dorester Cl BS10 .....28 C4
Dorian Cl BS7 .....18 E7
Dorian Rd BS7 .....18 E7
Dorington Cl GL6 .....148 B6
Dorington Way BS37 .....40 A8
Dormer Cl GL51 .....132 D2
Dormer Rd BS36 .....31 D6
Dormer Rd Bristol BS5 .....9 E3
  Cheltenham GL51 .....132 C2
Dormers The SN6 .....145 D3
Dorney Rd GL1 .....118 F4
Dorrit Cl GL1 .....118 F5
Dorset Ave GL51 .....133 A2
Dorset Cl BS9 .....8 D1
Dorset Ho GL53 .....49 B4
Dorset Rd
  Bristol, Kingswood BS15 .....20 D1
  Bristol, Westbury on Trym
   .....18 B6
Dorset St Bristol BS3 .....8 B3
  Bristol BS37 .....44 A3
Double View GL14 .....191 D3
Dovaston Cl GL54 .....143 E4
Doughemeadow Cotts
  WR12 .....184 F6
Douglas Ho GL50 .....193 B2
Douglas Rd
  Bristol, Horfield BS7 .....18 F7
  Bristol, Kingswood BS15 .....20 D7
Doulton Way BS14 .....3 B5
Douro Cl GL50 .....193 A2
Douro Rd GL50 .....193 A2
Dove Cl GL50 .....128 E8
Dove La Bristol, Redfield BS5 .....9 C7
  Bristol, St Pauls BS2 .....195 C4
Dove St BS2 .....195 A4
Dove St S BS2 .....195 A4
Dovecote BS37 .....32 F7
Dovedale BS35 .....51 D8
Dovedale Cl GL2 .....109 D8
Dover Hay GL51 .....129 F5
Dover Pl BS8 .....194 B3
Dover's View GL55 .....189 C2
Dovercourt Rd BS7 .....19 A6
Doverdale Dr GL2 .....127 D4
Doveswell Gr BS13 .....2 A4
Dovey Cl BS35 .....8 D4
Dowdeswell Cl BS10 .....27 F3
Dowding Way GL54 .....44 C2
Dowdy's La BS37 .....180 A8
Dowling Rd BS13 .....2 D3
Down Ampney CE Prim Sch
  GL7 .....143 F8

Down Ampney Rd GL7 .....143 D7
Down Farm Ho BS36 .....30 D6
Down Hatherley La GL2 .....173 C1
Down Leaze 2 BS35 .....51 A5
Marshfield SN14 .....25 C2
  Winterbourne BS36 .....30 F4
Down The Alveston BS35 .....50 F5
  Tockington BS35 .....50 D3
Down View Bristol BS2 .....18 F3
  Chalford GL6 .....148 C6
Downend Lower Sec Sch
  BS16 .....20 F5
Downend Park Rd BS16 .....20 D6
Downend Rd Bristol BS7 .....18 F5
Downend Rd
  Bristol, Fishponds BS16 .....20 D6
  Bristol, Horfield BS7 .....18 F5
  Bristol, Kingswood BS15 .....20 D1
Downend Upper Sec Sch
  BS16 .....20 F7
Downfield GL4 .....119 F6
Downfield Cl GL12 .....16 A5
  Keynsham BS31 .....4 A5
  Stroud GL5 .....98 F3
Downfield Cl BS35 .....51 A5
Downfield Dr BS36 .....31 A8
Downfield Ho BS15 .....129 D2
Downfield La BS20 .....182 A8
Downfield Lodge BS8 .....18 A1
Downfield Rd Bristol BS8 .....18 A1
  Stroud GL5 .....98 F3
Downhams The NP25 .....154 A7
Downland Cl BS4 .....2 D6
Downleaze
  Bristol, Downend BS16 .....20 D8
  Bristol, Stoke Bishop BS9 .....17 F3
Downleaze Dr BS37 .....33 B8
Downleaze Rd BS9 .....17 F3
Downman Rd BS7 .....19 A6
Downs Cl BS35 .....51 A5
Downs Cote Ave BS9 .....17 F6
Downs Cote Dr BS9 .....17 F6
Downs Cote Gdns BS9 .....18 A6
Downs Cote Pk BS9 .....18 A6
Downs Cote View BS9 .....18 A6
Downs Ct BS9 .....18 A6
Downs Mill GL16 .....148 E4
Downs Pk E BS6 .....18 A4
Downs Pk W BS6 .....18 A4
Downs Rd Bristol BS9 .....18 A6
  Dundry BS41 .....1 D2
Downs The GL12 .....53 F7
Downside Cl BS30 .....10 F5
Downside BS8 .....18 A1
Downsview Cr Bristol BS37 .....18 E8
  Bristol BS37 .....33 A8
Downton Rd Bristol BS4 .....8 D1
  Stonehouse GL10 .....97 E6
Downy Pl BS8 .....7 F5
Downy Rd BS8 .....194 A2
Dowty Pl BS8 .....194 A2
Dowty Rd GL51 .....132 E2
Doynton La SN14 .....23 B3
Dozule Cl GL10 .....97 F3
Dr Brown's Cl GL6 .....91 F6
Dr Brown's Rd GL6 .....91 F7
Dr Cranford's Way GL6 .....91 F6
Dr Crouch's Rd GL6 .....148 C5
Dr Middletons Rd GL6 .....148 C5
Dr Newton's Way GL5 .....99 C6
Dr White's Cl BS1 .....195 B1
Drag Rd HR9 .....162 E3
Dragon Cl BS5 .....19 E1
Dragon Rd BS36 .....30 D5
Dragon Wlk BS5 .....19 F1
Dragons Hill Cl BS31 .....4 F5
Dragons Hill Ct BS31 .....4 F5
Dragons Hill Gdns BS31 .....4 F5
Dragonswell Rd BS10 .....28 A2
Drake Cl Innsworth GL3 .....127 F7
  Salford BS31 .....4 F2
Drake La BS37 .....88 C2
Drake Rd BS3 .....8 A3
Drakes Pl GL50 .....193 B3
Draper Ct BS5 .....9 C7
Draper's La GL19 .....172 D6
Draper's Cl GL52 .....138 B3
Draycott BS15 .....11 C5
Draycott Bsns Pk GL11 .....87 F7
Draycott Cres GL11 .....87 F7
Draycott Rd BS7 .....18 F5
Draydon Rd BS4 .....2 D8
Drayton Cl Bristol BS14 .....3 B8
  Cheltenham GL51 .....133 B6
  Gloucester GL4 .....117 C1
  Keynsham BS31 .....5 A6
Drayton Rd Bristol BS9 .....17 C8
  Cheltenham GL51 .....129 E8
Drayton Way GL11 .....119 C5
Drews Cl BS13 .....1 C5
Drews Cl GL33 .....128 C4
Driffield Cross Rds GL7 .....151 B1
Driffield Rd GL15 .....92 C5
Drift Cl GL7 .....190 A2
Drift Ct SN14 .....69 D4
Drifton Hill SN14 .....25 F7
Drive The
  Bristol, Hengrove BS14 .....3 C6
  Bristol, Henleaze BS9 .....18 B5
  Dursley GL11 .....87 F4
Drivemoor GL4 .....119 D3
Droveway GL4 .....119 D3
Drovers End GL14 .....191 C4
Drug-gers End La WR13 .....180 C8
Druid Cl BS9 .....17 E5
Druid Hill BS9 .....17 E5
Druid Rd BS9 .....17 D4

Druid Stoke Ave BS9 .....17 D5
Druid Woods BS9 .....17 C5
Druids Cl GL4 .....119 C7
Druids La GL4 .....119 C7
Druids Oak GL2 .....109 F8
Drummond Ct BS30 .....10 F4
Drummond Rd
  Bristol, Fishponds BS16 .....19 F3
  Bristol, St Pauls BS2 .....18 E1
Drury La GL19 .....179 D2
Dry Meadow La GL3 .....127 C7
Drybrook Rd GL17 .....164 B4
Drybrook Sch GL17 .....164 B4
Dryland Mews GL3 .....120 B6
Drylaze Keynsham BS31 .....4 E7
  Wootton-u-E GL12 .....68 A7
  Yate BS37 .....43 C7
Drylaze Ct GL12 .....68 A7
Drylaze Gdns GL12 .....68 A7
Drylaze Ho GL12 .....68 A7
Drylaze Rd BS16 .....19 F6
Dubbers La BS5 .....19 E2
Dublin Cres BS9 .....18 B1
Duchess Rd BS8 .....18 A1
Duchess Way BS16 .....19 D6
Ducie Rd
  Bristol, Redfield BS5 .....9 B7
  Bristol, Staple Hill BS16 .....20 E5
Ducie St GL1 .....118 F7
Duck St GL12 .....52 C5
Duckmoor Rd BS3 .....8 A3
Duckworth Ct GL14 .....130 D5
Dudbridge Hill GL5 .....99 F6
Dudbridge Mdw GL5 .....98 F5
Dudbridge Rd GL5 .....98 F5
Duderstadt Cl GL5 .....98 F8
Dudley Cl 4 E4
Dudley Cnr GL7 .....151 C5
Dudley Ct BS30 .....10 D4
Dudley Farm GL7 .....151 C5
Dudley Gr BS7 .....19 A8
Dudley Rd WR11 .....188 C7
Duffield's La NP25 .....154 C5
Dugar Wlk BS6 .....18 C4
Dugdale Rd GL7 .....190 C5
Duglynch La GL4 .....183 E1
Duke of Beaufort Ct
  GL1 .....118 D5
Duke Of York Rd GL16 .....154 C7
Duke St GL52 .....133 F1
Dukeries The GL1 .....196 A3
Dukes Field GL14 .....143 F8
Dukes Way GL20 .....192 D1
Dulverton Pl GL50 .....187 B7
Dulverton Rd BS7 .....18 D4
Dumaine Ave BS34 .....29 E5
Dumbleton Gr GL51 .....129 B6
Dunalley Par GL50 .....133 D3
Dunalley Prim Sch
  GL50 .....133 E3
Dunalley St GL50 .....193 B4
Dunbar Cl GL11 .....132 D4
Duncombe La BS15 .....20 B2
Duncombe Rd BS15 .....20 B2
Duncroft Rd GL3 .....127 F1
Dundas Cl BS10 .....27 E2
Dundonald Rd BS6 .....18 B3
Dundridge Gdns BS15 .....10 A6
Dundridge La BS15 .....10 A6
Dundry CE Prim Sch BS41 .....1 D2
Dundry Cl BS15 .....10 D6
Dundry La BS41 .....1 C3
Dundry View BS4 .....9 A1
Dunford Rd BS3 .....8 D3
Dunkeld Ave BS34 .....28 F2
Dunkerry Rd BS3 .....8 D3
Dunlin Cl GL2 .....117 D3
Dunmail Prim Sch BS10 .....28 C2
Dunmail Rd BS10 .....28 C2
Dunmore St BS2 .....8 F4
Dunns Copse BS18 .....178 F8
Dunromin La SN14 .....24 B5
Dunsmore Gn GL19 .....181 B3
Dunstall Ho GL56 .....187 A3
Dunster Glen GL3 .....128 D4
Dunster Cl
  Cheltenham GL51 .....132 D3
  Gloucester GL4 .....118 B1
Dunster Gdns Bristol BS30 .....11 B2
Dunster Gr GL51 .....132 D3
Dunster Rd Bristol BS4 .....2 F8
  Keynsham BS31 .....132 D3
Dunstone GL4 .....164 D5
Durand Cl GL12 .....127 C6
Durand Rd GL12 .....68 A7
Durban Rd BS34 .....28 F8
Durbin Wlk BS5 .....9 A8
Durley Ct GL11 .....179 C1
Durdham Pk BS6 .....18 A3
Durham Cl BS11 .....130 A5
Durham Gr BS31 .....4 D4
Durham Rd Bristol GL52 .....67 A2
  Charfield GL12 .....67 A3
  Gloucester GL4 .....119 C8
Durleigh Cl BS13 .....2 A7
Durley Hill BS31 .....4 C7
Durley La BS31 .....4 D7
Durn's Rd GL12 .....68 C7
Durncourt Cotts GL7 .....151 C5
Durnford Ave BS3 .....8 A4
Durnford St BS3 .....8 A4

Dursley CE Prim Sch
GL11 ....80 C8
Dursley Cl BS37 ....43 E1
Dursley Cl GL11 ....88 A1
Dursley Rd Bristol BS11 ..16 E5
Dursley Rd Bristol GL11 ...87 E3
Slimbridge GL2 ....95 F3
Durville Rd BS13 ....2 B6
Durweston Wlk BS14 .....3 C8
Dutton Cl BS14 ....3 D6
Dutton Leys GL54 ....168 A1
Dutton Rd BS14 ....3 D6
Dutton Wlk BS14 ....3 D6
Duttons La GL17 ....163 F3
Dye House Rd GL12 ....67 F5
Dyer St 190 D4
Dyer's La
Chipping Campden GL55 .198 B7
Yate BS37 ....43 A4
Dyers Cl BS13 ....2 C4
Dyke House La GL18 .....179 F4
Dylan Thomas Ct **4**
BS30 ....11 A5
Dynevor St GL11 ....118 F7
Dynevor Terr GL7 ....152 D4
Dyrham BS16 ....30 C1
Dyrham Cl
Bristol, Henleaze BS9 ....18 D6
Bristol, Kingswood BS15 ..10 F8
Thornbury BS35 ....64 C3
Dyrham Par SN14 ....29 C4
Dyrham Park* SN14 .....23 F5
Dyrham Rd BS15 ....10 F8

E

Eagar Ho GL53 ....131 B4
Eagle Cl GL6 ....148 B6
Eagle Cres BS16 ....22 C5
Eagle Dr BS34 ....28 E8
Eagle Mill Cl GL5 ....99 D5
Eagle Rd BS4 ....9 D2
Eagle Way GL4 ....119 C5
Eagles Wood Bsns Pk
BS32 ....40 C3
Eagly Hill GL7 ....107 C5
Eardisland Rd GL4 .....118 E2
Earl Russell Way BS5 .....9 B7
Earl St BS1 ....195 A4
Earls Cnr SN16 ....141 F4
Earlsmead BS16 ....19 E4
Earlstone Cl BS30 ......11 A4
Earlstone Cres BS30 .....11 A4
Early Way BS7 ....18 E8
Earthcott Rd BS35 ......51 F1
Easedale Cl BS10 ....28 D2
East Allcourt GL7 ......153 E2
East Approach Dr GL52 .133 F4
East Court Mews GL52 ..131 C5
East Croft BS9 ....18 C7
East Ct BS3 ....7 F3
East Dr GL51 ....43 F2
East Dundry La BS41 ....2 A1
East Dundry Rd BS13,BS14 .2 F2
East End GL54 ....131 C5
East End Flats GL53 ....131 C5
East End Rd GL52,GL53 .131 C5
East Gable GL52 ....188 B3
East Gr BS6 ....18 F1
East Hill BS9 ....18 E7
East Link GL17 ....164 D5
East Par BS9 ....17 C6
East Park Dr BS5 ....9 C2
East Pk
Bristol, Lower Easton BS5 ..9 C2
Bristol, Rose Green BS5 ....9 C2
East Priory Cl BS9 ......18 A7
East Ridge Dr BS13 .....18 B2
East Shrubbery **3** BS6 .18 B2
East St Avonmouth BS11 ..26 A1
Bristol, Bedminster BS3 ....8 A4
Bristol, St Pauls BS2 ....195 C4
Moreton-in-M GL56 .....187 A3
St Briavels GL15 ....146 F7
Tewkesbury GL20 ....192 C4
East View Bristol BS16 ..20 F6
Newnham GL14 ....156 F7
East Wlk BS37 ....43 E1
Eastbourne Rd **3** BS5 ...9 D8
Eastbourne Terr GL7 ...152 E3
Eastbrook Rd GL4 ......119 C8
Eastbury Cl BS35 ....64 C1
Eastbury Rd Bristol BS16 ..20 A4
Eastbury Rd GL5 ....64 C1
Eastcote Pk BS14 ....54 B8
Eastcott Way GL3 ......128 A6
Eastern Ave
Gloucester GL4 ....119 B8
Mitcheldean GL17 ......164 D5
Eastern Way GL14 ......156 C6
Eastfield
Ashton Keynes SN6 .....142 F5
Bristol BS9 ....18 B7
Eastfield Dr BS37 ....43 E4
Eastfield Rd
Bristol, Eastfield BS9 ....18 B7
Bristol, Montpelier BS6 ..18 D2
Bristol, Westbury on Trym
BS9 ....18 A8
Minchinhampton GL6 ...148 A3
Eastfield Terr BS9 .....18 B6
Eastgate Ctr BS5 ....19 83
Eastgate Office Ctr BS5 ..19 83

Eastgate St GL1 ....196 B2
Eastholm Lawns GL3 ...128 C5
Eastington Prim Sch
GL10 ....97 A8
Eastington Rd GL54 ...168 A1
Eastington Trad Est
GL10 ....100 F1
Eastlake Cl BS7 ....19 87
Eastland Ave BS35 ......64 C2
Eastland Rd BS35 ....64 C2
Eastleach CE Prim Sch
GL7 ....153 D8
Eastleigh Cl BS16 ......20 C6
Eastleigh Rd
Bristol, Brentry BS10 ....28 D1
Bristol, Staple Hill BS16 ..20 C6
Eastley Cl GL12 ....67 F7
Eastlyn Rd BS13 ....2 88
Eastmead Ct BS9 ....17 E4
Eastmead La BS9 ....17 E4
Eastnor Castle* HR8 ..179 B7
Eastnor CE Prim Sch
HR8 ....179 88
Eastnor Ho **14** GL51 ..132 E2
Easton Bsns Ctr BS5 ....3 A3
Easton Bsns Ctr BS5 ....9 88
Easton CE Prim Sch BS5 ..9 A8
Easton Hill Rd BS35 ....64 D1
Easton Rd Bristol BS5 ...9 88
Pill BS20 ....16 C4
Easton Sq SN16 ....58 D1
Easton Town SN16 ......58 D1
Easton Way BS5 ....9 A8
Eastover Cl BS9 ....18 A8
Eastrop SN6 ....145 D3
Eastrop Cty Inf Sch
SN6 ....145 D3
Eastview Terr SN6 .....145 D3
Eastville GL4 ....119 88
Eastwood Cres BS4 ......9 F3
Eastwood Rd Bristol BS4 ..9 F3
Harrow Hill GL17 ......164 83
Eaton Cl
Bristol, Fishponds BS16 ..20 84
Bristol, Stockwood BS14 ..3 E5
Eaton Cres BS8 ....194 A4
Eaton Gr BS13 ....193 82
Eaton St **3** BS3 ....8 C3
Ebenezer La **3** BS9 ..18 C7
Ebenezer St BS5 ....9 D7
Ebley Ind Pk GL5 ....98 B6
Ebley Rd GL10 ....98 B6
Ebor Rd GL2 ....127 C1
Ebrington GL55 ....189 D3
Ebrington Cl GL11 .....189 D3
Eccleston Ho **1** BS5 ..9 B6
Echo La GL11 ....87 82
Eclipse Ct BS16 ....20 C4
Eclipse Office Pk BS16 ..20 C4
Eddys La GL17 ....163 E3
Eden Gr BS7 ....29 A1
Eden's Hill GL18 ....171 D6
Edencroft SN6 ....145 D4
Edendale App GL51 ....129 C8
Edendale Rd GL51 .....132 C1
Edenwall Cl GL15 ......155 85
Edenwall Rd GL16 .....155 85
Edge End Rd **11** GL16 ..155 86
Edge Hills Cl GL14 ....191 D5
Edge Hills Rd GL14 ....191 D5
Edge La GL6 ....103 C8
Edge Rd GL6 ....103 E8
Edgecombe Rd BS10 ....28 A1
Edgecorner La SN14 ...36 A3
Edgecume Rd BS6 ......18 D2
Edgefield Cl BS14 ....2 F3
Edgefield Rd BS14 ....2 F3
Edgeware Rd
Bristol, Southville BS3 ....8 C4
Bristol, Staple Hill BS16 ..20 D4
Edgewood Cl
Bristol, Hengrove BS14 ....3 C8
Bristol, Longwell Green
BS30 ....11 A3
Edgeworth BS37 ....32 C6
Edgeworth Cl
Cirencester GL7 ....190 82
5 Gloucester GL4 ....119 C5
Edinburgh Pl **1**
Cheltenham GL51 ......132 E2
3 Coleford GL16 .....155 85
Edinburgh Rd BS31 .....4 E4
Edington Gr BS10 ......28 A2
Edmond Rd NP16 ....61 88
Edmund Cl BS16 ....20 D6
Edmund St BS34 ....28 A7
Edna Ave BS4 ....9 E3
Edward Bird Ho **7** BS7 .19 B6
Edward Ct BS31 ....4 F4
Edward Pl GL20 ....192 D1
Edward Rd
Bristol, Arno's Vale BS4 ....9 E3
Bristol, Kingswood BS15 ..10 E8
Edward St
Bristol, Eastville BS5 ....19 D2
Bristol, Redfield BS5 ......9 C7
Cheltenham GL52 ......193 B1
Edward Wilson Ho **2**
GL51 ....132 C3
Edwards Cl
Joy's Green GL17 ....163 D3
Poulton GL7 ....151 E3
Edwards Ct **10** BS16 ..20 F6
Edwards' Coll GL17 ....142 F8
Edwin Short Cl BS30 ....5 E8
Egbey Par GL1 ....196 B4
Effingham Rd BS6 ......18 E2
Egerton Brow BS7 ......18 D3

Egerton Rd BS7 ....18 D4
Eggshill La BS37 ....43 D1
Eglin Croft BS13 ....2 84
Egypt Rd GL6 ....91 84
Eighth Ave
Bristol, Filton BS7 ....29 87
Bristol, Hengrove BS14 ....3 A7
Eirene Terr BS20 ....16 D4
Elberton BS35 ....11 A8
Elberton Rd Bristol BS9 ..17 87
Elberton BS35 ....49 F5
Elbridge Ho **3** BS2 ..195 C3
Elbury Ave BS15 ....10 C8
Elderberry Mews GL3 ..127 F6
Elderberry Wlk BS10 ...28 C3
Eldersfield Cl
Quedgeley GL2 ....117 E2
Winchcombe GL54 .....174 A8
Eldersfield Lawn CE Sch
GL19 ....180 F1
Elderwood Dr BS13 .....11 A3
Elderwood Rd BS14 .....3 87
Elderwood Way GL4 ...118 C2
Eldon Ave GL52 ....134 A1
Eldon Rd GL52 ....133 F1
Eldon Terr BS3 ....183 F1
Eldon Way BS4 ....9 C5
Eldonwall Trad Est BS4 ...9 C5
Eldorado Cres GL50 ....133 81
Eldorado Rd GL50 .....133 81
Eldred Cl BS9 ....17 D5
Eleventh Ave BS7 ....29 87
Elf Mdw GL7 ....151 F4
Elfin Rd BS16 ....20 45
Elgar Cl Bristol BS4 .....2 D6
Ledbury HR8 ....178 E8
Elgar Ho GL51 ....132 E2
Elgin Ave BS7 ....28 F1
Elgin Hall GL10 ....97 F7
Elgin Rd BS16 ....18 82
Eliot Cl Bristol BS7 .....29 A1
Gloucester GL2 ....118 C4
Elizabeth Cl BS35 ......51 D8
Elizabeth Cres BS34 ....29 E4
Elizabeth Gdns
Meysey Hampton GL2 ..152 83
5 Tetbury GL8 ....140 84
Elizabeth Ho BS20 .....16 D4
Elizabeth Way
Bristol BS16 ....21 83
Siddington GL7 ....152 B2
Elizabeths Mews **12** BS4 ..9 F6
Elkstone Wlk BS30 .....11 C2
Ellacombe Rd BS30 ....10 F2
Ellan Hay Rd BS34 .....30 A6
Ellbridge Cl BS9 ....17 A5
Ellenborough Ho BS8 ..194 A2
Ellenborough Rd GL52 ..138 A2
Ellendene Dr GL20 ....182 E4
Ellenor Dr GL20 ....183 E4
Ellencroft Rd
Kingswood GL12 ....67 F8
Wotton-u-E GL12 ....68 A8
Ellesmere BS35 ....51 C8
Ellesmere Cl GL3 ......119 F8
Ellesmere Gr GL50 ....130 86
Ellesmere Rd
1 Bristol, Hengrove BS4 ..9 D1
1 Bristol, Kingswood BS15 ..10 D8
Ellfield Cl BS13 ....1 F6
Ellicks Cl BS32 ....40 E2
Ellicott Rd BS7 ....18 F4
Ellingham Cl GL52 ....133 E3
Ellinghurst Cl BS10 ....28 A2
Elliott Ave BS16 ....30 C1
Elliott Pl BS51 ....129 F7
Elliott Rd BS7 ....190 E1
Ellis Ave BS13 ....2 A8
Ellison Cl GL4 ....120 A6
Ellison Rd GL51 ....132 E2
Elliston La BS6 ....18 C2
Elliston Rd BS6 ....18 C2
Elsbridge Cl BS31 ....5 85
Elsbridge Ho Norton
Radstock GL18 ....5 85
Ellsworth Rd BS10 .....27 F2
Ellwood Prim Sch
Ellwood GL16 ....155 83
Sling GL16 ....155 83
Ellwood Rd GL16 ......155 83
Ellyott Ct **5** BS16 .....19 E3
Elm Cl Bristol BS34 .....29 D7
Cheltenham GL51 ....3 D4
Chipping Sodbury BS37 ..44 A1
King's Stanley GL10 ....98 A4
Prestbury GL52 ....134 A5
Tutshill NP16 ....73 A2

Elm Rd continued
Stroud GL5 ....98 E8
Tutshill NP16 ....73 A2
Elm Side GL2 ....173 83
Elm St GL51 ....133 84
Elm Terr GL5 ....98 D6
Elm Tree Ave BS16 .....21 A2
Elm View GL7 ....142 C6
Elm Wood BS37 ....32 E8
Elmbridge Inf Sch GL2 ..127 C2
Elmbridge Jun Sch GL2 ..127 C3
Elmbridge Rd GL2 .....127 C3
Elmbury Dr GL20 ......192 F5
ElmCroft Cres BS7 .....19 A4
Elmdale NP16 ....73 E3
Elmdale Cres BS35 .....64 C1
Elmdale Gdns **2** BS16 ..20 A4
Elmdale Rd Bristol BS8 ..194 A3
Bristol, Bedminster BS3 ...8 82
Elmdean GL14 ....191 C5
Elmfield Bristol BS15 ...10 B8
Cheltenham GL50 ......193 A3
Elmfield Ave GL51 .....133 C4
Elmfield Cl BS15 ....10 E6
Elmfield Jun Sch GL51 ..133 C4
Elmfield Rd Bristol BS9 ..18 A8
Cheltenham GL51 ......133 C4
Elmfield Sch for Deaf
Children BS10 ....18 88
Elmgrove Ave **10** BS5 ..9 88
Elmgrove Dr BS37 ......43 F2
Elmgrove Pk GL52 .....109 E2
Elmgrove Pk W GL52 ..109 D7
Elmgrove Rd
Bristol, Fishponds BS16 ..19 E3
Bristol, Redland BS6 ....18 D1
Gloucester GL3 ....120 A6
Elmgrove Rd E GL52 ...109 E2
Elmgrove Rd W GL12 ..109 D7
Elmhirst Gdns BS37 ....44 A2
Elmhurst Ave BS5 ....19 D3
Elming Down Cl BS32 ..29 D6
Elmira Rd GL4 ....118 F4
Elmlea Ave BS9 ....17 F5
Elmlea Jun & Inf Schs
BS9 ....17 F5
Elmlea Rd GL10 ....98 D6
Elmleaze GL2 ....127 D3
Elmleigh Ave BS16 .....21 85
Elmleigh Cl BS16 ......21 85
Elmleigh Rd BS16 .....21 85
Elmley Rd WR11 ....183 D8
Elmore Bristol BS15 ....10 B8
Yate BS37 ....32 D8
Elmore La E GL2 ......117 F3
Elmore La W GL2 ......117 D2
Elmore Rd
Bristol, Horfield BS7 ....19 A6
Bristol, Patchway BS34 ..39 F1
Elms Gr BS34 ....40 81
Elms Rd GL10 ....97 E8
Elms The
Bristol, Frenchay BS16 ..30 C1
Bristol, Henbury BS10 ...27 F2
Highworth SN6 ....145 C3
Elmsdale Rd **14** BS8 ..178 E8
Elmtree Cl BS15 ....20 D1
Elmtree Cotts GL12 ....68 D3
Elmtree Dr BS13 ....1 A5
Elmtree Way GL15 ......20 D1
Elmvil Rd GL20 ....182 84
Elphick Rd GL7 ....190 88
Elsbert Dr BS13 ....1 E6
Elstree Rd BS5 ....19 E1
Elstub La GL11 ....87 E5
Eltham Lawn **5** GL50 ..130 88
Elton Ho **2** Bristol BS2 ..195 C3
Huntley GL19 ....165 D7
Elton La BS7 ....18 E1
Elton Rd Bristol BS8 ...194 C3
Bristol, Bishopston BS7 ..18 D2
Bristol, Kingswood BS15 ..20 C1
Elton GL14 ....157 A8
Cheltenham GL14 .....156 D8
Elton St BS2 ....195 C4
Elvard Cl BS13 ....2 A4
Elvard Rd BS13 ....2 A4
Elvaston Rd BS3 ....8 E3
Elwell La BS40,BS41 ....11 A1
Ely Gr BS9 ....17 87
Embassy Rd BS5 ....19 E1
Embassy Wlk BS5 ......19 E1
Embleton Prim Sch BS10 ..28 C2
Embleton Rd BS10 .....28 C2
Embrook Cls GL4 ......177 C4
Emerald Cl GL4 ....118 C3
Emerson Green Prim Sch
BS16 ....21 87
Emerson La BS16 ......21 86
Emersons Green La BS16 ..21 B6
Emersons Way BS16 ...21 C7
Emery Rd BS4 ....9 F1
Emet Gr BS16 ....21 86
Emet La BS16 ....21 86
Emlyn Rd BS5 ....19 C1
Emma-Chris Way BS34 ..29 C2
Emmanuel Cr BS8 .....194 A4
Emmanuel Gdns GL3 ..130 C6
Emmerson La GL4 .....149 A4
Emmett Wood BS14 ....3 A3
Emperor Cl **7** GL51 ..132 D2
Empire Cres BS15 ......10 E4
Empire Way BS15 ......118 C5
Emra Cl BS5 ....19 F1
Enborne Cl GL4 ....118 83
Enfield Rd BS16 ....20 A3
Enfield Villas GL51 ....133 F5
Engine Common La BS37 ..43 C5

England's Cres BS36 ....
English Bicknor CE Prim S
GL16 ....
Englishcombe Rd BS13 ..
Ennerdale Ave GL2 ....
Ennerdale Rd Bristol BS10 ..
Cheltenham GL51 ....
Enterprise Way GL11 ....
Epney Cl BS34 ....
Epney Rd GL4 ....
Epsom Cl BS16 ....
Epworth Rd BS10 ....
Equinox BS32 ....
Erin Pk GL5 ....
Erin Wlk BS4 ....
Ermin Pk GL3 ....
Ermin Pl GL7 ....
Ermin St
Broad Blunsdon SN26 ...
Brockworth GL3 ....
Ermin Way GL3 ....
Ermine Par GL3 ....
Ermine Way BS11 ......
Erminster Dr GL2 ......
Ermleet Rd **3** BS6 ....
Ernest Barker Cl **14** BS5 ..
Ernestville Rd BS16 ....
Eros Cl GL5 ....
Errington GL56 ....
Ervine Terr BS2 ....
Eskdale BS10 ....
Esland Pl GL7 ....
Essery Rd BS5 ....
Essex Ave GL51 ....
Essex Cl GL3 ....
Essex Pl GL54 ....
Esson Rd BS15 ....
Estate Rd GL14 ....
Estcote Rd GL7 ....
Estcourt Cl GL11 ......
Estcourt Gdns BS16 ...
Estcourt La GL11 ......
Estcourt Rd GL11 ......
Estoril BS37 ....
Estune Wlk BS41 ......
Etheldene Rd GL5 .....
Etheridge Pl GL1 ......
Etloe Rd BS6 ....
Eton Rd BS4 ....
Ettington Ct GL51 .....
Ettricke Dr BS16 ......
Eugene Flats **7** BS2 ..
Eugene St
Bristol, Kingsdown BS2 ..
Bristol, St Pauls BS2,BS5 ..
Evans Cl BS4 ....
Evans Rd BS6 ....
Eve Rd BS5 ....
Evelyn Cl GL53 ....
Evelyn Ct GL54 ....
Evelyn Rd BS10 ....
Evening Post Rdbt The
BS2 ....
Evenlode Ave GL52 ...
Evenlode Gdns
Bristol BS11 ....
Moreton-in-M GL56 ...
Evenlode Rd
Gloucester GL4 ....
Moreton-in-M GL56 ...
Evenlode Way BS31 ...
Evercreech Rd BS14 ..
Everest Ave BS16 ....
Everest Cl GL6 ....
Everest Rd Bristol BS16 ..
Cheltenham GL53 .....
Evergreen Ind Pk GL7 ..
Everlands GL11 ......
Everside Cl GL11 ....
Everside La GL11 ....
Everyman Theatre The
GL50 ....
Evesham Rd
Bishop's Cleeve GL52 ..
Cheltenham GL50,GL52 ..
Greet GL54 ....
Stow-on-t-W GL54 ....
Evington Ct **7** GL51 ..
Evington Rd **8** GL51 ..
Evens Rd GL52 ....
Evlyn Rd GL51 ....
Exchange Ave BS1 ...
Exeter Bldgs BS6 ....
Exeter Rd BS3 ....
Exley Cl BS30 ....
Exmoor St BS3 ....
Exmouth Cl GL53 ....
Exmouth Rd BS4 ....
Exmouth St GL53 ....
Exploratory (Science Ctr)
The* BS1 ....
Exton Cl BS14 ....
Eyer's La BS2 ....
Eyford Cotts GL54 ....
Eynon Cl GL53 ....

F

Faber Gr BS13 ....
Fabian Dr BS34 ......
Factory Rd BS36 .....
Failand Cres BS9 ....
Failand La BS20 ......
Failand Wlk BS9 .....
Fair Furlong BS13 ....
Fair Furlong Prim Sch
BS13 ....
Fair Lawn BS30 ......

Foxwell Dr GL3 .....120 A8
Foye Ho BS8 .....7 E6
Fraley Rd BS9 .....18 E5
Frampton Cotterell CE Sch BS36 .....31 A8
Frampton Cotts GL20 .....183 E3
Frampton Cres BS16 .....20 C4
Frampton Ct
  8 Bristol, Longwell Green BS30 .....66 C5
  Bristol, Redfield BS5 .....9 D7
Frampton Dr WR12 .....188 B2
Frampton End Rd BS37 .....42 D2
Frampton Mews GL1 .....129 B7
Frampton on Severn CE Prim Sch GL2 .....100 A6
Frampton Rd GL1 .....118 D7
France La GL9 .....63 C3
Frances Ct GL52 .....133 F1
Frances Greeves Ct BS10 .....27 F1
Francis Ct BS5 .....9 F7
Francis Ho BS2 .....195 A4
Francis Pl BS30 .....10 F4
Francis Rd
  Bristol, Bedminster BS3 .....8 C2
  Bristol, Westbury on Trym BS10 .....18 C8
Francis St BS13 .....193 B1
Francis Way BS30 .....11 D6
Francombe Gd BS10 .....18 E6
Francombe Ho BS10 .....195 A1
Frank Brookes Rd GL51 .....133 A4
Franklin Ct BS1 .....195 B1
Franklyn Ct
  6 Bristol BS16 .....19 E3
  8 Cheltenham GL51 .....132 E2
Franklyn La BS2 .....18 F1
Franklyn St BS2 .....18 F1
Fraser St BS3 .....8 D3
Frayne Rd BS3 .....8 A4
Frazier's Folly GL7 .....150 E2
Freame Cl GL6 .....148 B6
Frederick Pl BS8 .....194 B3
Frederick Thomas Rd GL11 .....87 E4
Fredrick St BS4 .....9 A4
Free Tank BS2 .....195 C2
Freeland Bldgs 1 BS5 .....7 C2
Freeland Pl BS8 .....7 F6
Freeling Ho BS1 .....195 B1
Freemans Cl GL20 .....181 F8
Freemantle Gdns BS5 .....19 C3
Freemantle Ho BS2 .....195 A4
Freemantle Rd BS5 .....19 C3
Freeminers Way GL14 .....191 D5
Freestone Rd BS2 .....9 A6
Freezinghill La BS30 .....13 B4
Fremantle La 6 BS6 .....18 D1
Fremantle Rd BS6 .....18 D1
Fremantle Sq BS6 .....18 D1
French Cl NP25 .....154 C4
Frenchay CE Prim Sch BS16 .....20 B7
Frenchay Cl BS16 .....20 B7
Frenchay Hill BS16 .....20 C8
Frenchay Hospl BS16 .....20 C7
Frenchay Park Rd BS16 .....19 F6
Frenchay Rd BS16 .....20 B8
Freshland Way BS15 .....10 B8
Fretherne Rd GL4 .....118 D3
Frewin Cl GL51 .....132 D2
Frewins La GL18 .....165 D3
Friars Cl GL51 .....130 B5
Friars Ho 4 BS37 .....27 F1
Friary Grange Pk BS36 .....30 E6
Friary Rd Bristol BS7 .....18 D4
  Gloucester GL4 .....119 C6
Friday St Arlingham GL2 .....137 C6
  Minchinhampton GL6 .....148 A3
  Painswick GL6 .....103 F8
Fridays Ham La BS6 .....143 A5
Friendly Row BS20 .....16 C5
Friendship Rd BS4 .....9 B2
Friezewood Rd BS3 .....8 A4
Fripp Cl BS5 .....9 B6
Frith La GL12 .....53 F3
Frith The GL6 .....148 B6
Frithwood Cl GL6 .....148 B6
Frithwood Cl GL6 .....148 B6
Frithwood Pk GL6 .....148 B6
Frobisher Mews GL3 .....127 F8
Frobisher Rd BS3 .....8 A3
Frocester Hill GL10 .....89 C8
Frog Furlong La GL2, GL3 .....117 A7
Frog La Bristol BS1 .....194 C2
  Coalpit Heath BS36 .....31 E7
  Frocester GL10 .....97 A3
  Huntley GL19 .....165 D6
  Ilmington CV36 .....189 F6
  North Nibley GL11 .....79 C5
Frogmarsh La GL5 .....91 A8
Frogmore Rd GL19 .....165 D6
Frogmore St BS1 .....194 C2
Frome Ave GL5 .....99 A6
Frome Ct BS35 .....51 C8
Frome Gdns GL5 .....98 E6
Frome Glen BS36 .....30 E4
Frome Park Rd GL5 .....99 A6
Frome Rd 1 BS16 .....19 E5
Frome Rd BS37 .....44 C1
Frome St BS2 .....195 C4
Frome Valley Rd BS16 .....19 F8
Frome View BS36 .....31 B7

Frome Villas BS16 .....20 C7
Frome Way BS36 .....30 E5
Fromebank Jun Sch BS37 .....43 D3
Fromeside Cl GL6 .....99 C6
Fromeside Dr BS16 .....98 D6
Fromeside Pk BS16 .....20 B7
Front La SN26 .....144 D2
Front St Ilmington CV36 .....189 C6
  Nympsfield GL10 .....89 E5
Froomshaw Rd BS16 .....20 A7
Frowens La HR9 .....170 B4
Fry Ct 2 BS3 .....8 C4
Fry's Cl BS16 .....19 D4
Fry's Hill BS4 .....9 D2
Frys Hill BS15 .....20 E2
Fulbrook Cl GL51 .....132 D5
Fulford Rd BS13 .....2 C5
Fulford Specl Sch BS13 .....2 B5
Fulford Wlk BS13 .....2 B5
Fuller's La GL19 .....172 B4
Fullers Ave 6 SN6 .....143 E4
Fullers Ct GL1 .....196 A3
Fulmar Cl BS35 .....64 D2
Furber Ct BS5 .....10 B6
Furber Rd BS5 .....10 B6
Furber Ridge BS5 .....10 B6
Furber Vale BS5 .....10 B6
Furlong Cl 3 GL6 .....148 B8
Furlong Ho HR8 .....178 E7
Furlong La GL52 .....137 F3
Furlong Rd GL1 .....118 E7
Furlong The BS6 .....18 C8
Furlongs The GL12 .....69 C3
Furnace Cl GL44 .....191 C4
Furnace La GL18 .....171 A5
Furnace Valley GL15 .....156 D1
Furnwood BS5 .....10 A6
Furze Croft GL2 .....109 F7
Furze La BS5 .....189 B4
Furze Rd BS16 .....20 C3
Furze The GL4 .....119 A4
Furzewood Rd BS15 .....10 F8
Fussell Ct BS15 .....10 F8
Fylton Croft BS14 .....3 B7

G

Gabb La GL19 .....173 B7
Gable Cl BS35 .....39 A2
Gable Cotts GL47 .....152 E3
Gable Point GL52 .....138 B3
Gable Rd 7 BS5 .....19 A1
Gable Row GL20 .....182 F8
Gadshill Dr BS34 .....36 C7
Gadshill Rd BS5 .....19 C2
Gadwell Rd GL20 .....192 E3
Gages Cl BS15 .....10 F7
Gages Rd BS15 .....10 F7
Gainsborough Dr GL4 .....118 C2
Gainsborough Rd BS31 .....4 F5
Gainsborough Sq BS7 .....19 B7
Gainsborough Terr GL55 .....189 A1
Gales Ct GL7 .....153 E2
Gallagher Ret Pk GL51 .....132 F5
Galleries The BS1 .....195 B3
Galley Orch SN6 .....143 F4
Gallivan Cl BS34 .....29 B8
Gallops La GL52 .....134 D4
Gallops The GL2 .....118 B6
Galway Rd BS4 .....8 E1
Gambier Parry Gdns GL2 .....126 F4
Gambles La GL52 .....138 C4
Gambril La GL3 .....65 F5
Ganborough Rd GL56 .....176 D8
Gander Cl BS13 .....2 B5
Gander La Teddington GL20 .....183 A4
  Tewkesbury GL20 .....192 C3
Gannaway La GL20 .....192 F5
Gannet Cl BS13 .....120 C5
Gannicox Rd GL5 .....99 A7
Ganzell La GL11 .....80 C7
Garamond Ct BS1 .....195 B1
Garden City Way NP16 .....60 E8
Garden Cl Bristol BS9 .....17 C5
  Cirencester GL7 .....190 C3
  Dumbleton WR11 .....183 F7
  Mickleton GL55 .....189 A6
Garden Cotts GL19 .....172 A2
Garden Ct BS8 .....194 A4
Garden Rd GL53 .....131 B4
Garden Suburb GL11 .....88 A1
Garden The GL5 .....99 A2
Garden Way GL2 .....127 B4
Gardeners Way King's Stanley GL10 .....98 A4
  Newent GL18 .....170 F4
Gardens Wlk BS41 .....27 B1
Gardenia Gr GL51 .....129 F5
Gardens The
  Bristol, Frenchay BS16 .....29 F1
  4 Bristol, Upper Sounwell BS16 .....30 A2
  Cheltenham GL50 .....133 E4
  Monmouth NP25 .....154 A8
Gardiner Cl GL6 .....148 C6
Gardiners Ct BS13 .....128 A6
Gardner Ave BS10 .....27 E3
Gardner Ct GL7 .....190 D3
Gardner's La GL11 .....133 C4
Garfield Rd BS5 .....10 C5
Garland Ct GL7 .....190 C3
Garlands Rd GL15 .....147 D3
Garlandstone Wlk GL11 .....118 C6

Garnalls Rd GL4 .....119 C4
Garnet St BS3 .....8 B3
Garnett Pl BS16 .....37 C7
Garns Ct GL11 .....89 B1
Garren Heve HR9 .....162 C7
Garrett Dr BS32 .....29 D7
Garretts The GL7 .....152 D4
Garton Ho BS16 .....20 D5
Garvey Ct NP16 .....60 F4
Garvey Ho BS15 .....9 C7
Gas La Bristol BS2 .....9 A6
  Cricklade SN6 .....143 F4
Gasferry Rd BS1 .....194 B1
Gaskins The BS7 .....19 A5
Gassons Rd GL7 .....153 E3
Gassons Way GL7 .....153 E2
Gaston Ave BS31 .....4 F6
Gaston La SN16 .....58 D1
Gastons The BS11 .....17 A8
Gastrells Com Prim Sch GL5 .....99 A4
Gasworks La GL54 .....168 F7
Gasworks Villas GL2 .....118 B4
Gatcombe Cl GL52 .....137 E3
Gatcombe Dr BS34 .....29 E4
Gatcombe Rd BS13 .....2 B5
Gatehouse Ave BS13 .....2 A5
Gatehouse Cl BS13 .....2 A5
Gatehouse Ct BS13 .....2 B5
Gatehouse Sh Ctr BS13 .....2 B5
Gatehouse Way BS13 .....2 A5
Gatesby Mead BS34 .....29 E5
Gathorne Rd BS3 .....8 B4
Gatmeres Rd GL4 .....119 C3
Gatton Rd BS2 .....19 A1
Gatton Way GL3 .....127 F1
Gatwick Cl GL14 .....157 E8
Gaunt's La BS1 .....194 C2
Gaunts Earthcott La BS32 .....41 B5
Gaunts Rd BS37 .....33 B8
Gay Elms Prim Sch BS13 .....2 A4
Gay Elms Rd BS13 .....2 A4
Gayner Rd BS7 .....29 D1
Gays Rd BS15 .....10 B4
Gaythorne Cres BS34 .....43 D2
Gaywood Ho 7 BS2 .....8 B3
Gazelle Rd GL2 .....117 F2
Gazzard Cl BS36 .....30 E7
Gazzard Rd BS36 .....30 E7
Gee Moors BS15 .....10 E5
Gefle Ct BS1 .....194 B1
General Hospl Sch of Nursing GL53 .....193 C1
Genista Way 3 BS15 .....129 F5
Geoffrey Cl BS13 .....1 F5
George & Dragon La 11 BS5 .....9 D7
George Ct 12 Bristol BS6 .....8 D5
  Painswick GL6 .....103 F8
George Dowty Dr GL20 .....182 B1
George La Chipping Campden GL55 .....189 A1
  Cinderford GL14 .....164 E1
  Marshfield SN14 .....24 E1
George Naisey Ho 3 GL52 .....134 A3
George Pl 4 GL16 .....155 A7
George Rd GL15 .....156 A2
George Readings Way GL51 .....133 A4
George St Bisley GL6 .....105 A1
  Bristol BS5 .....9 C8
  Gloucester GL1 .....196 C3
  Nailsworth GL6 .....91 C4
  6 Stroud GL5 .....8 E5
George Whitefield Cl GL4 .....119 C4
George Whitefield Ct GL4 .....119 C4
Georgia Rd GL7 .....152 E2
Georgian Cl GL4 .....119 E3
Georgian House (Mus)* BS1 .....194 C2
Gerald Rd BS3 .....8 B3
Geralds Way GL4 .....148 C6
Gere Cl GL4 .....118 D2
Gerrard Cl BS4 .....2 D7
Gerrish Ave
  Bristol, Redfield BS5 .....9 C8
  Bristol, Staple Hill BS16 .....20 F5
Gervase Rd GL4 .....174 A8
Gibbet La BS14 .....3 D1
Gibbs Ct 14 BS5 .....9 D7
Gibbsfold Rd BS13 .....2 C4
Gibraltar Way NP16 .....61 B4
Gibson Cl GL5 .....99 F7
Gibson Ct GL7 .....190 D3
Gibson Rd Bristol BS6 .....18 D1
  Innsworth GL3 .....127 E7
Giddyngap La GL5 .....91 C5
Giffard Ho BS34 .....29 D6
Giffard Way GL53 .....130 D4
Gifford Cl Gloucester GL2 .....127 D5
  Rangeworthy BS37 .....43 A8
Gifford Ct BS34 .....29 D2
Gifford Rd BS10 .....27 F4
Giffords Pl BS13 .....2 A7
Gilbert Hill GL13 .....85 E4
Gilbert Rd
  Bristol, Kingswood BS15 .....20 D1
  Bristol, Redfield BS5 .....9 C8
  Gloucester GL2 .....127 C5
Gilberts La GL4 .....110 F6
Gilda Cl BS14 .....3 C5
Gilda Cres BS14 .....3 B6
Gilda Par BS14 .....3 C5

Gilda Sq W BS14 .....3 B5
Gilder Rd GL52 .....138 A2
Gilders Paddock GL52 .....134 A2
Giles Ave SN6 .....143 E3
Giles Cox GL2 .....109 F8
Gill Ave BS16 .....20 B6
Gillard Cl BS15 .....10 D8
Gillard Rd BS15 .....10 D8
Gillebank Cl BS14 .....3 D5
Gillett Cl GL54 .....139 F5
Gillingham Hill 6 BS15 .....10 B5
Gillingstool BS35 .....51 C8
Gillingstool Prim Sch BS35 .....51 B8
Gilray Ct GL19 .....19 B6
Gilpin Ave GL3 .....127 F1
Gilpin Cl BS15 .....20 F1
Gilroy Cl BS30 .....11 B3
Gilslake Ave BS10 .....28 B3
Gilton Ho BS4 .....9 E2
Gimson Cl GL4 .....118 D2
Gingell's Gn 4 BS5 .....10 A8
Gipsy La Chalford GL6 .....148 D4
  Leonard Stanley GL10 .....97 E2
Gipsy Patch La BS34 .....36 C7
Glades The BS5 .....19 E2
Gladfield Gdns GL5 .....98 E6
Gladfield Sq GL5 .....98 E6
Gladiator Cl GL3 .....120 C5
Gladstone Dr BS16 .....20 F2
Gladstone La BS36 .....31 C7
Gladstone Rd
  Bristol, Hengrove BS14 .....3 B6
  Bristol, Kingswood BS15 .....20 D1
  Charlton Kings GL53 .....131 A5
  Gloucester GL1 .....118 D6
Gladstone St
  Bristol, Bedminster BS3 .....8 B3
  Bristol, Kingswood BS16 .....20 D3
  4 Bristol, Redfield BS5 .....9 D7
Glaisdale Rd BS16 .....20 A5
Glamorgan Rd GL51 .....129 E6
Glanville Gdns BS15 .....10 E7
Glass House La BS2 .....9 B5
Glastonbury Cl BS30 .....100 C1
Glanum Works Trad Est GL1 .....118 F7
Glebe Cl Cirencester GL7 .....190 B8
  Long Ashton BS41 .....27 C2
  Mitcheldean GL17 .....164 D6
  Newent GL18 .....170 F5
  11 Stow-on-t-W GL54 .....176 F4
Glebe Farm Ct GL51 .....129 F5
Glebe Field BS32 .....40 A5
Glebe Ind Sch GL18 .....170 F5
Glebe La GL7 .....141 F8
Glebe Orch HR8 .....178 A3
Glebe Pl SN6 .....145 D3
Glebe Rd Bristol BS8 .....7 F6
  Long Ashton BS41 .....27 C2
  Minchinhampton GL6 .....148 A3
  Newent GL18 .....170 F4
  Prestbury GL52 .....134 B4
Glebe The Pilning BS35 .....38 C7
  Sapperton GL7 .....149 B6
Glebe View GL7 .....158 C4
Glebe Way GL18 .....170 F5
Glebe Wlk BS31 .....4 C4
Glebeland Dr GL20 .....182 C7
Glebelands GL11 .....87 F3
Glebelands Rd BS34 .....29 A3
Gledemoor Dr BS16 .....31 D7
Glen Brook BS9 .....17 C4
Glen Cl GL10 .....97 F8
Glen Dr BS9 .....17 D5
Glen Hospl The BS8 .....7 F8
Glen La BS4 .....9 D2
Glen Park Cres BS5 .....99 A4
Glen Park Gdns BS5 .....10 A8
Glen The
  Bristol, Eastville BS5 .....19 C2
  Bristol, St George BS5 .....10 A8
Glena Ave BS4 .....9 B2
Glenarm Rd BS4 .....9 E2
Glenarm Wlk BS4 .....9 E2
Glenavon Rd BS9 .....17 C4
Glenburn Rd BS15 .....20 B1
Glencairn Ave GL4 .....118 C1
Glencairn Ct GL50 .....130 A8
Glencairn Park Rd GL50 .....130 A8
Glencarn Pl BS16 .....155 A7
Glencoe La GL17 .....164 D4
Glencoyne Sq BS10 .....28 C2
Glendale 16 Bristol BS8 .....7 F6
  Bristol, Downend BS16 .....20 E8
  Bristol, Hillfields BS16 .....20 D5
Glendare St BS5 .....9 C6
Glendevon Rd BS14 .....3 A3
Glendower Cl GL3 .....127 F8
Gleneagles BS37 .....43 E1
Gleneagles Dr BS10 .....27 D3
Gleneagles Rd BS30 .....11 B6
Glenfall BS37 .....32 D7
Glenfall Com Prim Sch GL52 .....131 C6
Glenfall St GL52 .....131 B6
Glenfall Way GL52 .....131 B6
Glenfrome Prim Sch BS5 .....19 B4
Glenfrome Rd BS2 .....19 B3
Glenlea Gr GL51 .....129 F5
Glenroy Ave BS15 .....20 B1
Glensanda Ct GL50 .....193 B2

Glenside Cl BS16 20
Glenside Pk 3 BS16 20
Glentworth Rd
  Bristol BS8 19
  Bristol, Redland BS6 19
Glenview Rd BS4 9
Glenwood BS16 20
Glenwood Dr BS30 11
Glenwood Rd BS10 18
Glevum Cl GL2 12
Glevum Ct 11 GL51 12
Glevum Way GL4 11
Glevum Works (Trad Est) GL1 118
Gloster Ades Rd WR11 18
Gloster Ave GL51 12
Gloucester Bsns Pk GL3 12
Gloucester Cl BS34 2
Gloucester Coll of Arts & Tech
  Cheltenham GL50 13
  Gloucester GL1 19
Gloucester Cotts 5 GL50 19
Gloucester Docks The* GL1 19
Gloucester Ho 11 BS2 19
Gloucester House Mews GL12 19
Gloucester La
  16 Bristol BS2 19
  Mickleton GL55 18
Gloucester Mus & Art Gal* GL1 19
Gloucester Pl BS8 19
Gloucester Prison Mus* GL1 19
Gloucester Rd
  Almondsbury BS32,BS35 29
  Andoversford GL54 16
  Avonmouth BS11 17
  Bristol, Bishopston BS7 18
  Bristol, Patchway BS34 28
  Bristol, Staple Hill BS16 20
  Cheltenham GL51 13
  Coleford GL16 15
  Mitcheldean GL17 16
  Painswick GL6 10
  Staunton GL19 16
  Stone GL13 8
  Tadwick BA1 25
  Tewkesbury GL20 19
  Tutshill NP16 6
  Upleadon GL18 17
Gloucester Rd N BS7,BS34 28
Gloucester Road Prim Sch BS7 18
Gloucester Row
  6 Bristol BS8 7
  Kingswood GL12 6
Gloucester Royal Hospl GL1 19
Gloucester Rugby Football Gd GL1 11
Gloucester Ski Ctr* GL4 11
Gloucester St
  5 Bristol, Clifton BS8 7
  6 Bristol, St Pauls BS2 19
  Cirencester GL7 19
  Newent GL18 17
  Painswick GL6 10
  2 Stroud GL5 8
  Winchcombe GL54 13
  Wooton-u-E GL12 12
Gloucester Sta GL1 19
Gloucester & Warwickshire Rly* GL54 13
Gloucestershire Airport GL51 12
Gloucestershire Coll of Art & Tech GL1 19
Gloucestershire Constabulary HQ GL51 12
Gloucestershire Royal Hospl GL1 19
Glyn Terr GL51 13
Glyn Vale BS3 8
Glynbridge Gdns GL51 12
Glyndthorpe Gr 12 GL51 12
Glynfield Rise GL6 9
Glynrosa Rd GL53 13
Goddard Way GL4 11
Godfrey Cl GL51 12
Godfrey Ct 7 BS30 6
Godwin Dr 14 GL52 12
Godwin Rd GL54 13
Goffenton Dr BS16 2
Goldcrest Ct 6 GL10 9
Goldcrest Rd BS37 2
Golden Cl GL4 14
Golden Farm Rd GL7 19
Golden Hare WR11 18
Golden Hill BS6 1
Golden La GL12 5
Golden Miller Rd GL50 13
Golden Vale GL3 12
Golden Valley
  Brimscombe GL5 10
  Newent GL18 17
Golden Valley La BS30 1
Goldfinch Way BS16 2
Goldfoot Cl BS14 3

ey Ave
l, Clifton BS8 ....194 A2
l, Warmley BS30 ....11 C7
ey Ct 7 BS16 ....19 E3
ey Rd BS8 ....194 A2
borough Cl GL4 ....119 B6
bury Wlk BS11 ....27 A1
ham Rd GL51 ....132 E2
lub La
ham La
ith BS3 ....120 C5
ourd BS31 ....5 E2
ourse La BS34 ....28 F3
ourse Rd GL6 ....111 F2
Cl WR11 ....188 C7
Ct BS30 ....11 C4
Neighbours La
.........................154 B7
Shepherd Cl BS7 ....18 C4
ere Rd BS9 ....17 D3
hind St BS5 ....9 A8
e La GL20 ....182 A7
mans Terr 6 GL2 ....152 E4
noor Cres GL3 ....128 A6
neston Rd BS16 ....20 A3
ich Castle* HR9 ....163 A6
ich CE Prim Sch
.........................163 A6
rich Hill GL19 ....172 D4
ridge Ave GL3 ....9 AB
ridge Trad Est
.........................118 A4
ring Hill GL11 ....27 A1
win Ct GL1 ....118 E7
win Rd BS4 ....2 F4
wood Gdns BS16 ....96 F1
vere Sq GL1 ....196 C1
e St BS4 ....9 A3
e Acre BS32 ....29 F6
e Gn Bristol BS30 ....21 C1
BS3 ....43 E3
e Green Way BS37 ....43 E4
e La GL14 ....157 F8
eacre Ct GL7 ....190 C6
eacre La GL7 ....190 C6
egreen BS36 ....31 C8
eland Cl BS14 ....2 F3
elands SN16 ....141 B3
hill La GL54 ....183 E1
no Gdns BS20 ....16 B4
e an Ave BS5 ....19 E1
e Cn Cl Bristol BS5 .....19 E1
am GL2 ....125 E5
e Green Rd BS34 ....194 B3
istol, St Pauls BS2 ......18 F1
c, Whitehall BS5 ....19 D1
enham GL53 ....130 C5
en Terr GL5 ....99 D7
Rd BS3 ....8 A3
e Marsh Rd BS3 ....8 A2
ant BS11 ....27 C2
nds Rd BS37 ....44 C3
ngton Cl BS14 ....3 A7
e Bglws GL16 ....155 A6
e Cl
on-on-t-W GL4 ....169 A7
cester GL4 ....189 E8
he Cover Rd BS35 ....38 A7
e Hill BS16 ....20 C3
a La Bristol BS8 ....194 B2
Ashton BS30,SN14 ....13 D7
e Rd GL51 ....132 E2
c Mdw GL54 ....169 A6
e La GL54 ....169 A7
ey Gdns HR9 ....170 B4
ey Goff's Prim Sch
.........................170 B5

Graham Ct GL20 ....192 D5
Graham Gdns GL2 ....127 B3
Graham Pl GL51 ....132 D3
Graham Rd
  4 Bristol, Bedminster BS3 ..8 C3
  Bristol, Downend BS16 ......20 F6
  Bristol, Upper Easton
  ....19 B1
Grahamstown Rd NP16 ....61 B8
Grahamstown Rd NP16 ....61 B8
Grainger Cl BS14 ....2 F3
Grampian Cl BS30 ....11 C4
Granary Cotts GL56 ....186 C7
Granbrook La GL55 ....189 B7
Granby Hill BS8 ....7 F6
Grandmother's Rock La
  ....12 D2
Grange Ave, Hanham BS15 ...10 D5
  Bristol, Little Stoke BS34 ..29 C6
Grange Cl Bristol BS32 .....40 C2
  Highworth SN6 ....145 D3
  Minchinhampton GL6 ....91 F6
Grange Cl N BS9 ....18 B6
Grange Com Sch BS30 ......11 B7
Grange Court La GL19 ......165 D6
Grange Court Rd
  Bishop's Cleeve GL52 ......137 F3
  Bristol BS16 ....20 C6
Grange Jun Sch GL4 ....118 C3
Grange La GL8 ....140 B3
Grange Pk
  Bristol, Frenchay BS16 .....20 C8
  Bristol, Westbury on Trym
  BS9 ....18 B6
  Whitchurch HR9 ....162 D4
Grange Rd, Bishopsworth BS13 ..2 A5
  Bristol, Clifton BS8 ......194 A3
  Gloucester GL4 ....118 D1
  Northway GL2 ....182 C5
  Saltford BS31 ....5 C3
  St Arvans NP16 ....72 A6
Grange The BS37 ....19 D7
  Cheltenham GL51 ....129 B6
  Gloucester GL2 ....127 B2
  Moreton-in-M GL56 ....187 A3
Grange View GL5 ....93 A8
Grange Wlk GL53 ....131 B5
Grangefield Sch GL2 ....137 E3
Grangeville BS37 ....43 D3
Grangewood Cl BS16 ....20 C6
Granley Cl GL51 ....129 F8
Granley Dr GL51 ....129 F8
Granley Gdns GL51 ....129 F8
Granley Rd GL51 ....129 F8
Granna La GL52 ....138 D8
Granny's La GL15 ....10 E6
Gransmoor Grange GL3 .....127 A7
Grantham Rd BS15 ....20 C1
Grantham La BS15 ....10 C8
Grantley Cres GL7 ....190 C3
Grantson Cl BS4 ....9 F2
Granville Chapel 8 BS8 ....7 F5
Granville Cl BS15 ....10 B3
Granville St Bristol BS5 ..9 C6
  Cheltenham GL50 ....133 C3
  Gloucester GL1 ....118 D6
  Monmouth NP25 ....154 A7
Granville Terr NP16 ......73 A1
Grasby Cl GL4 ....119 F7
Grasmere Cl BS10 ....18 A8
Grasmere Rd
  Cheltenham GL51 ....129 F7
  Gloucester GL2 ....127 C4
Grasmere Way NP16 ......61 A4
Grass Meers Dr BS14 .....3 A4
Grassington Dr BS37 .....33 A8
Grassmere Gdns BS30 ....11 D6
Gratitude Rd BS5 ....19 C1
Gratton Rd GL50 ....193 A1
Gratton St GL50 ....193 B1
Gravel Hill Rd BS37 ....44 A5
Gravel Pit Cotts GL52 ..131 C6
Gravel Pit La GL32 ......134 C5
Gravel Pits Cl GL20 ....182 A5
Gravel Terr GL53 ....131 B5
Gravel Wlk
  Southam GL52 ....134 C8
  Tewkesbury GL20 ....192 D5
Graveney Cl BS4 ....9 D1
Graveney Rd GL54 ......168 A1
Gravney Ct GL51 ....132 E4
Gray Cl Bristol BS10 ....27 E2
  Innsworth GL3 ....127 F7
Gray Rd GL7 ....151 A2
Gray's La 18 GL36 .....187 A3
Grayle Rd BS10 ....28 A2
Grayling Cl 8 GL4 ......119 E5
Grayling Ho BS9 ....17 F7
Grayston Cl GL20 ......192 E6
Great Ann St BS2 ......195 C3
Great Brockeridge BS9 ..17 F6
Great Dowles BS30 .....11 A4
Great George St
  Bristol, Brandon Hill BS1 ..194 C2
  Bristol, St Pauls BS2 ....195 C4
Great Gr GL4 ....119 D7

Great Hayles Rd BS14 ....3 A6
Great Leaze BS30 ......11 A4
Great Mdw BS34 ....30 A6
Great Meadow Rd BS32 ..29 F6
Great Norwood St GL50 ..193 B1
Great Park Rd BS32 ....40 C3
Great Rissington Prim Sch
  GL54 ....169 D4
Great Rose La SN26 ....144 D3
Great Stoke BS34 .....30 A5
Great Stoke Way
  Bristol, Great Stoke BS34 ..30 A5
  Bristol, Harry Stoke BS34 ..29 D3
Great Western BS34 ....29 D3
Great Western La BS5 ..9 C6
Great Western Rd
  Cheltenham GL50 ......193 A5
  Gloucester GL1 ....196 C3
  Sharpness GL13 ......93 B1
Great Western Terr
  GL50 ....193 A4
Great Weston Bsns Pk
  BS37 ....43 B3
Great Witcombe Roman
  Villa* GL3 ....120 F1
Greatfield Dr GL53 ....130 F5
Greatfield La GL53 ....129 E5
Greatfield Park Prim Sch
  GL51 ....129 F5
Grebe Cl GL4 ....119 C5
Grebe Sq GL54 ....169 D6
Green Acre Bream GL15 ..147 D8
  Brockworth GL3 ......120 E5
Green Bank GL3 ....120 E4
Green Barn GL3 ....120 C6
Green Int Sch GL14 ...118 C2
Green Cl Bristol BS7 ..18 B4
  Brockworth GL3 ......120 E4
  Honeybourne WR11 ...188 C6
  Uley GL11 ....89 C2
Green Colley Ct HR9 ..163 B6
Green Cotts BS35 .....20 A1
Green Dell Cl BS10 ...27 D3
Green Dragon Rd BS36 ..30 D5
Green Gdns BS37 .....33 C8
Green La Avonmouth BS11 ..26 B1
  Chedworth GL54 ......159 B6
  Churchdown GL3 ......128 C4
  Easter Compton BS35 ..38 C1
  Evenlode GL56 ....177 C7
  Gloucester GL2 ......120 A6
  Hardwicke GL2 ....190 E6
  Little Witcombe GL3 ..121 C3
  Marshfield SN14 .....14 E8
  Naunton Valence GL2 ..101 A6
  Naunton WR8 ....180 A7
  Rangeworthy BS37,GL12 ..53 B2
  Severn Beach BS35 ...38 B8
  Sherston SN16 ....58 C1
Green Lane Bsns Pk
  BS37 ....43 B3
Green Lane Cl GL54 ...168 F8
Green Meadow Bank
  GL52 ....137 E3
Green Pastures NP25 ..154 A3
Green Pippin Cl GL52 ..127 C2
Green Side BS16 .....21 A6
Green St Bristol BS3 ..8 F4
  Brockworth GL3 ......120 E4
  Bushley Gn GL20 .....181 B5
  Chepstow NP16 ......60 E8
  Dursley GL11 ....88 C5
Green The
  Bishop's Cleeve GL52 ..137 F3
  Bristol, New Cheltenham
  BS15 ....20 E2
  Bristol, Stoke Gifford BS34 ..29 E4
  1 Broadway WR12 ....185 B8
  Chepstow NP16 ......60 85
  Chipping Campden GL55 ..189 A1
  Cirencester GL7 .....190 C5
  Cromhall GL12 ....53 B8
  Fairford GL7 ....152 D4
  Frampton on Severn GL2 ..157 F2
  Great Wolford CV36 ..168 C7
  Highworth SN6 ......145 C3
  6 Moreton-in-M GL56 ..187 A3
  Newnham GL14 ......156 F6
  Oaksey SN16 ....141 F4
  Olveston BS35 ....39 D8
  Pill BS20 ....16 D4
  Tetbury GL8 ....140 C4
  Uckington GL51 .....132 D6
  Uley GL11 ....89 C2
Green Way GL4 ....119 F6
Green's Green SN6 ...9 A1
Green's Ct GL4 ......169 C4
Greenacre Rd BS14 ..3 A3
Greenacres Bristol BS9 ..17 E7
  Twyning GL20 ....181 B8
Greenacres Park Homes
  BS36 ....31 E5
Greenacres Pk GL7 ...152 A3
Greenaways GL18 ....170 F5
Greenbank Ave BS5 ..19 C1
Greenbank Ave W BS5 ..19 C1
Greenbank Cl GL17 ..164 B3
Greenbank Rd
  Bristol, Hanham BS15 ..10 D5
  Bristol, Lower Easton BS5 ..19 D2
  Bristol, Southville BS3 ..8 A4
  Greenbank View BS5 ..19 D2
Greenbanks NP25 ....146 B7
Greendale Rd
  Bristol, Bedminster BS3 ..8 E2

Greendale Rd continued
  Bristol, Redland BS6 ..18 B3
Greenditch Ave BS13 ..2 C5
Greenditch St BS35 ..49 D1
Greendown BS5 ......10 A7
Greenfield Ave BS10 ..18 D6
Greenfield Cl GL17 ..163 D3
Greenfield Rd
  Bristol BS10 ....28 D1
  Coleford GL16 ......155 A6
  Joy's Green GL17 ...163 D3
Greenhaven 5 BS5 ..19 C1
Greenhill BS35 ......51 A4
Greenhill Cl GL14 ...191 E5
Greenhill Down BS35 ..51 A5
Greenhill Dr GL2 ....118 A3
Greenhill Flats GL5 ..99 E3
Greenhill Gdns GL15 ..51 A5
Greenhill Par 8 BS35 ..51 A5
Greenhill Rd GL53 ...130 F3
Greenhills Cl GL53 ..130 E5
Greenhills Rd GL53 ..130 F5
Greenhouse La GL6 ..104 A7
Greenings The GL51 ..129 F5
Greenlands Way BS10 ..27 F4
Greenlands Way BS10 ..27 F4
Greenleaze BS4 ......9 81
Greenleaze Ave BS16 ..30 D1
Greenleaze Cl BS16 ..30 D1
Greenmore Rd BS4 ..9 B2
Greenore GL15 ......10 C7
Greenpark Rd BS10 ..28 E1
Greenridge Cl BS13 ..1 E4
Greens Cl BS10 .....27 D3
Greensplott Rd BS11 ..26 E7
Greenstreet GL10 ...97 F8
Greenview Bristol BS30 ..11 A2
  Quenington GL7 .....152 D7
Greenway GL2 ....138 B3
Greenway Bush La BS3 ..8 B4
Greenway Cl GL51 ...129 D1
Greenway Dr BS10 ..18 D8
Greenway Ho 10 BS6 ..18 B2
Greenway La
  Charlton Kings GL52 ..131 C7
  Cold Ashton SN14 ....13 D5
  Gretton GL54 ....183 F1
  Llandogo NP25 ......146 A3
  Shurdington GL51 ....129 D1
Greenway Pk BS10 ..18 D8
Greenway Rd
  Blockley GL56 ....186 C6
  Bristol BS6 ....18 B2
Greenway The GL4 ..191 C3
Greenway The BS16 ..20 C3
Greenways
  Aylburton GL15 ......147 F5
  Bristol BS23 ....21 A1
  Wynchcombe GL54 ...178 A8
Greenways Dr GL16 ..155 B4
Greenways Rd BS37 ..43 E3
Greenwood Cl Bristol BS7 ..18 E7
  Gloucester GL2 ......120 B6
Greenwood Dr BS35 ..50 F4
Greenwood Rd BS4 ..9 A1
Greet Rd GL54 ......174 A8
Gregory Ct BS30 ....11 A6
Grenadier Cl GL4 ...119 F6
Grenadier Rd GL51 ..132 E4
Grenville Cl Bristol BS5 ..9 F4
Grenville Ct BS8 ....127 D5
  Innsworth GL3 ......127 F8
Grenville Pl 7 BS1 ..7 F5
Grenville Rd BS6 ....18 E3
Gresham Cl 5 GL51 ..132 E2
Gretton Prim Sch GL54 ..183 E1
Gretton Rd
  Gotherington GL52 ..134 C8
  Winchcombe GL54 ...178 A8
Greve Ct 6 BS30 ....10 F4
Grevel Cl GL55 ......189 A2
Grevel La GL55 .....132 C4
Greville Cl GL2 .....126 E4
Greville Ct GL51 ....129 F8
Greville Rd BS3 .....8 B4
Greville St BS3 .....8 C4
Greyfriars 6 BS1 ....196 B2
Greyfriars Church*
  GL1 ....196 B3
Greyfriars Wlk GL7 ..190 B2
Greyhound Gdns GL2 ..127 D5
Grigg Cres GL20 ....192 E3
Greylands Rd BS13 ..1 F7
Greyrick Ct GL54 ...189 A6
Greys 10 GL51 .....146 B6
Greystoke Ave BS10 ..18 A8
Greystoke Gdns BS10 ..18 A8
Greystone Lodge GL53 ..120 B7
Greystones Rd GL54 ..30 E1
Greystones La GL54 ..169 A7
Grierson Cl GL2 ....120 B6
Griffin Cl GL51 .....177 A4
Griffin Ct GL54 .....177 A4
Griffith Mill Est GL51 ..99 D4
Griffiths Ave GL51 ..132 F1
Griffon Cl GL2 .....117 F3
Griggfield Wlk BS14 ..3 A7
Griggs Cl GL4 ......119 D5
Grimsbury Park Specl Sch
  BS30 ....11 B7
Grimsbury Rd BS15 ..11 A7

Grimwade Cl GL51 ..132 F1
Grindell Rd BS5 .....9 D7
Grinfield Ave BS13 ..2 C4
Grinfield Cl BS13 ...2 C4
Grinfield Ct BS13 ...2 C4
Grisedale Cl GL2 ....127 D5
Grist Mill Cl GL51 ..132 D5
Grittleton Rd BS7 ...18 E8
Grosvenor Ct 2 BS6 ..18 B1
Grosvenor Ho GL1 ..196 B3
Grosvenor Pl S GL52 ..193 C3
Grosvenor Rd Bristol BS2 ..18 F1
  Gloucester GL2 ......127 B2
  Stonehouse GL10 ....101 F1
Grosvenor St GL52 ..193 C3
Grosvenor Terr GL52 ..193 C3
Grove Ave Bristol BS1 ..195 A1
  Bristol, Coombe Dingle BS9 ..17 C7
  8 Bristol, Fishponds BS16 ..19 F4
  Honeybourne WR11 ..188 C2
Grove Bank BS16 ....30 C1
Grove Cotts GL5 ....98 F8
Grove Ct
  4 Coleford GL16 ....155 A6
  Gloucester GL4 .....127 D1
Grove Ct BS9 ....17 E5
Grove End Cotts GL2 ..109 A7
Grove Gdns GL8 ....140 B5
Grove Hill SN6 ......145 C4
Grove Ind Est The BS34 ..29 B8
Grove La Cirencester GL7 ..190 D5
  Hinton SN14 ....13 C6
  Lydney GL15 ....92 B6
  Whitminster GL2 ....100 F4
Grove Leaze BS11 ...16 D6
Grove Orch SN6 ....145 C4
Grove Park Ave BS4 ..9 D2
Grove Park Rd Bristol BS4 ..9 D2
  Stroud GL5 ....99 C8
Grove Pk
  Bristol, Brislington BS4 ..9 D2
  Bristol, Redland BS6 ..18 A2
  Bristol, Coombe Dingle BS9 ..17 D8
  Bristol, Fishponds BS16 ..19 F4
  Bristol, Redland BS6 ..18 A2
  Innsworth GL3 ......127 F6
  Whitecroft GL15 ....155 F7
Grove St
  Cheltenham GL50 ....193 A4
  Gloucester GL1 .....196 C1
Grove The Avening GL6 ..68 B7
  Bristol BS1 ....195 A1
  Bristol, Oldland BS30 ..11 A4
  Bristol, Patchway BS34 ..29 B7
  Bristol, Battledown
  GL52 ....134 A1
  Cheltenham, Lansdown
  GL50 ....130 B8
  Chelworth SN16 ....141 E5
  Moreton-in-M GL56 ..187 B3
  Rangeworthy BS37 ..43 A8
  Selsley GL5 ....98 E4
  Sheepscombe GL6 ..94 D6
Grove View Bristol BS16 ..19 E6
  Greet GL54 ....184 A1
Grovefield Cl GL19 ..180 D4
Grovefield Way GL51 ..129 B7
Grovelands Cl GL4 ..127 E1
Grovelands Cl 1 GL53 ..131 B6
Groves The BS13 ....2 D4
Gryphons The 15 GL52 ..133 F2
Guardian Cl GL3 ...130 F6
Gubbrook Ave GL1 ..9 F4
Guernsey Ave BS4 ..9 F4
Guest Ave BS16 .....21 B7
Guestlos Cotts GL50 ..133 C5
Guggle La 7 GL54 ..168 A1
Guild Ct BS1 ....195 B2
Guildford Rd BS4 ...9 E6
Guildings Way GL10 ..98 A4
Guinea La Bristol BS16 ..20 A4
  Bristol BS16 ....20 A5
Guinea St Bristol BS1 ..195 A1
Gloucester GL1 .....196 C4
Guise Ave GL3 .....120 F2
Guise Cl GL2 ....109 F8
Gullimores Gdns BS13 ..2 B4
Gullivers Pl BS37 ..33 A8
Gullon Wlk BS13 ...1 F5
Gullons Cl BS13 ...2 A6
Gully La GL35 ......64 E7
Gully The BS36 ....30 F7
Gulleybrook La 3 BS5 ..9 B6
Gumstool Hill 10 GL8 ..140 C4
Gunhouse La GL5 ..99 D5
Gunnings Rd GL15 ..10 C6
Gunter's Hill BS5 ..10 A8
Gupshill Cl GL20 ..192 C2
Gurney Ave GL4 ...118 D2
Gustav Holst Birthplace
  Mus* GL52 ....193 C4
Guthrie Rd BS8 ....194 A4
Gwentlands Cl NP16 ..60 E7
Gwernant Rd GL51 ..129 F6
Gwilliam St BS3 ...8 D3
Gwinnett Ct GL51 ..129 E2
Gwyn Cl NP16 .....72 F1
Gwyn St BS2 ......18 E1
Gyde Rd GL20 .....111 F1
Gypsy La Gorsley GL18 ..170 C3

Gypsy La *continued*
Marshfield SN14 ....**14** F7

H

Haberdashers Sch for Girls
NP25 ....**154** A8
Haberdashers' Agincourt
Sch NP25 ....**154** A8
Haberfield Hill BS8 ......**16** E2
Haberfield Ho **1** BS8 ....**7** F6
Hacket Hill BS35 ....**51** F8
Hacket La BS35 ....**51** F8
Hadfield Cl Gl19 ....**172** A8
Hadley Cl BS30 ....**11** B6
Hadley Rd BL11 ....**87** E4
Hadley Rd **20** GL54 .....**154** A8
Hadnock Road Ind Est
NP25 ....**154** A8
Hadow Way GL2 ....**109** F8
Hadrian Cl Bristol BS9 ...**17** C4
Lydney GL15 ....**92** B4
Hadrians Way GL4 ......**119** F7
Hague Ave GL11 ....**87** F4
Haig Cl BS9 ....**17** B7
Hailes Abbey & Mus★
GL54 ....**184** D1
Hailes Green Barns
GL54 ....**174** C8
Hailes Rd GL4 ....**119** D7
Hailes St **20** GL54 ......**174** A7
Hakeburn Rd GL7 ....**190** C5
Halbrow Cres BS16 ......**20** C5
Haldon Cl BS3 ....**8** D1
Hale Cl BS15 ....**10** D4
Hale La GL6 ....**103** F8
Hale's Rd GL52 ....**134** A1
Hales Horn Cl BS32 .....**29** D6
Halfacre Cl BS14 ....**3** A3
Halfacre La BS14 ....**3** B4
Halford Ho GL2 ....**118** C4
Halfway Pitch GL6 ......**103** B4
Halifax Rd BS37 ....**34** D6
Hall End La BS37 ....**53** D2
Hall La
Cold Ashton BA1,SN14 ...**13** E2
Horton BS37 ....**45** E5
Lower Hamswell BA1 .....**13** B3
Hall Rd BS3 ....**130** D4
Hall St BS3 ....**8** C2
Halland Rd GL53 ....**130** D5
Hallards Cl BS11 ....**16** F8
Hallen Cl BS10 ....**27** D3
Hallen Dr BS9 ....**17** C7
Hallen Ind Est BS10 .....**27** A7
Hallen Rd BS10 ....**27** D4
Hallmead Cl GL51 ....**132** D5
Halls Rd BS15 ....**10** D8
Hallsfield SN6 ....**143** E4
Hallwood Dr HR8 ....**178** D8
Halmore La GL13 ....**86** A8
Halsbury Rd BS6 ....**18** B4
Halstock Ave BS16 ......**19** F3
Halston Dr BS2 ....**195** C4
Halswell Gdns BS13 ......**2** B4
Halt End GL3 ....**3** C3
Halwyn Cl BS9 ....**17** D5
Ham Cl GL52 ....**131** C7
Ham Farm La BS16 ......**31** B6
Ham Gn BS20 ....**16** D3
Ham La Bristol BS16 ....**19** E6
Doynton BS30 ....**22** E1
Dundry BS41 ....**1** D3
Kempsford GL7 ....**144** F7
South Cerney GL7 ....**142** F7
Thornbury BS35 ....**63** C7
Ham Mill La GL5 ....**99** E3
Ham Rd Ashleworth GL19 **172** E5
Charlton Kings GL52,GL54 **131** E7
Ham Sq GL52 ....**131** C7
Ham The GL11 ....**89** A6
Hambidge La GL7 ....**153** E3
Hambledon Cl GL7 .....**150** F2
Hamblin Cotts GL53 ....**123** A5
Hambrook La BS34 ......**30** A3
Hambrook Prim Sch
BS16 ....**31** D8
Hambrook St GL52 ......**131** B7
Hambutts Dr GL6 ....**103** E8
Hambutts Mead GL6 ....**103** E8
Hamer St GL1 ....**127** B1
Hamfallow Ct GL13 ......**85** D8
Hamfield La GL13 ....**85** D3
Hamilton Croft GL7 ....**152** A2
Hamilton Ct GL51 ......**132** D3
Hamilton Rd
Bristol, Southville BS3 ....**8** B4
Bristol, Upper Easton BS5 ..**9** B8
Hamilton St GL33 ......**131** A7
Hamlen Cl GL19 ....**165** D6
Hamlet Cl GL11 ....**132** E2
Hammersmith Bottom
GL7 ....**153** B7
Hammersmith Rd BS5 ...**9** D8
Hammett Ct NP25 ......**154** B7
Hammond Cl BS14 ....**9** E1
Hammond Ct GL53 ....**193** C1
Hammond St GL54 .....**168** A1
Hammond Sq BS9 ......**17** E7
Hammond Way
Cirencester GL7 ....**190** C4
Gloucester GL4 ....**127** D1

Hammonds SN6 ....**143** F4
Hampden Cl BS37 ....**43** D4
Hampden Rd BS4 ....**9** B3
Hampden Way GL1 ....**196** B2
Hampen Cotts GL54 ...**167** A7
Hampshire Gdns GL16 ..**155** A5
Hampshire Way BS37 ...**43** F4
Hampstead Rd BS4 .....**9** A5
Hampton Cl Bristol BS30 .**11** A5
Cheltenham GL51 ....**130** A5
Gloucester GL3 ....**120** B7
Hampton Cnr BS11 .....**16** E6
Hampton Ct BS6 ....**18** B1
Hampton Gr GL7 ....**152** A3
Hampton Hill GL8 ......**148** B1
Hampton La **20** BS6 ....**18** B1
Hampton Mews GL15 ...**92** B3
Hampton Pk BS6 ....**18** B1
Hampton Pl GL3 ....**128** A8
Hampton Rd BS6 ....**18** B1
Hampton St Bristol BS15 .**20** D1
Tetbury GL8 ....**140** B4
Hams Rd Keynsham BS31 ..**4** F7
Lydney GL15 ....**92** B3
Hanbury Cl BS15 ....**10** D5
Hanbury Ct BS8 ....**194** A4
Hanbury Ho NP16 ......**60** E8
Hanbury Rd BS8 ....**194** A4
Handel Ave **2** BS5 ......**9** D7
Handel Rd BS31 ....**4** E5
Handford Way BS30 .....**11** B3
Hanford Ct BS14 ....**3** D7
Hang Hill Rd GL15 .....**155** D1
Hangerberry New Rd
GL17 ....**163** D1
Hanham Abbots Jun Sch
BS15 ....**10** C4
Hanham Bsns Pk BS15 ..**10** B5
Hanham Hall Hospl BS15 .**10** D4
Hanham High Sch BS15 ..**10** C4
Hanham Rd BS15 ....**10** D7
Hankerton Rd SN16 ...**142** B1
Hanley La NP16 ....**73** E6
Hanman Rd GL1 ....**118** F7
Hanman Villas GL2 ....**124** C8
Hanna Ct GL50 ....**193** B4
Hannah Boote Ho **8**
GL52 ....**134** A3
Hannah Cres GL7 ......**150** F2
Hannah More Prim Sch
BS1 ....**195** B2
Hannan Cl GL11 ....**87** F7
Hannam Cl GL53 ....**130** E4
Hanover Cl NP16 ....**72** D1
Hanover Ct Bristol BS1 ..**195** B3
Bristol, Filton BS34 ......**29** A3
10 Cheltenham GL51 ..**130** B8
Cirencester GL7 ....**190** D4
Tewkesbury GL20 ......**192** C4
Tutshill NP16 ....**61** A8
Hanover Gdns GL6 ......**91** B4
Hanover Ho Bristol BS2 ...**9** B7
Highworth SN6 ....**145** C3
Hanover Lodge GL5 ......**98** D7
Hanover Pl BS1 ....**194** B1
Hanover St
2 Bristol BS1 ....**195** A2
Bristol, Barton Hill BS5 ....**9** C7
Cheltenham GL50 ......**133** D3
Hanover Way **11** GL2 ...**128** A7
Hanstone Ct GL7 ......**190** B2
Happerton La BS20 .....**16** D2
Harbour Rd GL15 ......**144** B8
Harbour View GL20 ....**192** D5
Harbour Wall BS9 ......**17** B4
Harbury Mews GL51 ....**194** C1
Harbury Rd BS9 ....**18** C7
Harcombe Hill BS36 ....**30** E4
Harcombe Rd BS36 .....**30** D5
Harcourt Ave BS5 ....**10** A6
Harcourt Cl BS31 ....**5** E2
Harcourt Hill BS6 ....**18** C5
Harcourt Rd BS6 ....**18** B3
Harden Rd BS14 ....**3** E5
Hardenhuish Rd BS4 ....**9** D5
Harding Pl BS31 ....**5** B5
Hardings Dr GL11 .....**188** A1
Hardington Dr BS31 .....**5** A2
Hardwick Ave NP16 .....**60** E7
Hardwick Bank Rd GL20 .**182** B5
Hardwick Bldg (Cheltenham
& Gloucester Coll of H Ed)
GL50,GL51 ....**133** C3
Hardwick Cl
Bristol, Brislington BS4 .....**9** E3
Bristol, North Common
BS30 ....**11** D5
Hardwick Hill NP16 .....**60** E8
Hardwick Hill La NP16 ..**60** E8
Hardwick Rd BS20 ......**16** C5
Hardwicke BS37 ....**32** C7
Hardwicke Prim Sch
GL2 ....**109** E6
Hardy Ave BS3 ....**8** A4
Hardy Ct BS30 ....**11** D6
Hardy La BS32 ....**50** A1
Hardy Rd
Bishop's Cleeve GL52 ....**138** A4
Bristol BS3 ....**8** B2
Hare La GL1 ....**196** B3
Harebell Pl GL4 ....**119** E5
Hareclive Prim Sch BS13 ..**2** C4
Hareclive Rd BS13 ....**2** C4
Harefield Cl BS15 ....**10** C2
Harescombe BS37 ....**32** E7
Haresdown Hill GL7 ...**141** C8

Haresfield GL7 ....**190** B8
Haresfield CE Prim Sch
GL10 ....**110** B1
Haresfield Ct GL10 .....**110** A1
Haresfield La GL2,GL10 .**109** F5
Haresfield Lodge GL4 ..**119** B4
Harewood Cl GL4 ......**118** C1
Harewood Ho BS6 ....**18** A3
Harewood Jun & Inf Sch
GL4 ....**118** C1
Harewood Rd BS5 ......**20** A1
Harford Cl BS9 ....**17** C7
Harford Dr BS16 ....**30** C1
Harlech Way BS30 ......**11** B2
Harleston St **1** BS5 ....**9** A8
Harley Ct **8** BS8 ....**7** F6
Harley Mews **8** BS8 .....**7** F7
Harley Pl **4** BS8 ....**7** F7
Harleys Field GL4 ......**119** D7
Harling Ct **12** HR8 .....**178** E8
Harmer Cl BS10 ....**27** F3
Harness Cl GL2 ....**118** B6
Harnham La GL54 ......**166** E2
Harnhill Cl BS13 ....**2** B4
Harold Rd BS15 ....**156** B2
Harolds Way BS15 ......**10** C6
Harp Hill GL52 ....**134** B1
Harper Rd GL5 ....**98** E8
Harpfield Cl GL52 ......**137** F3
Harpfield Rd GL52 .....**137** F2
Harptree Ct **6** BS30 ....**11** A4
Harptree Gr BS3 ....**8** B2
Harptres Way GL17 ....**164** D6
Harrier Way GL20 .....**192** E2
Harrington Ave BS14 ....**3** E6
Harrington Cl BS30 ......**5** E8
Harrington Dr GL51 ....**129** F7
Harrington Gr BS14 .....**3** E6
Harrington Rd BS14 .....**3** E6
Harrington Wlk BS14 ....**3** E6
Harris Barton BS36 .....**31** B7
Harris Cl GL3 ....**128** C5
Harris Ct BS30 ....**10** F4
Harris Gdns GL54 .....**169** D6
Harris Rd SN6 ....**143** A5
Harrison Cl Bristol BS16 ..**21** B6
Newnham GL14 ....**156** F6
Harrison Rd GL1 ......**128** A6
Harrison Way GL15 .....**92** C2
Harrow Rd BS4 ....**9** D3
Harrowdene Rd BS4 .....**9** B3
Harry Stoke Rd BS34 ...**29** E2
Harry Yates Way GL51 .**132** D4
Hart Gn GL4 ....**191** C2
Hart La GL17 ....**163** F4
Hartbury Cl GL51 ......**132** C3
Hartcliffe Rd BS4 ....**2** E8
Hartcliffe Sch BS13 ......**2** E8
Hartcliffe Way BS3,BS4,
BS13 ....**2** F8
Hartcliffe Wlk BS4 ......**2** F8
Hartfield Ave BS6 .....**194** C4
Hartgill Cl BS13 ....**3** C2
Hartington Pk BS6 .....**18** C2
Hartington Rd GL4 ....**118** C6
Hartland Ho BS5 ....**9** C6
Hartland Rd GL1 ......**118** F6
Hartlands **22** GL18 ...**171** A4
Hartlebury Way GL52 .**131** C6
Hartley Cl
Cheltenham GL53 ......**130** F4
Chipping Sodbury BS37 ...**44** C1
Hartley CE Prim Sch
GL19 ....**172** C3
Hartpury Coll
Hartpury GL19 ....**172** A1
Longhope GL17 ....**165** A4
Harts Barn Flower & Craft
Ctr★ GL17 ....**164** E5
Harts Croft BS37 ....**43** F4
Harvard Ave WR11 ....**188** C2
Harvest Cl BS32 ....**40** D1
Harvest Gr BS11 ....**15** D8
Harvest Way GL2 ......**109** F7
Harvesters View GL7 ..**137** D4
Harvey Cl GL2 ....**118** C5
Harvey's La GL54 ......**139** F5
Harwell Cl GL4 ....**118** D1
Harwood Ho **8** BS5 .....**9** B7
Haselbury Gr BS31 ......**5** E2
Hasfield Cl GL2 ....**117** E1
Hasfield Rd GL19 ......**172** C6
Haskins Ct **2** BS30 .....**11** D5
Haslemere Ind Est BS11 ..**26** C2
Haslette Way GL4 ......**129** E5
Hasnett Rd HR8 ....**178** E8
Hassall Dr BS2 ....**9** A7
Hastings Cl BS3 ....**8** B3
Hastings Pl BS30 ....**192** C2
Hastings Rd Bristol BS3 ...**8** C1
Cinderford GL14 ....**191** C4
Hatcher's Cres SN26 ..**144** D1
Hatchet La BS34 ....**29** E4
Hatchet Rd BS34 ....**29** E5
Hatchmere BS35 ....**51** D8
Hatfield Rd GL1 ....**119** A7
Hathaway Cl GL2 ......**118** C4
Hatherley BS37 ....**32** E7
Hatherley Brake GL51 .**129** E7
Hatherley Court Rd
GL51 ....**130** B7
Hatherley Ct GL51 ....**130** B8
Hatherley Gate GL51 ..**130** B8
Hatherley Hall GL51 ..**130** A7
Hatherley Inf Sch GL51 .**130** B8
Hatherley Inf Sch GL1 .**119** A7
Hatherley La GL51 ....**129** D7

Hatherley Rd Bristol BS7 ..**18** E4
Cheltenham GL51 ......**129** F7
Gloucester GL1 ....**119** A7
Hatherley St GL50 .....**130** B7
Hatherop GL7 ....**152** E8
Hatheroop Castle Sch
GL7 ....**152** E8
Hatherop Rd GL7 ......**152** E4
Hathaw Rd BS3 ....**120** B6
Hathway Wlk BS5 ....**9** A8
Hatters' La BS37 ....**44** C1
Hatton Cl GL17 ....**163** D1
Havelock Rd GL3 ......**120** A8
Haven Ave GL10 ....**97** E6
Haven Ct GL17 ....**127** C3
Haven The BS15 ....**20** E1
Haverstock Rd BS4 ......**9** F3
Haviland Ho **7** BS2 ...**195** C3
Haw La BS35 ....**50** B3
Haw Rd GL16 ....**155** C8
Haw St Coaley GL11 ....**80** D4
Wooton-u-E GL12 ....**68** A7
Hawburn Cl BS4 ....**9** E2
Hawcombe Mews **1**
GL51 ....**129** F5
Haweswater Cl BS30 ...**11** D6
Haweswater Rd GL51 ..**129** F6
Hawk Cl **5** Chalford GL6 .**148** C6
Gloucester GL4 ....**119** D5
Hawkesbury Rd GL17 ..**164** D5
Hawker Sq GL54 ....**169** D6
Hawkers Hill GL7 ......**160** A1
Hawkesbury Grange GL9 .**56** A2
Hawkesbury Prim Sch
GL9 ....**55** F3
Hawkesbury Rd
Bristol BS16 ....**19** E3
Hillesley GL12 ....**55** D6
Hawkesley Dr BS34 .....**29** D6
Hawkfield Bsns Pk BS14 ..**2** D5
Hawkfield Cl BS14 ....**2** D5
Hawkfield Rd BS13 ......**2** D5
Hawkfield Way BS14 ....**2** D5
Hawkins Cl BS30 ....**11** C5
Hawkins Cres BS32 ....**29** E8
Hawkins La GL14 ......**157** A7
Hawkins St BS2 ....**195** C3
Hawkley Dr BS32 ....**40** D3
Hawkmoor La BS16 .....**19** E8
Hawkmoth Cl GL20 ...**192** E2
Hawkridge Dr BS16 ....**22** C5
Hawksmoor Cl BS14 ....**3** A5
Hawkswood Rd GL51 .**130** B5
Hawksworth Dr BS15 ..**10** B5
Hawkwell Cotts GL17 .**164** B3
Hawkwood Coll GL6 ...**103** D2
Haworth Cl GL2 ....**117** F2
Hawthorn Ave BS15 ....**10** B6
Hawthorn Cl Bristol BS34 .**28** E7
Charfield GL12 ....**67** A4
Portishead BS20 ....**60** E4
Hawthorn Cres BS35 ...**64** C2
Hawthorn Ct GL15 .....**92** B3
Hawthorn Dr
Innsworth GL3 ....**127** F6
Sling GL16 ....**155** B2
Woodmancote GL52 ....**118** A8
Hawthorn Rd BS11 .....**132** E3
Hawthorn Ridge GL6 ...**90** F5
Hawthorn Rise GL15 ....**98** D8
Hawthorn Way
Bristol BS34 ....**29** E5
Northway GL20 ....**182** C5
Hawthorne Ave GL4 ..**119** C6
Hawthorne Cl BS16 ....**22** C2
Hawthorne Gdns BS16 ..**20** F4
Hawthorne Gr GL18 ...**170** D5
Hawthorne St BS4 ....**9** A3
Hawthornes The
Bristol BS16 ....**20** F4
Cheltenham GL51 .....**129** D6
Hawthorns La BS31 .....**4** E5
Hawthorns Rd GL17 ...**164** B5
Hawthorns The
Bishop's Cleeve GL52 ..**137** E4
Bussage GL6 ....**148** B6
Coalpit Heath BS36 .....**37** F6
Lydney GL15 ....**87** F5
Hay Ct BS20 ....**16** A4
Hay La Ablington GL7 .**159** E1
Horsley GL6 ....**83** A7
Hay Leaze BS37 ....**43** D4
Hay St SN14 ....**8** A3
Hay's Cotts GL53 .....**130** E6
Haycombe BS14 ....**2** F6
Haycroft Cl GL52 ......**137** E4
Haycroft Dr GL4 ......**119** D3
Haycroft La GL13 ....**79** A3
Haycroft Rd Bristol BS34 .**29** A3
Northleach GL54 ......**168** F2
Haydale Gdns GL2 ....**127** C5
Hayden La GL51 ....**132** A3
Hayden Rd GL51 ......**132** B3
Haydock Cl BS16 ....**30** F1
Haydon Cl **12** BS8 ....**129** B9
Haydon Gdns BS7 ......**19** B5
Haydons Cl GL15 .....**189** A2
Haye's La GL9 ....**46** F2
Hayeley Dr BS32 ....**24** D2
Hayes Cl BS2 ....**195** C3
Hayes Ct Bristol BS34 ..**29** A7
Cheltenham GL52 .....**134** A2
Gloucester GL2 ....**126** F6
Hayes La GL7 ....**158** B4
Hayes Rd
Cheltenham GL52 .....**134** A2

Hayes Rd *continued*
Nailsworth GL5 ....**1**
Hayes The
Prestbury GL52 ....**1**
Sedbury NP16 ....**1**
Hayfield SN14 ....**1**
Hayfield Way GL12 ......**1**
Haygarth Cl GL7 ....**1**
Hayhedge La GL6 ......**1**
Haylea Rd GL52 ....**1**
Hayleigh Ho BS13 .....**1**
Haymarket The BS13 ...**1**
Haymarket Wlk **8** BS1 ..**1**
Haymead La GL8 ......**1**
Haymes Dr GL52 ......**1**
Haymes Rd GL52 ......**1**
Haynes Ho **6** BS16 .....**1**
Haynes La BS16 ....**1**
Hays Cl WR12 ....**1**
Haysum's Cl GL55 .....**1**
Hayter Cl BS10 ....**1**
Hay Rd GL16 ....**1**
Haythorne Ct **8** BS16 ..**1**
Haytor Pk BS9 ....**1**
Hayward Cl GL4 ....**1**
Hayward Ind Est **1** BS16 .**2**
Hayward Rd
Bristol, Barton Hill BS5 ...**1**
Bristol, Staple Hill BS16 ...**1**
Hayward's Rd GL52 ....**1**
Haywards La GL52 .....**1**
Haywood Pitch HR9 ...**1**
Hazebrouck Cl GL51 ...**1**
Hazel Ave BS6 ....**1**
Hazel Cl GL2 ....**1**
Hazel Cote Rd BS14 ...**1**
Hazel Cres BS35 ....**1**
Hazel Ct GL4 ....**1**
Hazel Gdns BS35 ......**1**
Hazel Gr BS7 ....**1**
Hazel La Alveston BS35 .**1**
Tockington BS32 ....**1**
Hazel Rd GL17 ....**1**
Hazelbury Dr BS30 ....**1**
Hazelbury Rd BS14 ....**1**
Hazelcroft GL3 ....**1**
Hazeldean Rd GL14 ...**1**
Hazeldene Rd BS34 ....**1**
Hazelgrove BS36 ......**1**
Hazelhurst Bglws HR9 ..**1**
Hazels The GL4 ....**1**
Hazelton Cl GL4 ......**1**
Hazelton Rd BS7 ......**1**
Hazelwood **1** GL10 ...**1**
Hazelwood Ct BS9 ....**1**
Hazelwood Rd BS9 ....**1**
Hazle Cl HR8 ....**1**
Hazlecote La GL6,GL8 ..**1**
Hazledean Rd GL51 ...**1**
Hazlewood Cl GL51 ...**1**
Hazlitt Croft GL51 ....**1**
Headford Ave BS5 .....**1**
Headford Rd BS4 ......**1**
Headington Cl BS15 ...**1**
Headlam Cl GL4 ....**1**
Headland The NP16 ...**1**
Headlands The GL5 ....**1**
Headley Cl BS13 ......**1**
Headley La BS13 ......**1**
Headley Park Ave BS13 ..**1**
Headley Park Prim Sch
BS13 ....**1**
Headley Park Rd BS13 ..**1**
Headley Wlk BS13 ....**1**
Healey Dr SN14 ....**1**
Heapey Cl **8** GL51 ....**1**
Hearne Cl GL53 ....**1**
Hearne Rd GL53 ......**1**
Hearn Mears BS14 ....**1**
Heath Cl BS36 ....**1**
Heath Ct BS16 ....**1**
Heath Gdns Bristol BS16 ..**1**
Cheltenham GL51 ......**1**
Heath House La BS7,BS16 .**1**
Heath House Priory Hospl
BS16 ....**1**
Heath Lo **5** GL52 ....**1**
Heath Rd BS8 ....**1**
Bristol, Downend BS16 ...**1**
Bristol, Eastville BS5 .....**1**
Bristol, Hanham BS15 ....**1**
Heath Ridge BS41 ....**1**
Heath Rise BS30 ......**1**
Heath St Bristol BS5 ...**1**
Monmouth NP25 ......**1**
Heath Wlk BS16 ......**1**
Heathcote Dr BS36 .....**1**
Heathcote La BS36 ....**1**
Heathcote Rd
Bristol, Chester Park BS16 .**1**
Bristol, Staple Hill BS16 ...**1**
Heathcote Wlk BS16 ...**1**
Heathdean Rd GL14 ...**1**
Heather Cl Bristol BS15 ..**1**
Chepstow NP16 ....**1**
Stroud GL5 ....**1**
Heatherdene BS14 ....**1**
Heathfield Cl BS31 ....**1**
Heathfield Cres BS14 ..**1**
Heathfield Rd GL53 ...**10**
Heathfields BS16 .....**2**
Heathville Rd GL1 ....**1**
Heazle Pl GL5 ....**9**
Hebden Cl GL53 ......**10**

Holly Gn BS15 ....21 A1
Holly Gr BS16 ....20 C3
Holly Gr The GL2 ....109 F8
Holly Hill BS37 ....42 E3
Holly Hill Rd BS15 ....20 F1
Holly Ho BS11 ....27 C2
Holly La GL16 ....155 C5
Holly Lodge Cl BS5 ....20 A2
Holly Lodge Rd BS5 ....19 F2
Holly Tree Gdn GL5 ....98 D6
Holly Tree Pl GL11 ....156 B1
Holly Wlk BS31 ....4 D4
Hollybush Cl GL9 ....36 A6
Hollybush La Bristol BS9 .17 E5
  Bristol BS9 ....17 E4
Hollydean GL14 ....191 C5
Hollyguest Rd BS15 ....10 C6
Hollyhill Pk GL14 ....191 B5
Hollyhill Rd GL14 ....191 B5
Hollyhock La GL4 ....103 F8
Hollyleigh Ave BS34 ....34 C4
Hollymead La BS9 ....17 E4
Hollyridge BS14 ....3 C6
Hollywell Rd GL17 ....164 D6
Hollywood La BS10,BS35 ..28 A7
Hollywood Rd BS4 ....9 D2
Holm La BS35 ....49 B2
Holmdale Rd BS34 ....29 C3
Holme Rd GL20 ....192 C5
Holmer Cres GL51 ....129 D6
Holmes Ct BS9 ....18 B5
Holmes Gr BS9 ....18 B5
Holmes Hill Rd BS5 ....9 F8
Holmes St BS5 ....9 F8
Holmesdale Rd BS3 ....8 C1
Holmfield Dr NP25 ....146 B7
Holmleigh Rd GL14 ....118 C3
Holmoak Cl GL20 ....192 C2
Holmoak Rd BS31 ....4 C4
Holmsleigh Par GL4 ......118 C2
Holmwood BS15 ....10 C6
Holmwood Cl
  Gloucester GL4 ....118 C2
  Winterbourne BS36 ....30 D6
Holmwood Dr GL4 ....18 C2
Holmwood Gdns BS9 ......18 B5
Holroyd Ho BS3 ....8 D3
Holsom Cl BS14 ....3 F6
Holst Gdns BS4 ....118 C3
Holst Way GL51 ....18 D3
Holt The
  Bishop's Cleeve GL52 ....137 E2
  Gloucester GL4 ....119 E7
Holtham Ave GL3 ....128 B7
Holton Rd 19 A6
Holts Rd GL18 ....170 F4
Holy Apostles CE Prim Sch
  ....131 A8
Holy Cross Catholic Prim Sch
  BS3 ....8 C4
Holy Family Prim Sch
  BS34 ....29 B8
Holy Trinity Prim Sch
  Bristol BS32 ....40 C2
  Cheltenham GL52 ....193 C4
Holy Well Cl BS4 ....9 E6
Holymead Inf Sch BS4 .....9 D2
Holymead Jun Sch BS4 ....9 D3
Holyrood Cl BS34 ....29 B8
Holyrood La Dursley GL11 ..88 A4
  Wootton-u-E GL12 ....68 C8
Home Cl Bristol BS10 ......28 E2
  Cheltenham GL51 ....132 E3
  Upper Oddington GL56 ..177 C5
Home Cl GL20 ....192 C4
Home Farm Ct GL52 ......131 A7
Home Farm Dr BS8 ....7 B2
Home Farm Way BS35 .....39 A1
Home Field Cl BS16 ....21 B6
Home Ground
  Bristol, Eastfield BS9 ......8 A1
  Bristol, Shirehampton BS11 ..16 D7
  Cricklade SN6 ....143 E4
Home Mead
  Bristol, Cadbury Heath
  BS30 ....11 A4
  Bristol, Filwood Park BS4 ....8 D7
Home Orch BS37 ....43 D2
Homeabbey Ho GL20 .....192 C5
Homeapple Hill BS30 ......11 F6
Homeavon Ho BS31 ....4 B5
Homeberry Ho GL7 ....190 C4
Homecroft Dr GL51 ....132 E6
Homefarm SN6 ....145 E3
Homefield Nailsworth GL6 ..91 A3
  Thornbury BS35 ....51 D8
  Yate BS37 ....43 E3
Homefield Cl BS31 ....5 E3
Homefield Rd BS16 ....20 A5
Homefield Rd
  Pucklechurch BS16 ....22 B5
  Saltford BS31 ....5 F3
Homeground BS16 ....21 B6
Homeground La GL7 ....152 F4
Homelea Rd BS10 ....35 B1
Homemead Dr BS4 ....9 D1
Homend Cres 2 HR8 .....178 B8
Homend The 16 HR8 ......178 F8
Homepiece SN6 ....145 E3
Homespa Ho 5 GL50 ......133 A1
Homespring Ho GL52 .....134 A2
Homestead Cl GL20 ....182 C7
Homestead Gdns BS16 ....20 B8

Homestead Rd BS34 ....29 A3
Homestead The BS31 ....4 F2
Honey Garston Cl BS13 ....2 B4
Honey Garston Rd BS13 ....2 B4
Honey Hill Rd BS15 ....10 F8
Honey Suckle La BS31 .....10 C3
Honeyborne Way GL12 ....54 B5
Honeybourne Airfield Ind Est
  WR11 ....188 C5
Honeybourne Fst Sch
  WR11 ....188 C4
Honeybourne Rd WR11 ..188 C7
Honeybourne Sta WR11 ..188 C7
Honeybourne Way SN14 ....3 C6
Honeysuckle Cl
  Bristol BS32 ....40 C2
  Prestbury GL52 ....137 D3
Honeysuckle Dr GL14 ....119 E5
Honeysuckle La GL6 ......91 C4
Honeythorn Cl GL2 ....118 B7
Honister Ho BS34 ....24 C4
Honiton Rd BS16 ....44 C1
Honyatt Rd GL1 ....196 C4
Hoo La
  Chipping Campden GL55 ..188 B2
  Tewkesbury GL20 ....173 E8
Hook's La GL18 ....171 D5
Hookshouse La
  Doughton GL8 ....71 E4
  Tetbury GL8 ....140 A3
Hooper Cl GL4 ....119 B6
Hooper Rd BS14 ....3 D5
Hoovers La HR9 ....164 B8
Hop Gdn The NP16 ....60 F4
Hope Cotts GL5 ....99 D6
Hope Ct BS1 ....194 B1
Hope Mill La GL5 ....99 E2
Hope Orch GL4 ....132 D4
Hope Rd Bristol BS3 ....8 C1
  Yate BS37 ....43 A2
Hope Sq GL5 ....7 F6
Hope St GL5 ....133 B3
Hope Villas GL5 ....99 C8
Hopechapel Hill 10 BS8 ....7 A6
Hopes Cl GL15 ....92 C2
Hopes Hill Com Prim Sch
  GL17 ....165 A5
Hopetoun Rd BS2 ....50 A8
Hopewell GL14 ....191 E5
Hopewell Cl NP16 ....61 A4
Hopewell Colliery Mus*
  GL16 ....155 D6
Hopewell Gdns BS11 ......16 C8
Hopewell St BS1 ....196 C1
Hopkin Cl BS35 ....51 D7
Hopkins Ct 18 BS6 ....49 F1
Hopkins Orch 5 SN6 ......143 E4
Hopland Cl BS30 ....11 B3
Hopp's Rd GL15 ....10 D1
Hopton Rd GL11 ....88 B4
Hopwood Gr 6 GL52 ......134 A1
Hoppard La GL18 ....171 A5
Hopyard The GL4 ....182 B5
Horcott Ind Est GL7 ....152 F2
Horcott Rd GL7 ....152 D3
Horesham Gr BS13 ....2 C5
Horfield CE Prim Sch
  BS10 ....18 D7
Horfield Rd BS2 ....18 E4
Horfield Rd BS2 ....195 A4
Horley Rd BS2 ....19 A2
Horn La GL56 ....177 C7
Hornbeam Mews GL2 ....127 B5
Hornbeam Wlk BS31 ....4 C2
Hornbeam The BS16 ....30 B1
Hornbury Cl BS11 ....142 D1
Hornbury Hill SN16 ....142 D1
Horns Rd GL5 ....99 D6
Horsbere Rd GL3 ....120 B8
Horse Fair La SN6 ....143 F4
Horse La BS35 ....40 A7
Horse Lane Orch HR8 ....178 F8
Horse Pool La HR9 ....162 E2
Horse St BS37 ....43 A7
Horsecroft Gdns BS30 ....11 A6
Horsefair Cl GL53 ....131 A5
Horsefair La GL18 ....170 F5
Horsefair St GL53 ....131 A5
Horsefair The BS1 ....195 B3
Horsepool La
  Doynton BS30 ....12 F8
  St Briavels GL15 ....146 E6
Horsepool The 6 GL16 ..155 A7
Horseshoe Dr Bristol BS9 ..17 C4
  Gloucester GL2 ....126 B4
Horseshoe La BS37 ....44 B1
Horseshoe Way GL2 ....118 B6
Horsford Rd GL12 ....11 C3
Horslea GL17 ....163 D3
Horsley CE Prim Sch GL6 ..90 F1
Horsley Hill GL6 ....91 A1
Horsley Rd GL6 ....91 A2
Hortham La BS32 ....40 A5
Horton Ct* BS37 ....45 D5
Horton Hill GL52 ....45 C5
Horton Prim Sch BS37 .....45 C5
Horton Rd
  Chipping Sodbury BS37 ..44 C2
  Chipping Sodbury, Little
  Sodbury GL18 ....44 D4
  Gloucester GL1 ....127 A2
Horton St BS2 ....195 C3
Horwood Cl 8 BS30 ....11 A4
Horwood La GL12 ....54 B4
Hosey Wlk BS13 ....2 A5

Hospital Rd GL56 ....187 A3
Host St BS1 ....195 A3
Hot Water La BS15 ....21 A3
Hottom Gdns GL7 ....19 A7
Hotwell Rd BS8 ....194 B1
Hotwells Prim Sch BS8 .....7 F6
Houlton St BS2 ....195 C4
Hounds Cl BS37 ....44 B1
Hounds Rd BS37 ....44 B1
Howard Ave BS5 ....9 F8
Howard Cl
  Bristol, Southville BS3 .....8 A4
  Bristol, Staple Hill BS16 ..20 D4
  Bristol, Westbury Park BS6 ..8 E1
  5 Coleford GL16 ....155 B6
  Northway GL20 ....182 C4
  Thornbury BS35 ....64 C2
Howard St Bristol BS5 .....19 E1
  Gloucester GL1 ....118 F7
Howcroft GL3 ....128 C4
Howcroft Cl BS37 ....17 E4
Howcroft Gdns BS9 ....17 E4
Howell Rd
  Cheltenham GL51 ....132 E4
  Cheltenham GL51 ....132 F4
Howell's La GL15 ....156 E3
Howells Mead BS16 ....21 B7
Howells Rd GL20 ....192 D4
Howes GL7 ....11 A6
Howett Rd 18 BS5 ....9 C7
Howgate Cl 1 GL4 ....119 F5
Howmead GL13 ....85 E4
Howsmoor La Bristol BS16 ..21 B8
  Bristol BS16 ....21 C8
Hoylake BS37 ....32 E8
Hoylake Dr BS30 ....11 D6
Hucclecote La GL3 ....128 D2
Hucclecote Mews GL3 ....127 A7
Hucclecote Rd GL3 ....120 E7
Huckford La BS36 ....31 A4
Huckford Rd BS36 ....30 C5
Huckley Way BS32 ....29 F6
Hudd's Hill Gdns 2 BS5 ....9 F8
Hudd's Hill Rd BS5 ....9 F8
Hudd's Vale Rd BS5 ....9 E8
Huddleston Rd GL54 ......174 A8
Hudman's Cl GL20 ....192 C6
Hudnalls View NP25 ......146 B7
Hudson Cl
  Chipping Sodbury BS37 ..32 F8
  Honeybourne WR11 ......188 C7
Hudson La GL14 ....191 C5
Hudson Way GL50 ....133 D3
Hudsons View GL14 ....191 C1
Hughenden Rd
  Bristol, Clifton BS8 ....18 A2
  Bristol, Horfield BS7 ....18 E5
Hughes Cl GL20 ....182 C5
Hughes Cres NP16 ....60 F7
Hughes Terr GL15 ....155 E3
Hulbert Cl Bristol BS4 .....10 A2
  Swindon SN25 ....133 A7
Hulbert Cres GL51 ....129 F5
Hulse Rd BS4 ....10 A2
Humber Pl GL3 ....120 F5
Humber Rd GL52 ....134 A2
Humber Way BS11 ....26 D5
Humberstan Wlk 16 E8
Humberston Rd GL54 ....3 B1
Humbley Barton BS4 ....9 F5
Hung Rd BS11 ....16 E5
Hunger Hill GL11 ....80 A8
Hungerford Cl BS14 ....3 E8
Hungerford Gdns BS14 ....3 E8
Hungerford Rd
  Bristol BS14 ....3 E8
  Bristol St GL50 ....133 D3
Hungerford Wlk BS16 ....44 C1
Hunter's Way
  Andoversford GL54 ....166 C6
  Bristol BS34 ....29 B3
Hunters Cl Bristol BS15 ..10 C5
  Stroud GL5 ....98 D7
Hunters Dr BS15 ....20 F1
Hunters Gate GL14 ....119 D4
Hunters Mead GL9 ....56 A2
Hunters Rd
  Bishop's Cleeve GL52 ....137 E4
  Bristol BS15 ....10 C5
Hunters Rd E BS15 ....10 C4
Hunters Way GL7 ....98 B7
Huntfield Rd NP16 ....60 D8
Hunthill GL14 ....165 E1
Huntingdon Cl GL5 ....99 D6
Huntingham Rd BS13 ....1 F4
Huntings The 7 WR12 ...185 B8
Huntley CE Prim Sch
  GL19 ....165 C6
Huntley Cl GL4 ....119 E5
Hunts Ground Rd BS34 ...29 F4
Hunts Grove View GL10 ..107 B7
Hunts Hill SN26 ....144 D1
Hunts La BS7 ....18 E6
Huntscote Rd GL54 ....133 A1
Huntsfield Cl GL50 ....133 E4
Huntsmans Cl GL54 ....138 A4
Huntsmans Meet GL54 ...166 D6
Hurcombe Way GL4 ....120 C6
Hurle Cres BS8 ....18 B1
Hurle Rd BS8 ....18 B1
Hurlingham Rd BS7 ....18 F2

Hurn La BS31 ....5 A3
Hurricane Rd GL3 ....120 C5
Hursley Hill BS14 ....3 D1
Hursley La BS14 ....3 A1
Hurst Cl GL2 ....127 D5
Hurst Rd BS5 ....9 C7
Hurst Wlk BS4 ....10 A2
Hurston Rd BS4 ....2 D7
Hurstwood Rd BS16 ....20 D5
Hutton Cl Bristol BS9 ......17 E7
  Keynsham BS31 ....4 D7
Huxley Cl GL7 ....143 A8
Huxley Rd GL1 ....118 F7
Huxley Way GL52 ....137 D4
Huyton Rd BS5 ....19 E1
Hyatts Way BS16 ....138 A3
Hyde Ave BS35 ....64 B3
Hyde Cl GL1 ....127 A2
Hyde Cotts GL54 ....139 F4
Hyde La Gloucester GL1 ..127 A2
  Newnham GL14 ....156 F7
  Swindon GL50,GL51 .....133 D7
  Whitminster GL2 ....100 F6
Hyde Park Cnr GL19 ......179 D2
Hyde The GL14 ....156 E6
Hyde View GL16 ....154 F3
Hyde's La SN14 ....14 A6
Hyett Cl GL10 ....103 F8
Hyett Rd GL5 ....98 E7
Hygrove La GL2 ....125 B1
Hyland Gr BS9 ....17 F8

I

Icehouse La GL56 ....186 D1
Icombe Cl GL52 ....137 F3
Ida Rd 2 BS5 ....50 B8
Idaho St GL7 ....152 E2
Idesleigh Rd BS6 ....18 B3
Idsall Dr GL3 ....134 C4
Idstone Rd BS16 ....20 B4
Iford Cl BS31 ....5 E3
Ilchester Cres BS13 ....8 B1
Ilchester Rd BS13 ....2 B8
Iles Cl BS15 ....10 C4
Ilex Cl BS13 ....2 A5
Ilmington CE Prim Sch
  CV36 ....189 F6
Ilminster Ave BS4 ....2 D7
Ilminster Avenue Prim Sch
  BS4 ....3 A8
Ilsom Cotts GL8 ....140 D5
Ilsyn Gr BS14 ....3 E8
Imber Court Cl BS14 ....3 B8
Imjin Rd GL52 ....134 B2
Imperial Arc BS3 ....8 D4
Imperial Cir GL50 ....193 B3
Imperial Gr GL50 ....193 B3
Imperial Rd
  8 Bristol, Clifton BS6 .....18 B1
  Bristol, Knowle BS14 ....3 D8
Imperial Sq GL50 ....193 B2
Imperial Wlk BS14 ....3 D8
Inchbrook CE Prim Sch
  Inchbrook GL5,GL6 ....91 A6
  Inchbrook Trad Est GL5 ..91 A7
India Ho 2 GL51 ....132 E2
India Rd GL1 ....119 A8
Ingleside Rd BS15 ....20 C1
Ingmire Rd BS6 ....19 B3
Ingmire Rd BS5 ....49 B3
Ingst Hill BS35 ....49 B3
Ingst Rd BS35 ....49 D4
Inkerman Cl BS7 ....18 E7
Inkerman La 18 GL50 ......19 D8
Inn Cotts BS11 ....17 A7
Inner Ctyd GL1 ....190 B4
Inner Down The BS12 .....50 D3
Inner Loop Rd NP16 ....61 A6
Innerstone La GL19 ....171 D4
Innocks Est GL12 ....11 D3
Innox Gdns BS13 ....2 A5
Inns Court Ave BS4 ....2 D7
Inns Court Dr BS4 ....2 D6
Innsworth Ave BS10 ....35 D1
Innsworth Gdns GL3 ......127 D7
Innsworth La GL3 ....127 D6
Innsworth Tech Pk GL3 ..127 C6
Insley Gdns GL3 ....119 F8
Insley Rd GL3 ....119 F8
Instow Wlk BS4 ....2 E8
International Sch of
  Choueifat SN14 ....15 C4
International Trad Est
  BS11 ....26 B2
Interplex 16 BS32 ....40 C3
Inverlea Ct GL15 ....189 A6
Ipswich Dr BS4 ....9 E6
Irby Rd BS3 ....8 A3
Irena Rd BS16 ....19 F3
Ireton Rd BS3 ....8 B3
Iron Acton CE Prim Sch
  BS37 ....42 B3
Iron Acton Way BS37 ......42 C4
Iron Hogg La GL12 ....65 C3
Iron Mills GL6 ....91 E3
Ironchurch Rd BS11 ....26 C5
Ironmonger's La GL13 ....86 B4
Ironmould La BS4 ....4 D4
Ironstone Cl 2 GL15 ....147 D8
Irving Cl BS16 ....20 E4
Irving Ho BS1 ....195 A4
Irving Ho Bristol BS1 .....194 C3
  18 Cheltenham GL52 .....133 F2
Isbourne Rd GL52 ....134 B2
Isbourne Way GL54 ....174 B8
ISF Rd BS11 ....26 C3
Islamic Acad GL11 ....196 C2
Island Gdns BS16 ....19 C4

Islay Cres SN6 ....145 E4
Isleys Ct BS30 ....10 A5
Islington Rd BS3 ....8 A3
Ismay Rd GL51 ....1 C1
Ison Hill Rd BS10 ....17 B2
Itchington Rd
  Alveston BS35 ....50 F2
  Tytherington GL12 ....51 A2
Itton Rd BS15 ....20 C1
Ivanhoe No GL2 ....11 D1
Ivor Rd BS5 ....50 B1
Ivory Cl GL4 ....119 E8
Ivy Bank GL17 ....163 D3
Ivy House Est HR9 ....0 C3
Ivy House La HR9 ....0 C3
Ivy La Bristol BS16 ....20 A4
  Broad Blunsdon SN26 ....34 F4
Ivy Lodge Barns GL7 ......51 A3
Ivy Terr BS37 ....7 F8
Ivywell Rd BS9 ....17 D8
Izod's Cl GL55 ....18 E4

J

Jack Knight Ho BS7 ....18 E7
Jackbarrow Rd GL7 ....91 C4
Jackson Cl BS35 ....51 C5
Jackson Cres 2 GL15 ....155 C7
Jackson Rd
  Bledington OX7 ....178 B8
  South Cerney GL7 ....153 C5
Jacob St Bristol BS2 ......195 C3
Jacob's Ct BS1 ....194 B2
Jacob's Wells Rd BS8 ......7 A6
Jacobs Cl 4 GL8 ....8 C3
Jamaica St BS2 ....195 C4
James Cl BS16 ....18 E6
James Ct
  Cheltenham GL51 ....19 B5
  Yorkley GL15 ....154 F3
James Donovan Ct
  GL52 ....133 F2
James Grieve Rd GL4 ......18 E6
James Orch GL13 ....85 D4
James Rd BS16 ....21 E4
James St
  Bristol, Baptist Mills BS2 ..49 F2
  Bristol, St Pauls BS5 ......49 F1
James Way GL3 ....18 E7
James Wlk BS11 ....16 D7
Jameson Ct 22 GL56 ......187 A3
Jane St BS5 ....7 B6
Japonica Cl 5 BS32 ....40 C3
Japonica Dr GL52 ....134 A1
Jardine Dr GL52 ....18 E7
Jarvis St BS5 ....7 B5
Jasmin Way GL1 ....11 D1
Jasmine Cl GL4 ....119 E8
Jasmine Gr BS11 ....16 E5
Jasper St BS3 ....8 A3
Javelin Pk GL2 ....7 F8
Jay's Gn HR9 ....163 F2
Jay's Mead GL12 ....23 A2
Jays The GL17 ....163 C3
Jaythorpe GL4 ....120 C6
Jean Rd BS4 ....141 C3
Jefferies Cl 7 GL7 ....152 E2
Jefferies Hill Bottom
  BS15 ....10 C4
Jeffery Ct BS30 ....11 E6
Jeffreys Ct 9 BS16 ....20 A5
Jeffress Cl BS16 ....18 E6
Jellicoe Ave BS16 ....18 E6
Jena Ct BS31 ....4 D4
Jenkin's La GL6 ....91 C4
Jenner Cl
  Chipping Sodbury BS37 ..44 B1
  Gloucester GL3 ....128 C7
Jenner Ct GL13 ....85 E4
Jenner Mus* GL13 ....85 E4
Jenner Wlk GL50 ....133 B3
Jersey Ave Bristol BS4 .....9 F8
  Cheltenham GL51 ....132 F4
Jersey Rd GL1 ....119 F6
Jersey St BS2 ....10 B1
Jesse Mary Chambers
  Almshouses 7 GL50 ......193 C3
Jessop Ave GL50 ....193 B2
Jessop Rd GL50 ....193 F3
Jessop Cres BS10 ....35 C2
Jessop Dr 2 GL54 ....174 B8
Jessop Underpass BS3 ......8 B3
Jet Age Air Mus* GL2 .....127 E2
Jewson Cl GL4 ....119 B8
Jeynes Bldgs GL20 ....192 C5
Jeynes Row GL20 ....173 C4
Jim O'Neil Ho BS11 ....16 D7
Joan Hawley Mews
  GL52 ....133 F2
Job's La GL16 ....155 A7
Jobbins Ct GL7 ....152 E1
Jocelyn Rd BS7 ....18 D4
Jockey Stable Cotts
  GL56 ....187 A3
John Bevan Cl GL2 ....118 C4
John Buck Ho 8 GL52 ....193 F3
John Cabot Ct BS1 ....194 A1
John Cabot City Tech Coll
  BS15 ....10 A6
John Carr's Terr BS8 ....7 A6
John Cozens Ho 6 BS2 ..195 C3
John Daniels Way GL3 ....120 E6
John James Ct BS7 ....18 E7
John Lamb Ho GL51 ......132 D6

Masefield High Sch ...178 F8
Moore Countryside
* GL20 ...192 C4
Rushout Ct GL6 ...186 C7
St Bristol BS1 ...195 A3
ol, Baptist Mills BS2 ...19 A2
ol, Two Mile Hill BS15 ...10 C8
ed G5 ...99 C7
Tame Cl 4 GL7 ...152 E4
Wesley Rd BS5 ...10 B6
Wesleys Chapel ...195 B3
Woolfe Cl GL6 ...186 C7
son Rd BS30 ...10 F5
son Rd BS16 ...21 C6
sons La BS5 ...19 D1
sons Rd BS15 ...10 C8
sons Way GL15 ...156 B2
sston Cl GL19 ...172 A7
stone Rd 3 GL18 ...171 A4
ers La GL6 ...148 D8
e Ho NP25 ...154 A8
an Wlk BS32 ...29 D8
ans Cl WR12 ...188 B2
ans Way GL12 ...126 F5
cks Ind Est BS37 ...32 C4
and Cres GL19 ...172 F7
Hill BS8 ...9 C7
Green Prim Sch ...163 D3
ard Hill GL16 ...155 A8
er Rd GL51 ...133 A4
Green Rd GL17 ...163 D2
ee Ave GL11 ...87 F6
ee Cl Dursley GL11 ...87 F6
ury HR8 ...178 F7
tow-on-the-W GL54 ...176 F4
ee Cotts GL6 ...148 B5
ee Cres BS16 ...21 A6
ee Dr Bredon GL20 ...182 C7
nbury BS35 ...64 D1
ee Flats GL7 ...150 E2
ee Gdns
St Cerney GL7 ...142 F7
ee Ho BS34 ...29 C8
ee La GL12 ...53 B7
ee Maze™ HR9 ...162 E4
ee Pk™ HR9 ...162 E4
ee Pl Bristol BS1 ...195 A1
nton GL19 ...172 A4
ee Rd
ol, Baptist Mills BS2 ...19 A1
ol, Knowle BS4 ...9 C2
ol, St George BS5 ...9 F7
ol, Staple Hill BS15 ...20 E3
sley GL11 ...88 A2
dley GL15 ...92 C3
heldean GL17 ...164 D3
worth GL6 ...91 A5
ee St BS2 ...195 C2
ee Way
mouth BS16 ...26 B2
oness GL13 ...85 D8

Keelings The GL14 ...191 C5
Keels SN6 ...143 E5
Keepers GL45 ...38 C7
Keep The BS30 ...11 D5
Keepers Mill GL52 ...138 B3
Keil Cl 5 WR12 ...185 B8
Keinton Wlk BS10 ...28 A2
Keirle Wlk GL11 ...132 F5
Kelbra Cres BS36 ...31 B6
Kellaway Ave BS7 ...18 D5
Kellaway Cres BS9 ...18 D6
Kellaway Ct BS6 ...18 D5
Kells Meend GL16 ...155 A7
Kells Rd GL15 ...155 A7
Kelly's La NP16 ...146 F1
Kelston Cl Saltford BS31 ...5 D4
Yate BS37 ...32 D7
Kelston Gdns BS10 ...18 B8
Kelston Gr BS15 ...10 E6
Kelston Rd Bath BA1 ...6 E1
Bristol BS10 ...18 D8
Keynsham BS31 ...4 F3
Kelston Wlk BS16 ...20 C4
Kemble Boss Pk SN16 ...141 D6
Kemble Dr Bristol BS15 ...10 E6
Gloucester GL4 ...118 D2
Kemble Gdns BS11 ...16 F5
Kemble Gr GL51 ...129 B7
Kemble Ho BS34 ...39 F1
Kemble Prim Sch GL7 ...141 F8
Kemble Rd GL4 ...118 E2
Kemble St GL7 ...141 F8
Kemerton Rd
Bredon GL20 ...182 C7
Cheltenham GL50 ...130 B6
Westmancote GL20 ...182 D8
Kempe Cl GL20 ...
Kempsford Cl 5 BS41 ...7 F2
Kemperley Wlk BS32 ...29 D7
Kemps La GL6 ...103 F8
Kempsford Acre GL52 ...138 B3
Kempsford CE Prim Sch ...144 E8
Kempton Cl Bristol BS16 ...30 F1
Thornbury BS35 ...64 B3
Kempton Gr GL51 ...132 D2
Kencot Wlk BS13 ...2 B3
Kencourt Ct 2 GL2 ...127 B2
Kendal Rd Bristol BS7 ...19 A7
Gloucester GL2 ...127 C4
Kendall Gdns BS16 ...20 D4
Kendall Rd BS16 ...20 D4
Kendon Dr BS10 ...18 D7
Kendon Way BS10 ...18 D8
Kendrick St 4 GL5 ...99 C7
Kenelm Dr GL53 ...130 C6
Kenelm Gdns GL53 ...130 B6
Kenelm Rise GL54 ...174 A8
Kenilworth BS37 ...32 F8
Kenilworth Ave GL2 ...127 B3
Kenilworth Cl BS31 ...4 D4
Kenilworth Dr BS30 ...11 B2
Bristol BS11 ...16 D7
Kenilworth Ho 6 GL51 ...132 E3
Kenmare Rd BS4 ...18 C1
Kenmore Cres BS7 ...28 E1
Kenmore Dr BS7 ...28 E1
Kenmore Gr BS7 ...28 E1
Kenn Court Bsns Pk BS4 ...2 E7
Kennard Cl BS15 ...10 C7
Kennard Ct BS15 ...10 C8
Kennard Rise BS15 ...10 C8
Kennedy Cl GL3 ...127 F1
Kennedy Way BS37 ...43 F1
Kennedy Way GL7 ...46 E2
Kennel La
Broadwell GL56 ...177 A6
Brockworth GL3 ...129 C2
Kennel Lodge Rd BS3 ...7 E4
Kennerwell La GL12 ...68 E3
Kennet Cl GL20 ...182 B4
Kennet Rd BS31 ...5 A4
Kennet Way 4 BS35 ...51 D8
Kenneth Cl GL53 ...130 E4
Kenneth Rd BS4 ...9 D2
Kennett Gdns GL4 ...119 F4
Kennington
Bristol, Bishopston BS7 ...18 F4
Bristol, Two Mile Hill BS5 ...
Kennion Rd BS5 ...20 D1
Kennmoor Ct BS30 ...11 A6
Kensal Ave BS3 ...8 E3
Kensal Rd BS3 ...8 E3
Kensington Ave GL50 ...130 A8
Kensington Cl BS35 ...64 B2
Kensington Ct BS8 ...194 A3
Kensington Park Rd BS4 ...9 C2
Kensington Pl BS8 ...194 A3
Kensington Rd
Bristol, Redland BS6 ...18 C1
Bristol, St George BS5 ...10 A8
Bristol, Staple Hill BS16 ...20 D4
Kensley Vale GL4 ...191 C3
Kent Ave BS37 ...43 F3
Kent Cl Bristol BS34 ...29 D4
Churchdown GL3 ...128 D5
Kent End SN6 ...143 A5
Kent End Cl SN6 ...143 A5
Kent Rd BS7 ...18 E4
Kent St BS3 ...8 C3
Kentmere Cl GL51 ...129 E7
Kenton Dr GL20 ...127 C5
Kenton Ho BS34 ...39 F1
Kenton Mews BS9 ...18 C5

Kents Gn BS15 ...20 E2
Kenulf Rd 2 GL54 ...174 F4
Keppel Cl BS31 ...5 D2
Keriston Ave GL3 ...128 A6
Kerr Way GL56 ...187 C3
Kerrin La GL15 ...147 C2
Kerris Ct 7 GL3 ...128 A7
Kerry Rd BS4 ...8 F1
Kersteman Rd BS6 ...18 C3
Kerstin Cl GL50 ...133 C5
Kestrel Cl Bristol BS34 ...28 E8
Cheltenham GL53 ...130 C5
Chipping Sodbury BS37 ...32 F8
Thornbury BS35 ...64 D2
Kestrel Ct 8 GL10 ...97 F8
Kestrel Dr BS16 ...22 C4
Kestrel Gdns GL2 ...117 F3
Kestrel Par GL3 ...127 D6
Kestrel Way GL20 ...182 B5
Keswick Cl GL2 ...127 B3
Keswick Rd GL51 ...129 E7
Keswick Wlk BS10 ...28 C2
Ketch Rd BS3 ...8 E3
Kevin Cl GL4 ...127 D1
Kew Cl NP25 ...193 B1
Kew Wlk BS4 ...3 C8
Kewa La GL5 ...170 D4
Kewstoke Rd BS9 ...17 F4
Keynes Carry Pk* GL7 ...142 D7
Keynsham By-Pass GL... ...4 E7
Keynsham Hospl BS31 ...4 F4
Keynsham La GL15 ...147 B2
Keynsham Prim Sch ...4 D5
Keynsham Rd
Bristol BS30,BS31 ...5 A8
Cheltenham GL53 ...193 C2
Keynsham St GL52 ...130 F8
Keynsham Sta BS31 ...4 E6
Keynshambury Rd GL52 ...193 C2
Keys Ave BS7 ...18 F7
Keys Gate BS15 ...189 D3
Kibble's La GL14 ...191 C1
Kidnalls Rd GL15 ...155 F1
Kidnams Wlk GL2 ...100 F5
Kidnappers La GL53 ...130 B4
Kidney Hill BS37 ...32 A3
Kitsgate Court Gdns* GL55 ...
Kilbirnie Rd BS14 ...3 A3
Kilburn St 17 BS5 ...9 B8
Kilburn St 19 BS5 ...9 B8
Kilda Rd SN6 ...145 C4
Kildare Rd BS4 ...8 D1
Kilham La GL14 ...166 E5
Kilkenny St BS2 ...195 C2
Killcott Rd GL12 ...55 E8
Kilmersdon Rd BS13 ...2 B4
Kilminster Ct 11 GL43 ...12 F7
Kilminster Rd
Bristol BS11 ...16 D7
Stroud GL5 ...99 F7
Kilmore Rd GL20 ...181 F7
Kiln Cl BS15 ...20 B2
Kiln Ct BS5 ...9 B8
Kilnhurst Ct BS30 ...10 F2
Kilvert Cl BS4 ...9 D5
Kimberley Ave BS16 ...20 C5
Kimberley Cl Bristol BS16 ...20 C7
Gloucester GL2 ...127 D4
Lydney GL15 ...92 B3
Kimberley Cres BS16 ...20 C5
Kimberley Dr GL15 ...92 B3
Kimberley Rd
Bristol, Fishponds BS16 ...20 C5
Bristol, Kingswood BS15 ...20 D1
Kimberley Wlk GL52 ...134 C2
Kimbrose GL1 ...194 B2
Kimbrose Way GL1 ...196 A2
Kimmins Rd GL10 ...96 A8
Kimbor La GL52 ...134 B4
Kindrick La 11 GL51 ...99 C7
King Alfred Way GL3 ...130 E8
King Alfreds Rd NP16 ...61 A8
King Arthur Cl GL53 ...130 F7
King Dick's La 3 BS5 ...9 F8
King Edmund Com Sch
BS37 ...43 E1
King Edward Cl BS14 ...3 A6
King Edward's Ave GL11 ...118 E7
King George Cl GL53 ...130 F4
King George V Pl 6
BS1 ...195 A2
King George's Rd BS13 ...1 F5
King Georges Field
GL54 ...176 F4
King Henry GL53 ...130 F6
King John's Cotts GL2 ...192 C5
King John's Rd BS15 ...20 E3
King Johns Ct GL20 ...192 C5
King Rd BS37 ...45 A7
King Rd BS4 ...9 C1
King Road Ave BS11 ...26 B2
King Sq BS2 ...195 A4
King Square Ave BS2 ...195 A4
King St Avonmouth BS11 ...26 B4
Bristol, Lower Easton BS5 ...19 C1
Bristol BS1 ...195 A2
Cheltenham GL50 ...193 B4
Cirencester GL7 ...190 D7
Minchinhampton GL6 ...148 A3
Stroud GL5 ...99 D7
King Street Par 4 GL5 ...99 C7
King William Ave 1 BS1 ...195 A2
King William Dr GL53 ...130 F6
Gloucester GL4 ...119 A5
King William St BS3 ...8 B4
King's Ave BS6,BS7 ...18 F7

King's Barton St GL1 ...196 C2
King's Ct BS1 ...195 A2
King's Head La GL13 ...1 E7
King's Mill La GL6 ...103 E7
King's Parade Ave 1
BS8 ...18 B1
King's Parade Mews BS8 ...18 A1
King's Rd
Bristol, Clifton BS8 ...194 A3
Bristol, Kensington Park BS4 ...9 C3
Cheltenham GL52 ...133 F1
Stonehouse GL10 ...101 F1
Stroud GL5 ...99 B6
King's Sch The GL1 ...196 B3
King's Sq GL1 ...98 A4
King's Stanley CE Jun Sch
GL10 ...98 A4
King's Stanley Inf Sch
GL10 ...98 A3
Kingcomb La GL55 ...188 F2
Kingfisher Cl Bristol BS32 ...40 E2
Thornbury BS35 ...64 D2
Kingfisher Dr BS16 ...19 E6
Kingfisher Pl GL2 ...143 A8
Kingfisher Rd BS37 ...33 A8
Kingfisher Rise GL2 ...117 E1
Kingham La GL54 ...177 F1
Kingley Rd GL5 ...98 F2
Kings Ave Bristol BS7 ...18 F7
Kings Chase BS37 ...33 C8
Kings Ct GL7 ...33 C7
Kings Ave Bristol BS15 ...10 B4
Kings Chase BS15 ...10 D8
Kings Cl GL1 ...
Kings Ct Bristol BS1 ...195 A2
Bristol, Little Stoke BS34 ...29 C6
Bristol, St Pauls BS1 ...195 B4
Kings Dr Bristol BS15 ...10 B4
Dursley GL11 ...88 A2
Kings Elm GL2 ...123 B3
Kings Gate GL20 ...192 F4
Kings Head La GL54 ...166 F2
Kings Mdw
Bourton-on-h GL54 ...168 F8
Crudwell SN16 ...143 B3
Kings Mead GL14 ...156 F6
Kings Park Ave BS2 ...9 C6
Kings Sq BS30 ...5 D8
Kings Well La GL54 ...176 C1
Kings Weston Ave BS11 ...16 E8
Kings Weston La BS11,
Avonmouth BS11 ...26 E3
Bristol BS11 ...17 A8
Kings Weston Rd BS11,
BS10 ...27 C1
Kings Wlk Bristol BS13 ...1 E7
Kingscote Cl
Cheltenham GL51 ...129 D7
Churchdown GL3 ...128 D4
Kingscote Dr GL14 ...119 E5
Kingscote Pk BS5 ...10 B6
Kingscote Rd E GL51 ...129 D7
Kingscote Rd W GL51 ...129 D6
Kingscourt Cl BS14 ...3 A4
Kingscourt La GL55 ...99 A4
Kingscroft Rd GL3 ...120 A7
Kingsdale Cl WR12 ...185 C8
Kingsditch La GL51 ...133 A5
Kingsditch Ret Pk GL51 ...133 A5
Kingsdown GL11 ...88 A3
Kingsdown Par BS6 ...195 A4
Kingsfield
Bristol, Longwell Green
BS15 ...10 E5
Bristol, Mount Hill BS30 ...10 E4
Kingsfield Sch BS15 ...11 A8
Kingshill Cl GL51 ...190 F4
Kingshill Ho BS37 ...9 B1
Kingshill La
Cirencester GL7 ...150 F4
Dursley GL11 ...88 A2
Kingshill Pk GL11 ...88 A3
Kingshill Rd Bristol BS4 ...9 B1
Kingsholm CE Prim Sch
GL1 ...196 C4
Kingsholm Ct GL1 ...126 C4
Kingsholm Rd
Bristol GL1 ...18 D8
Gloucester GL1 ...196 B4
Kingsholme Rd BS15 ...20 D1
Kingsland Cl 1 BS2 ...9 A6
Kingsland Rd BS2 ...9 A6
Kingsland Road Bridge 3
BS2 ...9 A6
Kingsland Trad Est BS2 ...195 C3
Kingsleigh Cl BS15 ...10 F7
Kingsleigh Gdns BS15 ...10 F7
Kingsleigh Pk BS15 ...10 F7
Kingsley Gdns GL51 ...129 E8
Kingsley Ho GL52 ...195 C2
Kingsley Rd
Bristol, Lower Easton BS5 ...19 C1
Bristol, Montpelier BS6 ...18 D2
Gloucester GL4 ...119 A5
Kingsmark La NP16 ...72 D1
Kingsmead

Kingsmead
Cirencester GL7 ...190 E2
Gloucester GL4 ...119 F4
Lechlade on T GL7 ...153 E3
Painswick GL6 ...103 E8
Kingsmead Ave GL51 ...132 F4
Kingsmead Ct GL51 ...132 F4
Kingsmead Ind Est
GL51 ...133 A4
Kingsmead Rd Bristol BS5 ...20 A1
Kingsmead Rd GL51 ...132 F4
Kingsmead Wlk BS5 ...20 A1
Kingsmill BS9 ...17 D5
Kingston Ave BS31 ...5 C3
Kingston Cl BS16 ...21 A7
Kingston Dr Bristol BS16 ...21 A7
Cheltenham GL51 ...132 C1
Kingston Rd Bristol BS3 ...8 C4
Northway GL20 ...182 C4
Slimbridge GL2 ...79 F8
Kingstone Ave GL3 ...127 F1
Kingstree St BS4 ...9 A4
Kingsville Rd GL51 ...133 A4
Kingsway
Bristol, Little Stoke BS34 ...29 C6
Bristol, St George BS5 ...10 B7
Cirencester GL7 ...150 F3
Coleford GL16 ...155 B6
Dursley GL11 ...88 A3
Kingsway Ave BS5 ...10 C8
Kingsway Cres BS15 ...10 C8
Kingsway La GL7 ...163 F4
Kingsway Sh Prec BS5 ...10 B7
Kingsway Rd BS3 ...8 A4
Kingsweston Down Nature
Res* BS9,BS11 ...27 C1
Kingsweston Specl Sch
BS11 ...17 A8
Kingswood Abbey
Gatehouse* GL12 ...67 F5
Kingswood Cl GL52 ...137 F3
Kingswood Cty Prim Sch
GL12 ...67 F5
Kingswood Rd GL12 ...55 D8
Kingswood Trad Est 6
BS15 ...20 D1
Kington La BS35 ...63 E1
Kington Rd BS35 ...63 E3
Kinmoor GL4 ...119 D3
Kinsale Rd BS14 ...3 C7
Kinsale Wlk BS4 ...8 E2
Kinsham La GL20 ...182 E7
Kinvara Rd BS4 ...2 E8
Kipling Cl GL2 ...118 C4
Kipling Rd Bristol BS7 ...29 B1
Cheltenham GL51 ...132 C1
Dursley GL11 ...80 C7
Kirby Rd GL54 ...169 E6
Kirkby Rd BS11 ...27 A1
Kirkbride Gdns BS10 ...28 C2
Kirkstone Ho BS34 ...29 A8
Kirtlington Rd BS5 ...19 B3
Kitchener Ave GL1 ...118 E5
Kite Hay Cl BS16 ...19 E5
Kitefield 18 SN6 ...143 E4
Kites Cl BS32 ...40 C2
Kitesnest La GL54 ...158 A6
Klondyke Ave GL15 ...92 B3
Knap La Cromhall GL12 ...66 B3
Painswick GL6 ...103 F7
Knapp Cl HR9 ...163 A6
Knapp Cotts GL18 ...179 B3
Knapp La
Brimscombe GL5 ...148 A4
Cheltenham GL50 ...193 A4
Coaley GL11 ...89 B5
Dursley GL11 ...87 F4
Netherend GL15 ...147 D3
Stroud GL5 ...104 B2
Knapp Rd
Cheltenham GL50 ...193 A4
Thornbury BS35 ...64 D2
Thornbury,Crossways BS35 ...64 C2
Wotton-u-E GL12 ...68 C7
Knapp The Dursley GL11 ...88 B1
Yate BS37 ...43 F5
Knapps La BS5 ...19 E2
Knighton Rd BS10 ...28 E1
Knights Cl BS9 ...18 B6
Knights Cres GL18 ...170 F4
Knights Way
Newent GL18 ...170 F4
Tewkesbury GL20 ...192 E4
Knightsbridge Bsns Ctr
GL51 ...173 F5
Knightsbridge Cres
GL53 ...130 F7
Knightsbridge Rd GL51 ...173 F5
Knightsbridge Pk BS13 ...22 E4
Knightshill HR9 ...164 D8
Knightstone Cl BS4 ...19 D2
Knightstone Gdns BS4 ...9 B2
Knightstone Mount BS5 ...10 A6
Knightstone Rise 4 BS5 ...9 F8
Knightstone Sq BS14 ...3 C5
Knightwood Rd BS34 ...29 F5
Knockdown Rd SN16 ...58 C1
Knockley Patch GL15 ...155 D1
Knole Cl BS32 ...39 F4
Knole La BS10 ...28 B3
Knole Pk BS32 ...39 F3
Knoll Cl GL19 ...172 F4
Knoll Hill BS9 ...17 D3
Knoll The Kempsford GL7 ...144 E8

Knoll The continued
Stroud GL5 ....99 D7
Knollys End GL2 ....109 F8
Knovill CI BS11 ....27 B2
Knowlands SN6 ....145 D4
Knowle Jun Sch BS4 ......9 A3
Knowle Park Jun & Inf Schs
BS4 ....9 A1
Knowle Rd BS4 ....8 F3
Knowles Rd GL1 ....118 F7
Knowsley Rd BS16 ....19 E3
Knox Rd GL15 ....147 E8
Kydermister Rd GL4 ....174 A8
Kyght CI BS15 ....11 A8
Kylross Ave BS14 ....3 B5
Kymin La NP25 ....154 A7
Kymin Rd NP25 ....154 B7
Kynges Mill CI BS16 .....20 A7
Kyngstone Ct 10 BS16 ...19 E3

L

La Maison BS5 ....20 A2
Labbott The BS31 ....4 E5
Laburnum Cres GL4 ....102 F2
Laburnum Ct GL1 ....132 C2
Laburnum Gdns GL2 ....117 F2
Laburnum Gr BS16 ....20 B4
Laburnum Mews GL10 ...97 E7
Laburnum Rd Bristol BS15 .10 C5
Stonehouse GL10 ....97 E7
Laburnum Way GL10 .....60 E5
Laburnum Wlk
Keynsham BS31 ....4 C3
Stonehouse GL10 ....97 E7
Lacca CI GL2 ....127 D5
Lacey Rd BS14 ....3 F6
Lacock Dr BS30 ....10 F5
Lacy CI GL2 ....127 C6
Ladbarrow Cotts GL54 ..161 A4
Lad CI BS15 ....17 C7
Ladden Ct BS35 ....51 C8
Ladder The GL6 ....91 C4
Ladies Mile BS8 ....17 F1
Ladman Gr BS14 ....3 A6
Ladman Rd BS14 ....3 E5
Lady Chapel Rd GL4 ....119 E6
Lady La SN26 ....144 D1
Lady Margaret Ct NP16 ..60 F4
Lady Mead SN6 ....143 E4
Ladybellegate St GL1 ...196 A2
Ladygrove Bsns Pk
GL17 ....164 E5
Ladysmith Rd Bristol BS6 ..18 B4
Cheltenham GL52 ....134 B2
Gloucester GL1 ....118 E3
Ladywell CI GL2 ....118 B7
Laggar La GL6 ....98 F1
Laines Est The GL54 ....158 F6
Lake CI GL2 ....124 B3
Frampton on Severn GL2 .157 F3
Lake Rd BS10 ....18 C8
Lake Side GL18 ....171 A5
Lakers Rd GL16 ....155 E2
Lakers Sch GL16 ....155 B7
Lakeside Bristol BS16 ...19 E3
Fairford GL7 ....152 D3
South Cerney GL7 ....143 A8
Lakeside Ave GL15 ....92 C2
Lakeside CI GL52 ....133 F4
Lakeside Dr GL15 ....92 C2
Lakeside Jun Sch GL51 .122 E7
Lakewood Cres BS10 ....18 B8
Lakewood Rd BS10 ......18 B8
Lamb Hill BS5 ....9 E7
Lamb La GL4 ....191 D4
Lamb St BS2 ....195 C3
Lambert Ave GL51 ....129 C1
Lambert CI GL51 ....129 D1
Lambert Dr GL51 ....129 C1
Lambert Gdns GL51 .....129 D1
Lambert PI BS4 ....2 D6
Lambert Terr GL51 ......129 D2
Lamberts Field BS35 ....169 A7
Lambeth CI BS15 ....9 E8
Lambourn CI Bristol BS3 ..8 D2
Gloucester GL52 ....127 E3
Lambourn Rd BS31 ....5 A4
Lambourne Ave GL51 ...165 D6
Lambourne Ct 11 HR8 ..178 F8
Lambrook Rd BS16 ....20 A4
Lambs Barn Pitch GL8 ..171 A5
Lambs Cross HR9 ....170 B4
Lambsdowne GL11 ....87 F3
Lambsquay Rd GL16 ....155 A3
Lamord Gate BS34 ......29 E5
Lampern View GL11 ......89 B1
Lampeter Rd BS9 ....18 A7
Lampreys The GL4 ......119 B6
Lampton Ave BS13 ....2 E3
Lampton Gr BS13 ....2 E3
Lampton Rd BS41 ....7 A1
Lanaway Rd BS20 ....26 B6
Lancashire Rd BS7 ......18 C2
Lancaster CI BS34 ....29 D4

Lancaster Ct
2 Cheltenham GL50 ....130 B8
Lydney GL15 ....92 B5
Lancaster Dr Lydney GL15 .92 B5
Upper Rissington GL54 ..169 D6
Lancaster Rd Bristol BS2 .19 A2
Kempsford GL7 ....144 F7
Newport GL20 ....192 D2
Yate BS37 ....43 E3
Lancaster St 10 BS5 .....9 C7
Lancaster Terr GL18 ....171 A5
Lancaster Way NP16 ....60 D8
Lancaut La NP16 ....72 F6
Lancelot Ct GL2 ....95 D4
Lancelot Rd BS16 ....19 E8
Land The BS36 ....31 C7
Landgate Yd 2 GL54 ....176 F4
Landor Gdns 10 GL52 ..133 F2
Landseer Ave BS7 ....19 B7
Lane End GL54 ....169 C4
Lane The
Broadway WR12 ....184 F7
Chastleton GL56 ....177 E8
Easter Compton BS35 ...38 F2
Randwick GL6 ....102 D2
Lanercost Rd BS10 ......28 C2
Lanes CI GL20 ....192 C3
Lanes The GL53 ....130 B4
Lanesborough Rise BS14 ..3 D7
Lanescourt GL20 ....192 D3
Langdale BS37 ....29 A8
Langdale Gdns GL2 ....127 C5
Langdale Rd Bristol BS16 .19 F4
Cheltenham GL51 ....129 F6
Langdon Rd GL53 ....125 E5
Langdown Ct BS14 ....3 E5
Langet GL7 ....142 F7
Langetts Rd 4 GL16 ....155 A5
Langfield CI BS10 ....27 E3
Langford Rd BS13 ....1 F8
Langford Way BS15 .....10 E7
Langham Ho NP16 ....60 F5
Langham Rd BS4 ....9 B2
Langhill Ave BS4 ....2 D7
Langley CI GL54 ....139 F5
Langley Gdns GL53 ....7 F1
Langley Mow BS16 .....21 D7
Langley Rd
Gloucester GL4 ....119 B5
Winchcombe GL54 ......139 D5
Langsdown Ho 2 BS2 ...8 F1
Langston Priory Workshops
OX7 ....177 F1
Langthorn CI BS36 ....31 C7
Langworth Rd GL5 ......199 E3
Langton CI GL4 ....119 E8
Langton Court Rd BS4 ...9 D5
Langton St 10 BS16 .....19 E3
Langton Grove Rd GL2 .131 A7
Langton Ho 6 BS2 .....195 C3
Langton PI BS9 ....8 B3
Langton PI BS13 ....131 A7
Langton Way BS4 ....9 F6
Lanham Gdns GL2 ......109 F7
Lanham La GL52 ....118 F7
Lansdown Stroud GL5 ....99 C7
Yate BS37 ....32 E8
Lansdown Castle Dr
GL51 ....129 D2
Lansdown CI Bristol GL15 .20 D2
Cheltenham GL50 ......130 A8
Lansdown Cotts GL18 ..168 F8
Lansdown Cres GL50 ..193 A2
Lansdown Crescent La
GL50 ....193 A2
Lansdown Ct GL10 ....97 D6
Lansdown Ho GL15 ......20 D2
Lansdown Ind Est GL51 .133 A1
Lansdown La GL3 ....12 C1
Lansdown Lodge Dr
GL51 ....130 A8
Lansdown Par GL50 ....130 B8
Lansdown PI Bristol BS8 .194 A3
Lansdown PI GL50 ....193 A2
Lansdown Place La
BS2 ....193 A2
Lansdown Terr
Bristol BS8 ....18 D5
Cheltenham GL50 ......193 A3
Cheltenham GL50 ......193 A3
Lansdown Terrace La
GL50 ....193 A2
Lansdown Villas 10 GL10 .97 F8
Lansdown Wlk
15 Bream GL15 ....147 D8
Cheltenham GL50 ......193 A3
Lansdowne BS15 ....9 B8
Lantern CI Berkeley GL13 .89 C7
Cinderford GL14 ....191 C4
Lapdown La GL9 ....34 D1
Laphams Ct 11 BS30 ....9 E7
Lapwing CI BS32 ....40 D2
Northway GL20 ....182 B5
Lapwing Gdns BS16 .....19 F6
Larch CI GL53 ....131 C5
Larch Rd Bristol BS15 ...20 E3
Colerne SN14 ....15 F6

Larch Rise GL53 ....130 B4
Larch Way BS34 ....28 E7
Larches The GL4 ....119 E5
Larchmere Gr 8 GL51 ..129 E5
Larchwood Dr GL4 ......118 E3
Larkin Rise Chalford GL6 .148 C6
Coleford GL16 ....155 A6
Yate BS37 ....43 F2
Lark's Field BS16 ....19 E5
Lark's La BS37 ....42 B7
Larkfield BS36 ....31 D7
Larkfield Ave NP16 ......60 E7
Larkfield Cty Inf Sch
GL13 ....127 E6
Larkfield Ho NP16 ....60 D7
Larkfield Pk NP16 ....60 D7
Larkham CI GL4 ....119 B3
Larkham PI GL4 ....119 B3
Larkham Rd GL3 ....120 A8
Larkhill CI NP16 ....60 E7
Larkrise GL11 ....87 F5
Larksfield Rd
Harrow Hill GL17 ....164 B4
Stroud GL5 ....99 A4
Larksleaze Rd BS30 .....10 F2
Larkspur CI GL18 ....155 E5
Larkspur CI BS35 ....64 D1
Larput PI GL50 ....133 D3
Lasanne Ct GL1 ....196 B2
Lasbury Gr BS13 ....2 C5
Lascelles Gr GL4 ....120 F4
Lassington Gr GL2 .....125 C5
Lassington La GL2 ......125 D6
Lassington Wood (Nature
Reserve) GL2 ....125 E5
Latchen CI GL7 ....164 F5
Latchen Orch GL17 ....164 F5
Latchmoor Rd BS13 .....2 A8
Latimer CI Bristol BS4 ...9 F2
Minchinhampton GL6 ..148 A3
Latimer CI GL54 ....175 B3
Latimer Rd GL14 ....191 E5
Latteridge La
Iron Acton BS37 ....42 A7
Tytherington BS35 ......51 F1
Latteridge Rd BS37 .....42 D4
Latton Rd BS7 ....18 F8
Latymer Croft GL3 ......128 B5
Launceston Ave BS15 ..10 B5
Launceston Rd BS15 ...10 A5
Laundry Cotts GL56 ...177 E5
Laundry Rd GL16 ......154 E4
Laura CI GL2 ....127 B4
Laurel Ave GL20 ....192 E2
Laurel Dr Colerne SN14 ..16 A6
Prestbury GL52 ....134 B4
Laurel Farm CI GL4 ....118 F4
Laurel Gate GL4 ....119 F5
Laurel Pk NP16 ....72 B6
Laurel Rd GL16 ....155 B3
Laureldene GL16 ....155 B3
Laurels The
Bristol, Catbrain BS10 ...28 A6
Bristol, Mangotsfield BS16 .21 A6
Castle Eaton SN6 ....144 F6
Quedgeley GL51 ....118 F7
South Cerney GL7 ......142 F8
Laurence CI GL51 ......129 D2
Laurie Cres BS9 ....18 C8
Laurie Lee Ct 3 BS30 ...64 D1
Lavender CI Bristol BS35 .19 F1
Lavender Cr BS31 ....19 C1
Cirencester GL7 ....190 C3
Lavender Ho GL7 ....190 C3
Lavender Mews GL52 ..137 E3
Lavender PI GL53 ....7 C1
Lavender View GL4 ....119 F4
Lavender Way BS32 ....29 F7
Lavenham Rd BS37 .....43 B2
Lavers CI BS15 ....10 E6
Lavington Dr GL2 ....127 B4
Lavington Rd BS5 ....10 B6
Lawford Ave BS34 ....29 C6
Lawford St BS2 ....195 C3
Lawfords Gate BS2 ....195 C3
Lawfords Gate Ho 19
BS2 ....195 C3
Lawn Ave BS16 ....20 B5
Lawn Cres GL51 ....129 E2
Lawn Rd
Ashleworth GL19 ....172 D4
BS16 ....20 B5
Lawns Pk GL5 ....98 F2
Lawns Rd BS37 ....43 F2
Lawns The Bristol BS16 ..16 E7
Gloucester GL4 ....119 D3
Gotherington GL52 .....138 B7
Stonehouse GL10 ....97 E8
Lawnside GL6 ....91 A4
Lawnside 6 HR8 ....178 E8
Lawnwood Ind Units 14
 ....99 B8
Lawnwood Rd 18 BS5 ...9 B8
Lawrence Ave BS5 .....19 B1
Lawrence CI Bristol BS15 .21 A2
Charlton Kings GL52 ...131 B6
Lawrence Ct BS37 ......43 B2
Lawrence Gr BS9 ....18 B5
Lawrence Hill BS5 ....9 B7
Lawrence Hill Ind Pk BS5 .9 B8
Lawrence Hill Rdbt BS5 ..9 A7
Lawrence Hill Sta BS5 ...9 B7
Lawrence Rd
Avening GL8 ....148 B1
Cirencester GL7 ....190 B3
Lawrence Way GL1 ....126 E4
Lawrence Way N GL1 ..126 E4

Lawrence Weston Rd
Avonmouth BS11 ....26 E5
Bristol BS11 ....27 A3
Bristol BS11 ....27 C1
Lawrence Weston Sch
BS11 ....27 B1
Lawrence's Mdw GL52 .138 A8
Lawson CI BS31 ....5 A1
Lawson Glade GL53 ....131 A4
Laxey Rd BS7 ....18 F7
Laxton CI BS35 ....50 A3
Laxton Dr GL12 ....67 F4
Laxton Rd
Cheltenham GL51 ......132 E2
Gloucester GL14 ....120 A6
Laymore Rd GL14 ......191 B5
Laynes Rd GL3 ....120 A7
Lays Bsns Ctr BS31 .....4 C4
Lea Bsns Pk GL11 ....4 C4
Lea CE Prim Sch The
HR9 ....164 C8
Lea Cres GL2 ....127 C5
Lea Croft BS13 ....2 A4
Lea Ct GL2 ....127 D5
Lea Rd GL3 ....120 F5
Leacey Ct GL3 ....128 A7
Leacey Mews GL3 ......128 A7
Leadon CI GL3 ....120 F5
Leadon Way HR8 ....178 E7
Leafield Rd GL7 ....152 E4
Leaholes CI GL7 ....190 D4
Leaholme Gdns BS14 ....3 A3
Leaman CI BS37 ....44 B1
Leap Vale BS16 ....21 A8
Leap Valley Cres BS16 ..21 A8
Leaping Stocks Rd HR9 .162 D3
Lear CI BS30 ....11 B5
Lears Dr GL52 ....138 A3
Leaside CI GL11 ....100 A8
Leasow La GL54 ....169 B5
Leasows The
Broadwell GL56 ....177 A6
Chipping Campden GL55 .188 F1
Mickleton GL55 ....189 B6
Leaze CI GL53 ....85 E3
Leaze CI GL13 ....92 C2
Leaze The
2 Ashton Keynes SN6 .142 F5
Leaze The GL7 ....142 F7
Yate BS37 ....43 D2
Leazes The GL5 ....99 D7
Lechlade Rd
Highworth SN6 ....145 D4
Lechlade on T GL7 .....152 C3
Southrop GL7 ....153 C6
Upper Inglesham SN6 ..145 D7
Lechmere Rd 1 GL51 ..132 E3
Leckhampton CE Prim Sch
GL51 ....130 D4
Leckhampton Farm Ct
GL51 ....130 B3
Leckhampton Gate
GL51 ....130 B3
Leckhampton Hill GL53 .130 D2
Leckhampton La GL53 ..130 A2
Leckhampton PI GL53 ..130 D5
Leckhampton Rd GL53 .130 D5
Leckhampton View
 ....129 F2
Leda Ave BS14 ....3 A7
Ledbury Heritage Ctr*
HR8 ....178 F8
Ledbury Pk 9 HR8 .....178 F8
Ledbury Prim Sch HR8 .178 E8
Ledbury Rd HR8 ....20 C4
Ledbury Road Cres
GL19 ....172 A8
Leddington Ct HR8 .....178 D7
Ledmore Rd GL53 ......131 B6
Ledwell Cl BS36 ....28 F8
Lee CI BS34 ....28 B8
Lee Rd GL20 ....182 C4
Leechpool Way BS37 ...43 E5
Leeming Way BS11 .....16 C8
Lees CI BS15 ....20 E1
Lees Hill BS15 ....22 F2
Lee La BS30 ....11 D5
Leicester Sq BS16 ......20 D3
Leicester St 6 BS3 .....8 D4
Leicester Wlk BS4 ....7 F5
Leigh CE Sch SN6 .....143 B3
Leigh Court Bsns Ctr
BS8 ....7 C2
Leigh La Cold Ashton BA1 .14 B3
Westerleigh BS37 ....32 E1
Leigh Rd BS8 ....194 B4
Leigh Woods Forest Walks*
BS8 ....7 D4
Leighterton Prim Sch
GL8 ....70 C3

Leighton Rd
Bristol, Knowle BS4 ......9 B2
Bristol, Southville BS3 ....8 B4
Cheltenham GL52 ......133 F1
Leinster Ave BS4 ....2 A2
Leinster CI GL51 ....132 D4
Leisure Cntr* GL7 .....190 B4
Leisure Rd BS15 ....10 E5
Lemon La BS2 ....195 C4
Lena Ave 8 BS5 ....19 C1
Lena St BS5 ....19 C1
Lennards Ct 7 BS1 .....143 A8
Lennox Way BS11 ....26 B1
Lenover Gdns BS13 ......2 B4
Lensbrook GL15 ....93 A8
Leonard La BS1 ....195 A3

Leonard Rd Bristol BS5 11
Gloucester GL1 11
Leonard Stanley CE Prim S
GL10 9
Leonards Ave BS5 1
Leopold Rd BS6 1
Lescren Way BS11 2
Letch Hill Dr GL54 16
Letch La 11 GL54 16
Leven CI GL2 12
Lever's Hill GL11 8
Lewin St 9 BS5 1
Lewington Rd BS16 2
Lewins Mead BS1 19
Lewis Ave GL2 12
Lewis CI BS30 1
Lewis Glade 2 GL16 ...19
Lewis La GL7 19
Lewis Rd Bristol BS13 .13
Cheltenham GL51 13
Lewis St BS2 ....
Lewis Way NP16 C
Lewisham Rd GL1 13
Lewisham Terr GL13 14
Lewiston Rd GL5 14
Lewton La BS3 ....
Ley La GS35 ....
Ley Orch WR12 16
Ley Rd GL2 11
Leyland Wlk BS13 ....
Leys The GL13 ....
Leysbourne GL55 16
Leyson Rd GL51 15
Leyton Villas BS6 ....
Libby's Dr GL5 ....
Libertus Ct GL51 13
Libertus Rd GL51 13
Liberty Ind Pk BS3 ......
Lichfield Dr GL1 13
Lichfield Rd Bristol BS4 ..
Gloucester GL4 13
Lidderdale Rd GL4 16
Liddington CI GL53 13
Liddington Rd
Cheltenham GL53 13
Gloucester GL2 13
Liddington Trad Est
GL53 13
Lifford Gdns WR12 18
Lightenbrook La GL2 ....
Lightfoot 10 GL3 12
Lightwood La GL6 10
Lilac CI Bristol BS10 ....
Cheltenham GL51 13
Lilac CE BS31 ....
Lilac Way Gloucester GL4 .
Quedgeley GL2 ....
Lillian St 5 BS5 ....
Lilliesfield Ave GL3 13
Lilliput Ave BS37 ....
Lilliput Ct BS37 ....
Lilly Hall La HR8 17
Lilstock Ave BS7 ....
Lilton Wlk BS13 ....
Lilymead Ave BS4 ....
Limber Hill GL50 ....
Limbury Hostels GL19 ..
Lime Ave GL9 ....
Lime CI Brentry BS10 ...
Prestbury GL52 13
Lime Ct BS31 ....
Lime Gr Alveston BS35 ..
Stroud GL5 ....
Lime Kiln CI BS34 ....
Lime Kiln Gdns BS32 ...
Lime Rd
Bristol, Hanham BS15 ...
Bristol, Southville BS3 ...
Tewkesbury GL20 1
Lime Tree Ave 3 WR12 .1
Lime Tree Gr BS20 ......
Lime Tree Rd GL20 .....
Lime Trees Rd GL3 .....
Lime Way GL15 ....
Limekiln Gr GL2 1
Limekiln La GL6 1
Limekiln Rd BS37,GL12 ..1
Limerick Rd BS6 ....
Limes PI SN6 ....
Limes Rd GL7 ....
Limes The Badminton GL9 .
Bristol BS16 ....
Gloucester, Barnwood GL4 .1
Gloucester, Kingsholm
GL2 ....
Limetree Ave NP25 1
Linacre Cres GL7 1
Lincoln Ave BS1 ....
Lincoln CI Keynsham BS31 .
Tewkesbury GL20 1
Upper Rissington GL54 ..1
Lincoln Green La GL20 .19
Lincoln St BS5 ....
Lincombe Ave BS16 ....
Lincombe Rd BS16 .....
Linden Ave GL3 ....
Linden CI
Bristol, Mayfield Park BS16 .
Chepstow NP16 ....
Colerne SN14 ....
Prestbury GL52 ....
Winterbourne BS36 .....
Linden Dr BS32 ....

en Ho BS16 .....19 C5
en Prim Sch GL11 ..118 D6
en Rd Bristol BS6 ...18 A4
ucester GL1 ......118 D6
on Ho BS9 ....9 E3
rea St ◼ BS3 .....8 B3
say Rd BS7 ....19 A4
The HR9 ....170 A3
gar Wood Rd GL14 .191 C1
ttock St GL1 ....8 A2
or Rd GL8 ....140 B4
riot Pk BS16 ......30 F2
Rd Bristol BS34 ....28 F3
well GL15 ....155 F1
kesbury GL20 .....192 D4
 〃 BS37 ....43 F1
nd Rd GL19 ....180 F2
s The GL16 ....155 A5
s View GL7 ....150 C7
ell GL5 ....111 B6
ell Cl BS7 ....19 B6
cl Bristol BS34 ....28 E8
ucester GL4 ....119 C5
ley Way GL4 ......118 D1
ern Cres BS30 ....11 B6
am Dr BS15 ....10 F6
on Ct GL5 ....193 C1
on Rd HR9 ....170 B4
ell Cl GL5 ....133 B5
orth Rd GL52 .....138 A3
Ct GL2 ....112 E4
on Rd GL51 ....132 E4
on Villas GL51 ....132 E4
arn Rd BS4 ....8 E1
PI GL12 ....68 A7
ore Rd SN6 ....145 C4
eld Rd BS8 ....7 F7
eld Rd BS8 ....7 F8
ow Rd GL54 ......169 D6
e Acorns GL52 ....137 E5
e Acre GL12 ....68 A8
e Ann St BS2,BS5 ..195 C4
e Bayshill Terr
 ....193 B3
e Birch Croft BS14 ..3 A3
e Bishop St BS2 ....195 B4
e Bristol Cl GL12 ..67 B4
e Bristol La GL17 ..67 B4
e Caroline PI ◼ BS8 ..7 F2
e Cleevemount
 ....133 F3
e Dowles BS30 ....11 A4
e Elmbridge GL2 ..127 E3
e Field GL4 ....119 D7
e Fishers GL5 ....99 A4
e George St BS2 ..195 C4
e Gn GL10 ....179 D2
e Green La BS35 ....38 A7
e Guillet Ct GL11 ..87 F4
e Hayes BS16 ......20 B6
e Headley Cl BS3 ...2 B7
e Herbert's Cl GL53 .131 B5
e Herbert's Rd GL53 131 B4
e Holbury GL2 .....100 E5
e Horcott La GL7 ..152 E3
e King St BS1 .....195 A2
e Lancarridge GL2 ..127 A6
e Marcle Rd HR8 ..178 E8
e Mdw BS34 ....30 A6
e Mus* GL20 ......192 C4
e Normans GL22 ..127 E5
e Oaks GL18 ......179 B4
e Orch GL52 ......137 E4
e Paradise BS3 .....8 D3
e Parr Cl BS16 ....19 C5
e Paul St BS2 .....194 C4
e Pheasants GL53 ..131 A5
e Rd WK11 ....188 B8
e Rose La SN26 ...144 C3
e Stoke La BS34 ...29 D6
e Stoke Prim Sch
 ....29 C6
e Stoke Rd BS9 ...17 E4
e Trewen La HR9 ..162 C5
e Withey Mead BS9 ..9 B9
e Wlk GL52 ....127 C5
ecote Cl GL52 ....137 E3
across Ho BS3 ......8 B4
edean St BS37 ....32 E7
edean CE Prim Sch
 ....156 E8
edean Hill* GL14 ..191 E4
edown Hill Rd GL53 130 F4
efield GL12 ....117 E2
e Wlk GL2 ....67 A6
eton Rd BS34 .....39 F1
eton La BS41 ....1 C1
eton Rd BS3 ......8 D3
eton St ◱ BS5 .....19 C1
ewood BS14 ....3 B3
ewurth GL15 .....188 F2
e Way GL11 ....92 B4
silo St ◱ GL11 ....118 D7
dilo St ◱ GL11 ...118 F7
Jogo Jun & Inf Sch
 ....146 B7
garron Bsns Ctr
 ....162 B7
grove CE Prim Sch
 ....162 B6
hony Cotts GL20 ..136 B7
hony Ind Est GL2 ..126 C1
hony Priory* GL2 ..126 C1
hony Rd GL2 ......126 C1
hony HR9 ....162 C5
ellyn Ct BS9 ....18 A8
el Baker Cl GL2 ...109 E7

Lobb Ct GL1 ......120 A1
Lobleys Dr GL4 ...120 A5
Lock Gdns BS13 ....1 F1
Lock's La GL7 ......41 E4
Lockemor Rd BS13 ..2 F4
Locking Hill GL1 ...99 C7
Lockingwell Rd BS31 ..4 D5
Lockleaze Rd BS7 ...19 A6
Lockleaze Sch BS7 ..19 C7
Locombe Hill GL7 ..153 D8
Locombe Rd GL2 ...68 C6
Lodersfield GL7 ....153 E2
Lodge Causeway Trad Ctr
 BS16 ....19 F3
Lodge Cswy BS16 ...20 A3
Lodge Ct BS9 ....17 E4
Lodge Dr Bristol BS30 .11 C2
 Long Ashton BS41 ...7 B2
Lodge Gdns GL15 ..146 E7
Lodge Hill BS15 ....20 C2
Lodge La GL15 .....147 D6
Lodge PI BS1 ......194 C3
Lodge Rd Bristol BS15 .20 C1
 Wick BS30 ....22 B1
 Yate BS37 ....27 F1
Lodge St BS1 ......194 C3
Lodge Wlk BS16 ....20 D6
Lodgemore Cl GL5 ..99 A7
Lodgemore La GL5 ..99 A7
Lodgeside Ave BS15 .20 C1
Lodgeside Gdns BS15 .20 C1
Lodore Rd BS16 ....19 F3
Lodway Cl BS20 ....16 C4
Lodway Gdns BS20 .16 C4
Lodway Rd BS4 ......9 C2
Logan Rd BS7 ......18 D3
Logus Ct ⓯ BS30 ..10 F4
Loiterpin GL5 .....156 D2
Lombard St BS3 .....8 D4
Lomond Rd BS7 .....28 E1
London La WK11 ...142 E1
London Rd
 Bristol, St Pauls BS2 ..18 F1
 Bristol, Warmley BS30 ..11 D7
 Charlton Kings GL52,GL53 .131 C5
 Cheltenham GL52 ..130 F8
 Fairford GL7 ......152 F4
 Gloucester GL1,GL2 127 A2
 Moreton-in-M GL56 .187 B3
 Stroud GL5 ....99 E3
 Tetbury GL8 ......140 C5
 Thrupp GL5 ....99 E3
 Wick BS30 ....12 E6
London Road Terr BS37 .187 B3
London St Bristol BS15 .10 D8
 Fairford GL7 ......152 A5
Long Acres ⓯ HR8 ..178 E8
Long Acres Cl BS9 ...17 D7
Long Ashton BS41 ...7 B2
Long Beach Rd BS30 ..11 B3
Long Cl
 Bristol, Fishponds BS16 ..20 C6
 Bristol, Little Stoke BS34 ..29 E6
Long Croft GL7 .....43 D4
Long Cross BS11 ....27 B2
Long Dr GL16 .....155 B6
Long Eaton Dr BS14 ..3 D7
Long Eights GL2 ...182 C5
Long Field GL2 ....125 D6
Long Furlong GL2 ..127 B7
Long Furlong La GL8 .140 B3
Long Handstones BS30 .11 A4
Long Marston CV37,
 GL55 ....189 A8
Long Mdw BS16 ....19 E4
Long Mead BS37 ....43 E5
Long Mynd Ave GL51 .129 E6
Long Newnton Rd
 GL8 ....140 A3
Long Park Row BS1 .195 A3
Long Park St ⓰ GL54 .176 C4
Long Quay St GL1 ...80 B8
Lower Quay St GL1 ..196 A3
Long Row Bristol BS1 .195 B2
 Castle Eaton SN6 ..114 C1
 Tetbury GL8 ......140 B4
 Wooton-u-E GL12 ...68 B7
Longacre Rd BS14 ...3 A3
Longaston Cl GL4 ...95 A4
Longaston La GL4 ...95 E5
Longborough CE Prim Sch
 GL56 ....176 D8
Longborough Dr GL4 .119 E4
Longcross GL12 ....66 B1
Longden Rd BS16 ...20 D6
Longfield GL7 .....117 E2
Longfield Rd BS37 ...18 E3
Longford GL2 ......32 C8
Longford Ave BS10 ..18 D8
Longford Ct GL50 ..192 E3
Longford Ho GL2 ...127 A5
Longford La GL2 ...127 A5
Longford Mews GL2 .126 F6
Longhill Rd GL4 ...149 E8
Longhope CE Prim Sch
 GL17 ....164 F6
Longhope Cl GL4 ...119 E5
Longhope Rd GL19 .165 C6
Longland Ct GL2 ...127 A4
Longland Gdns GL2 .127 A4
Longlands GL8 .....140 B3
Longlands Ho ⓲ BS5 ..9 C7
Longlands Rd GL52 .138 B4
Longleat Ave GL4 ..118 C1
Longleat Cl BS9 ....18 C5
Longleigh La GL6 ...83 C6
Longlevens Jun & Inf Sch
 GL2 ....127 C4
Longmead Ave BS7 .18 D5

Longmead Croft BS13 ...1 F4
Longmead Rd BS16 ..31 B1
Longmeadow Rd BS31 ..4 C4
Longmoor Ct BS3 ....8 A2
Longmoor Rd BS3 ...8 A2
Longmore Ave GL54 .169 D6
Longney CE Prim Sch
 GL2 ....108 C5
Longney Rd GL4 ...118 D3
Longreach Gr BS14 ..3 D6
Longridge La GL19 ..155 A2
Longs Dr BS37 ......43 C2
Longs View GL12 ...67 A5
Longsmith St GL1 ..196 B2
Longstop Hill GL51 ..129 F6
Longtown Rd GL20 ..192 E2
Longtree Cl BS32 ..140 B5
Longville Ct GL4 ...119 F5
Longway Ave
 Bristol BS13,BS14 ....2 F4
 Charlton Kings GL53 .131 A4
Longwell Green Prim Sch
 BS30 ....10 F3
Longwell Ho BS30 ..10 F3
Longwood BS4 ......10 C4
Longwood La GL6 ..155 A7
Lonsdale Bsns Ctr BS15 ..20 C2
Lonsdale St SN26 ..144 E1
Loop Rd NP16 ....61 A3
Loran Wrik WS10 ....27 F2
Lord Eldon Dr NP16 ..60 F4
Lord's Hill GL5 ....155 A5
Lord's Hill Cl ⑤ GL5 .155 A5
Lords Gn GL52 .....138 C3
Lorimers Cl GL7 ...117 F2
Lorton Cl BS10 .....28 B1
Lorton Rd BS10 ....28 B1
Lotts The 〃 BS3 ..142 F5
Loughman Cl BS15 ..10 D8
Louisa St BS2 ......195 C2
Louise Ave BS16 .....21 A5
Love La
 Chipping Sodbury BS37 ..33 A8
 Cirencester GL7 ...207 D1
 Yate BS37 ....44 A4
Love Lane Ind Est GL7 .190 D2
Lovedays Mead GL5 ..99 C8
Lovell Ave BS30 ....11 D4
Lovell's Hill BS15 ...10 B5
Lovelinch Gdns BS41 ..1 C1
Lovers Wlk HR9 ....170 B4
Lovett Cl GL12 .....172 A8
Lowbourne BS14 .....2 F6
Lowdilow La GL51 ..136 E1
Lower Ashley Rd
 Bristol, Baptist Mills BS2,
 BS5 ....19 A1
 ⓫ Bristol, St Pauls BS2 ..18 F1
Lower Berrycroft GL7 .103 A8
Lower Castle St BS1 .195 B3
Lower Chapel La BS36 .37 C7
Lower Chapel Rd BS15 ..10 C5
Lower Cheltenham PI
 BS6 ....18 F1
Lower Church La BS2 .195 A3
Lower Church St NP16 ..72 F1
Lower Churchfield
 GL5 ....99 C6
Lower Clifton Hill BS8 .194 B2
Lower Cock Rd BS15 ..10 F7
Lower College St BS1 .194 C2
Lower Comn GL15 ..147 D5
Lower Court Rd BS32 .40 A5
Lower Croft GL7 ...152 E4
Lower Fallow Cl BS14 ..2 F3
Lower Gay St BS2 ..195 A4
Lower Grove Rd BS16 .19 F4
Lower Guinea St BS1 .195 A1
Lower Hanham Rd BS15 .10 C6
Lower High St
 Bristol BS11 ....16 D7
 Chipping Campden GL55 .189 A2
Lower House Cres BS34 .28 F2
Lower Kitesnest La GL6 .103 A3
Lower Knole La BS10 ..28 C2
Lower Lamb St BS1 .194 C2
Lower Leazes GL5 ...99 D7
Lower Lode La GL20 .192 A2
Lower Maudlin St BS1 .195 A3
Lower Mdw BS37 ...109 F7
Lower Mill St GL51 .133 A3
Lower Moor Rd BS37 .43 E4
Lower Newmarket Rd
 GL6 ....90 F4
Lower Park Row BS1 .195 A3
Lower Park St ⓱ GL54 .176 C4
Lower Quay St GL1 ..80 B8
Lower Quay St GL1 ..196 A3
Lower Redland Mews ◨
 BS6 ....18 B2
Lower Redland Rd BS6 .18 B2
Lower Sidney St BS3 ..8 A4
Lower Spillman's GL5 ..96 A6
Lower St Blockley GL56 .186 C5
 Stroud GL5 ....99 C6
 Whiteshill GL6 ....102 F3
Lower Station Rd
 ⓮ Bristol, Ridgeway BS16 .20 A4
 Bristol, Staplehill BS16 ..20 C4
Lower Stone Cl BS32 .31 C7
Lower Terr ⑧ GL56 .186 C5

Lower Thirlmere Rd
 BS34 ....29 A8
Lower Tockington Rd
 BS32 ....50 B1
Lower Tuffley La GL2 .118 B4
Lower Washwell La
 GL6 ....104 A8
Loweswater Cl GL51 .129 F7
Loweswater Rd GL51 .129 F7
Lowfield Rd GL8 ...140 B5
Lowlis Cl BS10 ......27 F3
Lowther Rd BS10 ...28 C2
Luxton Sq BS13 ......3 A6
Luxton Sq BS5 ....9 D1
Luccombe Hill BS6 ..18 B2
Lucinia Mews GL51 .132 F3
Luckington Court Gdns*
 SN14 ....47 F5
Luckington Cty Prim Sch
 SN14 ....47 E5
Luckington Rd BS7 ..18 E8
Luckley Ave BS13 ....2 C5
Luckwell Prim Sch BS3 .8 A3
Luckwell Rd BS3 .....8 B3
Lucky La BS3 ....8 D4
Ludgate Hill GL12 ..68 B7
Ludlow Cl
 Bristol, St Pauls BS2 ..18 F1
 Bristol, Willsbridge BS30 .11 B2
 Keynsham BS31 ......4 D5
Ludlow Ct BS30 .....11 B2
Ludlow Rd BS7 ......19 A7
Ludwell Cl BS36 ....30 D5
Luggs The GL10 .....98 A3
Luke La GL3 ....127 E6
Lullington Rd BS4 ...9 B2
Lulsgate Rd BS13 ....2 A8
Lulworth Cres BS16 .20 F8
Lulworth Rd BS31 ...4 E4
Lurgan Wlk BS4 .....8 E1
Lurks La GL6 ....103 B4
Lushill Cotts SN6 ..144 E5
Lux Furlong BS9 ....17 B7
Luxton St BS5 ....9 B8
Lych Gate Mews GL51 .92 A2
Lydbrook Cl BS37 ...32 D8
Lydbrook Prim Sch
 GL17 ....163 D2
Lyddington Rd GL51 .18 F8
Lyde Green Rdbt BS16 .21 B8
Lydfield Rd GL51 ...92 E3
Lydford Wlk BS3 .....8 D2
Lydiatt Croft BS15 ..10 C4
Lydney & District Hospl
 GL15 ....147 F6
Lydney CE Com Prim Sch
 GL15 ....92 A3
Lydney Ind Est GL15 ..84 C8
Lydney Junc Sta* GL15 .92 A1
Lydney Rd Bream GL15 .147 D8
 Bristol, Southmead BS10 ..28 D1
 Bristol, Staple Hill BS16 ..20 A4
Lydney Sta GL15 .....84 A8
Lydney Town Sta* GL15 .92 A3
Lydstep Terr BS3 .....8 C4
Lye La GL52 ....138 D1
Lyefield Rd E GL53 ..131 B6
Lyefield Rd W GL53 .131 A6
Lygon Cl GL52 .....152 E5
Lygon Wlk ⑨ GL51 .132 F3
Lyley Rd GL52 ....68 A7
Lynch Cl BS30 ....10 F4
Lynch Rd Berkeley GL13 ..85 D3
 Chalford GL6 ......148 D6
Lyncombe Wlk BS16 .20 B2
Lyncroft GL12 ......116 F7
Lycroft Farm Wkshps
 GL7 ....150 C8
Lyndale Ave BS9 ....17 D5
Lyndale Rd Bristol BS5 ..9 D8
 Yate BS37 ....43 D1
Lyndale Terr
 Cheltenham GL51 ..133 A2
 Norton GL2 ....173 B3
Lynde Cl BS13 ....2 B4
Lyndhurst Cl GL52 ..138 B3
Lyndhurst Rd Bristol BS9 ..17 F7
 Keynsham BS31 ......4 F6
Lyndhurst Chase GL52 .137 D4
Lyng Cl GL4 ....119 E8
Lynmouth Rd
 Bristol BS2 ....19 A2
 Gloucester GL3 ....119 F7
Lynn Rd BS16 ....19 D5
Lynt Farm Cotts SN6 .145 D7
Lynt Rd SN6 ....145 D7
Lynton ⓰ BS15 .....11 A8
Lynton PI ⓱ BS5 .....9 D8
Lynton Rd BS3 ......8 D2
 Gloucester GL3 ....119 F7
Lynton Way BS16 ....30 B1
Lynwood Rd Bristol BS3 .8 B2
 Lydney GL15 ....92 A5
Lynworth Ct ⑤ GL52 .138 C5
Lynworth Exchange
 GL52 ....134 A3
Lynworth La GL20 ..181 F8
Lynworth PI GL52 ..134 A3
Lynworth Terr GL52 .134 B4
Lyons Court Rd BS14 ..3 D7
Lyppiatt Dr GL50 ...193 A2
Lyppiatt Mews GL51 .193 A2
Lyppiatt Rd GL50 ...193 A2
Lyppiatt St GL50 ...193 A2
Lyppiatt View GL6 ..148 B6

Lyppiatt Rd BS5 ......9 D8
Lyppincourt Rd BS10 .28 A3
Lysander Cl GL3 ...128 C5
Lysander Rd BS10,BS34 .28 C6
Lysander Wlk BS34 ..29 D5
Lysons Ave GL1 ....118 D7
Lytchet Dr BS16 ....30 A4
Lytes Cary Rd BS31 ..5 A3
Lytton Gr Bristol BS7 ..19 A8
 Keynsham BS31 ......5 A5
Lyveden Gdns BS13 ..2 B5
Lyvedon Way BS41 ..7 B1

M

Mabel's Furlong ⓰ HR8 .178 F8
Macarthur Rd GL54 .168 A1
Macauley Rd GL51 ..19 A8
Macdonald Wlk ⑤ BS15 ..10 D8
Macey's Rd BS13 .....2 D3
Machen Rd GL16 ...155 B6
Machin Cl BS10 .....27 F3
Machin Gdns BS10 ..28 A3
Machin Rd BS10 ....28 A3
Mackenzie Way GL51 .133 A5
Mackie Ave BS34 ...29 B2
Mackie Rd BS34 ....29 B2
Mackie Rd BS34 ....29 B2
Macrae Ct BS15 .....10 E8
Macrae Rd BS20 ....16 E4
Madeline Rd BS16 ..19 F2
Madison Cl BS37 ....43 D2
Madleaze Ind Est GL1 .196 A1
Madleaze Rd GL1 ..196 A1
Madocke Rd NP16 ...61 A7
Maesbury BS15 ......10 E6
Maesbury Rd BS31 ..14 A3
Maesknoll La BS14 ...3 B1
Maesknoll Rd BS4 ...9 A2
Magdala Rd ⓵ GL1 .127 A1
Magdalen Rd GL8 ..140 B4
Magdalene PI BS2 ..18 F1
Maggs Cl BS10 ......28 C3
Maggs La Bristol BS5 .19 E2
 Whitchurch BS13 .....3 C4
Magnolia Cl NP16 ...60 F5
Magnolia Cl GL51 ..132 D2
Magnolia Wlk GL2 .117 E1
Magpie Bottom La
 Bristol BS15 ....10 C6
 Bristol BS5 ....10 B6
Magpie Ct GL10 .....97 F8
Maida Vale Rd GL53 .130 A5
Maiden Way BS11 ...16 C8
Maidencroft La GL7 .144 F7
Maidenhall GL2 ....125 D5
Maidenhead Rd BS13 ..2 D3
Maidenhill Sch GL10 .101 F1
Maidstone St BS3 .....8 F3
Main Rd Bristol BS16 ..21 D5
 Mile End GL16 .....155 B6
 Netherend GL15 ...147 D3
 Pillowell GL15 ....147 F1
 Tintern Parva NP16 .146 B3
 Whiteshill GL6 ....102 F3
 Woolaston GL15 ...147 C2
Main St Adlestrop GL56 .177 E6
 Beckford GL20 .....181 E4
 Bledington GL7 ....177 L1
 Bretforton WR11 ..188 A6
 Willersey WR12 ...188 B2
Main View BS36 .....37 D7
Mainard Sq GL2 ....127 C1
Maine St GL7 ....152 E2
Maisemore BS37 .....32 E6
Maisemore Ave BS34 .40 B1
Maitlands GL4 .....110 F5
Makin Cl BS30 ....11 C5
Malago Rd BS3 ....8 D3
Malago Vale Est BS3 .8 D3
Malago Wlk BS13 .....1 E4
Malden Rd GL52 ...133 E3
Maldon Gdns GL1 ..118 F7
Maldovers La BS35 ..10 A8
Malet Cl GL2 ....127 C5
Mall The Bristol, Clifton BS8 ..7 F7
 Bristol, Cribbs Causeway
 BS34 ....28 D6
Mallard Cl
 Bristol, Crofts End BS5 ..19 F1
 Bristol, Patchway BS32 ..40 D2
 Chipping Sodbury BS37 ..33 A8
 Quedgeley GL2 ....117 D1
Malleson Rd GL52 ..137 F8
Mallow Cl BS35 ......64 D2
Malmains Dr BS16 ...30 B1
Malmesbury Cl
 Bristol, Bishopston BS6 .18 C4
 Bristol, Longwell Green
 BS30 ....10 F5
Malmesbury Rd
 Cheltenham GL51 ..133 A5
 Gloucester GL4 ...119 B7
 Leigh SN6 ....143 C2
Malmesy Cl GL20 ..192 D1
Malthouse Cl SN26 .144 E1
Malthouse La
 Cheltenham GL51 ..133 D3
 Lower Slaughter GL54 .176 C1
 ⓱ Winchcombe GL54 .174 A7
Malthouse Wlk ⑧ GL8 .140 B4
Malvern Cl BS35 .....51 D8
Malvern Dr Bristol BS30 ..11 C5
 Thornbury BS35 .....51 D8

Malvern Gdns GL5 ....98 E7
Malvern Pl GL50 ....193 A3
Malvern Rd
Bristol, Brislington BS4 ....9 D3
Bristol, St George BS5 .....9 F7
Cheltenham GL50 ....133 B1
Gloucester GL1 ....126 F4
Staunton GL39 ....172 B8
Malvern St GL51 ....133 A4
Malvern View Bsns Pk
GL52 ....137 C4
Malvern Way GL14 ....155 C8
Malverns The GL4 ....118 B7
Manchester Ct ☒ GL56 ...187 A3
Manchester Pk GL51 ....133 B4
Manchester Way ☒
GL5 ....193 A4
Mancroft Ave BS11 ....16 F7
Mandalay Dr GL2 ....173 B3
Mandara Gr GL4 ....119 D4
Mandarin Way GL50 ....133 C5
Mandeville Cl GL2 ....127 C6
Mangotsfield CE Sch
GL3 ....21 B6
Mangotsfield Rd BS16 ....21 A5
Manilla Rd BS8 ....194 A3
Mankley Rd GL10 ....97 E4
Manley Gdns GL2 ....127 C5
Mannings Rd GL17 ....164 B4
Manor Ave Dursley GL11 ..87 F5
Lechlade on T GL7 ....153 F2
Manor Cl
Broad Blunsdon SN26 ....144 E1
Cirencester GL7 ....150 C7
Coalpit Heath BS36 ....31 C6
Dursley GL11 ....87 F6
Easton-in-G BS20 ....16 A4
Honeybourne WR11 ....188 C6
Sherston SN16 ....58 C1
Teddington GL20 ....183 A3
Tockington BS32 ....50 C1
Manor Ct The BS8 ....7 A8
Manor Cotts Pitt Ct GL11 ..79 F5
Sopworth SN14 ....57 D1
Manor Court Dr BS17 ....18 C7
Manor Ct
☒ Bristol, Fishponds BS16 ...19 E4
☑ Bristol, Upper Easton
BS5 ....19 B1
Gloucester GL4 ....119 B4
Swindon GL51 ....133 A4
Whitminster GL2 ....100 F5
Manor Farm Bristol BS32 ...29 D7
Little Rissington GL54 ....169 C6
Manor Farm Cotts GL8 ..141 A6
Manor Farm Cres BS32 ...40 D1
Manor Field GL54 ....183 F1
Manor Gardens Ho BS16 ...20 C4
Manor Gdns
Gloucester GL4 ....119 E8
Lechlade on T GL7 ....153 E2
Newnham GL14 ....156 F6
Woodchester GL5 ....99 A2
Manor Gr ☒ BS16 ....19 B1
Manor La
Bretforton WR11 ....188 A6
Charfield GL12 ....67 A4
Gotherington GL52 ....133 D2
Winterbourne BS36 ....30 F7
Wotton-u-E GL12 ....68 C7
Manor Orch SN6 ....143 F4
Manor Park Bsns Ctr
GL51 ....133 B4
Manor Pk Bristol BS6 ....18 B3
Cheltenham GL51 ....129 D5
Gloucester GL2 ....127 E4
Tewkesbury GL20 ....192 E6
Tockington BS32 ....50 C1
Manor Prim Sch The
BS36 ....31 D6
Manor Rd Abbots Leigh BS8 ...7 A8
Bristol, Bishopston BS7 ...18 E4
Bristol, Bishopsworth BS13 ...2 A6
Bristol, Fishponds BS16 ...20 A5
Bristol, Mangotsfield BS16 ...21 A4
Cheltenham GL51 ....133 A6
Lydney GL15 ....92 C3
Rangeworthy BS37 ....43 A7
Salford BS31 ....5 C2
Wick BS30 ....23 C5
Manor St GL6 ....105 A1
Manor Stables GL54 ....128 C4
Manor View
St Arvans NP16 ....72 B5
Stroud GL5 ....98 E4
Manor Way BS37 ....44 C2
Manor Wlk BS35 ....64 B3
Manse Gdns ☒ GL51 ....129 F7
Manse La The HR9 ....170 B5
Manse Rd GL17 ....164 B4
Mansel Cl BS31 ....5 C3
Mansell Cl GL2 ....118 C5
Mansell Ct GL2 ....118 C5
Mansfield Mews GL2 ....109 F7
Mansfield St BS3 ....8 C2
Manson's La NP25 ....162 A1

Manston Cl BS14 ....3 C7
Manworthy Rd BS4 ....9 D3
Manx Rd BS7 ....18 F8
Maple Ave Bristol BS16 ...20 C3
Chepstow NP16 ....60 E5
Thornbury BS35 ....64 C1
Maple Cl
Bristol, Little Stoke BS34 ...29 C7
Bristol, Oldland BS30 ....11 B4
Bristol, Stockwood BS14 ...3 D5
Dursley GL11 ....88 A1
Hardwicke GL2 ....109 E8
Maple Ct Bristol BS9 ....17 F8
Gloucester GL2 ....127 E4
☒ Bristol BS15 ....20 D1
Maple Dr
Brockworth GL3 ....120 D7
Charlton Kings GL3 ....131 B5
Stroud GL5 ....103 A1
Maple Leaf Ct BS8 ....194 A3
Maple Rd
Bristol, Horfield BS7 ....18 E5
Bristol, St Anne's BS4 ....9 B6
Maple Wlk Keynsham BS31 ...4 D4
Pucklechurch BS16 ....22 C5
Mapleleaze BS4 ....9 D3
Maplemeade BS7 ....18 C4
Mapleridge La BS37 ....44 D7
Maples The
Cirencester GL7 ....190 B1
Gloucester GL4 ....119 E6
Maplestone Rd BS14 ....3 A3
Mapstone Cl BS16 ....30 B3
Marbeck Rd BS10 ....28 B1
Marchant Cl GL51 ....132 F3
Mardale Cl BS10 ....28 C2
Marden Rd BS31 ....5 B5
Mardon Rd BS4 ....9 D7
Mardyke Ferry Rd BS1 ...194 B1
Marefield Cl GL4 ....117 F2
Marfells Way GL17 ....163 F3
Margaret Rd Bristol BS13 ...1 F4
☒ Ledbury HR8 ....178 E8
Tewkesbury GL20 ....192 D3
Margate St BS3 ....8 B3
Margery La GL15 ....154 F2
Margrett Rd GL50 ....133 D3
Marguerite Rd BS13 ....1 F4
Marian Cl GL1 ....196 A3
Marian La GL16 ....155 A7
Marians Wlk GL16 ....155 A7
Marigold Wlk BS3 ....8 A2
Marina Gdns BS16 ....19 E3
Marina The GL15 ....84 B8
Marina Gdns GL6 ....155 A5
Marine Par BS20 ....16 C5
Mariner's Way BS20 ....16 C5
Mariners Dr BS9 ....17 D4
Mariners' Path BS9 ....17 E3
Mariners Way NP16 ....61 A4
Marion Wlk BS5 ....10 A7
Marissal Cl BS10 ....27 E3
Marissal Rd BS10 ....27 E3
Mariston Way BS30 ....11 C6
Marjoram Cl ☒ GL4 ....119 F8
Marjoram Pl BS13 ....29 F7
Mark La BS1 ....194 C2
Market Cl GL54 ....168 F8
Market La GL54 ....184 A1
Market Par GL1 ....196 B3
Market Pl Berkeley GL13 ...
Cirencester GL7 ....190 C5
Coleford GL16 ....155 A5
☒ Fairford GL7 ....152 B8
Lechlade on T GL7 ....153 E2
☒ Tetbury GL8 ....146 C3
Market Sq Bristol BS16 ...20 C3
Minchinhampton GL6 ....148 A3
☒ Newent GL18 ....171 A4
Stow-on-t-W GL54 ....176 F4
Market St
Cheltenham GL50 ....193 A4
Cinderford GL14 ....191 D5
Ledbury HR8 ....178 E2
Nailsworth GL6 ....91 B3
Wotton-u-E GL12 ....68 B7
Market Way GL1 ....196 B2
Marketside BS2 ....9 B4
Markham Cl BS11 ....16 C7
Marklands BS9 ....17 E3
Marksbury Rd BS3 ....8 C1
Marlborough Ave ☒
BS16 ....19 E3
Marlborough Cl
Bishop's Cleeve GL52 ....137 E3
Charlton Kings GL53 ....19 A7
Marlborough Cres GL4 ...119 A7
Marlborough Dr BS16 ....19 E3
Marlborough Flats ☒
BS2 ....195 A4
Marlborough Hill BS2 ....195 A4
Marlborough Hill Pl
BS2 ....195 A4
Marlborough Pl GL2 ....133 F1
Marlborough St GL4 ....119 F7
Marlborough St
Bristol, Eastville BS5 ....19 E3
Bristol, Kingsdown BS2 .....4 B3
Marlbrook Prim Sch
BS35 ....64 C2
Marle Hill GL4 ....148 C5
Marle Hill Par GL50 ....133 D3
Marle Hill Rd GL50 ....133 D3
Marlepit Gr BS13 ....1 F6

Marley La GL6 ....148 D5
Marleyfield Cl ☒ GL3 ....128 A7
Marleyfield Way GL3 .....128 A7
Marlfield Wlk GL3 ....1 E7
Marling Cl GL5 ....91 C8
Marling Cres GL5 ....98 F7
Marling Rd BS5 ....9 B6
Marling Sch GL5 ....98 F7
Marlstone Rd GL11 ....88 A4
Marlwood Dr Bristol 28 A3
Marlwood Sch BS32 ....50 F5
Marmaduke St BS3 ....8 F3
Marment Rd GL11 ....87 E4
Marmion Cres BS10 ....27 F3
Marne Cl BS14 ....3 D5
Marram Cl GL4 ....119 F5
Marsh Cl
Cheltenham GL51 ....133 C3
Winterbourne BS36 ....30 E5
Marsh Comm BS35 ....38 D6
Marsh Dr ☒ GL56 ....187 A3
Marsh Dr BS31 ....133 C4
Marsh End BS35 ....133 C3
Marsh La
Bristol, Ashton Vale BS3 ...8 B2
Bristol, Avonmouth BS11 ...16 D4
Burton SN14, GL9 ....36 C4
Cheltenham GL51 ....133 C3
Easton-in-G BS20 ....16 A4
Frampton on Severn GL2 ...157 F1
Leonard Stanley GL10 ....97 F3
Marsh Mews GL10 ....97 F3
Marsh Rd Bristol BS3 ....F3
Chepstow NP16 ....60 F5
Leonard Stanley GL10 ....97 E4
Marsh St Avonmouth BS11 ...16 D1
Bristol BS1 ....195 A2
Marsh Terr GL51 ....129 D2
Marsh Way GL16 ....155 B2
Marshacre La BS35 ....49 F6
Marshall Ho ☒ BS16 ....19 F4
Marshall Wlk BS4 ....9 C6
Marshall's La GL14 ....191 D5
Marsland Rd GL51 ....132 D2
Marston Rd Bristol BS4 ...9 B3
Cheltenham GL52 ....133 F4
Martcombe Rd BS20 ....16 B3
Marten Cl GL4 ....120 A5
Marten Rd NP16 ....60 E6
Martin Cl Bristol BS34 ....28 E8
Cirencester GL7 ....190 C3
Martin St ☒ BS15 ....19 E3
Martin St ☒** BS3 ....8 F3
Martin's Rd BS15 ....10 C5
Martindale Rd GL3 ....128 B6
Martingale Rd BS4 ....9 D4
Martins Cl BS15 ....10 C5
Martins The Stroud GL5 ...98 D8
Tuffley NP16 ....60 E5
Martins Way HR8 ....178 E2
Martlock Cres BS3 ....8 C1
Martock Rd Bristol BS3 ...8 C2
Keynsham BS31 ....5 A3
Martor Ind Est SN14 ....35 A2
Marwood Rd BS4 ....2 E8
Mary Carpenter Pl ☒
BS2 ....18 F1
Mary Ct ☒ BS5 ....9 D8
Mary Godwin Ct ☒
GL51 ....132 F4
Mary Gr GL4 ....125 D5
Mary Rose Ave GL3 ....127 F7
Mary St BS5 ....9 D8
Marybrook St GL13 ....85 E3
Mascot Rd BS3 ....8 D3
Masefield Ave GL2 ....118 C4
Masefield Cl ☒ HR8 ....178 E3
Masefield Rd GL7 ....190 B2
Masefield Way BS7 ....19 A6
Maskelyne Ave BS10 ....28 A2
Mason Cl GL13 ....85 E3
Mason's Cl GL50 ....133 A5
Masons Wew BS16 ....30 F7
Massey Par ☒ GL1 ....118 F7
Massey Rd GL1 ....119 A7
Massey Sham Ave GL56 ...187 C3
Matchells Cl BS4 ....9 E6
Materman Rd BS14 ....3 E1
Matford Cl Bristol BS10 ...28 D4
Winterbourne BS36 ....30 E5
Matford La GL13 ....77 F4
Mathern Rd NP16 ....60 D5
Mathern Way NP16 ....60 D5
Mathews Way GL5 ....99 A8
Matson Ave GL4 ....119 C3
Matson La GL4 ....119 B3
Matson Pl GL1 ....119 A7
Matthew's Rd ☒ BS5 ....9 C7
Matthews Cl BS14 ....3 E3
Maud's Elm Ho GL51 ....133 B4
Maugersbury Cl GL54 ....176 F4
Maugersbury Pk GL54 ...176 F4
Maules La BS16 ....21 B3
Maunsell Rd BS11 ....27 B2
Maurice Rd BS6 ....18 E3

Mautravers Cl BS32 ....29 D7
Maverdine Ct GL1 ....196 A3
Mawdeley Ho ☒ BS3 .....8 C4
Mawley Rd GL47 ....152 D7
Maxse Rd BS4 ....9 C4
May Bush La HR9 ....162 E2
May Evans Cl GL11 ....87 F5
May Gr GL22 ....67 B5
May La Dursley GL11 ....88 A1
Ebrington GL55 ....189 D2
☒ May Meadow La GL17 ...146 F3
May Park Prim Sch BS5 ...19 C2
May St BS15 ....20 C1
May Tree Cl GL7 ....149 E3
May Tree Sq GL4 ....119 C7
May Tree Wlk BS31 ....4 C3
May Trees GL51 ....193 A2
Mayall Cl GL4 ....119 C3
Mayalls The GL7 ....172 F7
Mayalls The GL20 ....182 A7
Maybank Rd BS37 ....43 D1
Maybec Gdns BS5 ....10 A6
Maybourne BS4 ....10 A2
Maycliffe Pk BS6 ....18 F2
Mayfair Cl GL2 ....118 C8
Mayfield Ave BS16 ....20 A2
Mayfield Cl BS52 ....137 F2
Mayfield Cl BS16 ....20 A3
Mayfield Dr GL3 ....119 F8
Mayfield Ho GL50 ....130 B8
Mayfield Pk BS16 ....20 A2
Mayfield Pk N BS16 ....20 A2
Mayfield Pk S BS16 ....20 A2
Mayfields BS31 ....4 E4
Mayhill Ind Est NP25 ....154 A7
Mayland Cl GL51 ....129 E5
Maynard Cl BS13 ....2 C5
Maynard Rd BS13 ....2 C5
Mayors Bldgs BS16 ....20 B5
Maypole Gn ☒ GL15 ....147 D8
Maypole Rd GL15 ....147 D8
Maypole Terr GL15 ....98 F8
Mays La GL8 ....140 B8
Maythorn Dr GL31 ....132 D4
Maytree Ave BS13 ....2 B7
Maytree Cl BS13 ....2 B7
Maywood Ave BS34 ....29 A3
Maywood Ho BS16 ....20 B4
Maywood Cres BS16 ....20 B4
Maywood Rd BS16 ....20 C4
Maze St BS5 ....9 B6
Maze Wlk GL16 ....155 A7
McAdam Way BS1 ....7 F5
Mead Cl Bristol BS11 ....16 E6
☒ Moreton-in-M GL56 .....187 A3
☒ **Mead Ct** Bsns Pk BS35 ...130 E5
Mead La Aylburton GL15 ...147 F4
Lydney GL15 ....84 A8
Salford BS31 ....5 F4
Tockington BS35 ....49 D2
Mead Rd Bristol BS34 ....29 A4
Cheltenham GL53 ....133 F3
Chipping Sodbury BS37 ....44 C1
Gloucester GL4 ....119 E5
Mead Rise BS3 ....8 F4
Mead St BS3 ....195 C1
Mead The Alveston BS35 ...54 A1
☒ Ashton Keynes SN6 .....142 F4
Bristol BS34 ....29 B4
Cirencester GL7 ....190 B5
Dundry BS41 ....1 D2
Frampton Cotterell BS36 ....31 B8
☒ **Meade-King Gr** GL2 ...138 B3
Meadgate BS16 ....21 B7
Meadow Cl Bristol BS16 ...19 F1
Cheltenham GL51 ....132 C1
Cirencester GL7 ....190 C8
Tewkesbury GL20 ....192 E6
Viney Hill GL15 ....156 C1
Meadow Court Dr GL3 ...11 C3
Meadow Cl ☒ GL10 ....97 F8
Meadow La ☑ GL51 ....129 E5
Meadow La W GL5 ....98 E6
Meadow Mead
Frampton Cotterell BS36 ...31 B8
Yate BS37 ....43 E5
Meadow Orch ☒ WR12 ...185 B8
Meadow Rd
Chipping Sodbury BS37 ....44 A1
Cinderford GL14 ....191 D5
Cirencester GL7 ....190 C3
Crombhall GL12 ....66 E5
Honeybourne WR11 ....188 A6
Stonehouse GL10 ....97 F8
Meadow St
Avonmouth BS11 ....26 A1
Bristol BS2 ....195 B4
Meadow Vale BS5 ....20 A1
Meadow View
Dursley GL11 ....87 F4
Cirencester GL7 ....150 D7
Frampton Cotterell BS36 ....31 D7
Kempsford GL7 ....144 A2
Meadow Way Bristol BS32 ...29 E7
Churchdown GL3 ....128 B7
Kingham OX7 ....177 F2
Stroud GL5 ....98 E6
Meadow Wlk
Chepstow NP16 ....60 D8
Sling GL16 ....155 B2

Meadowleaze GL2 12
Meadows End GL17 16
Meadows Prim Sch The
BS30 ....
Meadows The BS15 1
Meadowside ☒ BS15 ....
Meadowside Dr BS14 ....
Meadowside Prim Sch
GL2 ....
Meadowsweet Ave BS34 ...2
Meads Cl
Bishop's Cleeve GL52 11
☒ Coleford GL16 15
Meads Ct NP16 ....
Meads The Bristol BS16 ...1
Burton SN14 ....
Leighterton GL8 ....
Meadvale Cl GL2 12
Meadway BS9 ....
Meadway Rd GL10 9
Meandor Rd BS14 ....
Mechanical Organ Mus*
GL17 16
Mede Cl BS1 16
Medical Ave BS2,BS8 ...19
Medina Cl BS35 5
Medoc Cl GL50 13
Medway Cl BS31 ....
Medway Cres GL3 12
Medway Ct
Cheltenham GL50 13
Thornbury BS35 ....
Medway Dr
Frampton Cotterell BS36 3
Keynsham BS31 ....
Meeks Hill GL17 15
Meeks Cl GL47 ....
Meeks Well La HR9 16
Meend Gardens Terr
GL14 ....
Meend La GL17 16
Meendhurst Rd GL14 15
Meend Way GL12 1
Meerbank BS12 ....
Meerstone Way GL4 ....
Meg Thatcher's Gdns
BS5 ....
Meg Thatchers Cl BS5 1
Melbourne Cl
Cheltenham GL53 13
Stonehouse GL10 10
Melbourne Dr
Chipping Sodbury BS37 4
Stonehouse GL10 10
Melbourne Rd BS7 ....
Melbourne St E GL1 11
Melbourne St W GL1 11
Melburn Rd BS5 ....
Meldon Terr GL1 ....
Melick Cl GL4 1
Melita Rd BS6 ....
Mellersh Ave BS13 ....
Mellersh Ho BS10 ....
Mells Cl BS31 ....
Melmore Gdns GL2 19
Melody Way GL2 1
Melrose Ave Bristol BS8 ...19
Yate BS37 ....
Melrose Cl BS37 ....
Melrose Pl BS8 ....
Melton Cres BS7 ....
Melville GL54 ....
Melville Rd Bristol BS6 ...
Churchdown GL3 ....
Melville Terr BS3 ....
Melvin Sq BS4 ....
Memorial Cl BS15 19
Memorial Cotts GL7 ....
Memorial Rd BS15 1
Mendip Cl
Cheltenham GL51 13
Keynsham BS31 ....
Quedgeley GL2 ....
Mendip Cres BS16 ....
Mendip Ho ☒ GL52 ....
Mendip Rd Bristol BS3 ....
Cheltenham GL53 13
Mendip View BS30 ....
Mendon Rd GL55 ....
Mercer Cl BS14 ....
Merchant St BS1 19
Merchants Mead GL2 ...1
Merchants Quay BS1 19
Merchants Rd
Bristol, Clifton BS8 19
Bristol, Hotwells BS8 19
Merchants The SN14 ....
Merchants Trad Pk BS2 ....
Merchant's Rd GL2 1
Mercia Dr BS2 ....
Mercia Rd
Gloucester GL1 ....
Winchcombe GL54 13
Mercian Cl GL7 13
Mercian Ct BS3 ....
Mercian Way NP16 ....
Mercury Way GL4 13
Meredith Cl BS1 ....
Merestones Cl GL50 15
Merestones Dr GL50 15
Merestones Rd GL50 15
Merevale Rd GL51 ....
Merfield Rd BS4 ....
Meridian Pl BS8 19
Meridian Rd BS6 ....

an Vale BS8 ....194 B3
t Ave BS13 ....2 B4
neth St BS3 ....8 F3
t St BS2 ....9 85
Cl Bristol BS9 ....17 F8
nshan GL53 ....130 C5
Ct BS10 ....18 B7
Dr GL7 ....117 F2
Haven GL12 ....68 A7
d Rd BS34 ....28 C6
Ridge BS16 ....22 C4
t Way
nham GL53 ....130 C5
ng Sodbury BS37 ....32 F8
t St BS7 ....19 86
t Orch GL2 ....95 D3
Glos BS15 ....195 A1
ks La NP16 ....146 D4
hans Rd BS11 ....16 D8
ile GL17 ....164 D5
ille Gdns GL51 ....133 A3
field GL51 ....133 A3
fields Gl10 ....110 B1
walks GL5 ....99 B7
walks Sh Ctr █ ....
....99 C7
weather Cl BS32 ....29 D8
wood Bsns 9 E2
wood Cl █ BS3 ....8 C4
wood Sch BS4 ....8 F1
The
Way GL2 ....134 42
ham Rd █ BS22 ....19 A2
ter Terr GL17 ....163 D2
t Cl GL10 ....98 86
t Rd BS7 ....18 E5
ns The GL14 ....156 F6
s Rd BS7 ....18 E4
Ct BS6 ....18 B1
d Gr BS6 ....120 E5
d Rd BS6 ....18 C3
d Rd BS6 ....18 C3
Way GL1,GL4 ....119 88
The
orth SN6 ....145 D3
sbury GL20 ....192 C4
y The GL21 ....
y Hampton CE Sch
elmas Ct GL1 ....152 A3
els Mead GL7 ....190 82
els Way GL16 ....125 B2
s Mead GL2 ....125 D5
ton Rd
bourne WR11 ....188 D7
ton CV36 ....189 F7
oucester Tech Coll
....190 D4
Haines Ct SN6 ....145 D3
Ave BS1 ....195 A4
t Croft GL4 ....119 D7
Farm Cl GL7 ....144 E8
e Ground SN6 ....143 E4
e Hill Chalford GL6 ....148 C6
....19 E7
e Hill Cres GL6 ....148 C6
e Leazes GL5 ....99 C7
Odds OX7 ....177 E1
t Rd Bristol BS15 ....20 F3
arrington OX18 ....161 D7
t GL5 ....99 A6
e Spillman's GL5 ....102 F3
t St Chepstow NP16 ....60 E8
t, Bowbridge GL5 ....99 D7
t, Uplands GL5 ....99 C8
e Tynings GL6 ....91 A4
e Way GL6 ....60 F5
ecroft GL10 ....96 F7
edown Rd SN14 ....24 C1
eford Ho BS13 ....2 C4
ehay Ct GL2 ....137 C3
emoor Mill GL5 ....91 A6
ton Lawn GL3 ....127 E6
s BS14 ....16 F8
d Ct GL7 ....190 D3
d Rd Bristol BS2 ....195 C3
t, Staple Hill BS16 ....20 E6
ester GL2 ....190 D2
use GL10 ....196 81
d St BS2 ....195 C2
d Way BS35 ....51 C7
mmer Wlk GL1 ....118 C5
n Gdns GL51 ....133 C3
ter Ave GL51 ....133 C5
er Gdns GL50 ....133 C5
ter Rd █ GL54 ....168 A5
t BS4 ....8 E8
s Cotts GL16 ....155 A3
t BS30 ....16 F4
t BS30 ....18 A1
one Sch The GL2 ....127 85
ne Wlk GL2 ....127 85
d Ave BS30 ....12 B7
e Cl BS14 ....8 C4
t St BS3 ....8 C4
e Bristol BS1 ....195 A2
way WR12 ....185 A8
ton Cotterell BS36 ....31 C7
Cerney GL7 ....143 A8
u-E GL12 ....68 C6
s BS37 ....32 B4

Mill Ct █ GL18 ....171 A4
Mill End GL17 ....164 D5
Mill Farm Dr GL5 ....98 E8
Mill Gr GL2 ....117 D1
Mill La Avening GL8 ....140 88
Mill Ho █ BS35 ....19 A1
Bitton BS30 ....5 E8
Bristol, Bedminster BS3 ....8 D4
Bristol, Warmley BS30 ....11 C5
Brockworth GL3 ....120 F6
Castle Eaton SN26 ....144 C6
Charlton Kings GL54 ....131 D8
Chipping Sodbury BS37 ....33 E6
Cranham GL4 ....112 D6
Doynton BS30 ....22 F1
Fairford GL7 ....152 D4
Falfield GL12 ....65 F7
Frampton Cotterell BS36 ....42 B1
Gorsley GL18 ....170 C3
Greet GL54 ....184 A1
Lechlade on T GL7 ....153 F2
Longhope GL17 ....165 A5
Lowbands GL19 ....179 F2
Lower Slaughter GL54 ....176 C1
Lower Swell GL54 ....176 C5
Mickleton GL55 ....189 A6
Prestbury GL52 ....134 C5
Stanton Fitzwarren SN6 ....145 A1
Staunton GL19 ....179 F1
Stoke Orchard GL51,GL52 ....136 D5
Tockington BS32 ....50 81
Upper Strensham WR8 ....180 C7
Upton Cheyney BS30 ....11 F1
Winchcombe GL54 ....174 A7
Mill Pitt Gdns GL3 ....120 A8
Mill Pl GL1 ....117 F2
Mill Rd BS35 ....30 D4
Mill Row Blockley GL56 ....186 D6
King's Stanley GL10 ....98 B1
Lower Lydbrook GL17 ....163 C3
Mill St St Gloucester GL1 ....127 A1
Prestbury GL52 ....134 C5
Tewkesbury GL20 ....192 84
Mill Stps BS36 ....30 C8
Mill View
Cirencester GL7 ....150 D7
Northleach GL54 ....168 A1
Mill Way GL17 ....87 F4
Millard Cl GL10 ....28 D2
Millbank GL11 ....88 A4
Millbank Cl BS4 ....9 E3
Millbrook Cl █ BS16 ....18 E1
Millbridge Rd GL3 ....120 A7
Millbrook Ave BS4 ....9 F3
Millbrook Cl Bristol BS30 ....11 C6
█ Gloucester GL1 ....127 A1
Millbrook Gdns BS4 ....193 A4
Millbrook Gdns
Cheltenham BS6 ....133 82
Lea HR9 ....164 D8
Millbrook Grn GL15 ....162 A6
Millbrook La GL16 ....177 A6
Millbrook Pl GL5 ....99 D7
Millbrook Rd BS37 ....45 C5
Millbrook St
Cheltenham BS6 ....193 C6
Gloucester GL1 ....127 A1
Millbury Way GL14 ....191 C4
Millend GL10 ....97 A7
Millend La GL10 ....97 A7
Millenium Row GL10 ....97 F7
Millennium Cotts GL19 ....172 A2
Millennium Ct GL20 ....192 E2
Millennium Way GL7 ....190 F5
Miller Cl
Ashleworth GL19 ....172 C6
Gloucester GL2 ....127 D5
Miller Craddock Way █
HR8 ....
Miller Ho BS8 ....194 A2
Millers Cl BS20 ....16 C4
Millers Dr BS30 ....11 F6
Millers Dyke GL2 ....117 D1
Millers Gn
Drybrook GL17 ....164 A4
Gloucester GL1 ....196 B3
Millers Way GL14 ....191 C4
Millfield BS35 ....64 C2
Millfield Dr BS30 ....12 A3
Millfields GL3 ....120 A8
Millground Rd BS13 ....1 F5
Millham Rd GL52 ....138 A4
Millhouse Dr GL54 ....154 F3
Millhouse Dr GL50 ....133 C5
Millican Cl BS13 ....2 F5
Millin Ave GL14 ....118 D2
Milling Cl SN6 ....143 A5
Millington Cres GL15 ....147 E5
Millmead Ho GL13 ....78 C3
Millpond End GL15 ....99 A2
Millpond St █ BS5 ....19 A1
Millpool Ct EPD GL19 ....188 B2
Mills Cl █ WR12 ....185 88
Millview GL56 ....186 C6
Millward Gr BS16 ....20 C6
Milne Pastures GL20 ....182 B4
Milne Wlk BS14 ....132 E4
Milner Gn BS30 ....11 E5
Milner Rd BS7 ....18 F5
Milo Pl GL1 ....118 E6
Milsom St Bristol BS5 ....9 A8
Cheltenham GL51 ....193 B4

Milton Cl BS37 ....43 D2
Milton Gr GL5 ....99 E7
Milton Pk █ BS5 ....9 C7
Milton Pl GL7 ....152 D3
Milton Rd Bristol BS7 ....18 E6
Cheltenham GL51 ....193 D2
late BS37 ....43 D2
Milton St GL7 ....152 D3
Miltons BS13 ....2 D4
Milverton Gdns BS6 ....18 F2
Milward Rd BS31 ....46 A6
Mimosa Ave GL51 ....130 A4
Mimosa Ct █ GL3 ....128 A7
Mina Rd BS2 ....19 A2
Minchinhampton Prim Sch
....6 1...
Mine Pitts La HR9 ....162 E3
Miners Wlk GL14 ....191 C4
Minerva Cl GL4 ....119 F6
Minerva Ct GL7 ....190 D4
Minerva Wlk GL15 ....92 85
Minerva Way GL54 ....138 A3
Minety CE Prim Sch
SN16 ....142 D1
Minety La SN16 ....142 A3
Miniature World Model
Village* GL54 ....168 F7
Minnow La OX18 ....161 D7
Minor's La BS10 ....27 A8
Minsmere Rd BS31 ....5 A4
Minster Cl GL52 ....137 E4
Minster St GL7 ....32 D7
Minster Gdns GL4 ....119 F6
Minsterworth CE Prim Sch
GL2 ....116 F7
Minstrel Way GL2 ....116 B6
Mint La BS22 ....19 A2
Minto Rd BS2 ....19 A2
Minto Road Ind Ctr █
BS2 ....19 A2
Minton Cl BS14 ....3 A1
Misarden Park Gdns*
GL6 ....106 B6
Misarden Park Woodland
Trail* GL6 ....106 D6
Misarden CEPrim Sch
GL6 ....106 A6
Misarden Rd GL51 ....132 D1
Miss Grace's La NP16 ....146 E2
Mission Rd BS37 ....43 B4
Mistletoe Mews GL3 ....127 F6
Mitcheldean Endowed Prim
Sch GL17 ....166 A8
Mitchell La BS1 ....195 82
Mitford Wlk BS30 ....11 D7
Mitford Villas GL56 ....187 A3
Mitre Pitch GL52 ....68 C7
Mitre St GL53 ....193 C2
Mitton Ct GL20 ....192 A5
Mitton Manor Prim Sch
GL20 ....192 E6
Mivart St █ BS5 ....19 82
Moat Bank GL20 ....180 C7
Moat Ho GL4 ....119 D6
Moat La Huntley GL19 ....165 E8
Staunton GL19 ....172 A8
Uckington GL51 ....132 D6
Moat Prim Sch The GL4 ....119 84
Moat The Kingham OX7 ....177 F3
Quedgeley GL7 ....117 F1
Mobley GL13 ....86 A3
Modecombe Gr BS10 ....27 F3
Moffat Rd GL4 ....119 D6
Mogg St BS2 ....19 A2
Mogridge Cl GL3 ....120 A7
Molesworth Cl BS13 ....2 A4
Molesworth Dr BS13 ....2 A4
Monarch Cl GL4 ....119 E4
Monica Dr GL50 ....133 E4
Monk Meadow Trad Est
GL2 ....118 C7
Monk Rd BS7 ....18 D4
Monk's Park Ave BS7 ....18 E8
Monkey Mdw GL20 ....182 C5
Monkey Puzzle Cl GL5 ....98 E6
Monks Ave BS15 ....10 B8
Monks Croft GL51 ....132 E1
Monks La GL20 ....182 C2
Monks Park Sch BS7 ....18 F8
Monks Park Way BS7 ....18 F8
Monks Wlk GL17 ....153 F2
Monkscroft Com Prim Sch
GL51 ....132 E1
Monkswell NP25 ....154 A8
Monkswell Rd NP25 ....154 A8
Monkton Rd BS15 ....10 B5
Monmouth Com Sch
NP25 ....154 A5
Monmouth Hill BS32 ....39 E4
Monmouth Rd Bristol BS7 ....18 D4
Edge End GL16 ....155 C8
Keynsham BS31 ....4 D5
Pill BS20 ....16 C5
Monmouth St BS3 ....8 D1
Monsdale Cl BS10 ....28 A2
Monsdale Dr BS10 ....28 A2
Monson Ave BS30 ....193 84
Montague Cl BS34 ....29 E5
Montague Ct BS2 ....195 A4
Montague Flats █ BS2 ....195 A4
Montague Hill BS2 ....195 A4
Montague Hill S █ BS2 ....195 A4
Montague Hill █ BS2 ....195 A4
Montague Pl BS6 ....195 A4
Montague Rd BS8 ....195 A4
Montague St
Bristol, Baptist Mills BS2 ....18 F1
Bristol, Barton Hill BS5 ....9 D1
Montague St BS1 ....195 A4
Monterey Cl GL20 ....192 E1

Montfort Rd GL2 ....127 B5
Montgomery Cl GL3 ....120 B6
Montgomery Rd GL51 ....129 D6
Montpelier BS37 ....8 F3
Montpelier Sta BS6 ....18 E2
Montpellier GL1 ....196 81
Montpellier Arc █ GL50 ....193 82
Montpellier Ave GL50 ....193 82
Montpellier Ct GL50 ....193 A2
Montpellier Dr GL50 ....193 82
Montpellier Gr GL50 ....193 82
Montpellier Ho GL50 ....193 82
Montpellier Mews GL1 ....196 81
Montpellier Par GL50 ....193 82
Montpellier Retreat
GL50 ....193 82
Montpellier Spa Rd
GL50 ....193 82
Montpellier Terr GL50 ....193 82
Montpellier St GL50 ....193 82
Montpellier Villas GL50 ....193 82
Montpellier Wlk GL50 ....193 82
Montreal Ave GL19 ....18 A8
Montreal Ho █ GL1 ....132 E3
Montreaux Ho █ BS5 ....11 A7
Montrose Ave BS6 ....18 C1
Montrose Ho BS10 ....11 86
Montrose Pk BS4 ....9 D2
Montserrat GL5 ....99 D3
Monument Ct BS1 ....195 84
Moon's La GL6 ....148 E7
Moor Court Dr GL52 ....133 F2
Moor Croft Dr BS30 ....10 F3
Moor End BS11 ....17 A8
Moor Hall Pl GL5 ....98 E8
Moor La
Bourton-on-t-W GL54 ....169 A8
Fairford GL7 ....152 E3
Tockington BS32 ....40 A8
Moor St Chepstow NP16 ....60 E8
Gloucester GL1 ....127 A2
Saul GL2 ....157 F4
Moordell Cl BS37 ....43 D1
Moore Cottage Hospl
GL54 ....168 F8
Moore Rd GL54 ....130 C6
Moorend Cres GL53 ....130 C6
Moorend Gdns BS11 ....16 F7
Moorend Glade GL53 ....130 C6
Moorend Gr GL53 ....130 C5
Moorend La GL52 ....95 C2
Moorend Park Rd GL53 ....130 C5
Moorend Rd
Charlton Kings GL53 ....130 C6
Cheltenham GL53 ....130 C5
Hambrook BS16 ....30 D3
Staunton GL19 ....180 C1
Moorend Terr GL53 ....130 C6
Moorfield Ave GL15 ....156 D1
Moorfield Rd GL23 ....95 C7
Moorfields Ho BS5 ....9 C7
Moorgate GL7 ....153 D2
Moorgrove Ho BS16 ....17 C7
Moorhen Ct GL2 ....117 D1
Moorhill St BS5 ....9 B7
Moorhouse La BS10 ....27 84
Moorings The BS20 ....16 C4
Moorland Rd BS37 ....43 D1
Moorlands Rd
Bristol, Mayfield Park BS16 ....20 A2
Bristol, Ridgeway BS16 ....20 A3
Moorpark Ave BS37 ....43 D1
Moors Ave GL51 ....133 A4
Moorslade La GL12 ....77 D1
Mopla Rd NP16 ....72 F2
Moravian Ct █ BS15 ....10 B6
Moravian Rd BS15 ....10 B6
Morcroft Pl GL15 ....155 F1
Morden Wlk BS14 ....3 D7
Morelands Gr GL1 ....118 E5
Morelands Trad Est
GL1 ....196 A1
Morestall Dr GL7 ....190 82
Moreton Cl
Bishop's Cleeve GL52 ....138 A2
Moreton La GL20 ....182 C8
Moreton-in-Marsh District
Hospl GL56 ....187 A3
Moreton-in-Marsh Sta
GL56 ....187 A3
Morgan Cl BS31 ....5 D2
Morgan St BS2 ....18 F1
Morgan's Way GL14 ....156 C6
Morgans La GL17 ....164 A3
Mork La GL15 ....146 E7
Mork Rd GL15 ....146 E7
Morlands Dr GL54 ....131 84
Morley Ave Bristol BS16 ....21 A4
Churchdown GL3 ....128 A6
Morley Cl
Bristol, Little Stoke BS34 ....29 C7
Bristol, Staple Hill BS16 ....20 D5
Morley Sq BS7 ....18 E4
Morley St
Bristol, Baptist Mills BS2 ....18 F1
Bristol, Barton Hill BS5 ....9 D1
Morley Terr █ BS15 ....20 D1
Norman Cl GL4 ....164 84
Morningside CI GL52 ....134 C4

Morningside Ctyd GL52 ....134 C4
Mornington Dr GL53 ....130 D6
Mornington Rd █ BS8 ....118 A2
Mornington St █ GL4 ....157 A6
Morpeth Rd BS4 ....2 D8
Morpeth St BS3 ....118 F7
Morris Cl GL15 ....156 82
Morris Ct GL17 ....165 A5
Morris Hill Cl GL51 ....133 86
Morris Orch GL11 ....87 F6
Morris Rd Bristol BS7 ....19 A5
Broadway WR12 ....185 88
Morse La GL17 ....164 A4
Morse Rd Bristol BS5 ....11 86
Drybrook GL17 ....164 84
Mortimer Rd
Bristol, Clifton BS8 ....194 A3
Bristol, Clifton BS8 ....29 82
Gloucester GL2 ....127 C5
Morton Mill BS35 ....64 C3
Morton St Bristol BS5 ....9 B7
Gloucester GL1 ....118 F7
Thornbury BS35 ....64 C1
Morwent Cl GL4 ....119 E6
Mosedale GL56 ....187 83
Moselle Dr GL3 ....128 A6
Mosley Cres GL5 ....98 E7
Mosley Rd GL5 ....98 E7
Motor Mus (The Bugatti
Trust)* GL54 ....138 E8
Motorway Distribution Ctr
BS11 ....26 C2
Mottershead Dr GL7 ....122 E6
Mottershead Rd GL7 ....120 B7
Moulder Rd GL20 ....192 E4
Mount Cl
Frampton Cotterell BS36 ....30 F8
Harrow Hill GL17 ....164 B7
Mount Craig Hall HR9 ....162 F8
Mount Cres BS36 ....30 E5
Mount Gdns BS15 ....10 D6
Mount Hill Rd BS15 ....10 D6
Mount Pleasant
Bisley GL6 ....148 D8
Blockley GL56 ....186 C6
Chepstow NP16 ....60 E8
Fairford GL7 ....152 E4
Hallen BS10 ....27 C4
Lechlade on T GL7 ....153 E2
Lydney GL15 ....92 C2
Pill BS20 ....16 C4
Stroud GL5 ....99 E7
Wootton-u-E GL12 ....68 C7
Mount Pleasant Ct
Lydney GL15 ....92 C2
█ Stow-on-t-W GL54 ....176 F4
Mount Pleasant Rd
Cinderford GL14 ....191 D3
Tewkesbury GL20 ....192 D4
Mount Pleasant Terr █ BS3 ....8 C4
Mount St Cirencester GL7 ....190 C3
Gloucester GL1 ....196 A3
Mount Way
Chepstow NP16 ....60 D8
Chepstow NP16 ....72 D1
Mountain View GL17 ....163 A4
Mountbatten Cl BS37 ....43 D3
Mounteney's La GL12 ....54 D7
Mountjoy's La GL14 ....191 D5
Mountjoy's Lane End
GL14 ....191 D5
Mounton Cl NP16 ....60 D7
Mounton Dr NP16 ....60 D7
Mounton House Sch
NP16 ....60 B7
Mounton Hts NP16 ....60 D8
Mounton Rd NP16 ....60 D8
Mousell La GL14 ....191 D4
Mousetrap La GL54 ....168 F8
Mow Barton Bristol BS13 ....1 F6
Yate BS37 ....43 D2
Mowbery Cl GL2 ....127 C5
Mowbray Ave GL20 ....192 D1
Mowbray Rd BS14 ....3 C7
Mowcroft Rd BS13 ....2 A4
Moxham Dr BS13 ....2 C4
Moyle Old School La
NP16 ....73 A4
Muirfield Bristol BS30 ....11 A6
Yate BS37 ....32 E8
Mulberry Cl Bristol BS15 ....10 E8
Hardwicke GL2 ....109 E8
Mulberry Ct █ GL51 ....132 D2
Mulberry Dr BS20 ....21 F1
Mulberry Gdns BS16 ....20 F1
Mulberry La GL54 ....177 C4
Mulberry Wlk BS9 ....17 C8
Mule St GL13 ....78 83
Muller Ave BS7 ....18 F4
Muller Rd BS5,BS7 ....19 A4
Mullings Cl GL7 ....190 C5
Mulready Cl BS7 ....19 C6
Mumbleys La
Thornbury, Alveston Down
BS35 ....
Thornbury BS35 ....50 E8
Munday CI BS16 ....148 86
Munsley Gr GL4 ....119 C3
Murford Ave BS13 ....2 84
Murford Wlk BS13 ....2 B4
Murray Cl GL52 ....137 F5
Murray St █ BS3 ....8 C4
Murrells Rd GL16 ....163 A4
Murvagh GL53 ....193 C1

St GL7 ....153 E2
Tree Ave BS16 ....22 B4
Tree CI Bristol BS15 ....10 C3
rwicke GL2 ....109 E7
Tree View GL4 ....119 C3
Tree Wlk BS14 ....4 D3
Way Huntley GL19 ......165 D6
dean GL14 ....156 E8
rn Cerney GL7 ....142 F7
ehouse GL10 ....97 F7
dean GL14 ....118 F4
brook Dr GL21 ....129 C3
roft Cl GL4 ....119 D3
ale Ave BS16 ....20 D8
ale CI BS16 ....20 E8
ale Dr BS16 ....20 D7
ale Rd
ol, Downend BS16 ......20 E8
ol, Hengrove BS14 ....3 A8
ean GL14 ....191 C5
ene
heltenham, Fairview

....134 A1

heltenham, Lansdown

....130 B8
ene Ave BS5 ....19 D3
ene Sch GL14 ....191 D4
nhill Rd BS4 ....9 E2
nhill Wlk BS4 ....9 E2
s La GL9 ....35 B5
eld Ave NP16 ....72 D1
eld Bsns Pk BS15 ......10 D7
eld Gr BS8 ....194 B4
eld PI BS8 ....194 B4
eld Rd
eld Bsns Pk BS15 ......10 D7
eld PI GL1 ....30 C2
eld Pitch GL15 ....146 F3
eld Prim Sch GL2 .....183 E4
eld Rd GL17 ....164 D5
unger La GL13 ....85 C4
urst CI GL3 ....126 C3
urst Rd BS9 ....17 F5
urst Rise GL52 ....131 A8
and Ave GL52 ....133 F3
and Bsn Pk BS37 ....43 B3
and Rd BS8 ....178 E8
and Rd
ristol, Redland BS6 ....18 B1
ol, St George BS5 ....9 E8
w Hill GL17 ....164 B3
and St GL53 ....131 A7
ends Cirencester GL7
GL16 ....155 B2
ands CI BS16 ....21 B5
ands Dr
ndsbury BS32 ....40 A4
ol, Frenchay BS16 ......20 A7
ol, Oldland Common
....11 C2
ands Pk GL55 ....155 E1
ands Rd BS16 ....21 A5
ands Rd GL15 ....156 B2
aze
eat Heath BS36 ....31 D7
ury SN16 ....142 D1
ge Ave BS5 ....64 C1
ge Rd BS9 ....19 D1
eigh Gdns BS30 ....11 C2
ry CI GL54 ....176 F4
ry Flats GL7 ....144 E7
ry Rd Bristol BS7 ....18 F7
enham GL52 ....24 E7
oncester GL7 ....190 C2
ry Way GL15 ....147 D8
eade Pk BS4 ....9 B2
ge Rd GL2 ....125 E5
dge CI Bristol BS15 ....11 A7
dge CI
oucester GL4 ....119 C5
dge Prim Sch GL4 .....148 E6
La GL18 ....170 C2
dge Rd
The Berry Hill GL16 ...155 A8
enham GL51 ....129 D6
ester GL4 ....119 E7
y CE Prim Sch

....141 F4
ey Rd SN16 ....142 B2
ee CI BS32 ....40 C2
ee Ct BS11 ....16 E7
ee Gdn GL4 ....119 C3
ee Gdns BS13 ....1 E5
ood Ave BS9 ....18 C6
ood CI Dream GL15 ....155 D1
rford GL14 ....191 D5
ood Dr GL3 ....119 F6
ood Pk BS16 ....20 A3
ood Rd
ol BS9 ....155 D1
ol BS9 ....18 B6
eld GL2 ....117 E2
eld Rd GL2 ....100 A6
ound GL12 ....68 C7
ll La GL7 ....141 A8
ands Ave BS14 ....3 A6
ys Cres 11 HR8 ....178 E8

Oatleys Rd HR8 ....178 E8
Oatleys Terr 10 HR8 ....178 E8
Oberon Ave BS5 ....19 E2
Ocker Hill GL6 ....102 E2
Octagon The NP16 ....60 F5
Octavia Pl GL3 ....92 B4
Oddfellows Row 3

....154 F4
Oddfellows Terr 18

....174 A7
Oddfellows' Terr 12

....187 A3
Oddington Rd GL54 .....176 F4
Odessa Rd GL20 ....173 F8
Offa's Mead Prim Sch

NP16 ....61 A8
Offa's Rd GL14 ....61 A1
Office Rd GL14 ....191 C3
Ogbourne CI GL2 ....127 E3
Ohio Ave GL7 ....152 E2
Okebourne CI BS10 .....28 B4
Okebourne Rd BS10 .....28 B4
Okus Rd GL33 ....131 A5
Old All Saints Sch

GL52 ....193 C4
Old Ashley Hill BS6 ....178 E8
Old Aust Rd BS32 ....40 C6
Old Barns The WB8 ....180 D7
Old Barrow Hill BS 16 D7
Old Bath Rd GL53 ......130 E5
Old Bell Chambers

GL51 ....195 C2
Old Bread St BS2 ....195 C2
Old Brewery La 8 GL8 .140 B4
Old Bristol Rd BS 91 B3
Old Bulwark Rd NP16 ..60 E7
Old Burford Rd OX7 ....177 E1
Old Cheltenham Rd

GL2 ....127 D4
Old Coach CI NP16 ....61 C2
Old Coach Rd GL16 ......61 C3
Old Coach The WR12 ..185 C8
Old Comm GL6 ....148 C6
Old Comm The GL6 ....148 B6
Old Court Dr GL19 ....171 D1
Old Dam Rd GL15 ....92 D7
Old Dean Rd GL17 ....164 D6
Old Dixton Rd NP25 ....154 A8
Old Down Hill GL9 ....50 B2
Old Down Rd GL9 ....35 C8
Old Elmore La GL2 ......117 F2
Old Farm CI SN16 ....141 E1
Old Farm La BS5 ....10 B6
Old Forge CI OX7 ....177 E1
Old Forge Cotts

Didbrook GL54 ....184 D2
Stoke Orchard GL52 ...136 E5
Old Forge The GL15 ...147 D3
Old Furnace CI GL15 ...147 D3
Old Gloucester Rd

Alveston BS35 ....51 B5
Bourton-on-H GL54 ....168 E7
Bristol BS16 ....30 D2
Bristol BS16 ....30 B4
Frampton Cotterell BS36 .41 D3
Staverton GL51 ....173 F1
Thornbury BS35 ....65 B2
Uckington GL51 ....132 B5
Old Gram School Mews The

GL55 ....189 A2
Old Hill Avening GL8 ...148 B1
Longhope GL17 ....165 A5
Old Horsley Rd GL6 ....91 B3
Old Hospital La GL20 ..192 D5
Old Inchbrook Sch GL6 ..91 A5
Old King Street Ct BS1 .195 B3
Old Kiln La GL16 ....21 C6
Old La (Simmonds La)

HR9,GL18 ....170 C4
Old Lodge Ct GL50 .....133 E3
Old London Rd GL1 ......80 C1
Old Manor CI GL2 ....67 A5
Old Manor Gdns GL55 .189 B6
Old Manor La GL20 ....192 E6
Old Market GL1 ....91 B4
Old Market St BS2 ....195 C3
Old Mill CI BS37 ....32 B4
Old Mill Mus The*

....176 C1
Old Mill The WR12 ......185 B8
Old Millbrook Terr 3

GL50 ....133 B2
Old Moat Ctyd GL2 .....172 F1
Old Monmouth Rd GL17 ...165 A5
Old Neighbourhood

GL6 ....148 C3
Old Oak CI NP16 ....60 F5
Old Orchard GL7 ....152 D7
Old Orchard The GL55 .189 D3
Old Painswick CI GL4 .119 B6
Old Painswick Rd GL4 .119 B6
Old Park Hill BS2 ....194 C3
Old Park Rd BS11 ....16 D7
Old Police Sta The BS4 ..9 A3
Old Priory Rd BS20 ....6 B4
Old Quarry Ind Units The

GL8 ....140 C2
Old Quarry Rd BS11 .....16 E7
Old Quarry Rise GL11 ...16 E7
Old Rd BS GL6 Coleford GL16 ..155 B5
Maisemore GL2 ....126 A8
Southam GL52 ....134 C8
Old Rectory CI GL15 ...189 B7
Old Rectory Gdns GL56 .176 D8
Old Rectory Rd GL12 ...67 F4
Old Reddings CI GL51 .129 C7
Old Reddings Rd GL51 .129 C7

Old Row GL11 ....196 C1
Old School CI GL6 ....91 B4
Old School Ho 3 GL30 .193 A4
Old School Mews The 4

GL53 ....131 B6
Old Sneed Ave BS9 ......17 D4
Old Sneed Cotts BS9 ...17 E4
Old Sneed Rd BS9 ....17 D4
Old Station Dr GL53 ...130 D5
Old Station Rd GL18 ..171 A5
Old Station Way GL16 .155 A5
Old Town GL17 ....68 B7
Old Town Mews GL15 .147 F5
Old Tram Rd GL1 ....196 A2
Old Vicarage Ct

BS37 ....34 B8
Old Vicarage CI

6 Coleford GL16 ....155 A6
Whitchurch BS14 ....3 C4
Old Vicarage Gn BS31 ...4 E6
Old Vicarage La GL7 ...141 F7
Old Vicarage The

Bristol BS6 ....18 E1
Olveston BS35 ....50 A3
Old Winding Wheel The

GL15 ....147 C8
Oldacre Dr GL52 ....138 A4
Oldacre Rd BS14 ....3 A3
Oldbridge Rd BS14 ....3 C7
Oldbury Chase BS30 .....11 A2
Oldbury CI GL11 ....132 D3
Oldbury Court Dr BS16 .20 B6
Oldbury Court Prim Sch

BS16 ....20 C7
Oldbury Ho GL11 ....192 D5
Oldbury La GL11 ....97 D8
Oldbury Orch GL3 ....128 D4
Oldbury Prim Sch BS35 .63 B5
Oldbury Rd

Thornbury BS35 ....64 B4
Wick BS30 ....12 D5
Oldcroft GL15 ....156 B1
Olde La GL54 ....184 B3
Oldends La GL10 ....97 D8
Oldfield GL20 ....192 D4
Oldfield Cres GL51 .....129 F8
Oldfield Girls Sch BA1 ...6 F1
Oldfield Rd BS8 ....7 F5
Oldfield Rd BS8 ....194 A1
Oldfields La BS35 ....41 D7
Oldhill GL15 ....98 D8
Oldlands Ave BS36 ......31 C6
Oldmead Wlk BS13 ....1 E7
Oldminster Rd GL13 ...192 D5
Olga Rd NP16 ....60 B5
Olympus CI BS34 ....29 D4
Olympus Pk GL2 ....118 A2
Olympus Rd BS34 ....29 D4
Onslow Rd GL18 ....171 A4
Oram Ct BS30 ....25 D8
Orange CI SN6 ....145 D3
Orange St BS2 ....195 C4
Orangery The GL4 ......119 E7
Orch The

Netherend GL15 ....147 C3
Oaksey SN16 ....141 F4
Orchard Ave Bristol BS1 .194 C2
Broadway WR12 ....185 C8
Cheltenham GL51 ....132 F2
Chepstow NP16 ....60 E5
Thornbury BS35 ....64 D1
Orchard Bank

Great Rissington GL54 .169 C4
Orchard Bvd BS30 ....11 B4
Orchard CI

Aylburton GL15 ....147 C4
Bredon GL20 ....182 D7
Bretforton WR11 ....188 A3
Bristol, Kingswood BS15 ..10 E8
Bristol, Westbury on Trym

....17 F5
Charfield GL12 ....67 A5
Clearwell GL16 ....154 F3
Dursley GL11 ....87 F5
English Bicknor GL16 ..163 A2
Gloucester GL2 ....54 B3
Hardwicke GL2 ....109 D7
Kemble GL7 ....141 F8
Keynsham BS31 ....4 D4
King's Stanley GL10 ......98 B3
Lea HR9 ....164 C8
Leonard Stanley GL10 ..97 F4
Mickleton GL55 ....189 B7
Mitcheldean GL17 ......164 D5
Winterbourne BS36 ......30 E5
Woodcroft NP16 ....24 D4
Yate BS37 ....43 F2
Orchard Cres BS11 ......16 D7

Orchard Ct

Bristol, Filton BS34 ......29 A2
18 Bristol, Redfield BS5 ..9 D7
Painswick Rd GL4 ......103 F8
Stonehouse GL10 ....97 E7
Tewkesbury GL20 ....192 D4
Yate BS37 ....43 B3
Orchard Dr Aust BS35 .49 A7
Churchdown GL3 ....128 D4
Twyning GL20 ....182 A7
Orchard End

Apperley GL19 ....173 C7
Monmouth NP25 ....154 A7
Orchard Farm CI NP16 .61 B7
Orchard Field GL8 ......140 B8
Orchard Gate GL15 ....156 D4
Orchard Gdns BS15 .....10 E8
Orchard Gr GL51 ....129 D1
Orchard Gr The GL51 ..129 D1
Orchard Grange BS35 .64 B2
Orchard Ho GL7 ....190 D5
Orchard Ind Est GL54 .184 A3
Orchard Ind Est BS1 ..194 C2
Orchard Lea

6 Alveston BS35 ....51 A5
Pill BS20 ....16 D4
Orchard Leaze GL11 ....87 D4
Orchard Mead

Nailsworth GL6 ....91 B4
Painswick GL6 ....103 F7
Orchard Pl

4 Ledbury HR8 ....178 F7
Stonehouse GL10 ....97 E7
Orchard Rd

Alderton GL20 ....183 E4
Bishop's Cleeve GL52 ..137 F3
Bristol, Ashley Down BS7 .18 E4
Bristol, Kingswood BS15 ..10 E8
Bristol, St George BS5 ...9 F8
Coalpit Heath BS36 ....31 D7
Coleford GL16 ....155 A6
Gloucester GL2 ....127 E4
Joy's Green GL17 ....163 D3
Lydney GL15 ....92 B2
Newent GL18 ....171 A7
Pucklechurch BS16 ......22 B5
Stroud GL5 ....98 C6
Winchcombe GL54 ......139 F6
Orchard Ridge GL20 ...118 C4
Orchard Rise

Chepstow NP16 ....60 B5
Dursley GL11 ....87 E7
Longborough GL56 .....176 D8
Newnham GL14 ....156 F6
Olveston BS35 ....50 A3
Tibberton GL19 ....171 E1
Orchard Springs GL6 ...91 A4
Orchard St Bristol BS1 .194 C2
Orchard St Bristol BS1 .194 C2
Wooton-u-E GL12 ....68 B7
Orchard The Bristol BS8 ..29 F5
Clapton-on-t-H GL54 ..168 F4
6 Fairford GL7 ....152 E4
Frampton Cotterell BS36 .31 C8
North Cerney GL7 ....158 D3
Pill BS20 ....16 C4
Tewkesbury GL20 ....192 D5
Tytherington GL12 ....51 E6
Uckington GL51 ....132 D7
Uley GL11 ....89 B1
Orchard Vale BS15 ......10 F7
Orchard View

Draycott GL56 ....186 E6
Sedbury NP16 ....90 A4
Orchard View Ham Green

Hospl BS20 ....16 C4
Orchard Way

17 Berry Hill GL16 ......155 A7
Cheltenham GL51 ....132 F3
Churchdown GL3 ....128 B7
Huntley GL19 ....165 D6
Kingham OX7 ....177 F2
Maisemore GL2 ....126 A8
Oridge Valley GL14 ....67 A5
Orielbar Gdns BS11 ......27 B2
Orlham La HR8 ....178 D6
Ormerod Rd Bristol BS9 .17 E5
Ormond PI GL50 ....193 B3
Ormond Terr GL50 .....193 B3
Ormsley CI BS34 ....29 C8
Orpen Gdns BS7 ....19 B5
Orpen Rd BS32 ....40 B3
Orpheus Ave BS32 ....29 D6
Oriskdale Terr GL53 ...129 C2
Orwell Dr BS31 ....5 A4
Orwell St BS3 ....8 E3
Osborne Ave BS11 ....18 F3
Osborne Ct BS34 ....29 D4

Osborne Terr

Bristol, Redfield BS5 ......8 B2
Thrupp GL5 ....99 E3
Osborne Villas BS2 ......194 C4
Osborne Wallis Ho BS8 .194 A1
Osbourne Ave GL4 ......118 C1
Osbourne Ho 6 GL50 ..130 B8
Osier CI GL4 ....119 A4
Osprey CI GL4 ....119 D5
Osprey Ct BS14 ....2 D5
Osprey Dr GL10 ....97 F8
Osprey Pk BS35 ....64 D3
Osprey Rd 18 Bristol BS5 .9 C7
Osprey Rd GL51 ....130 C5
Osric Rd GL1 ....118 F6
Othello CI GL51 ....132 E3
Otter Rd GL4 ....120 A5
Otterburn Ho GL50 .....118 C4
Otterford CI BS14 ....3 B5
Otters Field GL54 ....174 A8
Ottery CI BS11 ....27 A1
Ottrells Mead BS32 ......39 C1
Our Lady of Lourdes Prim RC

Sch BS5 ....19 D1
Our Lady of the Rosary Cath

Prim Sch BS11 ....17 A8
Our Lady of the Rosary Prim

Sch BS11 ....27 A1
Oval App GL12 ....152 F3
Oval The

Frampton on Severn GL2 .100 A3
Gloucester GL1 ....118 D6
Over Bridge* GL2 ....126 B4
Over Csvy GL1 ....126 C3
Over La GL5 ....39 D2
Over Old Rd GL19,GL2 .172 C3
Overbrook CI GL4 ....127 C1
Overbrook Rd GL52 ....133 F3
Overbury CE Fst Sch

GL20 ....182 F8
Overbury Rd GL1 ....119 A8
Overbury St GL53 ....131 A7
Overhill BS20 ....16 D4
Overhill Rd GL7 ....190 B8
Overn Rd GL7 ....149 E7
Overndale Rd BS16 ....20 C6
Overndale Sch BS37 .....34 A7
Overnhill CI BS16 ....20 D5
Overnhill Rd BS16 ....20 D5
Overnhurst Ct 8 BS16 .20 D5
Overton 5 BS4 ....9 D1
Overton CI GL50 ....193 B4
Overton La GL2 ....157 E5
Overton Park Rd GL50 .193 A3
Overton Rd Bristol BS6 .18 E2
Overton Rd GL50 ....193 A3
Owen Gdns 1 GL16 ....155 A6
Owen Sq BS5 ....18 B5
Owen St 10 BS5 ....9 B8
Owl CI GL4 ....119 A4
Owlpen Manor & Gdns*

GL11 ....89 E1
Owls End Rd GL52 ......138 A4
Owls Ewk 2 GL16 ....155 B6
Owls Head Rd BS15 .....20 A8
Oxbarton Ind Est GL52 .138 B4
Oxebode The GL1 ....196 B3
Oxen Leaze BS32 ....40 E2
Oxford CI 11 GL52 ......130 E8
Oxford Ho GL7 ....190 D4
Oxford Pas GL50 ....193 B4
Oxford PI

17 Bristol, Clifton BS8 ..7 F6
17 Bristol, Upper Easton

BS5 ....19 B1
Oxford Rd GL1 ....196 C2
17 Bristol, Barton Hill BS5 .9 C7
Bristol, Knowle BS3 ....8 F4
Bristol, Newton BS2 ......9 A6
Cheltenham BS2 ....130 E8
Chepstow NP16 ....60 E8
Gloucester GL1 ....196 C3
Lydney GL15 ....92 A2
Moreton-in-M GL56 .....187 A3
Oxford Terr

Gloucester GL1 ....196 C3
Stroud GL5 ....99 C8
Oxford Way GL51 ....130 A6
Oxford Wlk 8 GL2 ....130 F8
Oxleaze BS13 ....2 D4
Oxleaze Ct 4 GL8 ....140 B4
Oxleaze La BS41 ....1 E3
Oxleaze Rd Culkerton GL8 .140 E6
7 Tetbury GL8 ....140 B4
Oxmead CI GL52 ....138 B4
Oxmoor GL14 ....190 D4
Oxstalls Com Sch GL1 .127 A4
Oxstalls Dr GL2 ....127 A4
Oxstalls La GL2 ....127 A4
Oxstalls Way GL2 ....127 A3
Ozleworth BS15 ....11 A8

P

Packer's Rd GL14 ....191 D4
Packhorse La GL7 ....160 A4
Paddock CI

Bristol, Emerson's Green

....21 C6
Bristol, Patchway BS32 .40 E2
Paddock Gdn BS14 ....2 F4

Paddock Gdns
Alveston BS35 . . . . .51 A5
Gloucester GL2 . . . . .127 D5
Paddock Rise GL10 . . . . . .97 F8
Paddock The
Chepstow NP16 . . . . .60 D6
Coleford GL16 . . . . .155 B6
Highworth SN6 . . . . .145 D3
South Cerney GL7 . . . . . . .142 F7
Paddocks La GL50 . . . . . .133 D5
Paddocks The
Cirencester GL7 . . . . .150 D7
Monmouth NP25 . . . . .31 B5
Thornbury BS35 . . . . .64 D1
Padin Cl B GL6 . . . . . . .148 C6
Padmore St 7 BS5 . . . . . . .9 D7
Padstow Rd BS4 . . . . .2 F8
Paganhill La GL5 . . . . . . .98 F8
Paganhill La GL5 . . . . . . .98 E7
Page Ct BS16 . . . . .20 F4
Page Rd BS16 . . . . .20 D4
Page's La GL20 . . . . .181 F7
Pages Mead BS11 . . . . . . .16 A8
Pages Rd GL7 . . . . .190 D5
Pagets Rd GL52 . . . . . . .138 A2
Painswick Ave BS34 . . . . . .29 B8
Painswick Dr BS37 . . . . . . .43 E1
Painswick Old Rd GL6 . .103 C1
Painswick Rd
Brockworth GL3 . . . . .120 D3
Cheltenham GL50 . . . . . . .193 A1
Gloucester GL4 . . . . .119 C4
Stroud GL6 . . . . .103 B2
Painswick Rococo Gdn★
GL6 . . . . .111 E2
Pakistan Rd GL51 . . . . . .132 E2
Palestra La GL7 . . . . .190 C5
Palm Rd GL20 . . . . .192 E2
Palmdale Cl BS30 . . . . . . .11 A3
Palmer Ave GL4 . . . . .119 F5
Palmers Cl BS30 . . . . .11 A6
Palmers Leaze BS34 . . . . . .30 A6
Palmers Rd BS6 . . . . .18 C4
Palmerston St 6 BS3 . . . . .8 C3
Palmyra Rd BS3 . . . . .8 B2
Pancake La GL7 . . . . .173 E5
Paper Mill Cotts OX18 . .161 E7
Paquet Ho BS20 . . . . .16 D5
Parabola Cl GL50 . . . . . . .193 A3
Parabola La GL50 . . . . . .193 A3
Parabola Rd GL50 . . . . . .193 A3
Parade The
Bristol, Bishopsworth BS13 . . .2 A6
Bristol, Patchway BS34 . . . .39 F1
Bristol, Shirehampton BS11 . .16 C6
Brockworth GL3 . . . . .120 E5
Chipping Sodbury BS37 . . . .44 A1
Gloucester GL2 . . . . .127 D4
Paradise Row GL4 . . . . . .167 E2
Paragon Terr GL53 . . . . . .193 B2
Paragon The BS8 . . . . .7 F6
Parawell La GL15 . . . . . . .147 C8
Parbrook Ct BS14 . . . . .3 B5
Parfitt's Hill 8 BS5 . . . . . .9 F6
Park Ave
Bristol, Eastville BS5 . . . . .19 D3
Bristol, Knowle BS3 . . . . . . .8 E3
Bristol, Patchway BS32 . . . .40 A2
Bristol, St George BS5 . . . . .9 E8
Frampton Cotterell BS36 . . . .31 B6
Gloucester GL2 . . . . .127 C5
Highworth SN6 . . . . .145 D3
Winterbourne BS36 . . . . . . .30 E7
Park Brake GL2 . . . . .125 D4
Park Cl
Bristol, Cadbury Heath
BS30 . . . . .11 B5
Bristol, Kingswood BS15 . . .10 E7
Fairford GL7 . . . . .152 E4
Keynsham BS31 . . . . .4 D5
Northway GL20 . . . . .181 F6
St Briavels GL15 . . . . .146 F7
8 Tetbury GL8 . . . . .140 C4
Park Cres
Bristol, Cadbury Heath
BS30 . . . . .11 B5
Bristol, Frenchay BS16 . . . . .30 C1
Bristol, St George BS5 . . . . . .9 E8
Park Ct Lydney GL15 . . . . .92 A3
Stroud GL5 . . . . .99 D6
Park End 1 SN6 . . . . . . .142 F4
Park End Rd GL4 . . . . . . .196 B1
Park Farm GL54 . . . . .168 F8
Park Farm Ct 18 BS30 . . .10 E8
Park Farm Village Gn
BS36 . . . . .31 B6
Park Gate GL50 . . . . .193 A1
Park Glade NP16 . . . . . . .146 B4
Park Gr Bristol BS9 . . . . . .18 C5
Whitecroft GL15 . . . . .155 C1
Park Hill Bristol BS11 . . . .16 F6
Whitecroft GL15 . . . . .155 E1
Park Hill Comm GL15 . . . .147 A5
Park Hill La NP16,GL15 . .146 E2
Park Hill Rd
Tidenham Chase GL15 . . . .146 F2
Woolaston GL15 . . . . .147 A2
Park Ho GL50 . . . . .193 A1
Park Inf Sch The GL10 . . .97 F7
Park Jun Sch GL10 . . . . . .97 E7
Park La Bristol BS2 . . . . . .194 C3
Brockhampton GL54 . . . . . .174 A1
Cirencester GL7 . . . . .190 C4
Ilmington CV36 . . . . .189 E7

Park La *continued*
North Nibley GL11 . . . . .79 E7
Prestbury GL52 . . . . .134 B6
Winterbourne BS36 . . . . . . .31 B6
Woodchester GL5 . . . . .90 F6
Wooton-u-E GL12 . . . . .69 A8
Park Mews GL50 . . . . .130 C6
Park Par GL10 . . . . .97 E8
Park Pl
5 Ashton Keynes SN6 . . .142 F5
Bristol, Kingsdown BS8 . . . .19 A3
Bristol, Upper Eastville BS5 . .19 E3
Bristol, Victoria Park BS2 . .194 C3
Cheltenham GL50 . . . . . . .193 A1
Park Prim Sch The BS15 . . .10 E8
Park Rd Berry Hill GL16 . .155 E7
Bristol, Barton Hill BS5 . . . . .9 E8
Bristol, Cadbury Heath
BS30 . . . . .11 B5
Bristol, Kingswood BS15 . . .10 E8
Bristol, Northville BS7 . . . . .29 A1
Bristol, Shirehampton BS11 . .16 F6
Bristol, Staple Hill BS16 . . . .20 E5
Bristol, Stapleton BS16 . . . .19 D5
Chipping Campden GL55 . . .188 F1
B Coleford GL16 . . . . . .155 A6
Cromhall GL12 . . . . .66 B4
Gloucester GL2 . . . . .196 B2
Highleadon GL19 . . . . .171 F2
Keynsham BS31 . . . . .4 E4
Nailsworth GL6 . . . . .91 A8
Stonehouse GL10 . . . . .97 E8
Stroud GL5 . . . . .99 D6
Thornbury BS35 . . . . .64 B2
Park Road Cres GL6 . . . . .91 C3
Park Row Aylburton GL15 . .147 D4
Bristol BS1 . . . . .194 C3
Frampton Cotterell BS36 . . . .31 A8
Park St Bristol BS1 . . . . . .194 C3
Bristol, St George BS5 . . . . . .9 F8
Bristol, Totterdown BS4 . . . . .9 A3
Cheltenham GL50 . . . . . . .193 A4
Cirencester GL7 . . . . .190 C5
Fairford GL7 . . . . .152 E4
Gloucester GL1 . . . . .196 B3
Hawkesbury Upton GL9 . . . .56 A2
Iron Acton BS37 . . . . .27 D4
Stow-on-t-W GL54 . . . . . . .176 F4
Park Street Ave BS1 . . . . .194 C3
Park Terr 91 F6
Park The
Bristol, Frenchay BS16 . . . . .30 B1
Bristol, Kingswood BS15 . . .10 E8
Bristol, Patchway BS34 . . . .40 C3
Bristol, Willsbridge BS30 . . .11 B1
Cheltenham GL50 . . . . . . .130 B6
Keynsham BS31 . . . . .4 E4
Northway GL20 . . . . .182 B5
Stow-on-t-W GL54 . . . . . . .176 F4
Park View Bristol BS15 . . . .10 E7
Cheltenham GL51 . . . . . . .132 E4
Chepstow NP16 . . . . .60 D6
Cirencester GL7 . . . . .190 B8
Ruardean GL17 . . . . .163 F4
Saul GL2 . . . . .157 F4
Sedbury NP16 . . . . .61 B8
Yate BS37 . . . . .32 D8
Park View Ave BS35 . . . . .64 C2
Park View Dr GL5 . . . . . . .98 E8
Park View Rd GL13 . . . . . .85 D3
Park View Terr BS35 . . . . . .9 E8
Park Way Bristol BS30 . . . .11 B5
Gloucester GL2 . . . . .150 D2
Park Wood Cl BS14 . . . . . . .2 F4
Parkbury Ct GL51 . . . . . . .133 A2
Parkend Prim Sch GL15 . .155 F2
Parkend Rd Bream GL15 . .155 D1
Coleford GL16 . . . . .155 B6
Yorkley GL15 . . . . .156 A2
Parkend Sta GL15 . . . . . . .155 E3
Parkend Wlk
Coleford GL16 . . . . .155 B5
Sling GL16 . . . . .155 B3
Parker Pl 1 WR12 . . . . . . .185 B8
Parker St 5 BS3 . . . . .8 B3
Parkers Ave BS30 . . . . .12 C7
Parkers Barton BS5 . . . . . . .9 B6
Parkers Cl BS10 . . . . .18 C8
Parkers La GL56 . . . . .187 A3
Parkfield Ave 3 BS5 . . . . . .9 D7
Parkfield Cotts GL6 . . . . .112 A2
Parkfield Rd BS16 . . . . . . .22 A6
Parkhouse La BS31 . . . . .4 C2
Parkhurst Ave 4 BS16 . . . .20 B4
Parkland Mews 22 GL54 . .176 F4
Parkland Rd
Cheltenham GL50 . . . . . . .130 F4
Dursley GL11 . . . . .65 E7
Parkland Sq GL7 . . . . .190 B2
Parkland Way BS35 . . . . . .64 C3
Parklands Bristol BS15 . . . .10 E8
Churchdown GL3 . . . . .128 A6
Quedgeley GL2 . . . . .117 F1
Wooton-u-E GL12 . . . . .68 A7
Quedgeley GL2 . . . . .109 E8
Parklands Cl NP16 . . . . . . .60 B4
Parklands Rd BS3 . . . . .7 E4
Parkmill NP16 . . . . .162 C7
Parks Rd GL17 . . . . .164 D5
Parkside GL16 . . . . .155 A5
Parkside Ave BS36 . . . . . . .30 E6
Parkside Cl BS13 . . . . .127 F6
Parkside Ct BS3 . . . . .127 F6
Parkside Gdns BS5 . . . . . . .19 B4
Parkstone Ave BS7 . . . . . . .18 A3
Parkwall Cres BS30 . . . . . .10 E5
Parkwall Rd BS30 . . . . .11 A4

Parkway BS34 . . . . .30 A4
Parkway N BS34 . . . . .30 A4
Parkway Trad Est BS34 . . . .30 A4
Parkway Trad Est 10 BS2 . .128 F7
Parkwell Cty Prim Sch
BS30 . . . . .11 A4
Parkwood Cres GL15 . . . .119 F6
Parkwood Dr GL53 . . . . . .131 A4
Parliament Prim Sch GL5 . .99 F7
Parliament St Bristol BS4 . . .9 A4
Gloucester GL1 . . . . .196 B2
Stroud GL5 . . . . .99 D7
Parnall Cres BS37 . . . . .43 C2
Parnall Rd BS16 . . . . .20 A3
Parnall Road Ind Est
BS16 . . . . .20 A3
Parnell Rd BS16 . . . . .19 E7
Parr Cl GL54 . . . . .127 F7
Parr Ho GL54 . . . . .139 E5
Parragate Rd GL14 . . . . . .191 C5
Parry Rd GL51 . . . . .138 F6
Parry's Cl BS9 . . . . .17 E5
Parry's La BS9 . . . . .17 F5
Parrys Gr BS9 . . . . .17 E5
Parslow Barton 4 BS5 . . . .10 A7
Parson St BS3 . . . . .8 B2
Parson Street Prim Sch
BS3 . . . . .8 B2
Parson Street Sta BS3 . . . .8 B2
Parson's Cnr GL54 . . . . . .174 F6
Parsonage Farm 3 SN6 . .143 E4
Parsonage Rd GL4 . . . . . .197 F3
Parsonage St GL11 . . . . . .88 A1
Parsons Ave BS34 . . . . .29 F5
Parsons Ct GL6 . . . . .148 A3
Parsons La
Redmarley D'Abitot GL19 . .179 F2
Weston-s-E GL55 . . . . . . .188 D3
Parsons Paddock BS3 . . . . .3 A7
Parsons Wlk BS30 . . . . . . .11 D7
Partition St BS1 . . . . .194 C2
Parton Rd GL3 . . . . .128 C5
Parton Manor Inf Sch
GL3 . . . . .128 B6
Parton Mews GL3 . . . . . . .128 B6
Parton Rd GL3 . . . . .128 C6
Partridge Cl
Gloucester GL2 . . . . .118 C5
Stonehouse GL10 . . . . .97 F8
Partridge Rd BS16 . . . . . . .22 B7
Partridge Way GL7 . . . . . .190 E4
Parva Springs NP16 . . . . .146 B4
Passage Leaze BS11 . . . . . .16 D6
Passage Rd
Arlingham GL2 . . . . .157 B6
Bristol, Brentry BS10 . . . . . .27 F3
Bristol, Westbury on Trym
BS9 . . . . .18 A8
Saul GL2 . . . . .157 F4
Passage Road Brentry Hill
BS9,BS10 . . . . .28 A4
Passage St BS2 . . . . .195 B2
Pastor's Hill GL15 . . . . . . .147 D8
Pasture La GL56 . . . . .186 C5
Patch Ct BS16 . . . . .21 A8
Patch Elm La BS37 . . . . . . .42 F6
Patch La BS37 . . . . .43 A8
Patcham High Sch BS32 . . .40 B1
Patches The GL7 . . . . .163 F3
Pathway BS34 . . . . .29 B8
Pathway Brook BS32 . . . . .40 C2
Pathway Sta BS34 . . . . .29 C6
Pathway Trad Est BS34 . . . .28 F7
Paternoster Sch GL7 . . . . .190 D3
Paterson Rd GL7 . . . . .190 D3
Pates Ave GL51 . . . . .133 B2
Pates Gram Sch GL51 . . . .132 E3
Patseamur Mews GL2 . . . .127 E5
Patterdale Cl GL51 . . . . . .132 F5
Patterson Ho 8 BS1 . . . . .195 A1
Paul Mead GL6 . . . . .111 B1
Paul St Bristol BS2 . . . . . .194 C4
Gloucester GL1 . . . . .118 F7
Paul's Rise GL5 . . . . .99 A2
Pauls Croft SN6 . . . . .143 F5
Pauls Wlk GL10 . . . . .165 D6
Paulton Dr BS7 . . . . .18 C4
Paulton Rd BS3 . . . . .8 E3
Pauntley CE Prim Sch
GL18 . . . . .171 B8
Pauntley Court Dr GL19 . .171 C7
Pavey Cl BS13 . . . . .2 C4
Pavey Rd BS13 . . . . .2 C4
Pavilion Rd NP16 . . . . .61 C2
Pavilions The GL53 . . . . . .193 B2
Pawlett Rd BS13 . . . . .2 C3
Pawlett Wlk BS13 . . . . .2 C3
Paxhill La GL20 . . . . .182 A8
Paxton BS16 . . . . .5 A4
Paybridge Rd BS13 . . . . . . .1 F4
Paygrove La GL2 . . . . .127 D5
Paymans Terr GL7 . . . . . . .142 F7
Payne Dr BS5 . . . . .9 B7
Paynes Mdw GL2 . . . . . . .100 F5
Paynes Rd BS3 . . . . .8 A3
Peach Cl GL20 . . . . .192 E1
Peache Ct BS16 . . . . .21 D6
Peache Rd BS16 . . . . .20 F6
Peacock Cl
8 Cheltenham GL51 . . . . .132 D2
Gloucester GL4 . . . . .119 C5
8 Newent GL18 . . . . .171 A4

Peacock La GL14 . . . . . . .191 C1
Peacocks La BS15 . . . . . . .10 C7
Peak La GL11 . . . . .89 A7
Peakstile Piece GL52 . . . .138 B3
Pear Orch The GL20 . . . . .182 C5
Pear Tree Cl
Chipping Campden GL55 . . .189 A1
Hardwicke GL2 . . . . .109 E7
Lower Swell GL54 . . . . . . .176 D4
Woodmancote GL52 . . . . . .138 C3
Pear Tree Hey BS37 . . . . . .43 E5
Pear Tree Rd BS32 . . . . . . .40 C2
Pearce Way GL2 . . . . .118 B4
Pearces Hill BS16 . . . . .20 B7
Pearcroft Rd GL10 . . . . . . .98 A6
Pearl St BS3 . . . . .8 B3
Pearsall Rd BS30 . . . . .10 E2
Peart Cl Bristol BS13 . . . . . .1 E5
Gloucester GL1 . . . . .127 B1
Peart Dr BS13 . . . . .1 E4
Peartree La
Bristol, Lower Soundwell
BS15 . . . . .20 F2
Bristol, St George BS5 . . . . .10 B6
Pearwood Way GL4 . . . . . .118 C2
Pecked La GL52 . . . . .138 B5
Peel Cl GL53 . . . . .131 C5
Peel St BS5 . . . . .195 C4
Peg Hill BS37 . . . . .43 F4
Pegasus Bldg GL2 . . . . . . .118 A2
Pegasus Ct
Bourton-on-t-W GL54 . . . . .169 A8
Broadway WR12 . . . . .185 B8
Cheltenham GL51 . . . . . . .130 B7
Gloucester GL4 . . . . .127 E1
Pegasus Gdns GL2 . . . . . .117 F2
Peggotty Bglws GL4 . . . . .119 C7
Peghouse Cl GL5 . . . . .103 D1
Peghouse Rise GL5 . . . . . .103 D1
Pelham Cres GL3 . . . . .128 A6
Pemberton Cl BS16 . . . . . .20 C5
Pembery Rd BS3 . . . . .8 B3
Pembridge Cl GL52 . . . . . .131 C6
Pembridge Ct GL50 . . . . .193 A1
Pembroke Ave BS11 . . . . . .16 E6
Pembroke Gate BS8 . . . . . . .4 E1
Pembroke St BS2 . . . . . . .194 A3
Pembroke Jun & Inf Sch
NP16 . . . . .60 E6
Pembroke Mans BS8 . . . . .194 A4
Pembroke Pl BS8 . . . . .194 A1
Pembroke Rd
Bristol, Clifton BS8 . . . . . . .194 A4
Bristol, Kingswood BS15 . . .20 E2
Bristol, Southville BS3 . . . . . .8 C4
Bristol, Shirehampton BS11 . .16 E6
Chepstow NP16 . . . . .60 E6
Pembroke St Bristol BS2 . .195 B4
Cinderford GL14 . . . . .191 D4
Gloucester GL1 . . . . .196 C1
Pembroke Vale BS8 . . . . . .194 A4
Penbury Rd GL4 . . . . .118 E4
Pen Park Rd BS10 . . . . .28 D2
Pen Park Sch BS10 . . . . . . .28 D2
Penard Way BS15 . . . . .10 F7
Penby Lawn GL14 . . . . . . .156 F6
Pendil Cl NP16 . . . . .61 A8
Pendennis Ave BS16 . . . . .20 D5
Pendennis Ho 5 BS16 . . . .20 D5
Pendennis Pk BS4 . . . . .9 D2
Pendennis Rd BS16 . . . . . .20 D5
Pendil Cl GL50 . . . . .133 B6
Pendock Cl Prim Sch
GL19 . . . . .180 A4
Pendock Cl Bristol BS30 . . .11 C5
Quedgeley GL2 . . . . .117 E1
Pendock Ct BS16 . . . . .5 E3
Pendock Rd Bristol BS16 . .20 C6
Winterbourne BS36 . . . . . . .30 E5
Penfield Rd BS2 . . . . .19 A2
Penharva Cl GL51 . . . . . . .133 A3
Penhill Rd GL4 . . . . .119 C6
Penlea Ct BS11 . . . . .16 D7
Penmoel La NP16 . . . . .73 A3
Penmoyle Gdns NP16 . . . . .73 A4
Penn Dr BS16 . . . . .30 C1
Penn La GL10 . . . . .98 B2
Penn St BS1 . . . . .195 B3
Pennard Ct BS14 . . . . .3 A5
Penngrove BS30 . . . . .11 A3
Pennine Cl GL2 . . . . .109 E8
Pennine Rd Bristol BS30 . . .11 A3
Cheltenham GL51 . . . . . . .134 B3
Pennington Ct GL51 . . . . .132 E4
Pennlea BS13 . . . . .2 C7
Pennsylvania Ave GL51 . .132 F3
Penny Cl GL2 . . . . .127 D4
Penny La GL2 . . . . .99 B2
Pennyroyal Gr BS16 . . . . . .19 F6
Pennywell Ct 3 BS5 . . . . . .9 A8
Pennywell Rd BS5 . . . . .9 A8
Penpole Ave BS11 . . . . .16 E6
Penpole Cl BS11 . . . . .16 D7
Penpole La BS11 . . . . .16 D7
Penpole Pl BS11 . . . . .16 E6
Penrith Cl GL51 . . . . .129 F7
Penrith Gdns BS10 . . . . . . .18 D8
Penrith Rd GL51 . . . . .129 F7
Penrose Rd BS14 . . . . .2 E2
Penrose Cl GL54 . . . . .102 E3
Penrose Dr BS32 . . . . .29 D7
Penrose Rd GL3 . . . . .127 D6
Pensfield Pk BS10 . . . . .28 D4
Pensford Ct BS14 . . . . .3 D5
Pensile Rd GL6 . . . . .91 D4

Pentagon The BS9 . . . .
Pentathlon Way GL50 13
Penterry La NP16 . . . .
Penterry Pk NP16 . . . .
Pentire Ave BS13 . . . .
Pentland Ave BS35 . . . .
Penyworn Cl NP16 . . . .
Pentylands Cl SN6 14
Peppercorn Alley GL20 . . .18
Pepys Cl BS31 . . . .
Perch Dr GL14 19
Percival Rd BS8 . . . .
Percy St 8 Bristol BS3 . . . . .
Gloucester GL1 1
Percy Walker Ct BS16 2
Peregrine Cl GL2 1
Peregrine Rd GL3 1
Perretts Ct BS1 1
Perricks Cl GL14 16
Perrie Dr WR11 18
Perringit Rd BS36 . . . .
Perrinsfield GL7 1
Perrott Rd BS15 . . . .
Perry Cl
Charlton Kings GL53 1
8 Newent GL18 1
Winterbourne BS36 . . . .
Perry Court Inf Sch BS4 . . .
Perry Court Jun Sch BS14 . .
Perry Ctr The GL2 . . . .
Perry Field GL15 14
Perry Gr GL14 19
Perry Orch Stroud GL5 . . . . .
Upton St Leonards GL4 1
Perry Rd BS1 . . . .
Perry St BS5 . . . .
Perry's Cl BS15 . . . .
Perry's Court La GL17 . . . . .
Perrycroft Ave BS13 . . . . . .
Perrycroft Rd BS13 . . . .
Perryfield Cl 11 GL54 1
Perrygrove Rd GL16 1
Perrymans Cl BS16 . . . .
Perrys Lea BS32 . . . .
Persh La GL2 . . . .
Persh Way GL2 . . . .
Perwell Cl GL10 . . . .
Pesley Cl BS13 . . . .
Peter Pennell Cl GL51 . . . .
Peter's St GL10 . . . .
Peter's Terr BS5 . . . .
Petercole Dr BS13 . . . .
Peters Field GL2 . . . .
Peterson Sq BS13 . . . .
Petersway Gdns BS5 . . . . . .
Petherton Cl BS15 . . . .
Petherton Gdns BS14 . . . . .
Petherton Rd Inf Sch
BS14 . . . .
Pethick Ho BS4 . . . .
Pettigrove Gdns BS15 . . . . .
Pettigrove Rd BS15 . . . .
Petty La GL52 . . . .
Petty Marsh GL15 . . . .
Pettycroft GL17 . . . .
Petworth Cl GL4 . . . .
Pevelands GL11 . . . .
Pevensey Wlk BS4 . . . .
Peverell Cl BS10 . . . .
Peverell Dr BS10 . . . .
Peveril Ho GL2 . . . .
Pheasant La GL51 . . . .
Pheasant Mead GL10 . . . . .
Pheasant Rise HR9 . . . .
Pheasantry The GL7 . . . . . .
Phelps Way GL2 . . . .
Philadelphia Ct BS1 . . . . . .
Philip St
Bristol, Bedminster BS3 . . . .
Bristol, St Philip's Marsh
BS2 . . . .
Gloucester GL1 . . . .
Philip's Cl GL15 . . . .
Philippa Cl BS14 . . . .
Philips Ho 2 BS2 . . . .
Phillimore Gdns GL2 . . . . . .
Phillimore Rd GL11 . . . .
Phillips La GL19 . . . .
Phillips Rd WR12 . . . .
Phippen St 1 BS1 . . . .
Phipps St BS1 . . . .
Phoenix Cl GL16 . . . .
Phoenix Dr NP16 . . . .
Phoenix Gr BS6 . . . .
Phoenix Ho BS5 . . . .
Phoenix Trad Est GL5 . . . . .
Phoenix Way GL7 . . . .
Piccadilly
Guiting Power GL54 1
Stroud GL5 . . . .
Piccadilly Way GL52 . . . . . .
Pickedmoor La BS35 . . . . . .
Pickering Cl GL3 . . . .
Pickering Rd GL53 . . . .
Picklenash Jun Sch
GL18 . . . .
Picton Ho GL2 . . . .
Picton La BS6 . . . .
Picton St BS6 . . . .
Piece Hedge GL54 . . . .
Piece The
Cirencester GL7 1
Colin St Aldwyns GL7 1
Piercefield Ave NP16 . . . . . .
Piercefield Terr NP16 . . . . .

gate Ho BS5 .....20 A1
al Gate GL54 .....174 D3
ers CI BS30 .....18 C1
bey BS6 .....18 C1
ers The GL6 .....91 B4
ction Way GL51 .....129 F7
ing Stones GL55 .....189 A2
ing Way GL52 .....187 A2
an Amphitheatre* 190 B4
an Farm Ct BS11 .....27 C2
an Farm Rd BS4 .....2 E7
an Hackle Ave 133 C5
an Rd Bristol BS15 .....19 B1
eltenham GL51 .....133 A1
oucester GL4 .....119 E6
an Way
urton-on-t-W GL54 .....169 A8
stol BS9 .....17 C4
BS16 .....155 A5
shworth SN6 .....145 C3
hade of GL7 .....153 E3
edean GL14 .....191 F4
an Wlk
stol, Brislington BS4 .....9 C3
stol, Stoke Gifford BS34 .....29 E5
aney Ave BS7 .....19 B6
aney Avenue Inf Sch 19 B6
aney Avenue Jun Sch 19 B6
aney CI GL11 .....118 E5
aney Rd GL8 .....140 B4
Jones Ho B BS1 .....195 B4
ald Rd BS16 .....19 F6
ayne Wlk BS14 .....20 C6
kery La Pilning BS35 .....39 A6
kterhill BS30,SN14 .....22 F4
rjavels GL13 .....85 E7
njness GL15 .....154 F2
kery Rd Bristol BS4 .....9 A3
sworth GL3 .....127 D6
kery The GL54 .....159 A6
kery Way BS14 .....20 C6
ksmoor Hill GL5 .....99 A3
sevelt Ave GL52 .....131 A8
e Wlk The GL5 .....99 E3
sewalk GL20 .....192 D4
ary RC Prim Sch GL5 .....99 B7
ary The BS16 .....21 D7
e & Crown Ho GL50 .....193 F3
e & Crown Pas GL50 .....193 B4
bay Mead BS16 .....19 E5
ebony BS5 .....9 D8
ebony Rd BS5 .....9 C7
ebery Terr GL6 .....148 C5
ebery Ave Bristol BS2 .....19 A1
oucester GL1 .....118 E6
ebery Mount GL11 .....80 C8
ebery Pk GL11 .....80 C8
ebery Rd GL11 .....80 C8
ebery Terr BS8 .....194 B2
edale Ave GL10 .....98 A7
edale CI B 109 D8
edale Rd BS16 .....19 A3
field Cres GL20 .....192 F4
field Ct GL7 .....190 C7
hill Terr GL52 .....130 F8
hill Terr B GL52 .....130 F8
hip Ct GL51 .....130 A4
hip Way GL52 .....130 A4
elarge Gdns BS10 .....28 A2
emary CI Bristol BS30 .....29 F7
ucester GL4 .....119 D4
emary La BS30 .....11 C2
ant NP16 .....146 F1
emary Terr GL12 .....68 B7
emont Terr BS8 .....194 A2
emount Ct GL15 .....10 B8
ary CI BS9 .....18 D8
evear BS2 .....20 C3
evear Rd 9 A7
eville Ave BS30 .....11 A2
ewood Ave BS35 .....50 F5
ewar Rd E B BS5 .....19 B1
nni Gar W B BS5 .....19 B1
ng Rd BS7 .....19 B6
wn Rd BS6 .....18 C1
CI BS37 .....40 B1
Rd Berry Hill GL16 .....155 A8
heldean GL17 .....164 D6
ont GL18 .....170 F5
all Ave BS34 .....29 C6
all Rd BS4 .....7 D9
atter Wood Ct BS11 .....27 B2
iter's La BS5 .....10 A6
lyn Way BS35 .....64 C3
ermere CI GL51 .....129 F5
leigh GL51 .....129 E5
nda Terr GL50 .....193 A2

Rougemont Gr NP16 .....60 F4
Rounceval St BS37 .....44 A1
Roundabout La GL8 .....140 C8
Roundabouts The GL55 .....99 F1
Roundhills Mead SN6 .....145 D4
Roundmoor CI BS31 .....5 D3
Roundmoor Gdns BS14 .....3 D7
Roundways BS36 .....31 D6
Rousham Rd BS5 .....19 A3
Roves La SN6 .....145 D1
Row The Aust BS35 .....49 A7
  Lechlade on T GL7 .....153 C4
  Longborough GL56 .....176 F7
  Southrop GL7 .....153 C6
  St Arvans NP16 .....72 B6
Rowacres BS14 .....2 F6
Rowan CI BS16 .....20 A2
Rowan R B Bristol BS5 .....9 B7
  Yate BS37 .....43 C3
Rowan Dr NP16 .....60 E5
Rowan Gdns GL3 .....120 D6
Rowan Gr GL11 .....88 A3
Rowan Ho BS13 .....2 D4
Rowan Tree Ho BS16 .....20 F4
Rowan Way Bristol BS15 .....10 B3
 B Cheltenham GL51 .....129 E5
  Nailsworth GL6 .....90 F5
Rowan Wlk BS31 .....4 C4
Rowandean GL14 .....191 C5
Rowanfield Exchange 133 A2
Rowanfield Inf & Jun Schs 133 A2
Rowanfield Rd GL51 .....133 A1
Rowans The Bristol BS16 .....30 B1
  Pontshill HR9 .....164 B8
  Woodmancote GL52 .....138 B3
Rowberrow BS14 .....1 F7
Rowcroft GL5 .....99 B7
Rowcroft Retreat GL5 .....99 B7
Rowe CI GL50 .....193 A3
Rowland Ave BS16 .....19 D8
Rowlandson Gdns BS7 .....19 B6
Rowley GL11 .....88 A5
Rowley Mews GL11 .....88 A5
Rowley St BS3 .....8 C3
Rownham CI BS3 .....7 E4
Rownham CI BS8 .....194 A1
Rownham Hill BS8 .....7 D6
Rownham Mead BS8 .....194 A1
Rows The GL54 .....188 D4
Roxton Dr GL51 .....129 C7
Roy King Gdns BS30 .....11 C6
Royal Agricultural Coll GL7 .....150 B4
Royal Albert Rd BS6 .....18 A4
Royal CI BS10 .....27 D3
Royal Cres GL50 .....193 B3
Royal CI B GL51 .....132 D2
Royal Forest of Dean Coll GL16 .....155 B7
Royal Fort Rd BS2 .....194 C3
Royal Hospl for Sick Children BS2 .....194 C3
Royal La GL1 .....127 A2
Royal Oak Mews GL54 .....193 B4
Royal Oak Rd
  Gloucester GL4 .....196 A3
  Upper Lydbrook GL17 .....163 E3
Royal Oak Terr GL55 .....188 F1
Royal Parade Mews GL50 .....193 A2
Royal Pk BS8 .....194 A3
Royal Prom BS8 .....194 B3
Royal Spring GL17 .....165 A5
Royal Well La GL50 .....193 B3
Royal Well PI GL50 .....193 B3
Royal Well Rd GL50 .....193 B3
Royal West of England Acad BS8 .....194 B3
Royal York Cres BS8 .....7 A6
Royal York Ho BS8 .....194 A2
Royal York Mews BS8 .....194 A2
Royal York Villas BS8 .....194 A2
Royate Hill BS5 .....9 E7
Roycroft Rd BS34 .....29 B2
Royston Wlk BS10 .....28 D2
Rozel Rd BS7 .....18 F4
Ruardean CE Prim Sch GL17 .....163 E4
Ruardean Rd GL17 .....163 F3
Rubens CI BS31 .....5 A5
Ruby St BS3 .....8 B3
Rudford CI BS34 .....40 B1
Rudge CI BS15 .....10 E5
Rudge The GL2 .....126 B8
Rudgeway Rd BS35 .....50 F1
Rudgewood CI BS13 .....2 D2
Rudgleigh Ave BS20 .....16 C4
Rudgleigh Rd BS20 .....16 C4
Rudhall CI GL1 .....196 A3
Rudhall Rd GL8 .....18 E7
Rudhall View HR9 .....164 D8
Rudthorpe Rd BS7 .....18 E5
Ruffet CI GL16 .....155 B4
Ruffet Rd BS36 .....38 A4
Ruffet's CI NP16 .....60 D8
Ruffitt The GL14 .....191 F5
Rugby Rd BS4 .....9 D3
Rumsey CI GL4 .....119 C4
Runnings Rd GL51 .....133 A5
Runnings The GL51 .....133 A6
Runnymead Ave BS4 .....9 D2
Runnymede Bristol BS15 .....20 E1
  Cheltenham GL51 .....129 E5
Runswick Rd BS4 .....9 C3
Rupert St Bristol BS1 .....195 A3

Rupert St continued
  Bristol, Redfield BS5 .....9 C7
Ruscombe Rd GL6 .....102 E2
Rush CI BS32 .....40 D2
Rusham BS13 .....1 F4
Rushley La GL54 .....174 A7
Rushmead La SN14 .....24 F5
Rushton Dr BS36 .....31 D7
Rusworth CI GL51 .....132 D2
Rusworth Ho GL51 .....132 D2
Rushy BS30 .....11 A4
Rushy GL52 .....134 A4
Rushy Mews GL52 .....134 A4
Rushy Way BS16 .....31 A1
Rushyleaze GL15 .....92 B2
Ruskin GL BS7 .....19 A8
Ruskin Ho BS34 .....29 A8
Ruspidge CI GL4 .....119 E5
Ruspidge Rd GL14 .....156 C6
Russ St GL2 .....195 C2
Russell Almshouses GL20 .....192 C3
Russell Ave BS15 .....10 E7
Russell CI GL9 .....57 B3
Russell Gr BS6 .....18 C5
Russell PI GL51 .....133 C3
Russell Rd
  Cheltenham GL51 .....133 C3
  Gloucester GL1 .....196 B2
  Stroud GL5 .....99 C2
Russell Town Ave BS5 .....64 E8
Russell Town Ind Pk BB BS5 .....9 C7
Russet Ave GL7 .....153 F2
Russet CI Breedon GL22 .....182 C7
  Gloucester GL4 .....118 B3
  B Ledbury HR8 .....178 E7
  Olveston BS35 .....50 A3
Russet CI GL12 .....67 F4
Russet Rd GL51 .....132 F3
Russett Way ZB GL12 .....171 A4
Rustic CI GL4 .....119 C4
Rutherford CI BS30 .....11 A3
Rutherford Way GL51 .....133 A5
Ruthven Rd BS4 .....9 B2
Rutland Ave BS30 .....11 A2
Rutland CI GL4 .....133 B1
Rutland PI GL7 .....190 C3
Rutland Rd BS7 .....18 E3
Ryalls La GL2 .....95 A8
Rydal Ho BS34 .....29 A8
Rydal Rd GL2 .....127 B4
Rydal Wlk GL2 .....129 E7
Ryde Rd BS4 .....9 B2
Ryder CI GL11 .....88 A4
Ryder Row GL33 .....127 C6
Rye Ave GL53 .....132 D5
Rye CI BS13 .....1 E6
Rye Cres GL54 .....169 A7
Ryecliose GL54 .....169 A7
Ryecroft Ct BS36 .....31 C7
Ryecroft Rd BS36 .....31 C8
Ryecroft Rise BS41 .....7 B1
Ryecroft St GL1 .....196 C1
Ryedown La BS30 .....11 D2
Rylands GL4 .....118 C3
Rylands CI GL10 .....97 E8
Rylands Rd
  B Bream GL15 .....147 D8
  Stonehouse GL10 .....97 E8
Rylands The
  B Bream GL15 .....147 D8
  Randwick GL6 .....102 D1
Ryleaze GL15 .....99 C7
Ryleaze Rd GL5 .....99 C7
Ryeworth Dr GL52 .....131 B7
Ryeworth Rd GL52 .....131 B7
Ryland CI GL8 .....140 C5
Ryland PI B BS2 .....19 A2
Rylestone CI BS36 .....30 F8
Rylestone Gr BS9 .....17 F5
Rysdale Rd BS9 .....17 F6

S

Sabre CI GL2 .....118 A3
Sabrina Way Bristol BS9 .....17 C4
  Lydney GL15 .....92 B4
Sachi Ct GL51 .....132 E2
Sackville App GL50 .....133 D4
Saddlers La GL50 .....133 D4
Saddlers Rd GL3 .....117 F2
Saddlers CI GL52 .....130 F8
Sadlers Field B SN6 .....142 F5
Sadlier CI BS11 .....17 A8
Saffron CI GL4 .....119 A4
Saffron Rd GL20 .....192 C4
Sages Mead BS32 .....29 E8
Saintbridge CI GL4 .....119 B5
Saintbridge PI GL4 .....119 B5
SS Gt Britain* BS1 .....194 B1
SS Peter & Paul Catholic Sch BS8 .....194 C4
St Agnes Ave BS4 .....8 F2
St Agnes CI BS4 .....8 F2
St Agnes Wlk BS4 .....8 F2
St Aidan's CI BS5 .....10 B6
St Aidan's Rd BS5 .....10 B6
St Aidans CI GL52 .....132 C2
St Alban's Rd BS6 .....18 B4
St Albans CI GL51 .....130 A5
St Albans Rd GL2 .....118 C5

St Aldams Dr BS16 .....22 B5
St Aldate St GL1 .....196 B3
St Aldwyn Rd GL1 .....118 F6
St Aldwyn's CI BS7 .....18 F8
St Andrew CE Jun Sch SN26 .....144 E1
St Andrew's Ave NP16 .....60 E7
St Andrew's CE Prim Sch GL12 .....66 A1
St Andrew's Prim Sch GL54 .....159 A6
St Andrew's Rd
  Avonmouth BS11 .....26 B1
  Avonmouth BS11 .....26 B4
  Bristol BS6 .....18 E2
St Andrews
  Ashleworth GL19 .....172 D4
  Bristol BS30 .....11 B6
  Yate BS37 .....43 F1
St Andrews CI GL20 .....182 C4
St Andrews Gate Rdbt BS11 .....26 C2
St Andrews Gn GL3 .....128 B5
St Andrews Road Sta BS11 .....26 B4
St Andrews Trad Est BS11 .....26 C2
St Ann St GL1 .....72 F1
St Ann Way GL1 .....196 A1
St Ann's Cross ED GL15 .....147 D8
St Annal's Rd GL14 .....191 E4
St Anne's CI Bristol BS4 .....9 E5
  Cheltenham GL52 .....133 F2
St Anne's Ave BS31 .....4 D6
St Anne's CE Prim Sch BS30 .....11 C3
St Anne's CI Bristol BS4 .....9 E5
  Cheltenham GL52 .....133 F2
St Anne's Dr
  Coalpit Heath BS36 .....31 C5
  Wick BS30 .....12 B7
St Anne's Inf Sch BS4 .....9 E5
St Anne's Park Prim Sch BS4 .....9 E5
St Anne's Rd
  Bristol, St Anne's Park BS4 .....9 E6
  Bristol, St George BS5 .....10 B6
  Cheltenham GL52 .....193 C3
St Anne's Terr Bristol BS4 .....9 E5
  Cheltenham GL52 .....193 C3
St Annes CI Z Bristol BS5 .....9 F6
  Brockworth GL3 .....120 E6
St Annes CI BS4 .....9 D5
St Annes Dr BS30 .....11 C2
St Annes Rd BS15 .....146 E2
St Anthony's Dr BS30 .....12 B7
St Anthony's Sch GL14 .....191 D4
St Arild's Rd GL19 .....182 A8
St Aubin's Ave BS4 .....9 F3
St Augustine of Canterbury RC Sch BS16 .....20 F7
St Augustine's Par GL1 .....195 A2
St Augustine's PI B BS1 .....195 A2
St Barbara's CI GL20 .....182 C4
St Barnabas CE Prim Sch BS16 .....38 F1
St Barnabas CI
  Bristol, Knowle BS4 .....8 F1
  Bristol, Warmley BS30 .....11 C7
  Gloucester GL1 .....118 C4
St Bartholomew's Rd BS7 .....18 E3
St Bartholomews B GL18 .....171 A4
St Bartholomews CI GL11 .....87 F5
St Bede's RC Sch BS11 .....27 B2
St Bede's Rd BS15 .....10 C6
St Benedict's Catholic Sch B Sports Coll GL51 .....133 A3
St Bernadette RC Prim Sch BS14 .....3 B6
St Bernadette's Rd BS14 .....16 E6
St Bernard's Rd BS11 .....16 E6
St Birinus CI GL7 .....153 B8
St Blaize Ct GL7 .....190 C4
St Bonaventure's RC Prim Sch BS7 .....18 D4
St Brelades Gr BS4 .....9 F5
St Brendan's Rd GL1 .....99 E7
St Brendan's Sixth Form Coll BS4 .....9 E5
St Brendan's Way BS11 .....26 B1
St Brendans Rdbt BS11 .....26 C1
St Briavels Dr BS37 .....32 D8
St Briavels Parochial CE Prim Sch GL15 .....146 E7
St Briavels Rd GL15 .....147 B2
St Bruel's CI GL15 .....146 F7
St Cadoc Ho BS31 .....4 F5
St Catharine's RC Prim Sch BS6 .....18 B4
St Catherine St GL1 .....196 B4
St Catherine's Ind Est BS3 .....8 D3
St Catherine's Mead BS20 .....16 D3
St Catherine's Terr BS3 .....8 D3
St Catherines PI B BS3 .....8 D4
St Christopher's Specl Sch BS6 .....18 B4
St Clair Cotts GL51 .....173 F2
St Clement's Wlk GL2 .....190 C5
St Clements
  B Bristol BS16 .....20 D3

St Clements Ct continued
  Keynsham BS31 .....4 E4
St Clements Rd BS31 .....4 E4
St Cloe Mead GL5 .....91 B8
St Cloes Pitch GL5 .....91 A8
St Cyril's Rd GL10 .....97 F7
St David's Ave BS30 .....11 B5
St David's CI
  Chepstow NP16 .....60 E7
  Gloucester GL4 .....118 D3
St David's Cres BS4 .....9 F6
St David's CI GL56 .....187 A3
St David's Prim Sch GL56 .....187 A3
St David's Rd BS35 .....64 C1
St Davids CI GL51 .....130 A6
St Davids Rd GL20 .....182 C4
St Dominics RC Prim Sch GL5 .....91 A7
St Dunstan's Rd BS3 .....8 C2
St Edward's Rd BS8 .....194 B2
St Edward's Sch GL52 .....131 A7
St Edwards CI GL56 .....187 A2
St Edwards Dr GL54 .....176 F4
St Edwards Jun Sch GL52 .....131 B7
St Edwards Rd GL54 .....176 F4
St Edwards Senior Sch GL53 .....130 F6
St Edwards Wlk GL53 .....131 A6
St Edyth's Rd BS9 .....17 C6
St Ewens Rd NP16 .....60 E6
St Fagans CI BS30 .....11 B2
St Francis Dr Wick BS30 .....12 B7
  Winterbourne BS36 .....30 F6
St Francis RC Prim Sch BS1 .....194 B2
St Gabriel's Rd BS5 .....9 B8
St George CE Prim Sch BS1 .....194 B2
St George Com Sch BS5 .....9 C8
St George's Ave GL10 .....98 A4
St George's Bsns Pk GL31 .....133 A2
St George's CI
  B Cheltenham GL51 .....133 B2
  Dursley GL11 .....88 B3
  Gloucester GL4 .....118 C3
  B Moreton-in-M GL56 .....187 A3
St George's Dr GL51 .....133 B2
St George's Hill BS20 .....16 A3
St George's Ho BS8 .....194 B2
St George's PI GL50 .....193 B3
St George's Rd
  Cheltenham GL50 .....193 A3
  Dursley GL11 .....88 A3
  Keynsham BS31 .....4 D6
St George's Sq GL50 .....193 B3
St George's Ave GL BS5 .....9 F6
St Georges Ho B BS5 .....9 E8
St Georges Ind Est BS11 .....26 B3
St Georges Rd
  Ashchurch GL20 .....182 C4
  Bristol BS1 .....194 C2
  Brockworth GL3 .....120 E5
St Georges Twr GL50 .....193 B4
St Georges Way NP16 .....61 B4
St Giles Barton GL12 .....58 C8
St Giles' Rd GL4 .....182 C7
St Gregory's Rd BS7 .....18 F8
St Gregory's Wlk BS7 .....18 F8
St Helen's Wlk BS5 .....20 A1
St Helena Rd GL56 .....18 B4
St Helens Dr Bristol BS30 .....11 C2
  Wick BS30 .....12 C7
St Helier Ave BS4 .....9 F3
St Hilary CI BS9 .....17 D5
St Ivel Way BS30 .....11 C6
St James CE Prim Sch
  Cheltenham GL50 .....130 B6
  Chipping Campden GL55 .....189 A2
St James CI BS35 .....64 C3
St James Ct Bristol BS34 .....40 C3
  B Cheltenham GL50 .....193 A4
  Moreton-in-M GL56 .....187 A3
St James Pk GL56 .....155 B3
St James St
  Cheltenham GL50 .....193 B3
  Gloucester GL1 .....119 A8
  Monmouth NP25 .....117 F1
St James' & Ebrington CE Prim Sch GL55 .....189 A1
St James' Barton BS1 .....195 A4
St James CE Jun Sch GL1 .....119 A8
St James' CI GL2 .....117 F1
St James' Par W BS37 .....193 A1
St James' Sq
  Cheltenham GL50 .....193 B3
  Monmouth NP25 .....154 A7
St James' Ter NP25 .....154 A7
St James's PI GL50 .....193 B2
St James's PI BS16 .....21 A5
St James St BS16 .....21 A5
St John St
  Hawkesbury Upton GL9 .....57 B3
  Thornbury BS35 .....64 B1
St John's Bridge B BS1 .....195 A3
St John's CE Prim Sch
  Bristol BS8 .....18 A2

roke Rd GL1 ....196 C4
rook Rd GL14 ....3 B5
orne Rd BS11 ....132 D2
ey CI BS10 ....28 E1
e Court Ave BS4 ......9 E4
ans St BS35 ....8 D1
on Rd BS5 ....19 C1
s Rd BS9 ....17 D2
alls Rd BS9 ....17 D2
rt St GL1 ....196 C4
and Ave Bristol BS14 ...3 B7
ley GL11 ....80 C8
nd Way BS11 ....16 F7
on La GL1 ....196 B4
nda Way (Hempstead
Pass) GL2 ....118 C7
ury Barns Pk NP16 ...61 B8
ury La NP16 ....73 A1
on Rd BS2 ....19 A2
efield Gdns BS16 ...30 F1
ewick Gdns GL51 ...129 D6
ley CI GL4 ....118 C2
ley Rd GL52 ....137 F4
wick Ho BS11 ....16 E7
on Ho ■ GL50 .....133 B1
n Park Jun & Inf Schs
.........18 F3
ury Barns Pk NP16 ...18 F3
en Wlk GL11 ....129 D6
orne Rd 18 F5
op's Cleeve GL52 ...137 F4
ol BS7 ....18 F5
ooke Cres BS16 ....20 C6
e Rd BS5 ....19 F1
n Rd BS14 ....3 E5
rk CI GL52 ....133 F2
rk CI ■ GL52 .....133 F2
rk Gdns GL52 .....133 F2
rk Rd BS16 ....20 C1
rk St GL52 ....133 F2
s Rd GL2 ....109 D7
y Wlk BS13 ....2 A5
ry Rd BS13 ....98 F2
ol BS5 ....98 E4
orthy Bristol BS15 ...10 E7
enham BS11 ....129 E5
orthy CI BS31 ......4 D5
orthy Rd BS4 ......9 B2
on Way GL4 ....98 A5
n Rd GL4 ....118 F5
ca P ■ BS5 ....9 D7
ca St BS5 ....9 D7
ca Way GL50 .....133 B5
nus Bldgs BS14 ....2 D5
ol BS1 ....196 B4
dge La BS36 ....31 D4
Row GL7 ....149 E3
m ■ GL51 ....129 E5
Acres GL4 ....1 F5
Springs House (Sch)
.........123 B7
Stars Rd GL14 ....191 C6
Waters GL10 ......97 D4
fields SN6 ....145 D4
leaze La Edge GL4 .111 B2
eat GL4,GL6 .....111 D5
uth Ave 38 A6
ol, Filton BS7 .....29 B1
al, Hengrove BS14 ...4 D1
ester GL4 ....118 D2
n Ave NP16 ....73 A1
n Beach Prim Sch
.........38 A6
n Sta BS35 ....38 A6
n Cl Charfield GL12 ...67 A4
more GL2 ....126 B7
n Cres NP16 ....60 F7
n Dr Berkeley GL13 ...85 E4
n Grange BS10 .....27 D3
n La Berkeley GL13 ...84 E1
.........76 F8
n Oaks GL2 ....109 F7
n Rd
nouth BS11 ....26 C4
.........16 B6
enham GL52 ....134 A3
ey GL11 ....87 E4
ester GL1 ....196 A2
h BS10 ....27 A7
y GL15 ....92 B2
520 ....16 C5
n Beach BS35 ......37 F3
ness GL13 ....85 B8
house GL10 ....97 E8
n St GL14 ....157 A6
n Terr GL14 ....157 A6
n Vale Sch GL2 ...109 E8
n View GL14 ....191 E5
n View Rd
bury BS35 ....64 C2
aston GL15 ....147 B3
y GL15 ....156 B2
n Way
ley GL19 ....173 C7
nl BS34 ....39 F1
.........5 A5
bank Ave GL15 ...92 C3
banks Prim Sch
.........92 C3
leigh Gdns BS9 ...17 F3
side Trad Est
nouth BS11 ....26 C5
ester GL2 ....126 C1
nvale Dr GL2 .....117 E2
nwood Gdns BS35 ...38 A5
St BS2 ....18 F2

Seymour Ave BS7 ....18 E4
Seymour Cl ■ GL4 ...155 A7
Seymour Gate GL55 ...189 A2
Seymour Pl
Tewkesbury GL20 .....192 C3
■ Winchcombe GL54 ...174 A7
Seymour Rd
Bristol, Ashley Down BS7 ..18 E4
Bristol, Kingswood BS15 ...20 C1
Bristol, Staple Hill BS16 ...20 E4
Bristol, Upper Easton BS5 ..19 A1
Gloucester GL1 ....118 D7
Seyton Wlk BS34 ....29 E5
Sezincote ■ GL6 .....186 D2
Sezincote Cl GL6 .....148 B6
Shackel Hendy Mews
BS16 ....21 B5
Shackleton Ave BS37 ...32 F8
Shackleton Cl GL3 .....128 C5
Shadwell Rd BS7 .....18 D3
Shaft Rd BS35 ....38 A8
Shaftesbury Ave BS6 ...18 E1
Shaftesbury Hall ■
GL50 ....193 B4
Shaftesbury Ind Est
GL51 ....133 B6
Shaftesbury Pl ■ GL51 ...132 D2
Shaftesbury Terr ■ GL5 ...9 D7
Shakespeare Ave
Bristol BS7 ....18 A4
Gloucester GL2 ....118 C4
Shakespeare Cotts
GL51 ....129 B7
Shakespeare Rd BS20 ...192 C4
Shakespeare Rd
Cheltenham GL51 .....132 E1
Dursley GL11 ....80 C7
Shaldon Rd BS7 ....19 A4
Shalford Cl GL7 ....190 B3
Shallowbrooks La SN14 ...47 F8
Shallows The BS31 ......5 F3
Shambles Mus The ■
GL18 ....171 A4
Shambles The ■ GL55 ...99 C7
Shamrock Cl GL4 .....127 F6
Shamrock Rd BS5 .....19 D3
Shanklin Dr BS34 ....29 B3
Shannon Ct BS15 ....51 D8
Shannon Way GL20 ...182 B4
Shapcott Cl BS4 ....9 B1
Shaplands BS16 ......17 D4
Sharland Cl BS9 ....17 E3
Sharland Gr BS13 ......2 C4
Sharpness Prim Sch
GL13 ....85 D8
Sharps Way NP16 ......60 F5
Shaw Cl ■ BS5 ....9 B8
Shaw Green La GL52 ...134 C5
Shaymoor La BS35 .....32 A4
Shearmore Cl GL3 ....19 A7
Shearwater Gr GL3 ...127 E6
Sheene Ct ■ BS3 ....8 C3
Sheene La BS3 ....8 C3
Sheene Way BS3 ......8 C3
Sheenhill Rd GL51 .....188 B8
Sheeps Mdw GL14 ....156 F7
Sheep Fair La SN14 ....14 F8
Sheep St Cirencester GL7 ...190 C4
Highworth SN6 ....145 D3
Stow-on-t-W GL54 ...176 F4
Sheeps Croft BS13 ......2 A5
Sheepscombe Cl GL51 ...129 E8
Sheepscombe Cty Prim Sch
GL6 ....112 C1
Sheepwood Cl BS10 ...28 A2
Sheepwood Rd BS10 ...28 A2
Sheer Ho ■ WR12 .....185 C8
Sheevaun Cl GL2 .....127 D5
Sheiling Sch The BS35 ...64 B2
Shelburne Barton BS35 ...10 B7
Shelburne Rd GL51 .....193 C4
Sheldare Barton BS5 ...10 B7
Sheldons Cl GL12 .....193 C4
Sheldrake Dr BS16 ....19 E6
Shelduck Rd GL2 .....117 D1
Sheldrake Dr BS34 ....29 A2
Shellards La BS35 .....51 E2
Shellards Rd BS30 .....10 F3

Sheppard Rd BS16 ....20 C6
Sheppard Way
Minchinhampton GL6 .....91 F7
Newent GL18 ....171 A4
Shepperdine Rd BS35 ...75 D2
Sheppey Cnr WR12 .....184 F5
Shepton Wlk BS3 ......8 C2
Sherborne CE Prim Sch
GL54 ....169 A1
Sherborne Cl GL10 .....97 F8
Sherborne Ho ■ GL10 ...97 F8
Sherborne La GL54 ....169 C3
Sherborne Pl GL52 ....193 C3
Sherborne St
Bourton-on-t-W GL54 ...168 F7
Cheltenham GL52 .....193 C4
Gloucester GL1 ....196 C4
Lechlade on T GL7 ...153 E2
Sherborne Terr ■ GL54 ..168 F7
Sherbourne Ave BS32 ...29 E7
Sherbourne Cl BS15 ...20 F2
Sherbourne St BS5 .....9 E7
Sherbourne's Brake
BS32 ....29 E6
Shergar Cl GL4 ....119 D4
Sheridan Rd BS7 ......19 A8
Sheridan Way BS30 ...11 A2
Sherrin Way BS13 ......1 A3
Sherrings The BS34 ...29 B8
Sherry Covert GL54 ...175 B7
Sherry The GL54 ......175 B7
Sherston Cl BS16 ......20 B5
Sherston Rd Bristol BS7 ...18 E8
Luckington SN14 .....47 F5
Sherwell Rd BS4 ......9 E3
Sherwood Cl BS31 ......4 E5
Sherwood Gn GL2 .....126 F6
Sherwood Rd Bristol BS15 ...20 A1
Keynsham BS31 ....4 E5
Tetbury GL8 ....140 B4
Shetland Rd BS10 .....28 D1
Shield Ret Ctr BS34 ....29 A3
Shield Road Prim Sch
BS7 ....29 A1
Shields Ave BS7 ....29 A1
Shields Dr BS32 ....29 D7
Shilton Cl BS15 ....10 F7
Shimsey Cl BS16 ......20 C6
Ship La BS1 ....195 B1
Shipham Cl BS14 ....3 B5
Shipley Mow BS16 ....16 A8
Shipley Rd BS9 ......18 A8
Shipman Ct BS16 .....20 E4
Shipton's Grave La GL6 ...91 C1
Shipway Ct GL52 .....137 F4
Shire Gdns BS11 ......16 D8
Shire Way SN14 ......25 A7
Shire Way BS37 ......32 D6
Shirehampton Inf Sch
BS11 ....16 D6
Shirehampton Rd BS9 ...17 C6
Shirehampton Sta BS11 ...16 D5
Shooters End GL5 ......99 C8
Shop La Badminton GL9 ...46 E2
Brettonton WR11 .....188 A7
Shophouse Rd GL15 ...
.........155 A2
Shorland Ho BS8 ....18 A1
Short Hedges Cl ■
GL54 ....168 A1
Short La BS41 ....7 A2
Short St Bristol BS2 ....9 A5
Cheltenham GL53 .....130 C5
Short Way BS35 ....51 B7
Shorthill Rd BS37 ......32 C4
Shortlands Rd BS11 ...27 A1
Shortwood Hill BS16 ...21 E4
Shortwood Rd Bristol BS13 ...2 E3
Nailsworth GL6 ....91 A3
Pucklechurch BS16 ...22 A5
Shortwood View BS15 ...10 F8
Shortwood Wlk BS13 ...2 E3
Shotts La GL18 ....170 C3
Showering Cl BS14 ......3 D5
Showering Rd BS14 ......3 D5
Shrivenham Rd SN6 ...145 D2
Shrubberies Sch The
GL10 ....97 E8
Shrubbery Cotts ■ BS6 ...18 B2
Shrubbery Ct ■ BS16 ...20 D5
Shrubbery Cl ■ BS16 ...20 D5
Shrubbery Rd
Bristol, BS6 ....18 C5
Shrublands GL53 ....130 F5
Shrubbery The GL7 ...153 E2
Shurdington Prim Sch
GL51 ....129 D1
Shurdington Rd
Brockworth GL3 .....121 A5
Cheltenham GL53 ....130 B5
Cheltenham GL51 ....129 E2
Shute St GL10 ....98 A3
Shutehay Dr GL11 .....87 F1
Shuter Rd BS13 ....1 E5
Shutter La GL52 ......137 F8
Sibland BS35 ....51 D8
Sibland Cl ■ BS35 ....51 D8
Sibland Rd BS35 ......51 D8
Sibland Way BS35 ....51 D8
Sibree Cl GL6 ....148 B6
Sidcot BS14 ....10 A2
Siddington CE Sch GL7 ...190 D1
Siddington Hall GL7 ...190 D2
Sideland Cl BS14 ......3 E6
Sidelands Rd BS16 ....20 C6
Sidings The GL12 ......67 B5
Sidmouth Ct GL2 .....117 B5
Sidmouth Gdns BS3 ...8 D2
Sidmouth Rd BS3 ......8 E2

Sidney St
Cheltenham GL52 .....193 C3
Gloucester GL1 ....127 A1
Signal Rd BS16 ....20 F4
Silbury Rd BS3 ....7 E2
Silbury Rise BS31 ......5 A2
Silcock Cl GL3 ....127 A7
Silk Mill Ct ■ GL54 ....174 A7
Silk Mill La GL54 ....174 A7
Silklands Gr BS9 ......17 C6
Silley's Ct NP16 ....72 F5
Silver Birch Cl GL2 ...117 E1
Silver Cl Gloucester GL4 ...118 C3
Minety SN16 ....142 D1
Silver St Arlingham GL2 ...137 C6
Bristol BS1 ....195 A3
Cirencester GL7 .....190 C5
Coaley GL11 ....89 A7
Dursley GL11 ....88 B1
Littledean GL14 .....156 E8
Minety SN16 ....142 D1
South Cerney GL7 ...142 F8
■ Tetbury GL8 ....140 C4
Thornbury BS35 ......64 B1
Silverbirch Cl BS34 ...29 D7
Silverdale Par GL3 ...119 F6
Silverhill Brake BS35 ...50 E1
Silverhill Rd BS10 .....27 E4
Silverhill Sch BS37 ....50 E1
Silverhill Sch (Jun) BS36 ...30 E7
Silverthorne La BS2 ...195 C2
Silverthorne La GL52 ...9 A6
Silverthorne Wharf BS2 ...9 B6
Silverton Ct BS34 ......8 F1
Silvertree Gdns GL5 ...99 E3
Silverwood Way GL51 ...129 E5
Simmonds Cl GL6 ....148 A3
Simmonds Rd GL3 ....119 F6
Simmonds View BS34 ...29 F5
Simon Rd GL2 ....127 C5
Simplex Ind Est The
GL11 ....71 D4
Sims La GL2 ....117 F4
Sinclair Ho
Bristol, Clifton Wood BS8 ...194 A2
Bristol, Filton BS34 ...29 D4
Sinclair Rd GL51 .....129 D1
Sinderberry Dr GL20 ...182 C5
Sinope St GL1 ....196 C2
Sion Hill BS8 ....7 F7
Sion Pl BS8 ....7 F7
Sion Rd ■ BS3 ....8 C3
Sir Bernard Lovell Sch
BS30 ....11 C4
Sir Bernard Lovell Sch
(annexe) BS30 ....11 D5
Sir Beril Grenville's Mon*
.........13 A1
Sir John's La Bristol BS5 ...19 B4
Thomas Rich's Sch
GL2 ....127 D3
Sir William Romney's Sch
GL8 ....140 C5
Siskin Cl GL54 ....169 D7
Sissinghurst Gr GL51 ...130 A5
Sisson End GL2 ......127 D2
Sisson Rd GL2 ....127 C2
Siston Cl BS15 ....21 A2
Siston Cl BS15 ....21 A2
Siston Comm Bristol BS15 ...21 A2
Bristol BS30 ....21 B1
Siston Ctr The BS15 ...21 A2
Siston La BS30 ......21 F2
Siston Pk BS15 ......21 A2
Sivell Cl GL2 ....127 A6
Six Acres GL14 ....119 F3
Sixth Ave
Bristol, Filton BS7 ....29 B1
Bristol, Hengrove BS14 ...3 A7
Skillicorne Mews GL50 ...130 B8
Skinner St GL1 ....196 B4
Skinner's Cl SN6 ....145 D4
Skippon Ct BS15 ......10 E5
Skye Cl SN6 ....145 C4
Skylark Way GL4 .....119 B6
Slad La GL5,GL6 ......99 F8
Slad Rd GL5 ....99 D8
Slade Brook GL55 ....99 E8
Slade Rd GL15 ......156 B2
Slade The GL11 ......80 B8
Slaney St GL1 ....118 F7
Sleep La BS14 ....3 D3
Slimbridge Ct BS37 ...32 F7
Slimbridge La GL13 ...94 D2
Slimbridge Prim Sch
GL2 ....95 E2
Slimbridge Rd GL4 ...118 D3
Sloan St BS5 ....9 D8
Slough La SN14 ......13 F5
Slymbridge Ave BS10 ...28 A3
Small La BS16 ....19 E5
Small St Bristol BS1 ...195 A3
Bristol, St Philip's Marsh
.........9 A5
Smallbrook Rd WR12 ...188 A1
Smarts Gn BS37 ......33 C8
Smeaton Rd BS1 ....7 F5
Smith Barry Cir GL54 ...169 E6
Smith Barry Cres GL54 ...169 D6
Smith Barry Rd GL54 ...169 D6
Smith's Field GL7 ....190 A3
Smith's La GL20 ......192 C4
Smithcourt Dr BS34 ...29 D6
Smithmead BS13 ......2 B5

Smiths Ct GL20 ....192 C4
Smiths Hill GL16 .....155 C3
Smithville Cl GL15 ...146 F7
Smithville Pl GL15 ...146 F7
Smithwood Gr GL53 ...131 A4
Smithy Cl GL16 ......163 A2
Smithy La GL54 ......184 A1
Smithy The
Blakeney GL15 ....156 C2
Cirencester GL7 .....190 E3
Smithyman Ct GL14 ...157 A6
Smoke La BS11 ....26 D6
Smooth Stones NP16 ...60 A7
Smyth Rd BS3 ....8 A3
Smyth Terr ■ BS3 ......8 C4
Smythe Croft BS14 ....3 A3
Smythe Mdw GL6 ....148 B5
Smythe Rd GL51 .....133 B6
Smyths Ct BS31 ....26 B1
Snake Dr GL7 ....152 D7
Snead Pk GL4 ....119 F5
Sneedhams Rd GL4 ...119 B2
Snipe Rd GL54 ......169 D6
Snowberry Wlk BS5 ...19 E1
Snowdon Cl BS16 .....19 F4
Snowdon Gdns GL3 ...128 A7
Snowdon Rd BS16 ....19 F4
Snowdonia Rd GL20 ...192 E2
Snowdrop Cl ■ GL4 ...119 E5
Snowshill Cl GL4 ....119 D7
Snowshill Dr ■ GL52 ...137 F3
Snowshill Manor*
.........185 E7
Snowshill Rd
Broadway WR12 .....185 E7
Cheltenham GL51 ...129 E7
Snowswick La SN6 ...145 F8
Soapers La BS35 ......51 B8
Soaphouse Ind Est BS5 ...9 F8
Sodbury Rd GL12 .....54 A4
Soldiers of Gloucester Mus*
GL1 ....196 A2
Solent Way BS35 ....51 D7
Solon Ct BS13 ....1 F5
Solway Rd GL51 .....132 D4
Somerby Rd GL52 ....29 D7
Somerdale Ave BS4 ...9 A1
Somerdale Ave N BS30,BS31 ...4 F8
Somerford Ct BS10 ...27 F1
Somerford Rd GL7 ...109 C2
Somergate Rd GL51 ...132 D4
Somermead BS3 ......8 C1
Somerset Ave
Cheltenham GL51 ....133 A2
Dursley GL11 ....80 C7
Yate BS37 ....43 F3
Somerset Cl GL12 .....67 F4
Somerset Cres BS34 ...29 F5
Somerset Ho
■ Bristol BS2 ......195 C3
■ Cheltenham GL50 ...193 B4
Somerset Pl
Gloucester GL1 ....196 A1
Tewkesbury GL20 ...192 C3
Somerset Rd Bristol BS4 ...9 B3
Clinderford GL14 ....191 C4
Somerset Sq BS1 ....195 B1
Somerset St Bristol BS1 ...195 B1
Bristol, Kingsdown BS2 ...195 A4
Somerset Terr BS3 ...8 D3
Somerville Rd BS16 ...60 F4
Somerton Cl BS15 ....10 E7
Somerton Rd BS7 ....18 E6
Somerville Ct GL2 ....190 B2
Somerville Cl GL7 ...190 B2
Somme Rd GL52 .....137 C4
Somerville Rd BS7 ...18 E3
Somerville Rd S ■ BS6 ...18 F2
Sopwith Rd GL54 ....169 D7
Sopworth Rd SN14 ...47 E5
Soren Larsen Way GL4 ...118 C6
Sorrel Cl Gloucester GL4 ...119 A4
Thornbury BS35 ......64 D2
Soudley Prim Sch GL14 ...156 D5
Soundwell Coll
Bristol, Filton BS34 ...29 D3
Bristol, Upper Soundwell
BS16 ....20 C2
Soundwell Tech Coll
(Downend division)
BS16 ....21 A8
Soundwell Tech Coll
(Kingswood annexe)
BS15 ....10 E8
South Africa Ho ■
GL51 ....132 F4
South Ave
Ashchurch GL20 ....182 D4
Yate BS37 ....43 D8
So Bristol Trad Pk BS3 ...7 F3
South Cl GL2 ....127 B4
South Croft BS9 ......18 C7
South Ct BS32 ....40 D3
South Dene BS9 .....17 E6
South Farm Cotts GL7 ...153 B5
South Glos Central La GL54 ...169 D6
South Gloucestershire
Central Teaching Unit
BS16 ....21 A5
South Gr Bristol BS6 ...18 C5
Pill BS20 ....16 C4
South Green St ■ BS8 ...7 F6
South Hayes BS5 .....19 B4

South Liberty La BS3 ....8 A1
South Mdw La SN5 ....143 F2
South Meadow La SN5 ..144 A2
South Par
🔟 Ledbury HR8 ....178 F8
Yate BS37 ....43 E1
South Rd
Almondsbury BS32 ......40 E6
Bristol, Bedminster BS3 ..8 C3
Bristol, Kingswood BS15 ..10 D8
Bristol, Redland BS6 ....18 C2
Lydney GL15 ....92 A4
🔳 Coleford GL16 ....155 A6
Coleford, Broadwell GL16 .155 B5
Lydney GL15 ....92 A4
South St Bristol BS3 ......8 B3
Uley GL11 ....89 C1
South Street Prim Sch
BS3 ....8 B3
South Terr 🔟 BS6 ......178 E7
South View
Blockley GL56 ....186 C6
Bristol BS16 ....20 E5
Frampton Cotterell BS36 ..31 B7
Ripple GL20 ....183 D8
Stroud GL5 ....98 C7
South View Bsns Pk
BS16 ....20 F5
South View Cotts GL5 ....98 E8
South View Cres BS30 ....31 D6
South View Rise BS36 ....31 D6
South View Way GL52 ...134 C4
South Way GL7 ....190 C4
South Wlk
Mitcheldean GL17 ......164 D5
Yate BS37 ....43 E1
Southall Terr GL18 ......170 E2
Southam La GL52 ....134 B8
Southbank GL5 ....99 A2
Southbow Ho 🔳 BS3 .....8 A3
Southbrook Rd GL4 ....127 C1
Southcourt Cl GL53 ....130 D5
Southcourt Dr GL53 ....130 D5
Southdown Rd BS9 ......17 F8
Southern Ho GL12 ....54 A5
Southend La GL18 ......171 A4
Southend The HR8 .....178 F8
Southern Ave GL4 ......118 E4
Southern Rd GL53 ......130 E4
Southernhay
Bristol, Clifton Wood BS8 ..194 B2
Bristol, Staple Hill BS16 ...20 D4
Southernhay Ave BS8 ...194 B2
Southernhay Cres BS8 ..194 B2
Southey Ave BS15 ......20 D1
Southey Ct BS15 ....20 D1
Southey St BS2 ....18 F2
Southfield
Minchinhampton GL6 .....91 F6
Tetbury GL8 ....140 B3
Southfield App GL53 ...130 E4
Southfield Cl BS15 ......20 E1
Southfield Cl GL53 .....130 E4
Southfield Ct BS9 ....18 A7
Southfield Manor Pk
GL53 ....130 F3
Southfield Prim Sch
SN6 ....145 D3
Southfield Rd
Bristol, Cotham BS6 .....18 D1
Bristol, Westbury on Trym
BS9 ....18 A7
🔳 Coleford GL16 ....155 A6
Gloucester GL1 ....118 F5
Woodchester GL5 ....99 A2
Southfield Rise GL53 ...130 E4
Southgate Cres GL5 .....99 A5
Southgate Dr GL53 .....130 F7
Southgate Gdns GL5 ....99 A5
Southgate Mews GL7 ...190 D3
Southgate St GL1 ....196 A2
Southlands BS4 ....9 B8
Southleigh Rd BS8 .....194 B4
Southmead GL7 ....190 E2
Southmead Hospl BS10 ..18 E8
Southmead La BS10,BS34 .28 E1
Southmead Way BS10 ...18 D8
Southover Cl BS9 ....18 A8
Southrop CE Prim Sch
GL7 ....153 D6
Southsea Rd BS34 ....29 A8
Southside GL6 ....59 E7
Southside Cl BS9 ....17 B8
Southville Pi BS3 ....8 C4
Southville Prim Sch BS3 ..8 C4
Southville Rd BS3 ....8 C4
Southway Dr BS15 ....11 D5
Southwell St BS2 ....194 C4
Southwood Ave BS9 .....17 C8
Southwood Cl GL14 ....191 D5
Southwood Dr BS9 ......17 B8
Southwood Dr E BS9 ....17 C8
Southwood La GL50 ....193 A2
Sovereign Chase GL19 ..172 B8
Spa Cl SN6 ....145 D4
Spa Ct GL50 ....193 A3
Spa Gdns GL20 ....192 F4
Spa Rd GL1 ....196 B1
Spalding Cl BS7 ....19 A3
Spaniorum View BS35 ...38 F2
Spar Rd Avonmouth BS11 ..26 D4
Yate BS37 ....43 D2
Spark Hill GL11 ....87 F6
Sparrow Cl 🔳 GL6 .....148 C6
Sparrow Hill GL16 ......155 A5

Sparrows La HR9,GL18 ..170 B4
Spartan Cl GL4 ....119 E6
Spartley Dr BS13 ....1 F6
Spartley Wlk BS13 ....1 F6
Speculation Rd GL14 ...191 B7
Speech House Rd
Coleford GL16 ....155 D6
Ruspidge GL14,GL16 ...156 A7
Speedwell 🔳 GL16 ....155 B6
Speedwell Ave 🔳 BS5 ...9 D7
Speedwell Cl
Gloucester GL4 ....119 E5
Thornbury BS35 ....64 D2
Speedwell Rd BS5,BS15 ..20 A1
Speedwell Sch BS15 ....20 A1
Spencer Cl GL1 ....119 F7
Spencer Ct GL50 ....193 A4
Spencer Ho 🔳 BS1 ....195 B1
Spencer's Ct BS35 ......51 B5
Spenser Ave GL51 .....132 E1
Spenser Rd GL51 ......132 E1
Sperringate GL7 ....190 D3
Spey Cl Quedgeley GL2 .117 F2
Spider La GL5 ....99 E6
Spillman's Pitch GL5 ....99 A6
Spillman's Rd GL5 ......99 A6
Spindles The GL53 .....130 A4
Spine Rd W GL7 ....142 D5
Spine Road E GL7 ......143 B7
Spinnaker Ho GL2 .....118 C8
Spinnaker Rd GL2 .....118 C8
Spinners Ho 🔳 GL5 ....99 C7
Spinney Croft BS13 .....1 F5
Spinney Ct GL5 ....99 F1
Spinney Rd GL4 ....119 E7
Spinney The Bristol BS32 .29 E7
Cheltenham GL52 ......133 E4
Frampton Cotterell BS36 ..31 B7
Lechlade on T GL7 ....153 E2
Stroud GL5 ....105 C7
Spire Way GL4 ....119 D8
Spires View 🔳 BS16 ....19 E5
Spital La SN6 ....143 F4
Spitalgate La GL2 ......190 C5
Spittle Leys 🔳 GL54 ..174 F2
Spout Hill GL15 ....147 C3
Spout La GL17 ....164 A4
Spouthouse La GL11 ....88 A5
Spratsgate La
Siddington GL7 ....150 D2
Somerford Keynes GL7 ..142 D6
Spread Eagle Rd GL1 ...196 B3
Spring Cotts
Stonehouse GL10 ....98 A6
Stroud GL5 ....104 A2
Spring Dale GL2 ....165 F5
Spring Field Terr GL5 ...99 A6
Spring Gdns Bristol BS4 ..9 A1
Lechlade on T GL7 ....153 E2
Quenington GL7 ....152 D7
Tewkesbury GL20 ......192 D4
Spring Hill
Bristol, Kingsdown BS2 .195 A4
Bristol, Upper Soundwell
BS15 ....20 B2
Eastington GL10 ....97 A8
Newland GL16 ....91 B4
Spring Ho 🔳 BS35 ......51 C8
Spring La
Cleeve Hill GL52 ....138 E2
Dundry BS41 ....2 A1
Prestbury GL52 ....134 B6
Stroud GL5 ....99 D6
Thrupp GL5 ....99 E3
Spring Meadow Rd GL15 .92 A4
Spring Pl GL17 ....163 E4
Spring St 🔳 BS3 ....8 E4
Spring Street Pl BS3 .....8 E4
Springbank Cl GL51 ...132 D3
Springbank Dr GL51 ...132 C3
Springbank Gr GL51 ...132 C3
Springbank Rd GL51 ...132 C3
Springbank Way GL51 .132 D4
Springdale HR9 ....170 B4
Springdale Ct GL2 .....109 D8
Springfield
Bristol BS6 ....186 C6
Bourton-on-t-W GL54 ...168 F7
Dursley GL11 ....87 E4
Hardwicke GL2 ....109 E7
Horsley GL6 ....192 F5
🔳 Thornbury BS35 ......51 D8
Springfield Ave
Bristol, Horfield BS7 ....18 F5
Bristol, Mangotsfield BS16 .21 A7
Bristol, Shirehampton BS11 .16 D6
Springfield Bsns Ctr
GL10 ....97 C8
Springfield Cl
Bristol BS16 ....21 A7
Dursley GL11 ....129 C7
🔳 Coleford GL16 ....155 B5
Springfield Cotts BS30 ...6 A8
Springfield Dr GL14 ...191 C6
Springfield Gr BS8 .....18 C5
Springfield Ho
Bristol BS6 ....194 C4
Bristol GL15 ....132 E4
Springfield La WR12 ...185 B8
Springfield Lawn GL11 .116 D6
Springfield Pl GL4 .....121 F1
Springfield Rd
Bristol, Cotham BS6 ....18 D1
Bristol, Mangotsfield BS16 .21 A7
Cirencester GL7 ....190 B2

Springfield Rd continued
Lydney GL15 ....92 A4
Pill BS20 ....16 C4
Quenington GL7 ....152 D7
Stroud GL5 ....99 C8
Stroud, Westrip GL5 .....98 D8
Springfields Bristol BS34 .29 A2
Springfields 🔳 BS1 ....140 C4
Tetbury GL8 ....140 C4
Springfields Ct GL11 ...87 E4
Springhill GL11 ....88 C3
Springhill (Old Court)
GL11 ....88 B3
Springhill Cl GL6 ......91 B4
Springhill Cotts WR12 ..185 B4
Springhill Cres GL6 ....91 B4
Springhill Ct GL52 ....172 F1
Springleaze
Bristol, Knowle BS4 ......9 A1
Bristol, Mangotsfield BS16 .21 A7
Springs The GL15 ....92 A4
Springside GL11 ....88 F3
Springville GL BS30 .....11 A3
Springwater Cl GL20 ..182 C5
Springwater Park Trad Est
BS5 ....9 E7
Springwell Gdns GL3 ..128 B6
Springwood Dr BS10 ....27 D3
Spruce Ave GL16 ......155 C6
Spruce Ride
Coleford GL16 ....155 F6
Ruspidge GL14,GL16 ...156 A5
Spruce Way BS34 ......28 F7
Sq The GL56 ....186 C5
Square The Bibury GL7 ..160 A1
Bristol BS4 ....9 A1
Goodrich HR9 ....163 A6
Guiting Power GL54 ...175 B3
Ruardean GL17 ....163 E4
St Briavels GL15 ....146 E7
🔳 Stonehouse GL10 .....97 F8
Stroud GL5 ....99 C8
Toddington GL54 ......184 B3
Squires Cl GL4 ....148 B6
Squires Ct
Bretforton WR11 ......188 A6
Bristol BS30 ....10 F4
Squires Leaze BS35 ....64 D2
Squirrel Cl GL2 ....109 E7
Stable Cotts GL56 .....177 E5
Stable Yd GL15 ....99 C8
Stables The
Prestbury GL52 ....134 C4
Stow-on-t-W GL54 ....176 F5
Stackpool Rd BS3 ....8 C4
Stadium Rd BS6 ....18 C5
Stafford Cl 🔳 GL16 ....155 B6
Stafford Cres BS35 .....64 B1
Stafford Rd BS20 ....19 A2
Stafford St BS3 ....8 D4
Stag Hill GL15 ....156 A2
Stainer Cl BS4 ....2 D7
Staites Orch GL4 ......119 E3
Stamage's La GL6 .....103 F7
Stambourne La GL13 ...85 E8
Stamp's Mdw GL2 .....126 F5
Stanborough La GL54 ..167 F8
Stancombe La GL11 ....20 F6
Stanbridge Cty Prim Sch
BS16 ....20 F6
Stanbridge Rd BS16 ...20 F6
Stanbury Ave BS16 .....20 F6
Stanbury Mews GL3 ...120 B6
Stancombe La GL54 ...174 B7
Stancombe View 2️⃣
GL54 ....174 A7
Standfast Rd BS10 ......27 F3
Standish Ave BS34 .....40 C1
Standish Cl BS10 ....27 F1
Standish Ct GL10 ......101 E5
Standle La GL11 ....87 A2
Standon Way BS10 .....28 C2
Stane Way BS11 ....16 C7
Stanfield Cl BS7 ....19 C6
Stanford Cl BS36 ......30 F8
Stanford Pl BS4 ....2 D7
Stanford Rd Lydney GL15 .92 A3
Warmley GL20 ....182 C4
Stanhope Rd BS30 .....10 F2
Stanhope St BS2 ....9 A5
Stanier La GL2 ....109 C6
Stankleigh Terr GL17 ..126 A7
Stanley Ave
Bristol, Bishopston BS7 ..18 F6
Bristol, Filton BS34 ....29 B2
Stanley Chase BS5 .....19 F4
Stanley Cotts
Gloucester GL54 ......196 C1
Gretton GL54 ....183 E1
Stanley Cres BS34 .....29 B2
Stanley Gdns BS30 ....11 B4
Stanley Mead BS32 ....40 E2
Stanley Park Rd BS16 ..20 E3
Stanley Pk BS5 ....19 C1
Stanley Rd
Bristol, Cotham BS6 ....18 C1
Bristol, Warmley BS15 ..11 B8
Cheltenham GL52 ......134 B1
Gloucester GL1 ....118 E6
Stanley St 🔳 BS3 ....8 C3

Stanley St N 🔳 BS3 .....8 C3
Stanley St S BS3 ....8 C2
Stanley Terr Bristol BS3 ..8 C2
Gloucester GL1 ....118 E7
Stanley The GL4 ....119 F2
Stanley Way GL4 ....98 F5
Stanley Wlk GL4 ....119 F1
Stanmoor GL4 ....119 E3
Stansby Cres GL3 .....128 A6
Stanshaw Cl BS16 ......20 A7
Stanshaw Rd BS16 .....20 A7
Stanshawe Cres BS37 ..43 E1
Stanshawes Court Dr
BS37 ....32 E8
Stanshawes Dr BS37 ...43 D1
Stanshaws Cl BS32 .....40 C2
Stansted Ho GL1 ....196 A3
Stanthill Dr GL10 ....80 C8
Stanton Cl BS15 ....20 F1
Stanton Dr GL51 ......133 A7
Stanton Rd Bristol BS10 .28 A2
Stroud GL5 ....98 E8
Tewkesbury GL20 ......192 D5
Stanton Way GL51 .....129 E8
Stanway La GL14 ......157 E8
Stanway Rd BS30 ......11 C1
Stanway
Cheltenham GL51 .....129 D8
Gloucester GL4 ....119 C7
Stanton WR12 ....184 C1
Stanway Wood Dr GL52 .137 E3
Stanwick Cres GL51 ...133 B5
Stanwick Dr GL51 .....133 B5
Stanwick Gdns GL51 ..133 B5
Staple Gr BS31 ....4 D5
Staple Grove Cres BS5 ..10 B7
Staple Hill Cty Prim Sch
BS16 ....20 D4
Staplehill Rd BS16 .....20 D4
Stapleton Cl Bristol BS16 .19 D8
Highworth SN6 ....145 C3
Stapleton Rd
Bristol, Baptist Mills BS5 ..19 C3
Bristol, Eastville BS5 ...19 C3
Stapleton Road Junc
BS5 ....19 F3
Star Barn Rd BS36 .....30 E7
Star Ct 🔳 GL52 ....133 F2
Star Hill GL5 ....91 A5
Star La Avening GL8 ...148 B8
Bristol BS16 ....19 F3
Pill BS20 ....16 C4
Starling Cl 🔳 GL10 ....97 F8
Stars Pitch GL17 ......164 D5
Staton App
Gloucester GL1 ....196 C3
Minety SN16 ....142 E1
Station Avenue S 🔳
BS16 ....20 A4
Station Cl Bristol BS15 ..11 C8
Chipping Sodbury BS37 ..33 D8
Churchdown GL3 ....108 B7
Station Cotts GL20 ....177 C7
Station Dr BS30 ....9 E8
Station La GL20 ....182 C7
Station La Bristol BS7 ..19 A4
Longhope GL17 ....164 F5
Tewkesbury GL20 ......192 D5
Station Rd
Acton Turville GL9 .....35 H8
Andoversford GL54 ...166 D6
Ashton under Hill WR11 .183 E8
Beckford GL20 ....183 B6
Berkeley GL13 ....85 E5
Bishop's Cleeve GL52 ..138 B4
Blockley GL56 ....186 D6
Bourton-on-t-W GL54 ..168 F8
Bretforton WR11 ......188 A7
Bristol, Ashley Down BS7 ..18 F4
Bristol, Brislington BS4 ..9 D2
Bristol, Filton BS34 ....29 A3
Bristol, Fishponds BS16 ..20 A4
Bristol, Henbury BS10 ..27 F4
Bristol, Montpelier BS6 ..18 C2
Bristol, Newleaze BS34 ..29 B2
Bristol, Patchway BS34 ..29 B2
Bristol, Shirehampton BS11 .16 D5
Bristol, Staple Hill BS15 .20 E1
Bristol, Warmley BS30 ..11 C7
Broadway WR12 ....185 B8
Charfield GL12 ....67 B5
Chepstow NP16 ....69 B8
Chipping Campden GL55 .189 A2
Churchdown GL3 ......128 C5
Coalpit Heath BS36 ....31 C5
Dursley GL11 ....88 A5
Gloucester GL1 ....196 C2
Highworth SN6 ....145 C3
Honeybourne WR11 ...188 C7
Iron Acton BS37 ....42 D3
Kemble GL7 ....141 F8
Keynsham BS31 ....4 A6
Kingham OX7 ....177 F1
Kingham OX7 ....178 A1
Lechlade on T GL7 ....153 E3
Lydney GL15 ....84 A8
Milkwall GL16 ....155 B4
Moreton-in-M GL56 ...187 A3
Nailsworth GL6 ....91 C4
Newnham GL14 ....156 F7
Pill BS20 ....16 C4
Pilning BS35 ....38 F4
Ripple GL20 ....181 D8
Severn Beach BS35 ....38 A6

Station Rd continued
South Cerney GL7 1
Stroud GL5 1
Tewkesbury GL20 1
Wickwar GL12 1
Winterbourne BS36 1
Woodchester GL5 1
Woolaston GL15 1
Yate BS37 1
Station Road Bsns Ctr
BS15 1
Station Road Workshops
BS15 1
Station St
Cheltenham GL50 1
Cinderford GL14 1
Tewkesbury GL20 1
Station Terr
Cinderford GL14 1
Dymock GL18 1
Station Yard Ind Est
NP16 1
Staunton & Corse CE Prim
Sch GL19 1
Staunton Cl GL4 1
Staunton Fields BS14 1
Staunton Ho GL16 1
Staunton La BS14 1
Staunton Rd
Coleford GL16 1
Monmouth GL16,NP25 ...1
Staunton Way BS14 1
Staveley Cres BS10 1
Staverton Cl BS32 1
Staverton Connection
GL51 1
Staverton Tech Pk GL51 .1
Staverton Way BS15 1
Stavordale Gr BS14 1
Staynes Cres BS15 1
Steadings Bsns Ctr The
GL2 1
Steam Mills GL14 1
Steam Mills Prim Sch
GL14 1
Steam Mills Rd GL14 1
Stean Bridge Rd BS32 ...1
Steanbridge Cl GL6 1
Steel Ave GL15 1
Steel Ct BS30 1
Steel Mills BS31 1
Steep St NP16 1
Steeple Cl GL4 1
Steeple View GL15 1
Steevens Ho (almshouses)
BS2 1
Stella Gr BS3 1
Stella Way GL2 1
Stenders Cl GL17 1
Stenders Rd GL17 1
Stenders The GL17 1
Step's La GL8 1
Stepaside NP16 1
Stepbridge Rd GL16 1
Stephen St BS5 1
Stephens Pl GL16 1
Stephens Way WR11 ...1
Stepney Rd BS5 1
Stepney Wlk BS5 1
Stepping Stone La GL6 ..1
Stepping Stones The BS4 .1
Steps Cl GL1 1
Stepstairs La GL7 1
Sterling Cl GL54 1
Sterling Ct GL51 1
Sterncourt Rd BS16 1
Sterrys Cnr HR9 1
Sterrys Rd HR9 1
Stevans Cl GL2 1
Stevens Way GL6 1
Stevens Wlk BS32 1
Steward Rd GL20 1
Stewarts Mill La GL4 ...1
Stibbs Ct BS30 1
Stibbs Hill BS5 1
Sticky La GL2 1
Stidcot La GL12 1
Stidcote La GL12 1
Stile Acres BS11 1
Stillhouse La BS3 1
Stillingfleet Rd BS13 ...1
Stillman Cl BS13 1
Stinchcombe BS37 1
Stirling Cl BS37 1
Stirling Way
Gloucester GL4 1
Keynsham BS31 1
Stirling Way
Gloucester GL4 1
Stirrup Cl GL2 1
Stirrup The GL5 1
Stock Hill BS35 1
Stock La GL13 1
Stockdale Cl GL2 1
Stocken Cl GL3 1
Stockham Cl SN6 1
Stockholm Pl HR9 1
Stockley Way GL4,GL6 ..1
Stocks The GL6 1
Stockton Cl
Bristol, Oldland BS30 ...1
Bristol, Whitchurch BS14 .1
Charlton Kings GL53 1
Stockwell Ave BS16 1
Stockwell Cl BS16 1
Stockwell Dr BS16 1

Tennyson Rd continued
Cheltenham GL51 ...... 132 C1
Dursley GL11 ...... 80 C7
Tensing Rd GL3 ...... 130 E4
Tenth Ave BS7 ...... 29 B1
Tereslake Gn BS10 ...... 28 D4
Terhill GL52 ...... 133 F2
Tern Cl GL4 ...... 119 C6
Terrace The
Nailsworth GL6 ...... 91 A2
Wootton-u-E GL12 ...... 68 D8
Terrell Gdns 8 BS5 ...... 9 D7
Terrell St BS2 ...... 195 A4
Terris Ct BS34 ...... 29 E4
Terry Ho BS1 ...... 194 C3
Terry Ruck Cl GL51 ...... 132 D2
Tetbury Cl BS34 ...... 29 C7
Tetbury Hill GL8 ...... 140 B8
Tetbury Hospl GL8 ...... 140 C3
Tetbury La
Crudwell SN16 ...... 141 B3
Leighterton GL8 ...... 70 C3
Nailsworth GL6 ...... 91 C2
Tetbury Police Mus*
GL8 ...... 140 B4
Tetbury Rd Bristol BS5 ...... 10 B8
Cirencester GL7 ...... 150 B3
Cirencester GL7 ...... 190 B4
Gloucester GL4 ...... 118 C1
Sherston SN16 ...... 58 D1
Tetbury St GL6 ...... 148 A3
Teviot Rd BS31 ...... 5 A4
Tewkesbury CE Prim Sch
GL20 ...... 192 D4
Tewkesbury Hospl
GL20 ...... 192 D4
Tewkesbury Ind Est
GL20 ...... 192 F5
Tewkesbury Mus*
GL20 ...... 192 C4
Tewkesbury Rd
Bristol BS2 ...... 194 A2
Cheltenham GL51 ...... 133 A4
Gloucester GL2 ...... 126 F5
Newent GL18 ...... 171 B5
Northway GL20 ...... 182 B6
Stow-on-t-W GL54 ...... 176 C5
Uckington GL51 ...... 132 E6
Tewkesbury Sch GL20 ...... 182 B4
Tewther Rd BS13 ...... 2 D3
Texas Cl GL7 ...... 154 F2
Teyfant Com Sch BS13 ...... 2 E4
Teyfant Rd BS13 ...... 2 E4
Teyfant Wlk BS13 ...... 2 E4
Thackeray Wlk BS7 ...... 19 A8
Thames Cl GL12 ...... 67 A4
Thames Ho BS1 ...... 194 C2
Thames La SN6 ...... 143 F4
Thames Rd GL52 ...... 134 A2
Thames St GL7 ...... 153 E2
Thames View 5 SN6 ...... 142 F4
Thanet Rd BS3 ...... 8 B2
Thatcham Cl BS20 ...... 192 E1
Thatchers Cl BS5 ...... 10 B7
Thatchers End GL52 ...... 138 B3
Theatre Royal BS1 ...... 195 A2
Theescombe Hill GL5 ...... 91 B6
Theocs Cl GL20 ...... 192 C2
There-and-Back-Again La
BS1 ...... 194 C3
Theresa Ave BS7 ...... 18 E4
Theresa St GL1 ...... 118 D7
Thessaly Rd GL7 ...... 190 B8
Theyer Cl GL3 ...... 120 E5
Theynes Croft BS41 ...... 7 B1
Thicket Ave BS16 ...... 20 C3
Thicket Rd BS16 ...... 20 C4
Thicket Wlk BS35 ...... 64 C1
Thiery Rd BS4 ...... 9 E2
Thingwall Rd BS16 ...... 19 E3
Third Ave
Bristol, Filton BS7 ...... 29 A1
Bristol, Hengrove BS14 ...... 3 B7
Dursley GL11 ...... 80 C8
Third Way GL1 ...... 26 C2
Thirlestaine House Cotts
GL53 ...... 193 B1
Thirlestaine Rd GL53 ...... 193 C1
Thirlmere Cl BS30 ...... 11 C6
Thirlmere Rd Bristol BS34 ...... 29 A8
Cheltenham GL51 ...... 129 E7
Thistle Downs GL20 ...... 182 C5
Thistle St 1 BS3 ...... 8 A4
Thistledown Cl GL51 ...... 132 D4
Thomas Ave BS16 ...... 21 B8
Thomas Keble Comp Sch
GL6 ...... 148 C7
Thomas La BS1 ...... 195 B2
Thomas Paul Cl GL53 ...... 128 A8
Thomas Pring Wlk
BS5 ...... 20 A1
Thomas St
Bristol, Kingsdown BS2 ...... 195 B4
2 Bristol, Russell Town BS5 ...... 9 B7
Bristol, St Pauls BS2 ...... 18 F1
Chepstow NP16 ...... 60 E8
Cirencester GL7 ...... 190 C5
Gloucester GL1 ...... 196 C1
Thomas St N 12 BS2 ...... 18 D1
Thomas Stock Gdns
GL4 ...... 119 F4
Thomond Cl GL11 ...... 133 C4
Thompson Dr GL53 ...... 130 E6
Thompson Rd Bristol BS14 ...... 3 C6
South Cerney GL7 ...... 150 F2

Thompson Rd continued
Stroud GL5 ...... 99 D8
Thompson Way GL3 ...... 127 E6
Thompson Rd 7 BS5 ...... 9 B8
Thoresby GL52 ...... 133 E5
Thoresby Ave GL4 ...... 110 C8
Thorn Cl BS37 ...... 43 D1
Thorn Tree Dr NP16 ...... 60 F4
Thornbury Cl GL51 ...... 133 B2
Thornbury Hospl BS35 ...... 64 C2
Thornbury Ind Pk BS35 ...... 51 B7
Thornbury Mus* BS35 ...... 51 B8
Thornbury Rd BS35 ...... 51 A5
Thorncliffe 8 GL51 ...... 130 B8
Thorncliffe Dr GL51 ...... 130 B8
Thorndale BS8 ...... 194 A4
Thorndale Mews BS8 ...... 194 A4
Thornhaugh Mews 5
GL5 ...... 129 C5
Thornhaven Rd GL36 ...... 31 A8
Thornhill Cl GL11 ...... 118 D5
Thornhills The BS16 ...... 20 B6
Thornleigh Rd BS7 ...... 18 E5
Thornmead Gr BS10 ...... 28 D4
Thorns Farm BS37 ...... 43 E1
Thornwell Jun Sch NP16 ...... 60 F5
Thornwell Rd NP16 ...... 60 F5
Thornycroft Cl BS7 ...... 19 B7
Thorpe Lodge 8 BS6 ...... 18 D1
Threadneedle St 10 GL5 ...... 99 C7
Three Ashes La GL18 ...... 171 A6
Three Cocks La GL1 ...... 196 A3
Three Queens' La BS1 ...... 195 B2
Three Sisters La GL52 ...... 134 D3
Three Wells Rd BS13 ...... 1 F4
Thrissell St BS5 ...... 9 A8
Throgmorton Rd BS4 ...... 2 F8
Thrupp La GL5 ...... 99 E3
Thrupp Prim Sch The
GL5 ...... 99 E3
Thrush Cl GL4 ...... 119 D6
Thurlestone BS14 ...... 3 A6
Thurlow Rd GL5 ...... 19 C2
Thurston's Barton BS5 ...... 19 E1
Tibberton BS15 ...... 11 A8
Tibberton Com Prim Sch
GL19 ...... 171 E1
Tibberton Gr 2 BS16 ...... 129 B7
Tibberton La GL19 ...... 165 D6
Tibbiwell La GL6 ...... 103 F8
Tibbott Rd BS14 ...... 3 A5
Tibbott Wlk BS14 ...... 3 A5
Tiberius Ave GL15 ...... 92 B4
Tichborne Rd BS5 ...... 9 C7
Tide Gr BS11 ...... 17 A8
Tidenham Way BS34 ...... 39 F1
Tidling Cnr SN16 ...... 142 B3
Tidswell Cl GL12 ...... 109 F8
Tiffany Ct BS1 ...... 195 B1
Tilley Cl BS31 ...... 5 E2
Tilling Rd BS10 ...... 18 E2
Tilling Wlk BS10 ...... 18 E2
Tillis View GL16 ...... 154 D7
Tilney Rd GL50 ...... 133 D4
Tilnor Cres GL11 ...... 87 F4
Tilsdown GL11 ...... 87 F4
Tilsdown Cl GL11 ...... 87 F4
Tilting Rd BS35 ...... 64 B2
Timber Dene BS16 ...... 19 D4
Timbercombe La GL53 ...... 131 B3
Timbercombe Wlk BS14 ...... 3 C5
Timbrells Cl GL7 ...... 142 F8
Timbrells The GL7 ...... 142 B8
Timmis Cl GL4 ...... 119 E7
Timber Wood GL52 ...... 188 B2
Timperley Way GL51 ...... 129 E5
Timsbury Rd BS3 ...... 8 B2
Tindell St GL2 ...... 10 F4
Tinglesfield GL7 ...... 190 B8
Tinker's Cl 6 GL56 ...... 187 F3
Tinkley La GL10 ...... 90 B5
Tinmans Gn NP25 ...... 254 C5
Tintagel Cl BS31 ...... 4 D4
Tintern Abbey* NP16 ...... 146 C2
Tintern Ave 4 BS5 ...... 9 D7
Tintern Cl BS30 ...... 10 F6
Tintern Hts GL1 ...... 146 C3
Tintern Old Sta* NP16 ...... 146 C3
Tintern Rd GL4 ...... 118 E3
Tippett Rd BS15 ...... 10 D6
Tirle Bank Way GL20 ...... 192 F4
Tirlebrook Grange
GL20 ...... 182 A4
Tirlebrook Prim Sch
GL20 ...... 192 F4
Tirley Cl GL2 ...... 117 E1
Tirley Ho BS34 ...... 39 F1
Tirley St GL19 ...... 172 F7
Tithe Farm La GL19 ...... 165 E6
Tiverton Cl GL51 ...... 132 D3
Tiverton Wlk BS16 ...... 20 A2
Tivoli La GL50 ...... 193 A1
Tivoli Mews GL50 ...... 193 A2
Tivoli Pl GL50 ...... 193 A1
Tivoli Rd GL50 ...... 193 A1
Tivoli St GL50 ...... 193 A1
Tivoli Wlk 7 GL50 ...... 130 B8
Toadsmoor Rd GL5 ...... 148 A5
Tobacco Cl GL54 ...... 139 F4
Tobacconist Rd GL4 ...... 148 A5
Tobyfield Cl GL52 ...... 138 A3
Tobyfield La GL52 ...... 138 A3
Tobyfield Rd GL52 ...... 138 A3
Tockington Manor Sch
BS32 ...... 50 C2

Tockington Park La BS32 ...... 40 E8
Tocknell Ct GL11 ...... 87 F8
Toddington Cl BS37 ...... 32 D8
Toddington CE Prim Sch
GL54 ...... 184 C3
Toddington Sta* GL54 ...... 184 D3
Toghill La BS30 ...... 13 A8
Toll Down Way SN14 ...... 36 A3
Toll House Ct 4 BS3 ...... 8 F4
Tolsey La GL20 ...... 192 C4
Tom Price Cl GL52 ...... 193 C3
Tomlin Pl GL15 ...... 156 B1
Tone Dr GL3 ...... 120 F5
Tooke Rd GL6 ...... 91 E7
Top Rd Kempsford GL7 ...... 144 E8
Upper Soudley GL14 ...... 156 C5
Torchacre Rise GL11 ...... 88 A1
Tormarton Cres BS10 ...... 27 F4
Tormarton Intc GL7 ...... 34 B1
Tormarton Rd GL9 ...... 35 E6
Toronto Rd BS7 ...... 19 A8
Torpoint Rd BS3 ...... 8 D2
Torrance Cl BS30 ...... 11 D6
Torridge Rd BS31 ...... 5 A4
Torrington Ave BS4 ...... 2 F8
Tortworth Farming Mus*
Tortworth Prim Sch
GL12 ...... 66 C7
Tortworth Rd BS7 ...... 18 E5
Torwood House Sch BS6 ...... 18 A3
Totshill Dr BS13 ...... 2 E4
Totshill Gr BS13 ...... 2 E4
Tottenham Pl BS8 ...... 194 B3
Totterdown Bridge Ind Est
BS2 ...... 9 A4
Totterdown La GL7 ...... 152 E2
Touching End La SN14 ...... 14 F8
Touchstone Ave BS34 ...... 29 F5
Tower Cl GL4 ...... 119 D8
Tower Ho BS1 ...... 195 A2
Tower La Bristol BS1 ...... 195 A3
Bristol, Cadbury Heath
BS30 ...... 11 B6
Tower Rd Bristol BS15 ...... 20 C1
Yorkley GL15 ...... 150 D6
Tower Rd N BS30 ...... 11 B7
Tower Rd S BS30 ...... 11 B6
Tower St Bristol BS1 ...... 195 B2
Cirencester GL7 ...... 190 D4
Towerleaze BS9 ...... 17 D3
Townsend
Almondsbury BS32 ...... 39 F4
Mitcheldean GL17 ...... 164 D5
Ruardean GL17 ...... 163 D1
Townsend Cl Bristol BS14 ...... 3 F5
St Briavels GL15 ...... 146 F7
Townsend La BS32 ...... 9 C3
Townsend Rd BS32 ...... 40 A5
Townsend St GL51 ...... 133 C3
Townwell GL12 ...... 66 B2
Tozers Hill BS4 ...... 9 E3
Tracy Cl BS14 ...... 2 F7
Trafalgar Dr BS3 ...... 127 F8
Trafalgar Rd GL50 ...... 130 F2
Trafalgar St BS2 ...... 195 B4
Trafalgar Terr 3 BS3 ...... 8 B2
Traherne Cl 3 HR8 ...... 178 F7
Trajan Cl GL4 ...... 119 F6
Tralee Wlk BS4 ...... 8 A4
Tram Rd The 10 GL16 ...... 155 A5
Tramway Rd Bristol BS4 ...... 9 C3
Coderford GL14 ...... 156 C6
Upper Soudley GL14 ...... 156 C5
Tranmere Ave BS10 ...... 28 A4
Tranmere Gr BS10 ...... 28 A3
Tranmere Rd BS10 ...... 28 A3
Transport Mus* GL1 ...... 196 A3
Tranton La GL14 ...... 176 C4
Tratman Wlk BS10 ...... 27 F3
Travers Cl BS4 ...... 2 D6
Travers Wlk BS34 ...... 29 F5
Treasure Tram* GL16 ...... 155 A4
Tredegar Rd BS16 ...... 20 B3
Tredington Pk GL20 ...... 173 F8
Tredington Prim Sch
GL20 ...... 136 B6
Tredworth Jun & Inf Schs
GL1 ...... 118 F7
Tredworth Rd GL1 ...... 118 F6
Tree Leaze BS37 ...... 43 F2
Treefield Pl 8 BS2 ...... 19 A2
Treelands Cl GL53 ...... 130 D5
Treelands Dr GL53 ...... 130 D5
Tregarth Rd BS3 ...... 7 F1
Trelawney Ave 3 BS5 ...... 9 D8
Trelawney Pk BS4 ...... 9 D3
Trelawney Rd BS6 ...... 18 C1
Trelleck Rd NP16 ...... 146 B4
Trellick Wlk BS16 ...... 19 E8
Tremes Cl SN14 ...... 14 F8
Trench La BS32 ...... 40 E2
Trenchard Gdns GL7 ...... 150 F2
Trenchard Rd
7 Bream GL15 ...... 147 D8
Saltford BS31 ...... 5 D3
Stanton Fitzwarren SN6 ...... 145 A1
Trenchard St BS1 ...... 194 C3
Trendlewood Pk BS16 ...... 19 E5
Trenley Rd GL11 ...... 88 F7
Trent Dr BS35 ...... 51 D7
Trent Gr BS31 ...... 5 A4
Trent Rd GL3 ...... 120 F5
Trentham Cl 7 BS2 ...... 19 A2

Tresham Cl BS32 ...... 40 D2
Tresmore GL52 ...... 133 F2
Tretawn Gdns GL20 ...... 192 F4
Trevanna Rd BS3 ...... 7 F1
Trevelyan Wlk
Bristol, Henbury BS10 ...... 27 F3
Bristol, Stoke Gifford BS34 ...... 30 A5
Treverdowe Wlk BS10 ...... 27 D3
Trevethin Cl BS15 ...... 10 D7
Trevisa Cres GL13 ...... 85 E3
Trevisa Gr BS10 ...... 28 C4
Trevor Rd GL3 ...... 119 F7
Trewint Gdns BS4 ...... 2 F8
Trewsbury Rd GL7 ...... 149 E3
Triangle S BS8 ...... 194 B3
Triangle The
Hewelsfield GL15 ...... 146 D4
Longlevens GL2 ...... 127 C3
Triangle W BS8 ...... 194 B3
Tribune Pl GL4 ...... 119 E6
Trident Cl BS16 ...... 31 A1
Trier Way GL1 ...... 196 B1
Trim Mills BS1 ...... 195 A1
Trinder Rd BS20 ...... 16 B4
Trinity CE Prim Sch Gl9 ...... 36 A6
Trinity Coll BS9 ...... 17 E4
Trinity Dr GL6 ...... 148 A3
Trinity La GL52 ...... 193 C4
Trinity Mews 18 BS2 ...... 195 C3
Trinity Pl BS8 ...... 194 A2
Trinity Rd Bristol BS2 ...... 9 A7
Cirencester GL7 ...... 190 C3
Gloucester GL4 ...... 119 F6
Harrow Hill GL17 ...... 164 B7
Stroud GL5 ...... 99 D2
Trinity School La GL52 ...... 193 C4
Trinity St Bristol BS2 ...... 9 A7
Tewkesbury GL20 ...... 192 C4
Trinity Way GL14 ...... 191 D5
Trinity Wlk BS2 ...... 195 C3
Troon BS37 ...... 32 E8
Troon Dr BS30 ...... 11 B6
Troopers' Hill Rd BS5 ...... 10 A7
Trotman Ave GL4 ...... 87 F5
Troughton Pl GL20 ...... 192 E4
Trowbridge Rd BS10 ...... 28 C1
Trowbridge Wlk BS10 ...... 28 C1
Trowscoed Ave GL53 ...... 130 D6
Trubshaw Ct GL3 ...... 128 C5
Trull Cotts GL4 ...... 148 B7
Truro Rd BS3 ...... 8 B3
Tryes Rd GL50 ...... 130 C6
Trygrove GL4 ...... 119 D6
Trym Bank BS9 ...... 17 D7
Trym Cross Rd BS9 ...... 17 D7
Trym Rd BS9 ...... 18 A7
Trym Side BS9 ...... 17 C5
Trymleaze BS9 ...... 17 C5
Trymwood Cl BS10 ...... 27 F2
Trymwood Par BS9 ...... 17 C6
Tubular Cotts NP16 ...... 73 A1
Tucker St BS2 ...... 195 C3
Tuckett La BS16 ...... 20 C7
Tuckwell Rd GL4 ...... 144 F7
Tudor Cl BS30 ...... 11 D2
Tudor La GL1 ...... 97 E4
Tudor Dr NP16 ...... 72 C1
Tudor Lo GL4 ...... 130 C6
Tudor Lodge Dr GL50 ...... 193 A1
Tudor Lodge Rd GL50 ...... 130 C6
Tudor Pl GL20 ...... 192 C2
Tudor Rd
Bristol, Hanham BS15 ...... 10 C5
Bristol, Lower Easton BS5 ...... 19 C1
Bristol, St Pauls BS2 ...... 18 F1
Cirencester GL7 ...... 190 B4
Monmouth NP25 ...... 154 B7
Tudor St GL1 ...... 118 C6
Tudor Wlk GL4 ...... 118 B4
Tuffley Ave GL11 ...... 118 D5
Tuffley Cres GL1 ...... 118 C5
Tuffley La GL4 ...... 118 A5
Tuffley Prim Sch GL4 ...... 118 D1
Tuffley Rd GL1 ...... 118 D5
Tufthorn Ave GL16 ...... 155 A4
Tufthorn Cl GL16 ...... 155 B4
Tufthorn Ind Est GL16 ...... 155 B4
Tufthorn Rd GL16 ...... 155 B4
Tufton Ave BS11 ...... 17 A8
Tug Wilson Cl GL20 ...... 182 C5
Tugela Rd BS13 ...... 1 F7
Tulworths The GL2 ...... 127 B5
Tunacre GL2 ...... 125 D6
Tunbridge Way BS16 ...... 21 A8
Tuners La SN16 ...... 141 C3
Tunstall Cl BS9 ...... 17 E4
Turkdean Rd GL51 ...... 129 E8
Turley Rd BS5 ...... 19 D1
Turnberry Wlk 3 BS4 ...... 9 D1
Turnbridge Cl BS10 ...... 28 D4
Turnbridge Rd BS10 ...... 28 C3
Turnbury BS37 ...... 32 E8
Turner Cl BS31 ...... 5 F1
Turner Dr BS37 ...... 43 B1
Turner Gdns BS7 ...... 19 B6
Turner Rd GL11 ...... 87 E3
Turners Cl GL2 ...... 125 D4
Turners Ct 9 BS30 ...... 10 F6
Turnpike Ave GL12 ...... 68 C6
Turnpike Cl
Chepstow NP16 ...... 72 C1
28 Moreton-in-M GL56 ...... 187 A3
Yate BS37 ...... 27 E3
Turnpike End NP16 ...... 61 B4
Turnpike Gate GL12 ...... 54 B6
Turnpike Rd SN6 ...... 145 D3
Turnstone Dr GL2 ...... 117 D1

Turtlegate Ave BS13 ...... 1 ...
Turtlegate Wlk BS13 ......
Turville Barns GL7 ...... 1 ...
Turville Dr BS7 ......
Tuscany Ho BS6 ......
Tusculum Way GL17 ...... 16 ...
Tuthill Rise GL15 ......
Tutnalls St GL15 ......
Tutshill Gdns NP16 ......
Tweed Cl BS35 ......
Tweenbrook Ave GL1 ...... 1 ...
Tweeny La BS30 ......
Twenties The GL7 ...... 1 ...
Tweeny Acres Rd BS10 ......
Twickenham Rd BS6 ......
Twigworth CE Prim Sch
GL2 ...... 1 ...
Twinberrow La GL11 ......
Twixbears GL20 ......
Two Acres Rd BS14 ......
Two Hedges Rd GL52 ...... 1 ...
Two Mile Ct BS15 ......
Two Mile Hill Jun & Inf Sc
...
Two Mile La GL2 ...... 1 ...
Twomile Hill Rd BS15 ......
Twyning Manor GL20 ...... 1 ...
Twyning Rd WR8 ......
Twyning Sch GL20 ...... 1 ...
Twynings The BS15 ......
Twyver Bank GL4 ......
Twyver Cl GL4 ......
Tybalt Way BS34 ......
Tylea Cl GL51 ......
Tyler Cl BS15 ......
Tyler Ct 3 GL51 ......
Tyler St BS2 ......
Tyler's La BS16 ......
Tylers Way Chalford GL6 1
Sedbury NP16 ......
Tyne BS37 ......
Yorkley GL15 ......
Tyndale Ave Bristol BS16 ......
Yate BS37 ......
Tyndale Cl GL11 ......
Tyndale Ct 7 BS6 ......
Tyndale Mon The* GL11 ......
Tyndale Rd Bristol BS15 ......
Dursley GL11 ......
Gloucester GL3 ......
Slimbridge GL2 ......
Tyndale View BS35 ......
Tyndall Ave BS8 ......
Tyndall Ho 5 BS2 ......
Tyndall's Park Rd BS8 ......
Tyndalls Park Mews
BS2 ......
Tyndalls Way BS10 ......
Tyne Ho 8 BS35 ......
Tyne Rd BS7 ......
Tyne St BS2 ......
Tyning Cl Bristol BS14 ......
Yate BS37 ......
Tyning Cres GL2 ......
Tyning Hengrove Jun Sch
BS14 ......
Tyning Rd Bristol BS3 ......
Saltford BS31 ......
Tynings Ct GL3 ......
Tynings Cry Prim Sch
BS16 ......
Tynings Rd GL2 ......
Tynings The GL6 ......
Tynte Ave BS13 ......
Tyntesfield Rd BS13 ......
Tyrone Wlk BS4 ......
Tyrrel Way BS34 ......
Tythe Ct Dursley GL11 ......
Marshfield SN14 ......
Tythe Rd WR12 ......
Tythe Terr 10 GL54 ......
Tytherington Rd BS35 ......
Tythings Cres GL18 ......
Tythings Mews GL18 ......
Tythings The GL18 ......

U

Uley CE Prim Sch GL11 ......
Uley Long Barrow (Hetty
Pegler's Tump)* GL11 ......
Uley Rd GL11 ......
Ullenwood Court Bsns Pk
GL53 ......
Ullenwood Manor (Coll)
GL53 ......
Ullenwood Rd GL4 ......
Ullswater Cl Bristol BS30 ......
Ullswater Rd Bristol BS10 ......
Cheltenham GL51 ......
Underbanks BS20 ......
Undercliff Ave GL53 ......
Undercliff Terr GL53 ......
Underdown Ho BS1 ......
Underhill NP16 ......
Underhill Rd
Charfield GL12 ......
Gloucester GL4 ......
Underwood Cl BS35 ......
Underwood End GL2 ......
Unicorn Bsns Pk BS4 ......
Union Pl GL20 ......
Union Rd 2 Bristol BS2 ......
Coleford GL16 ......
Union St Bristol BS1 ......

on St continued
.eltenham GL52 ......193 C4
... 188 B8
.ucester GL1 ......196 C4
...wn-on-t-W GL54 ....176 F4
..nd GL5 ......99 C7
.y Ct BS31 ......5 A5
..y Rd BS31 ......5 A6
..y St
.stol, Canon's Marsh

......194 C2
.stol, Kingswood BS15 ...10 C8
.stol, Newton BS2 ....195 C3
. of Bristol BS8 ......194 C2
. of Bristol Dept of
.onomics BS8 ......194 C3
. of Bristol Dept of Ed
......194 C3

. of Bristol Sch of
.rinary Science BS2 ...194 C4
. of the West of England
.stol, Bower Ashton BS3 ..7 E4
.tol, Redland BS6 ....18 B2
. of the West of England
.culty of Health & Social
.e BS16 ......19 E5
. of the West of England
.enchay Campus BS16 ..29 E1
. of the West of England,
.Matthias BS16 ......30 C8
.ersity GL1 ......17 F4
.ersity Farm 10

......187 A3
.ersity Rd GL4 ......194 C3
.ersity Wlk BS8 ......194 C3
.water La GL14 ......157 A7
.e Ct GL51 ......129 C7
.in Rd GL2 ......129 C7
.atherley Way GL51 ....129 E5
.att Sta 143 E6
.old Prep Sch GL5 ....98 F8
.all Pl GL1 ......118 D5
.ll Rd Bristol BS7 ....18 F5
.sh Cres BS13 ......2 D3
.nds Com Prim Sch

......99 C8
.nds Dr BS31 ......5 F2
.nds Ho GL5 ......99 C8
.nds Rd BS16 ......20 D3
.ord BS31 ......5 F2
.nds Vw GL5 ......99 D8
.nds View Terr GL5 ....99 D7
.r Bath Rd BS51 ....51 B8
.r Bath St GL50 ......193 B1
.r Belgrave Rd BS8 ...18 A2
.r Belmont Rd BS17 ...34 A3
.r Berkeley Pl BS8 ...194 B3
.r Bilson Rd GL14 ....191 C6
.r Byron Pl BS8 ......194 B3
.r Chapel La BS5 ......31 C7

.r Cheltenham Pl

......18 E1
.r Church La BS2 ....194 C3
.r Church Rd GL5 ....113 B8
.r Church St NP16 ....60 F8
.r Cranbrook Rd BS6 ...18 B4
.r Cross 8 HR8 ......178 F8
.r Dorrington Terr

......99 D6
.r End Ct WR11 ......188 A6
.r Hayes Rd GL6 ......91 A4
.r Horfield Prim Sch

......19 A8
.r Kitesnest La GL6 ..102 F4
.r Leazes GL5 ......99 D8
.r Lynch Rd GL6 ....148 D6
.r Maudlin St BS2 ...195 A3
.r Mill La BS2 ......134 E5
.r Mills Ind Est GL10 ..97 F6
.r Myrtle Hill BS20 ....16 C4
.r Nelson St NP16 ....60 E8
.r Norwood St

......130 C6
.r Park Rd GL6 ......91 C3
.r Park St GL52 ......130 F8
.r Perry Hill BS3 ......8 C4
.r Poole Rd BS13 ....80 B8
.r Quay St GL1 ......196 A3
.r Queen's Rd 2

......97 F7
.r Rd Eastnor HR8 ....179 B8
.ndell GL15 ......155 F1
.r Rodley Rd GL14 ....137 B8
.r Sandhurst Rd BS4 ..9 D4
.r Springfield Rd

......99 C8
.r St Bristol BS4 ......9 A4
.ham SN14 ......22 C3
.r Station Rd BS16 ....20 D4
.r Stone Cl BS16 ......31 C7
.r Stowfield Rd

......163 C4
.r Sydney St BS3 ......8 B3
.r Terr BS11 ......27 B1
.r Tockington Rd

......50 A2
.r Tynings GL6 ......91 A4
.r Tynings The GL5 ....98 D8
.r Washwell GL6 ......111 F1
.r Wells St BS1 ......194 C2
.r York St BS2 ......195 B4
.r Shield Rd GL51 ....133 A5
.hall Cl 4 HR8 ......178 F8
.rpe GL11 ......88 B5
.rpe La GL11 ......88 B6
.r GL4 ......119 E7
.e Gdns GL8 ......140 B5

Upton St continued
Upton La
Brookthorpe GL4 ......111 B6
Gloucester GL4 ......119 F4
Maiden Head BS41 ....1 F1
Upton Rd BS3 ......8 B4
Upton St GL1 ......119 A8
Upton St Leonards CE Prim
Sch GL4 ......119 F3
Urfords Dr BS16 ......20 C6
Usk Ct 8 BS35 ......51 C8
Usk Way GL3 ......120 F5
Utah Dr GL7 ......152 E2

V

Vaisey Field GL2 ......100 F5
Vale Bank GL2 ......157 B6
Vale Ct Bristol BS8 ...194 A4
8 Cricklade SN6 ......143 E4
Vale La BS3 ......2 C8
Vale Rd GL7 ......190 B8
Vale St BS4 ......9 A4
Vale The BS16 ......21 F6
Valentine Cl Bristol BS3 ..3 B5
Chepstow NP16 ......61 A4
Valerian Cl Bristol BS11 ..16 F6
Gloucester GL2 ......126 F6
Valiant Way GL3 ......120 C7
Vallenders Rd GL20 ...182 C7
Valley Cl GL5 ......148 A5
Valley Cotts GL51 ....173 F1
Valley Ent Pk NP25 ..156 A8
Valley Gdns BS16 ....20 F8
Valley La GL4 ......120 A1
Valley Rd
Bristol, Bedminster Down
BS13 ......2 A8
Bristol, Mangotsfield BS16 ..21 A5
Cinderford GL14 ......191 C3
Leigh Woods BS8 ....7 C7
Lydney GL15 ......92 C2
Upper Lydbrook GL17 ..163 D1
Wooton-u-E GL12 ......68 C8
Valley View
Chedworth GL54 ......159 A6
Dursley GL11 ......87 F4
Valley View Rd GL3 ....99 F6
Valls The BS32 ......24 C3
Valma Rocks BS5 ....10 A6
Van der Breen St GL6 ..105 B1
Vandyck Ave BS31 ....4 F6
Varley Ave GL3 ......120 B6
Varnister La GL17 ....163 F4
Varnister Rd GL17 ....163 F4
Vassall Ct BS16 ......20 B5
Vassall Rd BS16 ......20 B5
Vatch View GL5 ......103 E1
Vattingstone La BS35 ..50 F5
Vaughan Cl BS10 ......27 F3
Vauxhall La GL14 ....170 F4
Vauxhall Rd
Chepstow NP16 ......60 D8
Gloucester GL1 ......196 C1
Vauxhall Terr
2 Bristol BS3 ......8 A4
Gloucester GL1 ......196 C1
Vayre Cl BS37 ......40 A8
Veldt House Barns HR8 .178 B5
Velhurst Dr 1 GL6 ....148 B6
Velthouse La GL17 ....163 L1
Vennings The GL11 ....87 F6
Venns Acre GL12 ......68 B6
Vensfield Rd GL2 ....117 E2
Vention La GL17 ......163 D3
Ventnor Ave 1 BS5 ...9 F8
Ventnor Rd
Bristol, Filton BS34 ....29 B3
Bristol, St George BS5 ..19 F1
Venton Ct 5 BS15 ...10 B5
Vera Rd BS16 ......19 F2
Verbena Ct 2 GL4 ....119 F5
Vernal Cl GL4 ......119 F5
Vernals La GL12 ......67 C8
Verney Cl GL53 ......130 E6
Verney Rd GL10 ......97 F7
Verneys The GL53 ....130 E6
Vernon Cl BS31 ......5 C3
Vernon Pl GL53 ......193 C3
Vernon St 5 BS2 ......8 F4
Verrier Rd GL7 ......9 C7
Vertican Rd GL3 ......127 D6
Vervain Cl GL3 ......128 A7
Verwood Dr BS30 ....11 C2
Vetch Cl GL4 ......119 A4
Viburnum Cl GL50 ....130 B6
Viburnum View 4 GL4 ..119 F5
Vicarage Ct
Churchdown GL3 ......128 C4
Lydney GL15 ......92 A2
Shurdington GL51 ....129 E2
Vicarage Cotts
Bristol BS16 ......20 D5
Chipping Campden GL55 ..189 A2
Vicarage Ct
8 Bristol BS1 ......10 B5
Brockworth GL3 ......120 E5
Vicarage La
Arlingham GL2 ......157 B5
Brockworth GL3 ......120 E6
Frampton on Severn GL2 ..157 F1
Highworth SN6 ......145 D3
Hillesley GL12 ......55 D8
Oliveston BS35 ......50 B3

Vicarage Rd
Bristol, Bishopsworth BS13 ..2 A6
Bristol, Hanham BS15 ..10 B5
Bristol, Southville BS3 ....8 B4
Bristol, Whitehall BS5 ....9 C8
Coalpit Heath BS36 ....31 C6
Gloucester GL1 ......119 A7
Leigh Woods BS8 ......7 C7
Pilning BS35 ......38 C7
Vicarage St GL4 ......104 A8
Vicars Cl BS16 ......20 B4
Vickers Rd GL54 ......169 D7
Victor Ho BS34 ......29 C7
Victor Rd BS3 ......8 B3
Victor St
2 Bristol, Barton Hill BS5 ..9 B6
Bristol, St Philip's Marsh
BS2 ......9 C7
Victoria Ave BS5 ......9 C7
Victoria Cl BS35 ......64 B3
Victoria Cotts
Quedgeley GL2 ......117 E3
8 Stonehouse GL10 ......97 F8
Victoria Cres BS35 ....38 A6
Victoria Ct
6 Bristol, Cotham BS6 ..18 D1
Bristol, Redland BS6 ....18 A3
Gloucester GL2 ......126 F6
Victoria Gr BS3 ......8 D1
Victoria Gr BS3 ......8 D1
Victoria Ho BS31 ......4 F4
Victoria Par BS5 ......9 C8
Victoria Park Com Jun & Inf
Schs BS3 ......8 E3
Victoria Pk
Bristol, Fishponds BS16 ..20 A5
Bristol, Kingswood BS15 ..20 D1
Cheltenham GL52 ......133 F1
Victoria Rd
Avonmouth BS11 ......16 B7
Brimscombe GL5 ......99 F1
Bristol, Hanham BS15 ..10 C5
Bristol, St Philip's Marsh
BS2 ......9 A5
Bristol, Warmley BS30 ..11 D5
Chepstow NP16 ......60 F5
Cirencester GL7 ......190 D4
Coleford GL16 ......155 A5
Gloucester GL2 ......126 F6
Ledbury HR8 ......178 E8
Lydney GL15 ......92 A3
Quenington GL7 ......152 D7
Saltford BS31 ......5 D3
Victoria Retreat GL50 ..193 B1
Victoria Sq BS8 ......194 A3
Victoria St
6 Bourton-on-t-W GL54 ..168 F7
Bristol BS1 ......195 B2
Bristol, Staple Hill BS16 ..20 D5
Cheltenham GL50 ......133 D3
Cinderford GL14 ......191 C4
Cinderford GL14 ......191 C4
Gloucester GL1 ......196 C1
Passage GL6 ......103 F8
Victoria Terr
6 Bourton-on-t-W GL54 ..168 F7
Bretforton WR11 ......188 A7
1 Bristol, Clifton BS8 ....7 F6
Bristol, St Philip's Marsh
BS2 ......9 B5
Cheltenham GL52 ......133 F1
Victoria Vale GL4 ......191 C4
Victoria Wlk BS6 ......18 D1
Victory Cl GL3 ......128 A8
Victory Rd
Gloucester GL1 ......118 F7
Whiteshill BS16 ......103 A3
Thornbury BS35 ......64 D1
Victory Villas GL7 ....152 F4
View Ct BS30 ......12 C6
Vigor Rd BS13 ......2 B5
Villa The GL4 ......191 C2
Villa Way HR8 ......178 E7
Village Ave GL4 ......175 D2
Village Cl BS37 ......40 A8
Village Farm GL7 ......150 F3
Village Rd GL51 ......132 F4
Villiers Rd BS5 ......19 B1
Vilner La BS35 ......51 B7
Vilvre Mead GL52 ....137 D4
Vimpany Cl BS10 ......27 F3
Vimpennys La BS10 ....38 E1
Vincent Ave GL4 ......118 D1
Vincent Cl BS11 ......27 C2
Vine Cl BS37 ......40 A8
Vine Cotts NP16 ......60 E8
Vine Ct GL50 ......133 C3
Vine Hall GL15 ......147 E4
Vine Terr GL1 ......196 C4
Vine Way GL30 ......192 D1
Vinecroft GL13 ......65 B8
Viner's La GL9 ......36 B5
Vineries GL33 ......130 C4
Vines The GL3 ......120 B7
Vineyard La GL12 ....67 F5
Vineyard St GL54 ....171 F2
Vineyards GL33 ......131 B4
Vining Wlk 4 BS5 ....9 B8
Vinney La BS37 ......44 F8
Vinny Ave BS16 ......21 A7
Vintery Leys BS9 ......18 F7
Virginia Ave GL7 ......152 E2
Virginia Cl BS37 ......44 A1
Virginia Rd GL20 ....182 C4
Vittoria Wlk GL50 ....193 B2
Vivian St BS3 ......8 D3
Vizard Cl GL11 ......80 B8

Vorda Rd SN6 ......145 D4
Vowell Cl BS13 ......2 B4
Voxwell La GL52 ......137 E3
Voyce Cl GL4 ......118 D2
Vulcan Way GL4 ......119 F6
Vyners Cl GL7 ......190 C2
Vyvian Ct GL1 ......196 B2
Vyvian Rd BS8 ......194 A3
Vyvyan Terr BS8 ......194 A3

W

Wade Ct GL51 ......129 C7
Wade Hill SN6 ......145 C3
Wade Rd BS37 ......43 A3
Wade St BS2 ......195 C3
Wadehurst Ind Pk BS2 ..9 A7
Wades La GL6 ......103 C2
Wades Rd BS34 ......29 B3
Wadham Cl GL51 ....153 C6
Wadham Dr BS16 ....30 B1
Wadham Gr BS16 ....21 B5
Waggons La GL19 ....172 C4
Wagtail Dr GL20 ....182 B5
Wainbridge Cres BS35 ..38 D7
Wainbrook Dr BS5 ...19 D2
Wainland Pl GL16 ....154 F3
Wainlode La GL2 ....173 A4
Wakefield Cl GL7 ....144 F7
Wakeford Rd 1 BS16 ..21 A7
Wakeman Cl GL20 ....192 E2
Walden Rd BS31 ......5 A4
Waldrist Cl GL51 ....132 F1
Walford Prim Sch HR9 ..163 C7
Walham La GL1 ......126 E4
Walk Mill La GL12 ....67 F4
Walk The GL12 ......67 F5
Walker Cl
Bristol, Dowend BS16 ..21 A7
Bristol, Upper Easton BS5 ..9 B8
Walker Ct BS16 ......20 F5
Walker St BS2 ......194 C4
Walker Way BS35 ......51 B7
Walker's La GL17 ......163 F4
Walkers Gdn 14 BS54 ..168 A1
Walkley Hill GL5 ......99 A5
Walkley Rd GL20 ....192 D5
Wallace Appartments 7
GL52 ......193 C4
Wallace Ho GL51 ....129 F6
Wallbank Ho GL1 ....127 A3
Wallbridge Stroud GL5 ..99 B6
Stroud GL5 ......99 B7
Wallcroft Ho BS6 ....18 A3
Walled Gdn The GL8 ..82 B5
Wallingford Rd BS4 ....2 D7
Walliscote Ave BS9 ...18 C6
Walliscote Rd BS9 ...18 C6
Wallow Gn Horsley GL6 ..90 F2
Wallscourt Rd BS34 ..29 B1
Wallscourt Rd S BS34 ..29 B1
Wallsend La SN14 ....24 C5
Wallsworth Hall Nature in Art
Mus* GL2 ......173 A1
Walmore Hill Prim Sch

......165 F1
Walnut Ave BS37 ......44 A2
Walnut Bank Dr GL20 ..183 A4
Walnut Cl Bristol BS31 ..20 F1
Broadway WR12 ......185 B8
Cheltenham GL52 ......133 E4
10 Coleford GL16 ......155 B5
Easton-in-G BS20 ......16 A3
Frampton Cotterell BS36 ..31 C6
Gloucester GL4 ......119 D3
Keynsham BS31 ......5 E4
Walnut Cres BS15 ....10 F8
Walnut Dr GL52 ......133 E4
Walnut Dr SN14 ......15 F6
Walnut La BS15 ......11 A8
Walnut Tree Cl BS32 ..40 A5
Walnut Wlk Bristol BS13 ..2 A6
Keynsham BS31 ......4 D4
Walsingham Rd BS6 ..18 E2
Walter Reynold Homes

......1 A7
Walter St BS3 ......8 A4
Walton Ave BS4 ......9 D5
Walton Cl Bristol BS30 ..11 C1
Keynsham BS31 ......4 D4
Upton St Leonards GL4 ..119 F1
Walton Dr GL20 ......192 F5
Walton Gdns GL20 ....192 F4
Walton Heath BS37 ....43 F1
Walton Ho BS37 ......132 E2
Walton House Bglws 8
GL54 ......168 A1
Walton House Ct 9
GL54 ......168 A1
Walton Rd BS11 ......16 D6
Walton Rise BS9 ......18 A7
Walton St BS5 ......19 B1
Walwyn Cl GL7 ......164 D5
Wandsdyke Prim Sch

......2 F4
Wansbeck Rd BS31 ....5 A4
Wanscow Wlk BS9 ....18 B6
Wansdyke Ct BS14 ....5 A6
Wansdyke Workshops

......5 A6
Wapley Hill BS37 ......32 E4
Wapley Rd BS37 ......33 B3
Wapping Rd BS1 ......195 A1

Ward Ave GL51 ......127 E6
Ward Cl GL52 ......138 A4
Ward Rd GL54 ......168 A1
Warden Hill Cl GL51 ..129 F6
Warden Hill Cty Prim Sch
GL51 ......130 A5
Warden Hill Rd GL51 ..130 A6
Warden Rd BS3 ......8 C4
Wardour Rd BS4 ......2 D8
Wards Rd GL51 ......129 D6
Ware Ct BS36 ......30 C5
Warend Hill Dursley GL11 ..80 A6
North Nibley GL11 ......79 F6
Waring Ho BS1 ......195 A1
Warman Cl BS14 ......3 F6
Warman Rd BS14 ......3 F6
Warmington Rd BS14 ..3 C8
Warminster Rd BS2 ..19 A2
Warmley CE Prim Sch

......11 C5
Warmley Tower Spec Sch
BS30 ......11 B7
Warneford Pl 20 GL54 ..187 A3
Warner Cl BS15 ......10 F6
Warns Cl 14 GL8 ......140 B4
Warns The BS30 ......11 A4
Warren Cl Bristol BS32 ..40 D3
Cheltenham GL51 ......129 F6
Innsworth GL3 ......128 A7
Warren Croft GL11 ......79 E4
Warren Dr 6 HR8 ......178 F8
Warren Gdns BS14 ......3 F5
Warren La HR9 ......170 A1
Warren Rd Bristol BS34 ..29 B3
Northway GL20 ......182 B4
Warren Slade NP16 ....60 F5
Warren Way BS37 ......43 E3
Warrens Gorse Cotts

......150 B8
Warrington Rd BS4 ....9 D2
Warth La Arlingham GL2 ..157 C6
Pilning BS35 ......48 D3
Warwick Ave
7 Bristol BS5 ......19 B1
Gloucester GL4 ......118 C1
Warwick Cl Bristol BS30 ..11 B2
Chepstow NP16 ......60 C6
3 Fairford GL7 ......152 E4
Stroud GL5 ......99 A4
Thornbury BS35 ......64 A1
Warwick Cres GL52 ....131 B6
Warwick Pl
Cheltenham GL52 ......193 C4
Tewkesbury GL20 ......192 D3
Warwick Rd
Bristol, Baptist Mills BS5 ..19 B1
Bristol, Redland BS6 ....18 B1
Keynsham BS31 ......4 D4
Washing Pound La BS14 ..3 A4
Washing's La NP25 ....154 C5
Washingpool Hill BS35 ..50 E1
Washingpool Hill Rd
BS32 ......50 D2
Washingpool La BS11 ..26 F7
Wasp Green La

......152 F1
Wasley Rd GL51 ......132 E1
Wash Elm Cl BS32 ....29 E6
Watchhouse Rd BS20 ..16 D4
Watchill Ave BS13 ....1 F6
Watchill Cl BS13 ......1 F6
Water Furlongs SN6 ..143 E4
Water La Brimscombe GL5 ..99 E1
Bristol BS1 ......195 B2
Bristol, Brislington BS4 ....9 D2
Bristol, Hanham Green
BS15 ......10 B2
Bristol, Knowle BS3 ....8 F3
Charlton Kings GL52 ..131 B6
Pill BS20 ......16 C4
Woodchester GL5 ......98 F3
Wooton-u-E GL12 ......68 B6
Water Mdw GL2 ......109 E7
Water St GL11 ......88 B1
Water's La BS9 ......18 A7
Waterbridge Rd BS13 ..1 F4
Watercress Rd GL2 ....18 F3
Waterdale Cl Bristol BS9 ..18 C7
Hardwicke GL2 ......109 D8
Waterdale Gdns BS9 ..18 C7
Waterfield Cl GL53 ....193 B1
Waterford Cl BS35 ....51 D8
Waterford Rd BS9 ....18 C6
Waterford Rd BS9 ....18 B6
Watergrip La GL20 ....183 A8
Waterloo Cl GL20 ....182 D2
Waterloo Ho BS20 ....16 D5
Waterloo La GL7 ......152 E3
Waterloo Pl 19 BS2 ..195 C3
8 Bristol, Clifton BS8 ....7 F7
Cheltenham GL51 ......133 B3
Waterloo The GL7 ....190 D5
Waterloo Way GL20 ..182 D7
Watermans Ct GL2 ....117 D1
Watermead GL15 ......92 A3
Watermill Cl GL52 ....65 E7
Watermoor Ct GL51 ..132 D4
Watermoor Ct BS35 ..128 B5
Watermoor Prim Sch

......190 D3
Watermoor Rd GL7 ..190 D3

Watermoor Way GL7 ....190 D3
Watermore Cl BS36 ....31 C7
Waters Rd BS15 ....10 C8
Waters Reach GL2 ....118 B6
Waters Way NP16 ....60 E7
Watershoot Cl GL52 ....134 A5
Waterside Cl
Andoversford GL54 ....166 D6
Quedgeley GL2 ....117 D1
Waterside Dr BS32 ....40 A1
Waterton Cl GL3 ....120 B6
Waterwells Dr GL2 ....110 A6
Waterwheel Cl GL2 ....117 D1
Watery La Aylburton GL15 ..147 F5
Doynton BS30 ....13 A8
Frampton on Severn GL2 ..157 F2
Gloucester GL4 ....111 F8
Lea HR9 ....164 C8
Minsterworth GL2 ....117 B7
Newent GL18 ....170 F4
Wathen Rd BS6 ....49 C5
Watkins Cnr SN5 ....143 E1
Watkins V BS9 ....18 A8
Watledge Bank GL6 ....91 B5
Watledge Cl GL20 ....192 D4
Watledge Rd GL6 ....91 B5
Watley's End Rd BS36 ..30 F7
Watling Way BS11 ....16 D7
Watson Ave BS4 ....9 D4
Watson Gr GL4 ....119 F5
Watson Ho ⬛ GL52 ....193 C4
Watson's Rd BS30 ....10 F3
Watters Cl BS36 ....31 C6
Watts Cl GL3 ....120 B7
Wavell Cl BS37 ....43 D3
Waveney Rd BS31 ....5 A3
Waverley Rd
Bristol, Cotham BS6 ....18 C1
Bristol, Shirehampton BS11 ..16 E6
Gloucester GL2 ....127 C2
Yate BS37 ....43 B2
Waverley St ⬛ BS5 ....19 A1
Waycroft Prim Sch BS14 ..3 A5
Wayford Cl BS31 ....5 A3
Waylands SN6 ....143 F4
Wayleaze
Coalpit Heath BS36 ....31 D7
Westerleigh BS37 ....32 F3
Wayridge The GL4 ....119 D4
Wayside Cl BS36 ....31 B7
Weald Cl GL4 ....119 C5
Weare Ct BS1 ....194 A1
Weathers The BS35 ....63 D5
Weavers Cl Dursley GL11 ..80 B8
Kingswood GL12 ....67 F4
Weavers Dr GL11 ....89 B1
Weavers Ho ⬛ GL52 ....99 C7
Weavers Rd
Cirencester GL7 ....190 E4
Quedgeley GL2 ....117 F2
Weavers Row GL5 ....99 F1
Weavings La GL14 ....156 C6
Webb Rd GL8 ....140 B5
Webb St BS5 ....9 A8
Webber Rd GL20 ....192 B3
Webbs Heath BS30 ....11 E8
Webbs Wood BS32 ....29 F7
Webbs Wood Rd BS32 ....29 F7
Webley Rd GL17 ....163 F3
Wedgewood Cotts
WR12 ....184 E5
Wedgewood Rd BS16 ....30 D1
Wedgwood Cl BS14 ....3 B5
Wedgwood Dr GL2 ....127 C4
Wedmore Cl BS15 ....10 F7
Wedmore Rd BS31 ....5 D4
Wedmore Vale BS3 ....8 B2
Weedon Cl ⬛ BS2 ....19 F2
Weigh Bridge Ct GL15 ..189 A2
Weight Rd ⬛ BS5 ....9 C7
Weir Bridge Cl GL4 ....119 E8
Weir La SN14 ....14 F8
Welch Ho GL51 ....129 D2
Welch Rd GL51 ....132 E4
Well Alley GL20 ....192 C5
Well Cl Chepstow NP16 ....60 F4
Long Ashton BS41 ....7 B1
Northway GL20 ....182 C5
Well Cross Rd GL4 ....119 A4
Well Hill GL6 ....6 A8
Well House Cl BS39 ....17 E3
Well La Badminton GL9 ..46 E5
Drybrook GL17 ....164 A4
Guiting Power GL54 ....175 B3
Stow-on-t-W GL54 ....176 F4
Well Pl GL50 ....133 B1
Well Vale La HR9 ....162 D3
Welland Ct GL52 ....134 A4
Welland Dr GL52 ....134 A4
Welland Lodge Rd GL52 ..134 A4
Welland Rd Keynsham BS31 ..4 F4
Quedgeley GL2 ....117 F2
Wellbrook Rd GL52 ....137 F5
Weller Bglws GL2 ....118 C4
Wellersley Prim Sch BS37 ..32 D6
Wellesley Rd GL50 ....133 E3
Wellesley St GL11 ....118 F6
Wellfield GL20 ....192 F5
Wellgarth Rd BS4 ....9 A2
Wellgarth Wlk BS4 ....9 A2
Welling Cl GL11 ....80 C7
Wellington Ave BS6 ....18 E1
Wellington Cres BS7 ....18 E6
Wellington Dr Bristol BS9 ..18 D6
Yate BS37 ....43 B2

Wellington Hill BS7 ....18 E6
Wellington Hill W BS9 ....18 D7
Wellington Ho GL7 ....190 D5
Wellington La Bristol BS6 ..18 E1
Cheltenham GL52 ....133 E2
Wellington Lodge Cl
GL20 ....182 D7
Wellington Mews BS11 ..16 D5
Wellington Par GL1 ....196 C3
Wellington Pk BS8 ....18 A3
Wellington Pl Bristol BS16 ..30 B1
Cheltenham GL52 ....193 C2
Wellington Rd
Bristol, Kingswood BS15 ..20 D2
Bristol, St Pauls BS2 ....195 C4
Cheltenham GL52 ....133 E3
Moreton-in-M GL56 ....187 B3
Upper Rissington GL54 ..169 D6
Yate BS37 ....43 E3
Wellington Sq GL50 ....133 E3
Wellington St
Cheltenham GL50 ....193 C3
Gloucester GL1 ....196 B2
Wellington Terr
⬛ Bristol BS8 ....7 F6
Moreton-in-M GL56 ....187 B3
Newnham GL14 ....156 F6
Wellington Wlk BS10 ....18 C7
Wellmeadow GL14 ....156 D7
Wellmeadow La GL16 ....155 A8
Wells Cl Bristol BS14 ....3 C5
Cheltenham GL51 ....133 C3
Wells Gdns ⬛ WR12 ....185 C8
Wells Rd Bisley GL6 ....148 D8
Bristol BS4 ....9 B2
Gloucester GL4 ....119 C8
Maiden Head BS41 ....1 E1
Wells St BS3 ....8 A4
Wellsprings Ho GL2 ....127 C3
Wellsprings Rd GL2 ....127 C3
Wellstead Ave BS37 ....43 D1
Wellsway BS31 ....4 F3
Wellsway Sec Sch BS31 ..5 A5
Welsford Ave BS16 ....19 D4
Welsford Rd BS16 ....19 C4
Welsh Back BS1 ....195 A2
Welsh House La GL18 ....170 F8
Welsh St NP16 ....72 D1
Welsh Way
Bagendon GL7 ....158 D1
Fairford GL7 ....152 B5
Sunhill GL7 ....151 F7
Welton Wlk BS15 ....20 C2
Welveland La GL4 ....127 E1
Welwyn Gdns BS11 ....2 C3
Welwyn Mews ⬛ GL51 ..129 E5
Wench Ford Forest Trail*
GL15 ....156 C2
Wend The GL17 ....164 F5
Wendover Gdns GL50 ....133 B1
Wenlock Rd GL20 ....192 D3
Wenmore Cl BS16 ....30 D1
Wentforth Dr ⬛ BS15 ....20 C2
Wentfield GL10 ....96 F7
Wentworth Bristol BS30 ..11 A6
Yate BS37 ....43 E1
Wentworth Cl
Cheltenham GL51 ....132 D3
Gloucester GL2 ....127 B5
Wentworth Rd BS7 ....18 D3
Werth La GL19 ....181 B1
Wescott Gr GL51 ....27 C2
Wesley Ave BS15 ....10 D5
Wesley Cl Aylburton GL15 ..147 E4
⬛ Bristol, Upper Soundwell
BS16 ....27 F1
Bristol, Whitehall BS5 ....19 D1
Wesley Ct
Gloucester GL1 ....196 C2
⬛ Stroud GL5 ....99 C7
Wesley Hill BS15 ....20 D1
Wesley La BS30 ....11 B5
Wesley Pl BS8 ....18 A2
Wesley Rd Bristol BS7 ....18 E8
Cinderford GL14 ....191 D5
Leonard Stanley GL10 ..97 E3
Whitecroft GL15 ....155 F1
Wesley St BS3 ....8 C3
Wesley Theological Coll
BS10 ....27 F1
Wessex Ave BS7 ....18 F7
Wessex Dr GL52 ....134 B2
Wessex Ho ⬛ BS2 ....195 C3
Wessex SN6 ....145 D4
West Allcourt GL7 ....153 E2
West Approach Dr GL52 ..133 E4
West Ave GL17 ....164 B4
West Broadway BS9 ....18 D6
West Coombe BS9 ....17 D2
West Country Water Pk*
BS36 ....40 F2
West Croft BS9 ....18 C7
West Dene BS9 ....17 E6
West Dr GL50 ....133 E3
West Dundry La BS41 ....1 E2
West End Avening GL8 ..140 A8
Bristol, Kingsdown BS2 ..195 A4
Bristol, Southville BS3 ..194 C1
Coaley GL11 ....96 D1
Kingham OX7 ....177 F2
Minchinhampton GL6 ..148 A3
Nailsworth GL6 ....168 A1
Ruardean GL17 ....163 E4
Thornbury BS35 ....8 B5
West End Gdns GL7 ....152 D4
West End La
Broadway WR12 ....185 B7
Gloucester GL3 ....120 B6

West Field GL2 ....125 D5
West Gr BS6 ....18 F1
West Grange Ct GL5 ....99 B8
West Hay Gr GL7 ....141 F8
West Hill SN26 ....144 D2
West La GL7 ....141 F8
West Leaze Pl BS32 ....29 E6
West Littleton Rd SN14 ..24 E2
West Mall BS8 ....7 F7
West Market Pl GL7 ....190 C5
West Mill La SN6 ....143 E4
West Par BS9 ....17 C7
West Park Rd BS16 ....20 E5
West Pk BS8 ....194 B4
West Point Row GL3 ....40 C3
West Priory GL7 ....18 A7
West Ridge BS36 ....31 C7
West Rocke Ave BS9 ....17 E6
West Shrubbery ⬛ BS6 ..18 B2
West St Bristol BS2 ....195 C3
Bristol, Bedminster BS3 ..8 C3
⬛ Bristol, Kingswood BS15 ..10 E5
Bristol, Oldland Common
BS30 ....11 C4
Kingham OX7 ....177 F3
Tetbury GL8 ....140 B4
Tytherington GL12 ....52 B5
West Town Ave BS4 ....9 D1
West Town Dr BS4 ....9 D1
West Town Gr BS4 ....9 D1
West Town La BS4 ....3 D8
West Town La BS4 ....9 D1
West Town Lane Jun & Inf
Schs BS4 ....9 D1
West Town Pk BS4 ....9 D1
West Town Rd BS11 ....16 C7
West Tynings GL6 ....91 A4
West View Alveston BS35 ..50 F4
Cinderford GL14 ....191 D3
Joy's Green GL17 ....163 D3
Newent GL18 ....170 F4
Newnham GL14 ....156 F7
Poulton GL7 ....151 F3
Wootton-u-E GL12 ....88 B3
West View Rd Bristol BS3 ..8 B3
Keynsham BS31 ....4 E5
West Way
Bristol BS10,BS34 ....28 E4
Cirencester GL7 ....190 C4
Lechlade on T GL7 ....153 E3
West Wlk BS37 ....43 E1
Westacre Cl BS10 ....28 A2
Westal Gn ⬛ GL50 ....130 B8
Westal Pk GL51 ....130 B7
Westbourne WR11 ....188 C7
Westbourne Ave BS31 ....4 E5
Westbourne Gdns BS8 ..18 A1
Westbourne ⬛ BS2,BS16 ..21 A7
Westbourne Dr
Cheltenham GL52 ....133 F2
Hardwicke GL2 ....109 C7
Westbourne Gr ⬛ BS3 ....8 C1
Westbourne Ho ⬛ GL52 ..133 F2
Westbourne Pl BS8 ....194 B3
Westbourne Rd
⬛ Bristol, Downend BS16 ..20 F8
⬛ Bristol, Upper Easton BS5 ..9 B8
Westbourne Terr BS16 ....20 B7
Westbrook Rd BS35 ....8 D8
Westbrook Ct BS16 ....20 B7
Westbury Court Rd BS9 ..17 E4
Westbury Cres BS9 ....18 A7
Westbury Hill BS9 ....18 A7
Westbury La BS9 ....17 C7
Westbury Park Prim Sch
BS6 ....18 B3
Westbury Pk BS6 ....18 A4
Westbury Rd Bristol BS6 ..18 A4
Cheltenham GL53 ....130 E4
Gloucester GL4 ....118 D3
Westbury-on-Severn CE
Prim Sch GL14 ....165 C1
Westbury-on-Trym CE Prim
Sch BS9 ....18 A8
Westcote Rd GL4 ....118 E1
Westcourt Dr BS30 ....11 B4
Westdowns Gdns GL52 ..133 F1
Westend GL11 ....97 D6
Westend Cross GL10 ....101 A2
Westend La GL11 ....96 D4
Westend Par GL11 ....126 C3
Westend Rd GL12 ....53 E5
Westend Terr
Chipping Campden GL55 ..188 F2
Gloucester GL1 ....126 C3
Westering Cl BS16 ....21 A5
Westerleigh Cl BS16 ....20 F7
Westerleigh Rd
Bristol BS16 ....20 F6
Henfield BS36 ....31 D2
Pucklechurch BS16 ....22 C7
Westerleigh BS36,BS37 ..32 B5
Yate BS37 ....32 C8
Westerley Cl GL14 ....191 D3
Western Approach
Distribution Pk BS35 ....38 C4
Western Ave
Chepstow NP16 ....60 F5
Frampton Cotterell BS36 ..42 A1
Mitcheldean GL17 ....164 D5
Western Ct ⬛ GL50 ....133 B1
Western Dr BS14 ....2 E6
Western Grange BS34 ....29 A3
Western Hill Rd GL20 ....183 B5
Western Rd Bristol BS7 ....18 E6
Cheltenham GL50 ....193 A3
Western Way GL18 ....170 D8
Westfield Dursley GL11 ....88 A2
Llangrove HR9 ....162 B6

Westfield Ave
Brockworth GL3 ....120 D6
Northway GL20 ....182 C4
Westfield Cl Bristol BS15 ..10 D5
Keynsham BS31 ....4 C5
Westfield Cotts GL51 ....136 B3
Westfield La GL14 ....191 D5
Westfield La BS34 ....29 E3
Westfield Pk BS6 ....18 B1
Westfield Pk S BS8 ....7 F7
Westfield Rd Bristol BS9 ..18 A8
Brockworth GL3 ....120 D6
Cinderford GL14 ....191 D5
Westfield Terr GL2 ....126 E5
Westfield Way BS32 ....40 D2
Westfields GL12 ....68 A7
Westgate St GL1 ....196 A3
Westhill Cl SN6 ....145 C3
Westland Ave BS30 ....11 C4
Westland Rd GL2 ....109 D7
Westlands Jun Sch
GL51 ....130 A7
Westleigh Cl Bristol BS10 ..28 D1
Yate BS37 ....43 C1
Westleigh Ct BS37 ....43 C1
Westleigh Pk BS14 ....3 B8
Westleigh Rd BS10 ....28 D1
Westmarsh BS35 ....63 B5
Westmarsh La BS35 ....63 B5
Westmead Rd Bristol BS5 ..30 B7
Gloucester GL2 ....127 D5
Westminster Cl
⬛ Bristol BS9 ....18 A7
Cheltenham GL53 ....130 F7
Westminster Dr ⬛ GL52 ..127 B2
Westminster Rd BS5 ....9 D8
Westmoreland Rd BS6 ....18 B3
Westmorland Ho BS6 ....18 B3
Westmorland Terr BS37 ..34 D7
Weston Ave ⬛ BS5 ....9 D7
Weston Cl BS9 ....17 C7
Weston Cotts SN7 ....145 E8
Weston Cres BS7 ....18 E6
Weston Ind Est WR11 ....188 D4
Weston Park Prim Sch
BS11 ....16 F8
Weston Rd
Bretforton WR11 ....188 B5
Gloucester GL1 ....196 B1
Honeybourne WR11 ....188 C6
Long Ashton BS41 ....7 A1
Westonbirt St GL8 ....58 D8
Westonbirt Arboretum*
GL8 ....58 B8
Westonbirt Sch GL8 ....58 E8
Weston La BS9 ....17 C4
Westons Brake BS16 ....31 A1
Westons Hill Dr BS16 ....31 A1
Westons Way BS15 ....10 F7
Westover Cl BS9 ....27 F1
Westover Ct GL3 ....128 B7
Westover Dr BS9 ....28 A1
Westover Gdns BS9 ....18 F8
Westover Rd BS9 ....28 A1
Westover Rise BS9 ....28 A1
Westpoint Trad Est BS15 ..10 D7
Westridge Rd GL12 ....68 A8
Westrip Pl GL5 ....98 D8
Westrop BS9 ....145 D3
Westrop City Prim Sch
SN6 ....145 C3
Westview GL19 ....173 C7
Westward BS41 ....7 B2
Westward Cl GL5 ....98 D6
Westward Dr BS20 ....16 C4
Westward Gdns BS41 ....7 B2
Westward Rd Bristol BS13 ..1 F7
Stroud GL5 ....98 D6
Westwick Rd GL19 ....165 D6
Westwing Sch BS32 ....50 E8
Westwood Cres BS4 ....9 D5
Westwood La GL52 ....134 D3
Westwood Rd BS4 ....3 D8
Wetherby Ct BS16 ....30 F1
Wetherell Pl BS8 ....194 B3
Wetherleigh Dr GL2 ....125 E5
Weybourne Cl GL52 ....99 D5
Weyhouse Cl GL5 ....99 D5
Weymouth Rd BS3 ....8 C2
Whaddon Ave GL52 ....134 A2
Whaddon Dr GL52 ....133 F2
Whaddon Prim Sch
GL52 ....134 B2
Whaddon Rd GL52 ....134 A2
Whaddon Road Ground
(Cheltenham Town FC)
GL52 ....134 A2
Whaddon Way GL4 ....118 D1
Wharf La Kempsford GL7 ..144 E7
Lechlade on T GL7 ....153 E2
Wharf Rd BS16 ....19 F4
Wharf The GL19 ....173 E6
Wharfdale Sq GL51 ....132 F3
Wharfdale Way
Hardwicke GL2 ....109 D2
Stonehouse GL10 ....97 E6
Wharfedale BS35 ....51 D8
Wharfings The GL7 ....144 E7
Wharncliffe Cl SN14 ....3 B5
Wharncliffe Gdns BS14 ....3 B5
Whartons ⬛ BS4 ....9 D1
Whatley Ct ⬛ BS8 ....18 B1
Whatley Rd BS8 ....18 B1
Wheat Cl GL56 ....177 A6
Wheat Hill ⬛ GL8 ....140 B4
Wheatfield Cl GL55 ....189 A6
Wheatfield Dr BS32 ....40 D1

Wheatfield Prim Sch
BS32 40
Wheathill Cl BS31 4
Wheatland Dr GL51 132
Wheatridge E The GL4 ..119
Wheatridge The GL4 119
Wheatsheaf Dr GL20 182
Wheatstone Cl GL20 182
Wheatstone Rd GL1 11
Wheatway GL4 119
Wheelers Wlk GL5 98
Whelford Rd GL7 144
Whimbrel Rd GL2 11
Whimsey Rd GL14 19
Whinchat Gdns BS16 1
Whip La GL6 9
Whippington Ct BS1 195
Whippington's Cnr
GL20 15
Whitby Rd BS4 9
Whitchurch District Ctr
BS14 ....
Whitchurch La
Bristol, Bishopsworth BS13 ..
Bristol, Hartcliffe BS13 ....
Bristol, Whitchurch BS14 ..
Dundry BS41 ....
Whitchurch Prim Sch
BS14 ....
Whitchurch Rd BS13 ....
Whitchurch Sch HR9 16
White Cotts GL5 9
White Cross Rd GL15 9
White Hart Cl GL7 13
White Hart Ho GL51 13
White Hart La ⬛ GL54 ..17
White Hart St GL51 13
White Horse La GL6 1
White Horse Rd SN6 14
White Lodge Rd BS16 ....
White St BS5 1
White Tree Rd BS9 ....
Whitebeam Cl GL12 12
Whitebeam Cotts BS5 ....
Whitechapel Rd ⬛
GL15 15
Whitecourt GL11 ....
Whitecroft GL6 ....
Whitecroft Rd GL15 1
Whitecroft Sta GL15 15
Whitecroft Way BS15 ....
Whitecross Ave BS14 ....
Whitecross Sch GL15 ....
Whitecross Sq GL53 ....
Whitecross St ⬛ SN25 ....
Whitefield Ave
Bristol, Hanham BS15 ....
Bristol, Speedwell BS5 ....
Whitefield Cl GL10 ....
Whitefields Rd
Bishop's Cleeve GL52 1
Chipping Sodbury BS37 ....
Whitefriars La SN6 ....
Whitegates BS36 ....
Whitehall GL5 ....
Whitehall Ave BS5 ....
Whitehall Gdns BS5 ....
Whitehall La GL2 ....
Whitehall Rd BS5 ....
Whitehall Trad Est ⬛ BS5 ..
Whitehill Rd GL17 1
Whitehouse La Bristol BS3
Gorsley HR9,GL18 1
Tetbury GL8 ....
Whitehouse Pk GL5 ....
Whitehouse Prim Sch
BS13 ....
Whitehouse Rd BS35 ....
Whitehouse St BS3 ....
Whitehouse Way GL52 ....
Whiteladies Rd BS8 ....
Whitelands La GL51 1
Whitelands Rd GL7 1
Whiteleaze BS10 ....
Whitemarsh Cl GL11 1
Whitemead Ho ⬛ BS3 ....
Whites Hill BS5 ....
Whiteshill BS16 ....
Whiteshill Prim Sch
GL6 ....
Whitethorn Cott GL51 1
Whitethorn Dr GL52 1
Whitewall La BS35 ....
Whitewater Rd GL8 ....
Whiteway GL11 ....
Whiteway La
Bristol, St Anne's Park BS4 ..
Bristol, St George BS5 ....
Whiteway Ct ⬛
Bristol GL7 ....
Cirencester GL7 ....
Whiteway Mews BS5 ....
Whiteway Rd
Bristol BS5,BS15 ....
Gloucester GL4 ....
Whiteway View GL7 ....
Whitewell Cl GL4 ....
Whitewood Rd BS5 ....
Whitfield Cl BS36 ....
Whitfield Fishponds Com
BS16 ....
Whitfield Rd GL11 ....
Whitfield St GL1 ....
Whitford Cl WR11 ....

DGERHURST D8 173

GLOUCESTER 196

Motorway with junction number	
Primary route – dual/single carriageway	
A road – dual/single carriageway	
B road – dual/single carriageway	
Minor road – dual/single carriageway	
Other minor road – dual/single carriageway	
Road under construction	
Pedestrianised area	
DY7 Postcode boundaries	
County and unitary authority boundaries	
Railway	
Railway under construction	
Tramway, miniature railway	
Rural track, private road or narrow road in urban area	
Gate or obstruction to traffic (restrictions may not apply at all times or to all vehicles)	
Path, bridleway, byway open to all traffic, road used as a public path	

The representation in this atlas of a road, track or path is no evidence of the existence of a of a right of way

185
106
196
192

Adjoining page indicators
(The colour of the arrow indicates the scale of the adjoining page - see scales below)

The map areas within the pink and blue bands are shown at a larger scale on the page, indicated by the red and blue blocks and arrows

Acad	Academy	Mkt	Market
Allot Gdns	Allotments	Meml	Memorial
Cemy	Cemetery	Mon	Monument
C Ctr	Civic Centre	Mus	Museum
CH	Club House	Obsy	Observatory
Coll	College	Pal	Royal Palace
Crem	Crematorium	PH	Public House
Ent	Enterprise	Recn Gd	Recreation Ground
Ex H	Exhibition Hall	Resr	Reservoir
Ind Est	Industrial Estate	Ret Pk	Retail Park
IRB Sta	Inshore Rescue Boat Station	Sch	School
		Sh Ctr	Shopping Centre
Inst	Institute	TH	Town Hall/House
Ct	Law Court	Trad Est	Trading Estate
L Ctr	Leisure Centre	Univ	University
LC	Level Crossing	Wks	Works
Liby	Library	YH	Youth Hostel

Railway station	Walsall
Private railway station	
Bus, coach station	
Ambulance station	
Coastguard station	
Fire station	
Police station	
Accident and Emergency entrance to hospital	
Hospital	
Place of worship	
Information Centre (open all year)	
Parking	
Park and Ride	
Post Office	
Camping site	
Caravan site	
Golf course	
Picnic site	
Important buildings, schools, colleges, universities and hospitals	Prim Sch
Water name	River Medway
River, stream	
Lock, weir	
Water	
Tidal water	
Woods	
Houses	
Non-Roman antiquity	Church
Roman antiquity	ROMAN FORT

■ The small numbers around the edges of the maps identify the 1 kilometre National Grid lines ■ The dark grey border on the inside edge of some pages indicates that the mapping does not continue onto the adjacent page

The scale of the maps on the pages numbered in blue is 3.92 cm to 1 km • 2½ inches to 1 mile • 1: 25344

The scale of the maps on the pages numbered in green is 1.96 cm to 1 km • 1¼ inches to 1 mile • 1: 50688

The scale of the maps on the pages numbered in red is 7.84 cm to 1 km • 5 inches to 1 mile • 1: 12672

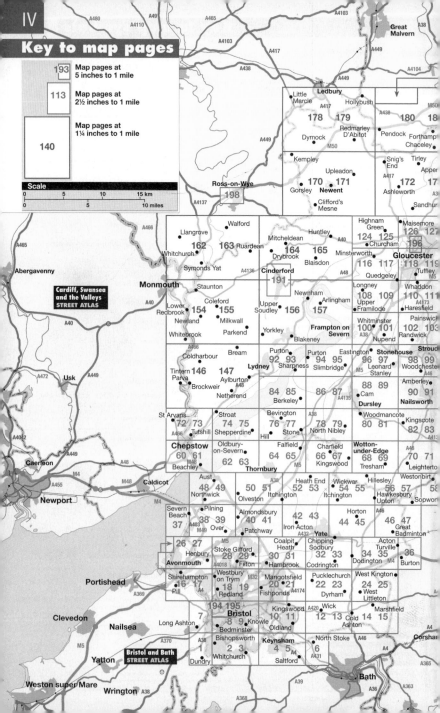